An Introduction to Chinese Politics

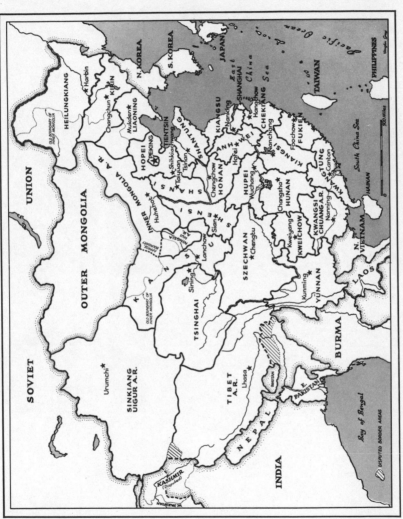

Map 1. Political Divisions of China

Reprinted by permission of the publishers from Theodore Shabad, China's Changing Map: National and Regional Development, 1949–71, rev. ed. (New York: Praeger, 1972, and London: Methuen & Co., Ltd., 1972). © 1956, 1972 by Theodore Shabad.

An Introduction to
CHINESE POLITICS

Harold C. Hinton

DAVID & CHARLES
NEWTON ABBOT

To the Memory

of

E. A. J. JOHNSON

0 7153 6321 1

Printed in Great Britain
by Redwood Press Limited Trowbridge Wiltshire
for David & Charles (Holdings) Limited
South Devon House   Newton Abbot   Devon

Contents

theoretical aspects of Mao's "thought"; political aspects of
Mao's "thought"; further readings

Preface

It hardly seems necessary to demonstrate in detail the importance and timeliness of contemporary China as a subject of intellectual curiosity and public concern. The U.S. Government, after two decades of trying with decreasing success to "contain and isolate" the People's Republic of China, has begun to shift to a more positive relationship with it, with spectacular results in the shape of President Richard M. Nixon's 1972 visit. Peking has reciprocated American overtures to an extent that few would have believed possible while the war in Indochina was still in progress and the United States was still committed to protecting Taiwan.

As if these things were not enough to stimulate intelligent curiosity, extraordinary developments have taken place recently on the mainland of China. The Cultural Revolution was a virtually unique exercise in political turmoil induced by the established political leadership of a major country. Nor has its termination brought an end to the flow of interesting, even startling, developments. Since September, 1971, it has gradually become known for certain that the Chinese Defense Minister, who had been the officially announced heir to Chairman Mao Tse-tung, has been purged under mysterious circumstances, and the official explanations that have been offered almost rival the works of Ian Fleming: Lin Piao is said to have tried to assassinate Mao and to have died while trying to defect to the Soviet Union.

China is a colorful object of interest and an important subject of inquiry. There is clearly a place for a general study of its political system that is introductory in the sense that it assumes no previous knowledge, only a serious interest and a willingness to work, but that tries to go significantly beyond the level of generalities, superficialities, or trivialities. With few qualifications (Derek J. Waller, *The Government and Politics of Communist China,* New York: Anchor Books, 1971, is a partial exception), there is no other recent book, to my knowledge, that fills this requirement. This lack was less surprising when I began serious study, almost purely independent study, of post-1949 China about twenty years ago, than it is today. I have often threatened to write a book that would try to fill this gap, for popular consumption and for student use. This book is offered in fulfillment of that threat. Whether it actually fills the gap must be judged by the reader.

This book is intended to serve as a textbook, for undergraduates and for beginning graduate students, that will give them at least a reasonably satisfactory overview of the complex subject of Chinese politics and will make it possible for them to go on to do their own study and research. It is also intended to be of interest and help to others who would like to know something about the subject, for one reason or another, and are willing to study at a level of analysis beyond that normally offered in the press and in general periodicals; for their purposes, the bibliographical portions can be omitted with no essential substantive loss.

The point of view here is not that of either a lover of China or a sympathizer with its regime. But this statement is not so negative as it has perhaps been made to appear for the sake of brevity. China as a subject has been the object of strong emotions, especially in the United States, where feelings were formerly mostly negative but are now, especially in the academic community, predominantly positive. (The reasons for this are discussed in Chapter 1.) In some cases, analysis of Chinese politics really begins with a highly negative view of existing conditions in the United States and consists, to a considerable extent, of a projection upon China, as (at least until recently) the most revolutionary of the world's major societies, of the assumed opposite of the defects perceived in American society. This approach has very little in common with sound political analysis. At the other extreme, it is equally unsound to make hostile criticism, rather than investigation for the sake of understanding, the major objective.

The approach adopted here is intended to fall about midway between these two extremes and within the range of what could reasonably be considered objective. It will probably be attacked more commonly from the left, since the sympathetic approach is more active and articulate now than its opposite; twenty years ago, I was accused by some critics of being a leftist. I basically reject the ideological and political values of the Chinese Communist system. Before this attitude is dismissed as hopelessly reactionary, let me point out that these values not only differ in many ways from those of pre-Communist China but also go beyond orthodox

Marxism-Leninism in some respects and are in the process of being rather drastically modified in China—a fact of which the invitation to President Nixon was one of the first more or less undeniable pieces of evidence. People who form a strong emotional attachment to transitory values and systems, especially foreign ones, that are in process of modification by their originators risk rapid obsolescence.

I refuse to take the regime in power in China more or less automatically at its own public self-valuation, but I would do the same for any regime, whether I sympathized with it or not. Why should the U.S. Government, which is subject to the (imperfect) control represented by a relatively free press and public opinion, suffer from a "credibility gap," but not the Chinese, which is subject to no such control and which can be publicly criticized, to the point of rebuttal if necessary, only from outside China? A refusal to take the Chinese regime automatically at its own self-valuation does not necessarily involve an effort at arbitrary imposition on the subject, with distorting effect, of non-Chinese (or non-Chinese Communist) values. Any value judgments expressed or implied in this book that are negative toward the regime could be matched, and more than matched, by views known to have been held by some Chinese on the mainland (including Communist Party members) during the brief interludes (in 1956–57, and to a lesser extent in 1961–65) when a degree of freedom of expression was permitted. Today, objectors to the regime on the mainland seem to belong to the left more than to the right: it is mainly disillusioned ex-Red Guards who make the dangerous swim to Hong Kong in increasing numbers, or maintain guerrilla resistance to the regime in some areas. The point again is that the regime is moving (although of course not all the way and not necessarily permanently) to the right, and that those who admired its former, more leftist stance must take account of this or risk being left behind by events.

Even so, it is a fair question, as it was of Stalin's Russia, whether methods much less drastic and dictatorial than those actually employed (in many cases admittedly) would have sufficed to produce a degree of national unity and a level of development comparable to what has actually been achieved. This is a difficult question; the answer may well be no, but one cannot be certain. But even if a negative answer is given, and if one agrees with Napoleon that it is necessary to break eggs in order to make an omelet, one can still spare a thought for the eggs in their unbroken condition while appraising the omelet and finding in it defects as well as virtues.

The discipline of political science is in the process of trying to make itself more truly scientific by importing and adapting concepts and methodology from the natural sciences and from computer technology; the result is rather similar to the effect of the computer on mathematics, which we call the "new math." Largely because of the "closed" nature of the societies involved, Communist studies has been one of the last areas to feel the impact of the new approach, but the process has begun. The progress made to date (or until recently) along these lines is indicated in Frederick Fleron and Eric Hoffman, eds., *Communist Studies and the Social Sciences: Essays in Methodology and Empirical Theory*, Chicago: Rand McNally, 1969.

This approach, usually called the "scientific" (as opposed to the older "classical" approach, which is less concerned with theory and quantification and more with qualitative analysis), has been applied to China in particular pieces of research. Some, although by no means a majority, of the sources cited at the end of the chapters of this book reflect it to one degree or another. An interesting article bewailing the limited extent to which the "scientific" approach has been applied to China is Chalmers Johnson, "The Role of Social Science in China Scholarship," *World Politics,* vol. xvii, no. 2 (January, 1965), pp. 256–71.

The approach adopted here is that of "classical" political analysis, based largely on historical method, primarily qualitative judgments, and (to the extent necessary) intuition. In this approach, the experience and judgment of the analyst, rather than a theory or methodology formulated outside the subject, receive the major emphasis.

In addition, a few comments are in order on a research method peculiarly appropriate to Communist (including Communist Chinese) studies that straddles the divide between the scientific and classical approaches and is sometimes known (especially to its critics) as Kremlinology or demonology. This methodology is more highly developed in the Soviet field, and regrettably little has been written on it in the Chinese context. It consists largely in the analysis, from the standpoint of the originators to the extent possible, of Communist "esoteric communications," with emphasis on content analysis applied to published Communist statements of various kinds. People in Communist countries who want to ensure their political survival and careers rapidly learn to practice this art, and there is no reason why it should be regarded as an irrelevant or unworthy subject by foreign analysts. For a good introduction to the subject, see the preface to Donald S. Zagoria, *The*

Sino-Conflict, 1956–1961, Princeton, N.J.: Princeton University Press, 1962, pp. viii–x. Another good summary is a comment by Uri Ra'anan in *The China Quarterly,* no. 50 (April–June, 1972), pp. 347–50. On the use of photographs as a means of "esoteric communication," see Roderick MacFarquhar, "On Photographs," *ibid.,* no. 46 (April–June, 1971), pp. 289–307; see also the exchange between him and Donald Klein in *ibid.,* no. 47 (July–September, 1971), p. 552. The use of chronology, in particular the scheduling (or apparent scheduling, since the purpose is rarely announced) of events on the anniversaries of similar (not identical) events with which some connection is intended to be suggested, for political effect, is an important aspect of the subject, and one to which some reference is made in this book, but one on which nothing has been published by way of systematic analysis.

All of this, of course, offers the student, especially the beginning student, no quick or easy answers to the problems of conceptualization and methodology. This is logical since, at least in the writer's opinion, there are no quick and easy answers in this field, whether there are in others or not. Understanding and analysis are greatly helped by experience, which of course is a function of time, provided that the time is spent with an open mind, as the principles of scientific method properly understood demand, rather than in a state of wedlock with some approach that screens out inconvenient facts, or probabilities, in order to leave the preexisting "model" unimpaired.

It is trite but true that no one who attempts, with whatever degree of success, to write a book like this one can fail to have accumulated a vast debt to his colleagues, many of whom he may not have met. This is of course true in the present case. The extent of my debt is indicated fairly accurately by the reading lists and the appendix, and it would be unnecessary and invidious to single out individuals for special acknowledgment. Probably none would agree with all the interpretations put forward; I can only hope that in each case they will see that there are serious reasons for the interpretation.

A special word of appreciation is due to Mervyn W. Adams of Praeger Publishers; she showed an interest in this book when it was proposed and helped enormously in the editorial passage from outline through manuscript to published end product.

Washington, D.C.
January, 1973

An Introduction to Chinese Politics

A muffled zone is, as it were, populated not by inhabitants of the earth but by an extraordinary corps from Mars: The people know nothing intelligent about the rest of the earth and are prepared to go and trample it down in the holy conviction that they come as "liberators."—ALEXANDER SOLZHENITSYN, Nobel Prize Lecture

1. Approaches to the Subject

The process of learning about a country as large, as complex, as interesting, and as important as contemporary China involves a major effort of the mind and can capture a part, or even all, of the emotions. This has proved to be so in many cases, and today probably more than ever. Since the subject is so far from being a neutral or purely technical one, there seems to be a place for some brief introductory comments that prepare the way for the substantive chapters that follow by laying some basic propositions for consideration—not for uncritical acceptance—about Western ways of looking at China, about the Chinese political outlook and system, about the manner in which this book deals with its subject, and about interpretations other than the author's. These comments are intended not as systematic analysis, which would obviously be impossible in such a short space, but as an effort to challenge certain fairly common presuppositions that can inhibit open-minded and fruitful thinking about contemporary China and to help open the way for the attempt made in the ensuing chapters to apply such thinking.

Western Views of China

There have been four basic Western ways of looking at China (apart from indifference and intellectual curiosity): the desire to help, the quest for profit, the effort to neutralize, and the urge to admire. (No modern state except Japan has seriously tried to dominate China.) The last of the four is the oldest, dating from about the time of Marco Polo, and it is the most important today. The other three are mainly of historical importance and can be dealt with briefly.

The desire to help embraces the work of the Christian missionaries, those who supported them morally and financially at home,

Western educators and medical personnel in China, and Western economists and planners who tried at various times to promote China's modernization. These people made an important contribution to China, and it is unfair to dismiss their work, as the Chinese Communists and some others do, as merely an aspect of Western "imperialism." At least some of the surprising (in view of the intensity of official anti-American propaganda over two decades) amount of goodwill in China toward individual Americans that has been displayed recently seems to reflect a lingering recognition of this contribution.

The quest for profit includes Western merchants, investors, and others. It is easy to criticize them, individually and collectively, for their motives and impact, but they too made a contribution by serving, not necessarily intentionally, as intermediaries between China and the world of modern science, technology, and industrial society. But unless China opens itself to the West in the future far more than it shows any intention of doing, this historic attitude and relationship, like the first, has little future.

By the effort to neutralize is meant activities by other powers aimed at preventing China from exerting a destabilizing influence on Asia and on international politics; this tendency occasionally gave rise to limited intervention (sometimes for purposes less creditable than neutralization) when China was weak, and to the American policy of containment when China was relatively strong. This sort of thing also appears to be in the past, in view of China's growing power and the new international balance in Asia, unless an unexpected weakening of the Chinese Communist system should open the way to Soviet influence and even intervention.

Admiration is another matter. Since the days of the eighteenth-century Jesuit missionaries, China has served intermittently as a New Jerusalem, a Shangri-La, for Western intellectuals alienated for various reasons from their own societies and the establishments thereof. China has been picked for this role because of the many admirable qualities of its people and culture, their huge differences from their Western counterparts, China's prolonged victimization by Western "imperialism," and (since 1949) the revolutionary dynamism of its society and political system. This attitude toward China has merged with a broader sympathy for left-wing nationalism, in its Communist and non-Communist forms, in the developing countries. There is a belief on the part of some that China has somehow found a path to development free of the usual evils lurking along such paths—inflation, corruption, coercion, and the like—and, although the Cultural Revolution cast some doubt on this view, the subsequent trend toward recovery has brought it back into fashion. There is a tendency to feel that if Communism, in China or elsewhere, is making impressive progress in important respects, this must be because of a superior ideology and program; the crucial importance of organization and coercion (often veiled), as well as innate Chinese qualities, are all too easily overlooked. Or if the coercion is recognized, it is often excused on the ground, implicit or perhaps subconscious, that violence is thoroughly bad only when it is employed by the right; this attitude seems to be one of the many unfortunate legacies of the career of Adolf Hitler. American China policy, until 1969 at any rate, and Vietnam policy as its major extension, have been widely regarded in the West as a vast wrong-headed rain dance on the part of the American Establishment, and opposition to them as a necessary concomitant to support for civil rights and social justice at home.

A strong objective case can be made for much of this, but it is far from airtight, and it is rarely made objectively by its proponents, who pride themselves on being "committed" or "concerned." Much of the talk by Communists and the New Left, as well as some others, about American "imperialism," for example, is not only politically biased but is also an example of the philosophical error known technically as reification—the attribution of concrete existence and systematic properties to something that is essentially an abstraction: one can concede the existence of specific behavior that could be called "imperialist" without agreeing to the existence of a general objective phenomenon with the attributes of "imperialism" in its usual sense.

The reasons for the kind of thinking that is being criticized here appear to be very deep-seated. Ever since the futilities of the eighteenth-century *anciens régimes* and the horrors of World War I discredited respectively the "feudal" and "bourgeois" systems in the eyes of many Western intellectuals, there has been a widespread desire for a political and social order in which the intellectual, in George Orwell's trenchant phrase, can get his hands on the whip. When intellectuals in the West complain that they are not free, as they sometimes do, what they usually mean is that they are not in power, or at least that they are not taken seriously by those who are. There may be valid reasons that they should not be, and it is a great mistake to think that intellectuals are in power in Communist countries, including China; the men in charge there either were never intellectuals or ceased to be able to function as such in proportion as their political careers developed. The fate of Leon Trotsky is the case of a brilliant and indeed competent intellectual who tried to serve in the leadership of the Soviet Communist Party while retaining the outlook of an intellectual. In China, a major political figure (P'eng Chen), who, while not an intellectual himself, tried to serve as the patron of intellectuals, was purged in 1966 when the mindless violence of the Red Guards was unleashed.

The Chinese Political Outlook and System

Chinese culture, at the elite level even more than at the popular level, has always placed heavy emphasis on human values and social relations, as contrasted with more abstract considerations such as theology and metaphysics. In Chinese thought and behavior, the family has tended to occupy the central place, partly no doubt because the size of the country and its population have encouraged an attitude of local self-sufficiency. The country has been thought of as a kind of vastly extended family, which was considered to be the Middle Kingdom, the only truly civilized state and one vastly superior, culturally if not necessarily in all other respects, to the rest of mankind. Although foreigners were thought of as generally barbarous, it was conceded that they could be dangerously strong, and that (especially in modern times) a state of confusion, disunity, and weakness within China could lead to foreign encroachments and even invasion. Even though it does not appear to be widely understood in China, the fact that these encroachments did not culminate in the establishment of Western colonial rule over China has meant among other things that Chinese intellectuals have been less modern-minded and cosmopolitan than those of some other Asian countries and have never been able to assert national political leadership, as have those in some other countries.

Turning to more strictly political matters, we see that there is no tradition in China of government by the people; at most, it has been to some degree for the people. Public opinion has been essentially passive, not active. There is a widespread belief that the only alternative to an undesired anarchy is unity and stability based on hierarchical authority, not government by active consent of the governed. Authority in Chinese eyes must rest on bureaucratic rule, a high degree of ritualization of public life, and a government of men (preferably good men, of course) more than of laws. The need for the state is generally accepted, the level of its power that is considered legitimate during any given period being roughly proportional to the need for, and the state's success at, defense of the country. There has been a normal preference for routinized over charismatic leadership, but the latter can be acceptable if it is unusually good at establishing and maintaining the unity of the country, pacifying and defending its border regions, and conducting relations with other states to China's advantage. Chinese tradition prefers civilian rule and civil pursuits over military; given the collapse of the traditional political system at the beginning of the twentieth century, this attitude on the part of educated Chinese amounted to abdication of political leadership in favor of military men shrewd and ruthless enough to perceive that they alone were in a position to fill the existing political vacuum.

China (the area inhabited predominantly by Chinese-speaking people) is essentially too big and diffuse to be readily governed as a single entity. For 2,000 years, nevertheless, educated Chinese have believed that their remarkable cultural unity required for its preservation a corresponding political unity. That this should be so is by no means self-evident. There are many other peoples (Turks, Kurds, Mongols, and so forth) who do not enjoy political unity and are likely never to. A serious effort by all German-speaking peoples in Europe to form a single state, which is roughly what happened in the 1930's, would create tremendous disruption in Europe now, as it did then. But the Chinese, mainly because of their enormous numbers absolutely and relative to their neighbors, have been able throughout most of their history to make good their claim to political unity. It could be made good, however, only under an authoritarian political system tempered informally by local autonomy protected by the absence of modern technology. An occasional trend toward anarchy brought not only weakness but fragmentation and foreign incursions. The resulting horror of anarchy and confusion (*luan*) remains in the Chinese psyche, including its Communist variant.

One of the most insidious distorting mechanisms affecting Western approaches to contemporary China is that, whereas everyone likes to have live contact with a country in which he is interested, it is very difficult to visit mainland China or hold meaningful communication with its leaders unless one has, or claims to have, views of which they approve or unless one can be useful to them in some way. China is not the only country where this problem exists, of course, but it is a country where it occurs to an unusual degree. Even apart from the familiar difficulty of getting a visa, examples of this "totalitarian thinking" (Orwell's phrase) are numerous.

For example, a high-ranking Chinese Communist diplomat recently assured a well-informed American that American Middle Eastern policy was made by the oil companies and that the companies supported Israel; the diplomat appeared badly shaken by the vigorous rebuttal of his absurd statement. This sort of thing, whether one is talking about manifestations of it on the part of the Chinese Communists or their foreign sympathizers, could be attributed to insecurity, or immaturity, or an excessive concern with self-image. Chou En-lai recently advised a foreign visitor not to take Chinese propaganda so seriously; this is good advice and should be more widely heeded, but it obviously does not answer the question why the regime should cultivate an image that is often far removed from reality. The cause, at least on the Chinese side, goes deep; it is again the problem of "totalitarian thinking," a current manifestation of the tendency that in the West began with the Zoroastrian division of the universe into the forces of light (one's own side, in practice) and the forces of darkness (the others) and has spattered the history of the West with religious and ideological violence.

Attitudes such as those just discussed lie more or less on the surface and are not hard to analyze. It is much more difficult to analyze the workings of the political system at the elite level, "closed" as it is to outside observation of the kind regarded as routine in the study of most Western (and also many non-Western) political systems. More has been done in an effort to overcome these obstacles in the study of the Soviet system, which of course is older than the Chinese Communist and (since the death of Stalin) slightly less "closed" to foreign observation. In the Soviet context, there have been two main schools of analysis of elite politics, one of which can be called the stable-dictatorship school and the other the constant-conflict school. The former assumes an unchallenged leader, the only significant competition within the elite being for his favor and for influence on him; in the Chinese case, this is sometimes referred to as the "Mao in command" interpretation. The other claims to detect, even though one member of the leadership is generally "more equal" than the others, a continual jostling for power and influence and a frequent forming and re-forming of combinations that may never aim at or succeed in threatening the top leader's position but still do not permit him to assume complacently that it is beyond challenge. The Great Leap Forward (see Chapter 3) and the Cultural Revolution (see Chapter 4) opened the eyes of most analysts to the possible validity of the constant-conflict model for China, but without entirely dispelling the influence of the other approach. In this study, the approach adopted is closer to the constant-conflict school than to the stable-dictatorship school, although it appears that, from the establishment of his ascendancy in the Communist Party of China (CPC), apparently in October, 1938, Mao Tsetung's position was never directly and seriously challenged, at least until 1966 (see Chapter 4). The constant-conflict approach, as long as it is not overdone, has the great advantage of permitting and encouraging the asking of more and better questions about elite politics than does the other.

A well-informed diplomat recently returned from an eighteen-month tour in Peking, when asked what he considered the major difference between Chinese realities as he perceived them and the dominant impressions of China current in the outside world, replied that most of the recent reportage by foreign travelers and journalists on brief visits was much too favorable. In particular, he felt that the regime could not possibly have produced a "new man," full of selfless enthusiasm for the "thought" of Mao Tsetung and for his concept of "uninterrupted revolution," to the extent that the regime claims and that many visitors infer from the responses that they get (for reasons already suggested) from Chinese to whom they talk. The problem becomes less puzzling when one remembers something probably relevant to it, the fact that traditionally the Chinese have developed a superb talent for what they call "outer obedience, inner rebellion," or, in other words, feigned political enthusiasm for the sake of national unity and/or personal survival. If this tendency is fairly widespread now, and it probably is, then it follows that the level of actual public support for the regime is significantly lower than appears on the surface. But inner apathy and disillusionment, to the extent that they exist, are one thing; active disaffection, let alone open opposition or organized resistance, are quite another, at least in a political system equipped with controls and sanctions as highly developed as those that Peking possesses as a result of the CPC's fifty years of experience in political activity. No manifestation of popular discontent that could threaten the regime is in sight; in spite of all the talk about revolution, modern states, once well established, are rarely overthrown from below, and the People's

Republic of China (C.P.R.) is essentially an established modern state (presiding, to be sure, over a largely nonmodern society). A more serious problem is possible centrifugal forces represented by regional and provincial military leaders whose power has increased greatly as a result of the Cultural Revolution; one of this book's main conclusions, however, is that this too is likely to prove a manageable problem for the regime.

Other Interpretations

Except perhaps when writing for a specialist audience, it is legitimate self-confidence and not conceit for an author to assume that the reader is mainly interested for the time being in the author's views and not those of others. Frequent references to the views of other authorities (except in footnotes, which are not used in this book) can become a device by which a writer minimizes, unconsciously perhaps, the need to do his own analysis and make his own judgments. Given this point of view, no effort is made in the text to explain and compare the views of various authorities on particular subjects; for one thing, the book would become too long in the process.

But this is not at all to say that the interpretation is presented with the idea that it is unquestionably correct or the only possible correct one. It can claim to be a considered viewpoint, and some effort has been made to indicate the evidence and reasoning on which it rests. But others with good qualifications have come to different conclusions, on general trends and on particular subjects. They, or many of them, are represented in the writings listed at the end of each chapter, and occasionally there are comments indicating what their viewpoints are. The object is not to conceal the existence of different views, but to present as much essential material as possible (from the writer's viewpoint) without allowing the book to become impossibly long.

As already indicated, in the Preface and earlier in this chapter, there is one school of thought on the subject of this book to which the writer does not subscribe. That is the school that regards the regime's ideology and political values as unquestionably valid at least for China, and perhaps for other countries as well, and that accepts the regime's self-valuation virtually without question. Toward, but not necessarily at, the other extreme is another school that shares, and in fact usually derives directly or indirectly from, the analytical approach (with or without the other views) of the

Chinese Nationalists, which stresses personal and power rivalries and hence weaknesses within the Chinese Communist leadership, to the point of minimizing the more important relative solidarity of most of the elite on major questions and the effectiveness of that elite's control over the "masses." The writer cannot accept either the thesis of the regime's transcendent rightness or that of its probable imminent decline or collapse. The writings of some representatives of both schools are included in the reading lists, however. Most of the writers represented in the lists would agree in general with the view expressed in this book that the C.P.R. deserves some strong criticism but gives every sign of being here to stay, although not to stay unchanged, and that the present evolution of its political system appears to be in an encouraging direction from the point of view of the outside world (apart from the extreme left and those who want or expect it to collapse).

FURTHER READINGS

There is no satisfactory over-all published treatment of historical Western attitudes toward China (and vice versa) and the history of Sino-Western relations down to, say, 1949; it is a subject that deserves more comprehensive and analytical treatment than it has so far received. The available works deal with the subject as part of some broader canvas (modern Chinese history, for example) or devote their full attention to some specialized aspect of the problem. A good start on the American side, although designed for professional historians and rather heavy going for the beginning student, is Ernest R. May and James C. Thomson, Jr., eds., *American–East Asian Relations: A Survey*, Cambridge, Mass.: Harvard University Press, 1972. The first three works cited at the beginning of the reading list for Chapter 2 contain chapters or sections of some value on this subject. For a collection of views on contemporary China and its relationship with the West, see Bruce Douglass and Ross Terrill, eds., *China and Ourselves*, Boston: Beacon Press, 1970.

The reference to George Orwell is a reminder that, although still much referred to and quoted, he is rather seldom read, especially by the young. He should be much more widely read for his intellect, honesty, courage, and powerful unadorned style. His excoriation of "totalitarian thinking" (mainly pro-Soviet views held by British intellectuals of his day) and the fat-bottomed British Establishment has much to say that is relevant by obvious analogy to today's conditions and is worthwhile and interesting in its own right. His political writings (apart from full-length books) are collected in Sonia Orwell and Ian Angus, eds., *The Collected Essays, Journalism and Letters of George Orwell*, 4 vols, New York: Harcourt, Brace & World, 1968,

London: Secker & Warburg, 1968, Harmondsworth: Penguin, 1970. Probably his most devastating attack on "totalitarian thinking" is "The Prevention of Literature" (vol. iv, pp. 59–72). A unique and valuable application of a viewpoint similar to Orwell's to Western thinking about China in the early 1950's can be found in Michael Lindsay, *China and the Cold War: A Study in International Politics,* Melbourne: Melbourne University Press, 1955.

For interesting, rather controversial analyses of the Chinese Communist political outlook and system, see the book by Lucian W. Pye cited at the end of Chapter 2 and Richard H. Solomon, *Mao's Revolution and the Chinese Political Culture,* Berkeley: University of California Press, 1971. Also valuable is John Wilson Lewis, ed., *Major Doctrines of Communist China,* New York: Norton, 1964.

The phrase "People's Middle Kingdom" was coined by Professor John K. Fairbank; see his *China: The People's Middle Kingdom and the U.S.A.,* Cambridge, Mass.: Harvard University Press, 1967, London: Oxford University Press, 1967.

The "Mao in command" (stable-dictatorship) model of Chinese politics is well presented by Michel C. Oksenberg, "Policy Making Under Mao, 1949–68: An Overview," in John M. H. Lindbeck, ed., *China: Management of a Revolutionary Society,* Seattle: University of Washington Press, 1971, pp. 79–115.

Richard C. Thornton has applied the constant-conflict model to the Chinese political system in the 1950's in "The Structure of Communist Politics," *World Politics,* vol. xxiv, no. 4 (July, 1972), pp. 498–517.

An example of the left-wing view of contemporary China, combining elements of a trip report with some political analysis, is Committee of Concerned Asian Scholars, *China: Inside the People's Republic,* New York: Bantam, 1972.

An example of the Nationalist-oriented school of analysis of recent developments on the mainland, although it does not go so far as to predict collapse, is Parris Chang, "Decentralization of Power," *Problems of Communism,* vol. xxi, no. 4 (July–August, 1972), pp. 67–75.

Some valuable essays on various aspects of the Chinese tradition can be found in Ping-ti Ho and Tang Tsou, eds., *China in Crisis,* vol. 1, book 1, Chicago: University of Chicago Press, 1968. A stimulating and controversial analysis of the Chinese political "style" is Lucian W. Pye, *The Spirit of Chinese Politics: A Psychocultural Study of the Authority Crisis in Political Development,* Cambridge, Mass.: The MIT Press, 1968.

2. The Legacy of the Past

It is not true that, as historians sometimes seem to assume, one must know almost everything about the past in order to understand anything of importance about the present. On the other hand, there are obviously some aspects of the past, remote and recent, that influence the contemporary life of every country. Even so revolutionary a society as that of China shows in many places, including its political attitudes and behavior, the marks of its past.

Traditional Politics

The traditional Chinese political system was in theory and in practice authoritarian. At its summit stood the emperor, the Son of Heaven, whose power was subject to no constitutional limits and could be very great indeed if he had the ability and energy to make it so. Normally, however, he had to consider not only his image as a nominally Confucian ruler but also the views, interests, and power of his family, his court, his generals, and above all perhaps the civil service and the gentry from whom it was mainly drawn. The support of the gentry and the civil officials was crucial to the survival of a dynasty. Gentry status was dependent largely on education, and specifically on knowledge of the Confucian classics as tested in officially administered examinations. Education was also the normal criterion for admission to the imperial civil service, so that the bureaucracy was staffed, in its classified career positions, largely by persons of gentry status. Official position conferred among other perquisites the opportunity to make money beyond one's salary, whether in socially tolerated ways ("squeeze") or through outright extortion. This money would typically be used to buy land, as the safest and most prestigious available form of investment, and to educate one's children to follow the same kind of career. Thus there was a considerable, although not a total, congruence among education, gentry status, officeholding, and landownership. Although there was no rigid, religiously sanctioned caste system as in India, a family tended to retain gentry status, once acquired, through successive generations and to feel a sense of solidarity with other gentry families, especially those of the same province. Thus the gentry had a corporate identity and a grip on civil officeholding that enabled it to survive the rise and fall of dynasties and on occasion to make or break them.

In the early stages of a dynasty, or at least of a major dynasty, emperors were generally more vigorous, the bureaucracy relatively efficient, and land fairly equitably distributed. Time always brought deterioration sooner or later, especially in the vigor of the hereditarily selected emperors and in the landholding situation. Land tended to become concentrated in the hands of strong provincial families, who could often get it left off the tax registers and thus pass the incidence of land taxes, which usually grew heavier as the dynasty aged, to less powerful or less well-connected landholders, and indirectly of course to their tenants. In time, more or less serious peasant rebellions would occur, to the accompaniment of famines and other disasters, external enemies would often seize the opportunity to attack, and the dynasty would collapse. Sooner or later a new one would emerge on the basis of a combination, in one proportion or another, of conquest and acceptance by the gentry. Such was the "dynastic cycle." Confucian theory rationalized this process by holding that the rise and fall of dynasties were determined by the gaining or loss of the "mandate of heaven" and popular support, and that these in turn were conditional on the morality or immorality (by Confucian standards, of course) of the rulers of the period.

The Western Impact and the Rise of Nationalism

The principal factor distinguishing modern from traditional China is the impact of a dynamic and, in critical respects, technologically superior West on a society already groaning from excessive long-term population growth (to perhaps 400 million by 1850). The pressure of population and the pressure of the West became acute about 1800, at which time a third complication appeared as the reigning dynasty (the Ch'ing, or Manchus, 1644–1911) entered the declining phase of its dynastic cycle. The decline was punctuated, especially in the third quarter of the nineteenth

century, by some major rebellions that the Manchus barely succeeded in suppressing, but did so to a large extent because they
made use of some Western innovations, including modern weapons.

The Western impact came in three major forms: economic and
technological, institutional, and ideological. Each deserves separate, if brief, examination.

Before the Industrial Revolution of the eighteenth and early
nineteenth centuries, the Western countries were at a disadvantage
in trying to trade with China. Chinese tea, silk, and porcelain were
in great demand in the West in the eighteenth century, but the
Chinese at first had little interest in any Western products, and
the Manchus imposed stringent controls that further restricted the
volume of trade. A breakthrough was made late in the eighteenth
century when opium-producing regions of India fell under British
control, and it was discovered that opium could be sold on a
large scale to eager buyers in China, although clandestinely because
the Manchus declared its importation illegal. A still more important change occurred when Western, and especially British, firms
began to produce large quantities of cheap cotton textiles in the
early nineteenth century. Their demands for easier access to the
supposedly vast China market pressed against the Manchus' basic
hostility to foreign trade. The balance of trade shifted against
China because of opium and cotton textiles, with serious effects
on the traditional Chinese economy and fiscal system. As the
Manchu dynasty weakened, foreign trade grew, and both foreign
and Chinese entrepreneurs began (in the second half of the nineteenth century) to operate modern enterprises of various kinds
(textile mills, steamship lines, and the like) in China. Modernization, in the usual sense, thus got under way, but the beginnings
were small in relation to the huge size of the country and its population. Small or not, they were sufficient to produce considerable
disruption—elimination of some traditional handicraft industries,
the growth of urban slum populations, the weakening of family
ties in areas most exposed to modernization, and other problems.

After its defeat by the British in the misleadingly named Opium
War (1839–42), the Manchu dynasty was progressively forced to
legalize the import of opium, permit the propagation of Christianity, limit its tariffs on foreign goods to a trifling maximum of 5
per cent, create "treaty ports" under the effective jurisdiction of
foreign consuls, permit foreigners on Chinese soil to be tried under
their own rather than Chinese law (extraterritoriality), and enter

into diplomatic relations with the foreign powers. In addition, most of the outlying states composing the traditional Chinese tributary system became the colonies of the major powers (Korea of Japan, Burma of Britain, and so forth). At the end of the nineteenth century, substantial parts of China itself were appropriated as commercial spheres of influence by the major foreign powers, other than the United States, which protested against this process in its Open Door Policy, while remaining technically under Chinese sovereignty and jurisdiction. These serious infringements of Chinese sovereignty were reluctantly but unavoidably sanctioned by the Manchus at each stage in a series of "unequal treaties," as the Chinese call them.

The dynasty made some largely ineffective efforts to beat the foreigners at their own game through using international law and partially modernizing its bureaucratic system and general performance in order to contain the Western impact and preserve its own authority. In the long run, these efforts were in vain. By the end of the nineteenth century, the Manchus were not only weakened beyond the point of no return, they were also increasingly discredited in the eyes of politically conscious Chinese as the representatives of an outmoded system and furthermore as non-Chinese. Confucianism, the philosophical sanction of the imperial system, had been progressively undermined by Christianity and by the spread of Western education, science, literature, and thought. While few Chinese advocated the complete scrapping of their own tradition in favor of some replacement of Western origin, increasing numbers favored radical modifications of Chinese tradition in one way or another. Whether reformist or revolutionary in tendency, they agreed not only that Chinese society was too backward but also that the Chinese state was too weak. It needed to be strengthened, they held, not so much to control the Chinese people more effectively as to cope with the foreign powers. The main engine of change, in other words, was a growing nationalism.

Nationalism nearly always has a significant negative, or antiforeign, component, and in the case of China it first became a major force as a result not of the inroads of the feared but respected Western powers but of defeat (in 1894–95) at the hands of the despised Japanese, who owed their victory not merely to innate qualities but to the fact that they had outstripped the Chinese in the mastery of Western technology. Once aroused by the Japanese, Chinese nationalism turned against the other foreign powers as well. But nationalism, if it was to be effective, required changes in China's political system.

Revolutionary Politics

The man who emerged, by virtue of his political integrity and the inferior quality of the competition, as the main spokesman for Chinese nationalism was Sun Yat-sen. With a half-baked mixture of Chinese and Western political ideas as the basis of his anti-Manchu platform, he succeeded in forming a movement, although not at first a true political party. When at the end of 1911 the Manchus collapsed, more than being overthrown, Sun was elected Provisional President of the Republic of China by a coalition of revolutionary groups. For a variety of reasons including naïveté, however, he soon yielded the presidency to Yuan Shih-k'ai, a powerful general and official who had been instrumental in compelling the abdication of the last Manchu emperor. Sun then proceeded to form for the first time, through his able lieutenant Sung Ch'iao-jen, his own political party, the Kuomintang (National People's Party), but it was outlawed by Yuan in 1913, when it tried to organize first a parliamentary and then an armed opposition to him. Yuan then tried to set up a dictatorship but at the time of his death in 1916 was failing to do so because of further domestic revolts and the energetic opposition of Japan, whose expansionist elements disliked the idea of a strong and united China.

After Yuan's death, an ineffective Republican government, with nominal Western-style institutions, operated in Peking, while military governors (often known as warlords) controlled the provinces, which in many cases they taxed destructively in order to fight one another. Meanwhile, Sun Yat-sen tried in various ways to become a significant force in Chinese politics again and move the country in a revolutionary direction. To him, this direction was the one indicated, rather vaguely, by his Three People's Principles: Nationalism (national unity, with a strong antiforeign aspect), Democracy (mainly the right of all citizens to vote for public officials), and People's Livelihood (a kind of welfare statism). He believed that his party could and should introduce these principles in three successive stages: military unification (defeat of the warlords and expulsion of foreign influence), political tutelage (a one-party Kuomintang-controlled state supposedly engaged in training the people in the arts of self-government), and constitutional government (the full realization of Sun's concept of democracy).

By 1922, Sun had come to realize that the help he needed would not come, reliably at any rate, from the selfish warlords or the capitalist West. He quickly became receptive to the message of Lenin's Bolshevik regime and Third International (or Comintern), which offered to help China throw off the influence of the "imperialist" powers and selected the Kuomintang as its best ally for this purpose. Under this influence, Sun's ideology became more radical, although he never fully accepted Marxism. In 1923, while based in Canton, he entered into a kind of alliance with the Soviet Union (as Bolshevik Russia soon came to be called) and the Comintern. From them he received funds, arms, and competent advisers who rapidly reorganized the Kuomintang more or less along the "democratic centralist" lines of a Communist Party and created, for the first time, a Kuomintang-controlled and revolutionary army complete with officer corps, political officers ("commissars"), and a military academy. The alliance included not only the Kuomintang and the Comintern but also the young (founded 1921) Communist Party of China (CPC). Sun, who naturally wanted to retain control over the alliance, insisted that the Chinese Communists must enter the Kuomintang as regular members, abide by its discipline, and refrain from operating as a disciplined bloc within it. The Communist leadership objected to these demands and finally accepted them only at the direct order of the Comintern, whose sense of stake in the alliance with Sun was greater than its interest in the views or even the fortunes of the CPC.

In spite of the Communists' reservations and political inexperience, their enthusiasm and the effectiveness of their Leninist political tactics were so great that they played a key role in organizing the masses into labor and peasant unions under the Kuomintang banner, penetrating the new officer corps (especially the political officers), and gaining high party posts in the Kuomintang. The anti-Communist General Chiang Kai-shek, who became the leading figure in the Kuomintang after Sun Yat-sen's death in 1925, feared the capture of the Kuomintang by a Comintern-orchestrated pincers, one arm operating from above (the Soviet advisers and the Communists in leading positions in the Kuomintang) and the other from below (the Communist-led mass organizations). In the spring of 1926, he used military force to contain the first of these arms, and a year later to crush the second. Stalin, who had hoped to the end that Chiang could be kept loyal to the alliance with the Comintern or at the worst expelled from it, had to recognize (in the summer of 1927) the end of the alliance, not only with Chiang but with the so-called Left Kuomintang, which had been anti-Chiang but had been alienated from the Comintern as well by Stalin's policies. He belatedly authorized Communist armed risings against Chiang, but those that were tried were disastrously unsuccessful. By mid-1928, Stalin had settled on protracted guerrilla warfare in the rural areas as the most promising Communist strategy for China, although he would have been glad to see a revival of Communist influence in the cities if possible, as it was not.

The Kuomintang in Power

By that time, Chiang Kai-shek had established control of the lower Yangtze Valley and nominally completed the so-called Northern Expedition through the capture of Peking. He then proclaimed the end of Sun Yat-sen's stage of military unification and the beginning of political tutelage. He established his capital at Nanking and was recognized by the foreign powers, including eventually the Soviet Union.

The new regime was faced with huge problems, over and above the ultimately fatal one that the Communist opposition had been scotched but not destroyed. The country in reality was far from united, and Chiang never succeeded in disarming the forces of some of the provincial warlords or in bringing them under effective control. China's underdevelopment remained massive, by modern standards. Worst of all, Japanese expansionists still looked with hostility on any strong leader who seemed to be making even limited progress toward unifying and modernizing China.

Given these obstacles, the Kuomintang government while in Nanking (1928–37) made some real progress along nation-building lines, and the difficulties that other developing nations have encountered recently make Chiang's achievements seem more impressive in retrospect than they appeared to critics at the time. The transportation network and industrial system were significantly enlarged. A unified national currency was introduced for the first time. With the aid of highly competent German advisers, a national army (distinct from the provincial forces) was created, although it lacked the political élan necessary to eliminate the Communists, and the firepower and mobility to match the Japanese. Some of the major provincial warlords were defeated by this army, and others (notably the one in Manchuria) gave their support to Chiang out of patriotic motives. Impressive progress was made toward abolishing the special privileges of the foreign powers under the "unequal treaties," with the exception of those of the major powers—Britain, Japan, and the United States.

On the other hand, the Nanking government's performance was also marked by failures and setbacks, under which it ultimately sank. The conservatism of Chiang and his most influential supporters permeated the political system and increasingly alienated the intellectuals. There was a strong official tendency to label any critic as Communist or pro-Communist and to employ police sanctions against him. The efforts made to institute self-government and constitutional government were meager in the extreme. What progressive social and economic legislation was promulgated remained largely on paper. While expensive but unsuccessful efforts were made to annihilate the Communists, the Japanese were repeatedly appeased, to the detriment of China's national interests and Chiang's prestige.

Which side of the Nanking government's balance sheet, the positive or the negative, would have come in time clearly to outweigh the other will never be known, for the necessary time was denied it. As a kind of tribute to the progress being made by the Kuomintang toward national unification and development, and in particular to its growing influence in Manchuria to the probable detriment of Japanese interests there, the Japanese military applied almost continuous military and political pressures to the Nanking government from 1931 on. They began by seizing all of Manchuria and extending their control down to the Great Wall. From this imposing base they rapidly increased their influence in North China south of the Wall. The more Chinese of various walks of life and political persuasions protested and demonstrated against this aggressive policy, the more the Japanese expansionists claimed to see the Nanking government as the pawn or victim of a Comintern and Chinese Communist plot to "bolshevize" China, a plot from which it needed deliverance through Japanese help. This self-serving line tended to galvanize Chiang into even more strenuous, although still unsuccessful, efforts to destroy the Communists, for the purpose among others of eliminating this plausible pretext for Japanese intervention.

But, under the pressure of Chinese public opinion and Soviet diplomacy and by force of circumstance—he was seized in the

December, 1936, Sian Incident by some of his own commanders who favored resistance to Japan and was bargained with under duress—Chiang reversed his policy and agreed in 1937 to a united front with the CPC against Japanese aggression. Partly to prevent this second Kuomintang-Communist alliance from having time to consolidate itself, as it would probably not have done in any case, the Japanese military enlarged a small clash in July, 1937, in North China into a major although undeclared war. Within a few months, Chiang's government lost most of its best troops and the key coastal regions of the country, including its capital city. It retreated up the Yangtze River and made its base in the remote but wealthy province of Szechwan. Deprived of the modernizing influence of direct contact with the coastal cities, it grew more conservative than ever, as well as more authoritarian and corrupt. During these difficult years, the most significant aid it received from abroad came from the Soviet Union, mainly via the Burma Road, because Stalin wanted to support a Chinese national resistance to Japan as a means of distracting the Japanese military from attacking the Soviet Far East, as they showed an occasional tendency to do, and he regarded the Kuomintang as a more useful instrument for this purpose than the CPC.

In 1941, because of Pearl Harbor and the German invasion of the Soviet Union, the United States replaced the Soviet Union as the main source of external military aid for the Chiang government and became its political patron as well. This benevolence, as well as increasingly effective American military operations in the Pacific, led the Chiang government to relax considerably its own efforts against the Japanese, which in any case had not amounted to much since 1938, on the assumption that the United States would ultimately take care of China's Japanese problem, while using some of its forces to blockade the Communist areas and husbanding others for a decisive test of strength with the Communists after the defeat of Japan. American efforts to modernize the Chinese army were resisted to the extent that they would have involved a reduction in size and other changes with disruptive effects on the Kuomintang's political machine. Given this uninspiring leadership and strategy and the various difficulties unavoidably created by the war, conditions in the Kuomintang areas deteriorated badly during the last years of the war, the most conspicuous aspect of the deterioration being a rampant inflation. American aid and support, in short, enabled the Kuomintang to survive the war as a nominally victorious power and even as a permanent (until 1971) member of the United Nations Security Council, but they did not alter the fact that Chiang's regime was in reality weaker, relative to its problems and its opposition, at the end of the war than it had been at the beginning.

The Rise of the Chinese Communist Movement

The disaster of 1927 fragmented the CPC so that its head, represented by the Central Committee headquarters operating underground in Shanghai and maintaining communication with the Comintern, had little direct contact with the body, represented by scattered pockets in Central and South China controlled by Communist-led military units. Mainly by championing the interests of the local peasants through various types of land reform and the building of guerrilla forces, the leaders of these pockets expanded them into areas known as soviets. The most successful and important was the one in southern Kiangsi led by Mao Tse-tung, a Hunanese of activist temperament and shrewd political intelligence. A desire to bring Mao's base area and forces under his own control was one reason Li Li-san, the energetic and overbearing de facto leader of the CPC, in the summer of 1930 drew on the contingents of the young Red Army in the various base areas to launch an offensive aimed at capturing the cities of the Yangtze Valley. The failure of this campaign led to the purging of Li by the Comintern and to a series of increasingly powerful Nationalist (or Kuomintang) offensives against the soviets; thereafter, the Red Army avoided the cities as a general rule.

In 1931–33, for a variety of reasons, the Central Committee moved its headquarters from Shanghai to Mao's soviet in Kiangsi. The political sequel is somewhat obscure, but it appears that personal rivalries and Nationalist military pressures contributed to something of a power struggle in Kiangsi during this period. Chou En-lai, a brilliant man of broader background and outlook than Mao's who had just arrived from Shanghai, objected to Mao's guerrilla strategy and his use of political officers of the Red Army as instruments of civil control, and insisted that they operate solely within the army and that civil functions be left to the civilian Party apparatus. On these and other issues, Chou asserted increasing control over the Red Army and its strategy.

Regardless of these disputes, the soviet areas as a whole were being increasingly blockaded and squeezed by superior Nationalist forces in a series of "encirclement" or "annihilation" campaigns.

By October, 1934, the plight of the Kiangsi Soviet was such that the Communists had to break out if they were to avoid destruction. They did break out, to the west, and set out on the famous one-year, 6,000-mile Long March. In January, 1935, at Tsuni in Kwei-chow, Mao Tse-tung succeeded in capitalizing on military mistakes that he attributed to Chou and others to gain effective control over the Party's military affairs, the important political and strategic aspects in particular. He did not, however, gain undisputed control over the Central Committee and its Political Bureau (Politburo) as is asserted in later (post-1943) official Party histories, all written from the Maoist standpoint. The remarkably agile Chou En-lai succeeded in accommodating himself to the altered situation.

A few months later, Mao debated a variety of issues with Chang Kuo-t'ao, then his principal rival and a man who had his own army and had led the second most important soviet (in the Yangtze Valley) until squeezed out by the Nationalists. Unable to agree, the two men with their respective followings split. Chang was effectively eliminated from contention soon afterward by defeats suffered at the hands of Muslim cavalry in Northwest China. Mao and his contingent settled, after many harrowing experiences, in northern Shensi, where they established a soviet centered (after December, 1936) upon the town of Yenan and were promptly blockaded from the south by Nationalist forces.

Since about 1932, both the Comintern and the CPC had been convinced of the need for a united front in China to resist Japanese aggression, a line that became increasingly popular with non-Communist Chinese as well. The critical question was whether the desired united front should include Chiang Kai-shek and the Kuomintang or be formed by isolating, excluding, and if possible destroying the Nationalist leadership and winning the remaining elements of the Kuomintang to a coalition headed by the CPC. At first, the objective was a united front of the latter type, but little real progress was made toward achieving it, and the Japanese menace grew more and more pressing. While the CPC leadership remained uncertain, and perhaps divided, as to what to do, Stalin inclined (in 1935–36) toward a united front of the first type. He took the political crisis created by Chiang Kai-shek's seizure in December, 1936, by some of his own commanders favoring a united front with the CPC as an opportunity to press his view on the CPC, which adopted it after a keen debate. The outcome was a complex series of negotiations lasting well into 1937 and an agreement on a united front under Chiang's leadership.

Each side made some political concessions, and there were important elements in the CPC that favored abiding by them and sincerely accepting Chiang's leadership against Japan. Mao Tse-tung disagreed, on the ground that such an approach would hamper and even endanger the CPC. He ultimately gained acceptance for his view that, while paying lip service to the united front and soft-pedaling class struggle (land reform in particular), the CPC should not only operate independently in reality but should also engage in revolutionary warfare against the Nationalists as well as against the Japanese as opportunity offered. This strategy brought a rapid expansion of Communist base areas behind (to the east of) the Japanese lines, often at the expense of local Nationalist units trying less effectively to do the same thing. (The nature of this strategy—"protracted war," "people's war," and so forth—is summarized in Chapter 5.)

At the cost of serious friction with the Nationalists just short of an open break, the CPC capitalized so effectively on its skills in revolutionary warfare and on the conditions created by the Japanese invasion (notably the drastic weakening of the Kuomintang and the hatred aroused by Japanese atrocities against the peasants) that by 1945 it controlled some twenty base areas (now known as liberated areas), located mainly in North and Northwest China and containing about 60 million people. There was even a possibility for a time that the Red Army might get arms directly from the United States under Lend-Lease, but this possibility did not materialize owing to objections from the Nationalists and the eventual American decision (in 1945) not to stage a landing on the China coast. The CPC thus received its foreign assistance in the form of Soviet intervention rather than American aid.

This was not an unmixed blessing for the CPC. Parallel with Mao's rise to power, which was probably irreversible from within the Party after 1938 and was formally proclaimed in 1943, and with the Party's growing strength had gone what the scholar Richard Lowenthal has called an "emancipation by conspiracy" of the CPC from Stalin's control. It was made possible by circumstances—notably China's size and remoteness and Stalin's preoccupation with the German invasion after 1941. It was apparently promoted by Mao as a conscious policy, but sufficiently unobtrusively so that Stalin never thought it necessary or worthwhile to take public notice of the process. A Soviet invasion of Manchuria, which Stalin decided on at least as early as 1943, offered the prospect of the defeat of Japan and an infusion of modern weapons for the rather skimpily armed Chinese Communist forces, but it also held the danger of satellitization. Mao escaped this disaster because Soviet forces, when they invaded Manchuria in August, 1945, did not actually come below the Great Wall; because Mao had taken care to eliminate or neutralize any possible rivals whom Stalin might have tried to substitute for him; and because Mao ignored the apparent Soviet preference that the CPC make its headquarters in Manchuria under the protecting (and dominating) wing of the Soviet Army. By preserving his party's autonomy, Mao was able to fend off Stalin's pressures on him to enter into a coalition government with the Kuomintang— a step that the United States was also urging on the Nationalists in 1945–46—except under conditions that would have given the CPC and parties friendly to it a veto over any major acts of the proposed coalition, which never came into existence.

The Kuomintang would not accept the CPC's terms and was rendered overconfident by its vast superiority on paper. The withdrawal of Soviet forces from Manchuria and of American forces from North China in the spring of 1946 weakened the influence of the United States, which had been trying to mediate the conflict, and the Soviet Union, which had been urging the CPC to form a coalition with the Nationalists. It was promptly followed by the outbreak of civil war. The Communists benefited from Japanese weapons and considerable territory turned over to them by Soviet forces while in occupation of Manchuria, but their main assets were superior leadership, morale, and organization, as well as the material and psychological damage inflicted on the Kuomintang by the war against Japan. In consequence, after a series of huge campaigns, the Red Army came into control of Manchuria and most of North China by the end of 1948, the Yangtze Valley by June, 1949, and the rest of China (except for Tibet, Hainan Island, and Taiwan) by the end of 1949. Among those surprised by the swiftness of the Communist victory was evidently Stalin, who would probably have preferred a Communist North China and a Nationalist South China, so that the CPC would be relatively amenable to his control. But what the disaster of 1927 had begun, the triumph of 1949 guaranteed: a Chinese Communist movement in no mood to take orders from Moscow where its vital interests were involved, especially now that it had become vigorous through struggle and confident by virtue of victory.

FURTHER READINGS

Two excellent introductions to China for the general reader or beginning student are available: John K. Fairbank's classic, *The*

United States and China, 3d ed., Cambridge, Mass.: Harvard University Press, 1971; and Lucian W. Pye, *China: An Introduction,* Boston: Little, Brown, 1972. Each contains a detailed reading list; the list given here will accordingly be kept brief.

Probably the best available general history of China is the relevant chapters of Edwin O. Reischauer, John K. Fairbank, and Albert M. Craig, *East Asia,* 2 vols., Boston: Houghton Mifflin, 1958, 1965, London: George Allen & Unwin, 1961, 1965. On the recent decades, O. Edmund Clubb, *Twentieth Century China,* 2d ed., New York: Columbia University Press, 1972, is useful.

Little of value is currently available on the Kuomintang. Two important exceptions are: Tuan-sheng Ch'ien, *The Government and Politics of China, 1912–1949,* Cambridge, Mass.: Harvard University Press, 1950 (paperback reprint, Stanford, Calif.: Stanford University Press, 1970); and Theodore H. White and Annalee Jacoby, *Thunder Out of China,* New York: William Sloane, 1946, London: Gollancz, 1947 (a brilliant journalistic account of the World War II period).

There is considerably more on the history of the Chinese Communist movement. One source of great value is Conrad Brandt, Benjamin Schwartz, and John K. Fairbank, eds., *A Documentary History of Chinese Communism,* London: George Allen & Unwin, 1947, New York: Atheneum, 1967. Every serious student should read Benjamin Schwartz's classic, *Chinese Communism and the Rise of Mao,* New York: Harper & Row, 1967, even though his version of Mao's rise is not in accord with the findings of later research. A fine new history is James Pinckney Harrison, *The Long March to Power: A History of the Chinese Communist Party, 1921–72,* New York: Praeger, 1972. Two important studies of the CPC's relations with Moscow are: Richard C. Thornton, *The Comintern and the Chinese Communists, 1928–1931,* Seattle: University of Washington Press, 1969; and Charles B. McLane, *Soviet Policy and the Chinese Communists, 1931–1946,* New York: Columbia University Press, 1958. A classic journalistic account of the Chinese Communists in Shensi is Edgar Snow, *Red Star Over China,* New York: Random House, 1938, London: Gollancz, 1937, 1968, Harmondsworth: Penguin, 1972, and other editions. An interesting although somewhat one-dimensional analysis of the Chinese Communist rise to power is Chalmers A. Johnson, *Peasant Nationalism and Communist Power: The Emergence of Revolutionary China, 1937–1945,* Stanford, Calif.: Stanford University Press, 1962, London: Oxford University Press, 1963. A. Doak Barnett, *China on the Eve of Communist Takeover,* New York: Praeger, 1961, London: Thames & Hudson, 1963, is a valuable firsthand account of the Nationalist collapse. An ambitious and useful, although tendentious and inaccurate, account of American policy is Tang Tsou, *America's Failure in China, 1941–50,* Chicago: University of Chicago Press, 1963. A useful recent study is Jacques Guillermaz, *A History of the Chinese Communist Party, 1921–49,* New York: Random House, 1972.

3. Political History to the Cultural Revolution

On coming to power after a struggle lasting two decades, the CPC enjoyed some valuable assets. As a result of Communist victory in a "protracted war" (Mao Tse-tung's phrase), the CPC's rival, the Kuomintang, was not only defeated but discredited, although of course it was still in control of the island of Taiwan. The country was more united, or at least more susceptible of being united, than it had been for many decades. The CPC enjoyed widespread and often enthusiastic popular support, although much more so in its older strongholds in North China than in the recently "liberated" provinces of the South. This support derived in part from the stress placed at that time in the CPC's propaganda on its short-run or "minimum" program, as against its long-term or "maximum" program (socialism and Communism). The minimum program, to which Mao Tse-tung had given the label New Democracy, emphasized the elimination through sweeping reforms of inequities that had existed under the old regime, such as the rural landlord system, and thus could command the approval of patriotic and progressive Chinese, most of whom in fact rallied to the CPC's leadership in 1949 or earlier. The main widely shared objection to the CPC related to its obvious ties with, and its suspected subservience to, the none-too-popular Soviet Union, a suspicion reinforced by the extraordinary lengths to which the CPC went in the early years after 1949 in proclaiming the Soviet Union as China's best friend, model, and ally.

Recovery and "New Democracy" (1949–52)

The CPC's principal initial domestic objectives were to eliminate remaining foci of actual or potential organized opposition to its rule, to bring the entire human and material resources of the country under its own effective control, to restore the battered economy roughly to the best levels it had attained before 1949, and to implement the Party's minimum program. Because of the CPC's unique and valuable experience of revolutionary social and political action acquired over the previous two decades, and because of the favorable conditions just mentioned, the Party was largely successful in achieving its initial objectives during the three years that its timetable allowed for the purpose.

The new regime's initial political organization and behavior were heavily influenced by the fact that it had come to power through a huge civil war necessarily fought, because of imperfect communications, in a rather decentralized manner. The organization of power after 1949 was correspondingly regional, and to a high degree military. This situation, which smacked of warlordism, was basically unacceptable, or at any rate was acceptable only as a transitional state of affairs, to the new central leadership in Peking, which set about substituting a more centralized and essentially civilian power structure whose key component would be the Communist Party apparatus. By the end of 1952, this process was well under way, although not complete. Among the levers used, in addition to Party discipline, were Peking's exclusive control of incoming Soviet economic and military aid and the opportunity created by the Korean War (1950–53) for drawing on and reshuffling the military resources available to the regional leaders.

Even the partial regionalization of power during the early years years did not prevent the general, although not uniform, implementation of programs that were desired by the center and were also acceptable to the regional authorities. These programs were promoted not only by local cadres (administrative personnel) but also through the CPC's tested strategy (the "mass line") of involving at least the poorer and more progressive sections of the populace (poor peasants, students, and the like) in a series of "mass organizations" (peasant associations, student groups, and so forth) and "mass campaigns." The latter were (and are) used to promote the regime's domestic objectives and to eliminate its perceived adversaries, actual or potential, who were considered such because of their "reactionary" class origins or political affiliations.

The first great mass campaign was the "agrarian reform" of 1950–52, whose announced purpose was to eliminate landlordism (exploitation of peasants by actual or alleged landlords) from the countryside, to divide up the landlords' land (chiefly among those defined as poor peasants), and to establish a system of free peasant landholding as a necessary preliminary to subsequent collectivization (or socialization). In reality, a great many rich peasants (landlords who farmed some land and rented out the rest) as well as landlords were caught up in the campaign, which featured the characteristic Chinese Communist procedure of the mass trial and was accompanied by a great deal of violence against its targets. Although with much overkill, the campaign achieved its objectives: the landlords were eliminated (although not always killed) as a social class and as an obstacle to Communist control of the countryside, and freeholding became virtually universal even if only temporary. Less violent, but perhaps of more lasting significance, was the marriage reform of 1950, whose general purpose was to begin, through the introduction of legal equality between the sexes, the process of "liberating" the Chinese woman from her traditional subordination to three successive males in her life (her father, husband, and eldest son) and involving her in public life, except at the policy-making level, on roughly the same footing as men. This massive assault on tradition aroused widespread discontent among women as well as men, but was nevertheless pressed vigorously and with increasing success since equality between the sexes could be taught to the youth through the school system. At the end of 1950, when tension was high owing to Chinese intervention in the Korean War, the regime introduced a two-year campaign against "counterrevolutionaries," who in effect were any real or suspected opponents, such as former Kuomintang supporters, who could not be otherwise classified or had not already been disposed of. More limited campaigns conducted during the same period were the "three-anti" campaign against corruption among Party cadres and the "five-anti" campaign against violations of increasingly stringent official regulations on the part of private businessmen. On the basis of the available evidence, including an unpublished portion of a speech delivered by Mao Tse-tung on February 27, 1957, an estimate of three-quarters of a million people executed at the CPC's instigation during this period appears reasonable. It is also worth noting that sources of foreign influence in China (diplomatic missions, trading companies, missions, and the like) were either eliminated or had their activities severely restricted, so that their Chinese contacts and constituencies would not be subjected to demands on their loyalties or sympathies competitive with those made by the CPC.

Victory in the civil war and its own elaborate organization conferred on the CPC a high degree of effective control over China's economic resources, as well as an opportunity unprecedented for many years to restore them to viability after the ravages inflicted by decades of warfare and disorder. The rampant inflation was soon checked through the introduction of rigid controls and the calculation of prices and wages in terms of "parity units" (each of which consisted of specified quantities of certain basic commodities) rather than cash. Existing communications, railways in particular, and factories were restored to approximately normal functioning with the help of several thousand Japanese engineers and technicians who had remained in China after their country's defeat in 1945; they were sent home in 1953, when the need for their services had ended, and a usefully favorable impression on Japanese public opinion was made at the same time. Prolonged and often difficult negotiations with the Soviet Union, beginning in 1949, resulted in Soviet commitments, some published and some secret, to extend economic and military aid on a substantial scale, but almost entirely on a reimbursable basis. Some of this had arrived by the end of 1952, but the greater part was to come later and was clearly related not to the reconstruction phase but to the succeeding phase of new industrialization discussed in the next section. In November, 1952, as prolonged negotiations over Soviet aid to the forthcoming Chinese First Five-Year Plan were in progress in Moscow, Peking accordingly proclaimed at least on paper the reduction of the regional governments to the level of mere agencies of the center and set up a powerful State Planning Committee to plan and supervise the projected drive toward industrialization.

The "Transition to Socialism" (1953–55)

The First Five-Year Plan (1953–57) represented primarily an ambitious effort to introduce a new heavy industrial system with the aid of Soviet advice, capital equipment, and credits. In addition, agriculture, handicrafts, and commerce and industry were to be socialized, with important variations from the Soviet model, such as a much lower level of agricultural mechanization.

Although it was to prove basically successful in the industrial sector, the plan was to be bedeviled by Soviet vacillation and disagreements within the Chinese leadership. Kao Kang, the boss of the Northeast region (Manchuria), which contained China's major existing heavy industrial facilities, was appointed chairman of the State Planning Committee when it was created in November, 1952. A man of overbearing personality, he soon developed differences with his colleagues over matters of political power and economic policy. He favored preferential treatment for the Northeast in the matter of new industrial investment and held out for a high level of regional autonomy, whereas the mainstream of the Party leadership, including Mao Tse-tung, favored a more geographically balanced investment program under centralized control. Kao advocated priority for the mechanization of agriculture over its socialization, a "soft" line because it would promote the enrichment of the peasants, whereas the mainstream preferred the opposite scheme of priorities. Kao enjoyed exceptionally close personal relations with the Soviet leadership and apparently counted on them to maximize the volume of Soviet aid. Some Sino-Soviet disagreement on the extent of Moscow's commitment to the Chinese First Five-Year Plan had evidently developed by the beginning of 1953, however, and after Stalin's death (announced on March 6, 1953) there continued to be uncertainty as to how much Soviet aid could actually be expected. Kao nevertheless hung on but was weakened, in the eyes of his colleagues, by repeated demonstrations of dissension and unreliability in Moscow, including the fall in late June, 1953, of Lavrenti Beria and the proclamation on August 8, 1953, by Georgi Malenkov, the most conspicuous member of the ensuing "collective leadership," of a "New Course" stressing consumer goods rather than capital equipment that, among other things, could be made available to the Chinese economy.

As soon as Beria's execution was announced in Moscow (December 24, 1953), esoteric indications, not publicized for several weeks, began to appear in Peking that Kao was in serious political trouble. At almost exactly that time, Mao was evidently taken seriously ill, and 'the desperate Kao tried by some means unknown to the Party constitution, possibly a military coup, not only to salvage his eroding position but also to make himself Mao's second-in-command in the Party and the state. He and Jao Shu-shih, the regional boss of East China who apparently supported him, failed by a wide margin; they were purged, together with some of their subordinates in the two regions, in the late winter or early spring of 1954, and Kao committed suicide soon afterward. Thus passed the most dangerous leadership crisis of the early years; had it turned out in Kao's favor, Soviet influence on the Chinese political and economic systems would probably not have fallen off as sharply as it actually did. The official version of the affair was not announced until April, 1955, by which time the resignation of Malenkov as Premier and the rising power of Nikita

Khrushchev, who had won the favor of the mainstream of the Chinese leadership by committing himself to a somewhat higher level of support for Chinese industrialization, had at last made it possible to put the First Five-Year Plan into purportedly final shape. Before then, presumably, an announcement of the Kao Kang affair, even though its Soviet aspect was not referred to publicly, might have endangered the desired increase in aid.

Mao's illness and the purge of Kao led to important changes in political organization (see Chapter 8). Among these were the completion of the process, which had begun earlier, of dissolving the various regional power structures and bringing the provinces under direct central control. During his convalescence, beginning in March, 1954, Mao supervised the drafting and later the adoption (in September, 1954) of a purportedly permanent state constitution under which he, as Chairman of the People's Republic of China (C.P.R.) enjoyed a prestige and political position matched in the Communist world at that time only by Yugoslavia's Tito, but under which the organization of the state otherwise resembled rather closely that of the Soviet Union.

This picture of seeming progress was marred in 1954 by rural unrest and a "blind influx" of peasants into the cities caused by summer floods in the Yangtze Valley and by the beginnings of agricultural collectivization under the rubric "lower-level" or "semisocialist" agricultural producers' cooperatives, in which land was worked, although not yet owned, collectively. This turbulence led the regime to tighten police controls and conduct a second major campaign against "counterrevolutionaries" that lasted into 1955; it was probably also the main cause of a food supply crisis that affected the cities by the spring of 1955. The latter in turn led to changes in the system of state procurement of grain and to what was probably the most acute debate on agricultural policy to date within the leadership. A majority of the Party's Politburo and Central Committee evidently favored decreasing the rate of formation of lower-level agricultural producers' cooperatives projected in the First Five-Year Plan, which had only recently been put into final shape. A minority led by Mao Tse-tung, who claimed with some exaggeration that the Chinese peasant had an innately socialist mentality, insisted that the answer to the problem was an increase in the rate. Instead of accepting the view of the adverse majority in good Leninist fashion, Mao got his way by taking his case on July 31, 1955, to a specially convened conference of provincial Party secretaries and to the massive Party propaganda machine, over which he took care to maintain a personal ascendancy. Once he had manipulated acceptance of his basic point in this way, Mao proceeded at intervals to raise his target for the number of cooperatives to be formed during the life of the First Five-Year Plan. In the winter of 1955–56, after the 1955 harvest had been gathered, the campaign escalated to the level of "higher-level" or "fully socialist" agricultural producers' cooperatives, in which the land was legally owned by the cooperative except for family private plots; by the end of 1956, nearly all agricultural land was held in this way. By insisting on getting his own way in a matter of such importance, Mao violated Leninist norms and set a dangerous precedent that was later to tempt him into even more spectacular violations.

In the private commercial and industrial sector, on the other hand, Mao endorsed a much more moderate approach. Beginning in 1955, private enterprises were "transformed" peacefully into "joint state-private" enterprises in which the original owner's capital was effectively confiscated; he was paid interest on it, however, and was usually retained as a salaried, sometimes highly salaried, manager or adviser. By Communist standards, this was a mild policy, and it aroused considerable high-level interest in Eastern Europe.

Mao and the De-Stalinization Question (1956–57)

Mao was probably encouraged in his increasingly arbitrary behavior (by orthodox Leninist standards), not only by his advancing age—he was born in 1893—but by his sense of superiority to and contempt for the post-Stalin leaders of the Soviet Union. Some of his principal colleagues, on the other hand, evidently including the second-ranking figure in the Party, Liu Shao-ch'i, regarded Mao's performance with growing reservations and drew support from the current deflation of Stalin's memory in the Soviet Union, culminating in Khrushchev's famous secret speech of February 25, 1956.

Almost immediately after the return from the Soviet Union of the Chinese delegation to the Party Congress at which Khrushchev had made his secret speech, the CPC leadership issued (on April 5) a major editorial giving in effect its reaction to the speech and to the broader question of de-Stalinization. The editorial, which did not mention the secret speech or Mao, hinted that he had been guilty of his own version of the "cult of personality" for which Stalin had been condemned by his successors and that appropriate measures would be taken. Encouraged no doubt by the memory of his success of the previous year, Mao promptly began to push back by trying to demonstrate his own political creativity and absolve himself of the implicit charge of having created a "cult of personality." In an unpublished speech delivered in April, 1956, he proposed among other things, although unsuccessfully, a two-thirds reduction of the Party and government bureaucracies, some of whose leaders were among those trying to clip his wings.

Shortly afterward, Mao effectively captured and escalated a campaign that had been in progress since the beginning of the year for improving, through better treatment, the loyalty and performance of intellectuals (in China, a broad term connoting virtually anyone with at least a secondary education who is not engaged primarily in political activity). Partly to humiliate his more bureaucratically oriented colleagues, who were trying to trim his cult, and over their reservations, Mao launched through the Party propaganda machine the famous Hundred Flowers campaign, which amounted to an invitation to intellectuals, and to a lesser degree others as well, to offer preferably constructive criticisms of the CPC. He probably hoped that he would be singled out for praise in contrast to his colleagues. But cowed by years of Communist pressures and probably sensing a division within the Party leadership on the question, the prospective critics were silent on all but the most routine administrative issues.

The CPC's main effort to cope with the problem of Mao and his cult was made, in an atmosphere of constitutionality, at its Eighth Congress in September, 1956. Among several manifestations of the effort that could be cited were the deletion from the Party constitution of all references to Mao and his "thought," his elimination from effective control over the Party Secretariat by the conferring of the post of General Secretary of the Central Committee on Teng Hsiao-p'ing, who was then the most rapidly rising figure in the Party leadership, and the creation of the title of Honorary Chairman of the Central Committee in the unfulfilled hope that Mao could be persuaded or pressured into retiring to it.

The Chinese leadership was shocked by the Hungarian crisis of October-November, 1956, which was in part a result of Khrushchev's attack on Stalin, and which evoked some strikes and disorders in China and suggested that the potential for another explosion of the Hungarian type might exist there. The pressures on

Mao eased, and by way of opening a small safety valve for discontent his colleagues agreed to support a modified, somewhat bureaucratized version of the Hundred Flowers campaign, now usually styled a "rectification" campaign. There still remained an important difference: the Party apparatus leaders preferred that the Party "rectify" itself, as it had done before, whereas Mao envisaged the unprecedented procedure (for a Communist Party or state) of the educated public and even the masses rectifying the Party from without. In an important speech, unpublished at the time, delivered on February 27, 1957, to launch the rectification campaign, Mao tried to blur the edges of the issue and encourage a breaking of the virtual public silence by describing the questions involved, in familiar if vague Leninist terminology, as "nonantagonistic contradictions" among the "people." Even though he gave no indication of any limits on his invitation to free speech, potential critics continued to hold back, perhaps because they realized that some of Mao's colleagues were still not fully behind him, until on April 13 the *People's Daily* (*Jen-min Jih-pao*) published an editorial that summarized and implicitly endorsed Mao's speech, although without referring to it. During the ensuing weeks, there occurred a variety of manifestations of public disapproval that the party leadership, except perhaps some of those who opposed the rectification campaign, had almost certainly not expected: strikes, student demonstrations, critical statements by prominent non-Communists at meetings convened by the CPC Central Committee's United Front Work Department, and the like. Hardly any criticism of the regime and of Mao that any non-Communist, or even anti-Communist, foreigner could think of failed to be expressed by one or more of these critics; the attacks centered on the Party's dictatorship, which it was (and is) pleased to call leadership, over the Chinese people and the draconian nature of its development program for "building socialism."

Although some of the opponents of the rectification campaign within the Party leadership may have been pleased, the regime as a whole was confronted with a most awkward dilemma, into which Mao at least cannot knowingly have gotten it in spite of later efforts by the Party to prove that it had expected the severity of the criticism from the start and had been trying to smoke out the critics. On the one hand, to tolerate the criticism, and still more to allow it to continue, would risk in Communist (including Chinese Communist) eyes the erosion of the party's claim to authority based on its alleged infallibility in major matters of "line" and policy. On the other hand, to silence, and still more to punish, the critics would be to break the clearly implicit promise of immunity given when the campaign was launched. The problem was especially acute because one of the "contradictions" mentioned by Mao in his February 27 speech was that with the Kuomintang, which he had said could be transformed from an "antagonistic" into a "nonantagonistic" contradiction capable of a compromise agreement through proper handling. But any hope, however faint, of an accommodation with the Kuomintang would be destroyed if it should appear that there was no political security for non-Communists under Peking's aegis. One obvious obstacle to such an accommodation was the Kuomintang's close ties with the United States; these must presumably be weakened as a first step in the desired direction. With this in mind, Peking probably welcomed the serious anti-American riots that broke out on "Black Friday" (May 24, 1957) in Taipei, over issues apparently not directly related to developments on the mainland, but was certainly disappointed when President Chiang Kai-shek personally ordered troops to suppress the disorders and thereby showed his determination not to let his relations with the United States pass the point of no return. The next day brought signs on the mainland that Mao and his colleagues had begun to consider that the ferment there, whose most alarming manifestations to the leadership were probably the student demonstrations, must also be suppressed, now that there appeared to be no chance of an accommodation with the Kuomintang in the near future. By early June, a large-scale program of silencing, "countercriticizing," and often punishing (usually more with administrative than with criminal sanctions) the "rightists" who had spoken against the regime during the previous weeks was getting under way. To justify this violation of the critics' promised immunity, a revised version of Mao's February 27 speech was published on June 18; it omitted certain passages, including the reference to the Kuomintang, and inserted certain new material, notably a caution that criticism must not go so far as to challenge the CPC's "leadership" over the country or the validity of its program for "socialist construction." Although the rectification campaign continued, it was now directed entirely from within the CPC, while an "antirightist struggle" raged against critics within and outside the Party who were alleged to have exceeded permissible limits during the earlier period of "blooming and contending."

This fiasco was a severe shock to the entire leadership, which had at least outwardly given its approval to the campaign, but to Mao more than the others, since he had been the campaign's main promoter. The trauma was all the greater for him because it contrasted painfully with a spectacular simultaneous triumph for Khrushchev, who had expressed some reservations the previous spring about the Chinese rectification campaign, over a powerful and dangerous "anti-Party group" led by Malenkov and Vyacheslav Molotov. Mao spent most of the summer away from Peking, apparently planning a comeback for himself and his regime from the colossal setback of the previous months.

The East Wind and the Great Leap Forward (1957–60)

Mao may have feared that, unless he could contrive some major successful political initiative, his colleagues would conclude that he was obsolete and superfluous and would push him into retirement as Honorary Chairman of the Party Central Committee. Having taken a moderate, almost liberal, stand during the preceding de-Stalinization phase, to a large extent in order to absolve himself of the clearly implicit accusation of having fostered a semi-Stalinist "cult of personality" focused on himself, and having sustained a serious setback in consequence, Mao was now determined to refute any possible charges that he had then become guilty of "revisionism" (a deviation by a Communist or Communists in the direction of moderation and to a degree perceived as unacceptable by other Communists applying the term). He undoubtedly wanted to avoid being considered responsible for the fiasco of 1957 in the way that Khrushchev had been held responsible for the East European crisis of 1956. From late 1957 to 1966, when his attention was pre-empted by the more urgent problems associated with the Cultural Revolution, Mao remained obsessed with the bogey of "modern revisionism" (as he called it) at home and abroad. The main personification of this abstraction to which he pointed at first was Tito; after 1959, it became Khrushchev and then his successors. A related attitude was Mao's increased distrust of intellectuals ("experts," in the sarcastic Maoist term) and their expertise and his enhanced faith in the political and nation-building potential of the masses (intrinsically "red," according to Mao) if given proper ideological guidance and political leadership—his own, of course. Given his innately radical propensities, Mao readily seized on the idea of exploiting even more intensively than hitherto the labor power of China's un-counted peasantry; accordingly, the agricultural slack season that fell during the winter of 1957–58 saw many millions of peasants put to work on a variety of capital projects, especially water-conservancy works. It was, of course, expected that in this way the output of the agricultural sector, which had grown relatively slowly during the First Five-Year Plan as compared with the impressive surge on the heavy industrial front, would be greatly increased.

Closely related to Mao's domestic preoccupations in late 1957, and of roughly equal importance in his mind, was his deter-mination to appear as the leading statesman of the Communist world even though for a long time to come his country could not equal in power the mighty Soviet Union. Prominent among the roots of this grand design was undoubtedly the consideration that increased personal influence within the international Communist movement would be helpful to Mao in re-establishing and enhanc-ing his position in China. An achievement that would obviously be very useful to Mao at home and abroad was readily visible progress toward the "liberation" of Taiwan. Now that an accom-modation with the Kuomintang was not in prospect, force and pressure were the obvious answer, but if these were to be effec-tive in the teeth of the United States Seventh Fleet, they would require the support of the Soviet Union, including at the minimum strong declaratory support and the transfer of modern (including nuclear) weapons to China. But Moscow had never shown any real enthusiasm for running risks in order to help promote the "liberation" of Taiwan by Peking. If he was to be persuaded to do more on this score, Khrushchev therefore needed to have his spine stiffened through exhortation and to be placated with con-cessions. This appeared to be all the more necessary since, at his Party's Twentieth Congress in February, 1956, he had shown (in Mao's eyes at least) a craven tendency to overestimate the *proba-bility* of thermonuclear war—an issue that Mao confused by pre-tending to minimize the *consequences* of such a war if it should occur—and had seemed only slightly more enthusiastic about the idea of active Soviet support for Communist revolutions in non-Communist countries than he had been about Stalin. But now that he had shed the restraining influence of his more cautious col-leagues, Malenkov and Molotov (purged in June, 1957) and Marshal Georgi Zhukov (purged in October, 1957), perhaps he might be more receptive to Mao's message. The prospects ap-

peared all the better because, several months in advance of the
United States, the Soviet Union had tested an ICBM in the summer of 1957 and orbited an earth satellite (Sputnik I) on October
4, thus enhancing the capabilities and morale of the "socialist
camp" and creating temporary disarray in the "imperialist camp."
Accordingly, at an important meeting held in Moscow in November, 1957, to celebrate the fortieth anniversary of the October
(Bolshevik) Revolution, Mao tried to placate Khrushchev by
insisting on the principle of Soviet "leadership" of the Communist
world and urged on him a strategy of more active confrontation,
short of actual war, with American "imperialism" on behalf of
other Communist Parties, whether in power like the Chinese or
not, under the slogan "The East wind has prevailed over the West
wind." Khrushchev soon came to realize that Mao was trying to
use him more than to follow his leadership, and that the international strategy urged by Mao would be excessively risky for the
Soviet Union whether or not it was advantageous to China.

Much as he was now to the left of Khrushchev, Mao was clearly
in advance of his principal colleagues, who in their policy statements during this period were contenting themselves for the most
part with relatively pragmatic and moderate positions such as a
program for decentralizing the control of industry to a large extent
to the provincial level (much as Khrushchev had done in the
Soviet Union), reducing the size of the agricultural producers'
cooperatives, and catching up with Great Britain in fifteen years
in the total (not per-capita) output of major industrial products.
Only Defense Minister P'eng Te-huai and Chief of Staff Huang
K'o-ch'eng seem to have opposed Mao's program outright, however. The others went along with it, in time and with varying
degrees of enthusiasm or reluctance, in part probably because of
a reluctance to face a leadership crisis so soon after the debacle of
the rectification campaign. There was general agreement with
Mao, furthermore, that, in spite of the rapid progress of the industrial sector during the First Five-Year Plan, the Soviet economic
model had proven itself unsuitable, or at least distasteful, from the
Chinese point of view and required modification in a direction
more appropriate to Chinese conditions and preferences. This
tendency was reinforced because the inflow of long-term industrial
credits from the Soviet Union came to an end during 1957, and
because Malenkov, the patron in the Soviet Union of the kind of
economic organization and planning that was being pronounced
unsuited to China, had fallen from power in mid-1957. Mao was

therefore able to get the general agreement of the central Party leadership to his radical program at a series of three major conferences held between December, 1957, and March, 1958. The provincial Party leaderships, which would have to implement the program, were not so easily convinced and were rather drastically purged during 1958. At a session of the National People's Congress held in February, 1958, the term "Great Leap Forward" began to be used publicly to describe the impending radical program, which it was officially predicted would yield sharp increases of agricultural and industrial output. At that same session, Chou En-lai turned over the Foreign Ministry to Ch'en Yi, probably in order to concentrate his efforts on his more important role as Premier and on the difficult task of helping to implement the Great Leap Forward, which to be sure was to be put into effect more through the Party apparatus than through the government bureaucracy, and perhaps also to dissociate himself to a degree from the more radical foreign policy that was to be the external counterpart of the Great Leap Forward.

In an atmosphere of considerable urgency and secrecy reflecting the tensions generated by the swing to the left in domestic and foreign policy, a second session of the Eighth Party Congress met in May, 1958. As in September, 1956, the major report was given by Liu Shao-ch'i, who in effect announced the start of the Great Leap Forward, which he said was to be marked by the generation of boundless enthusiasm for labor on the part of the masses through propaganda and by the establishment of many new small industrial enterprises. He did not mention the "people's communes," which at that time were in an experimental stage and may still have been controversial within the leadership. Marshal Lin Piao, who together with Teng Hsiao-p'ing was the fastest-rising figure in the upper ranks of the Party and a close political supporter of Mao Tse-tung, was added to the CPC's highest policy-making body, the Standing Committee of the Politburo.

During the ensuing weeks, people's communes were formed all over the country, allegedly at the demand of the peasants but actually under the direction of Party cadres. In August, the Party officially proclaimed them as the new unit of agricultural organization. On the average, a people's commune controlled a dozen agricultural producers' cooperatives (now renamed "production brigades"), and for a time it became the main unit of local administration. In keeping with the militant atmosphere of the time and Mao's emphasis on local "self-reliance," each people's commune was supposed to be as nearly self-sufficient as possible. Each one therefore set up and operated one or more local industries. The most celebrated of these were the "backyard furnaces," as they were called outside China, for converting locally available ore and scrap metal into "steel" (actually, pig iron). The people's communes had a powerful ideological aspect, necessarily so since one of their guiding ideas was to substitute nonmaterial incentives for material ones as well as to substitute massive new inputs of labor for new investment of capital that was not available. Furthermore, it was desired to imply that China was "building Communism" (the ultimate stage), not merely "socialism," and was therefore catching up with or even passing the Soviet Union in this respect even though the Chinese people were still, in Mao Tse-tung's words, "poor and blank" (that is, economically and educationally backward). Life on the people's communes was therefore lived communally to a high degree during the Great Leap Forward. Communal mess halls and nurseries were the rule. Food, clothing, and other necessities were issued from communal supplies and normally without charge, nominally at least. The family private plots were merged with the communal land and farmed collectively. There were even rumors that the sexes might be housed separately in barracks. The communal arrangements were supposed to have the practical advantage of releasing the younger women from their household tasks for work in agriculture and industry. The commune members were exhorted and driven by their Party cadres to work in the fields, in the local industrial enterprises, and so forth, for long and exhausting hours, with little reward but a necessary increase in their rations which, despite the good harvest of 1958, produced, together with the disruption of the transport system entailed by the Great Leap Forward, an urban food shortage by the end of the year. The regime was so confident of increasing output per acre through new methods, which included "close planting" and "deep plowing" as well as greatly increased applications of labor in other ways, that it directed a cut of one-third in the total sown area.

As already indicated, the Great Leap Forward was paralleled by a radical swing in foreign policy. Each of these shifts had its own logic, but the rationales were similar, and each acted on and reinforced the other. The period of the Party Congress in May, 1958, saw the launching of a violent Chinese propaganda offensive against Tito and his "modern revisionism" for effect, among others, on Khrushchev and the domestic Chinese political scene.

At the same time (May 27–July 22), Mao explained at length the implications of his new foreign strategy to a high-level conference of military men. Among its main aspects were increased support (propaganda, arms, and the like) for anti-"imperialist" wars of "national liberation" (notably the one in Algeria); a program for creating a Chinese nuclear-weapons capability with indispensable but still limited Soviet aid, and without the transfer of Soviet nuclear weapons (probably tactical) and delivery systems that Peking had requested in February or March, 1958; and a politico-military crisis in the Taiwan Strait, where the risks for Peking would be high but relatively controllable. The purposes of this crisis would be to dramatize the new Chinese approach and inspire anti-"imperialist" revolutions throughout the world, now that Khrushchev had shown himself reluctant to do so by recoiling before the implications of Mao's "East wind" line, to galvanize Khrushchev if possible into a more activist line, to weaken the tie between the Republic of China on Taiwan and the United States and thus promote the "liberation" of Taiwan, and to foster in China a "siege mentality" conducive to the prosecution of the Great Leap Forward. In particular, such a crisis would facilitate a mass campaign, which actually got under way in the summer of 1958, to enroll virtually all adults in militia units, to some extent for genuinely military or paramilitary purposes but even more as a labor force and a general control mechanism. There is no need for an account here of the crisis itself, which lasted from late August until early October, except to say that it failed to achieve its external objectives but did make a contribution to the creation of the desired atmosphere at home.

By the early autumn of 1958, it had become clear to the Party leadership that the Great Leap Forward had been carried to excess and required modification if it was not to turn into a disaster. Great Leap Forward approaches had been applied in other sectors than agriculture, but not so intensively. The peasants were exhausted and disaffected, and the entire economy was being dislocated to varying degrees by the general frenzy. Encouraged by the widespread slogan "politics in command," local cadres had reported fantastic increases in output and these had been duly cumulated, so that Peking was claiming by the end of 1958 an astronomical grain harvest of 375 million metric tons for the year (double the harvest claimed for 1957). The output of the backyard furnaces had proven to be almost useless and had to be dropped from the national figures for steel production.

The first major excess to go was the backyard furnaces, most of which were shut down. In addition, the ideological claims for the Great Leap Forward and the people's communes were modified. The latter were somewhat decentralized, and the stress was now on "consolidating" them rather than on further advances. Labor demands on the peasants were eased, and they were to be offered more in the way of material incentives to produce, although not as yet the return of the private plots. Participation in the communal mess halls and nurseries was no longer compulsory, although it was still officially favored. New housing was to be constructed along family rather than communal lines. These important modifications of the Great Leap Forward in the interest of its continued viability were formalized in December, 1958, at an important meeting of the Party Central Committee, which also however published the ludicrous claim of 375 million tons of grain harvested in 1958 and a target of 525 million tons for 1959.

The same meeting issued a rather cryptic announcement to the effect that Mao Tse-tung had decided not to be a candidate for a second term as Chairman of the People's Republic of China (that is, chief of state), although it was understood that he would retain his much more important post of Chairman of the Party Central Committee. The explanation offered was that he would have more time for "theoretical work" and for "dealing with questions of the direction, policy, and line of the Party and the state." It was correctly stated that Mao had expressed his desire to give up the chairmanship of the C.P.R. "more than once" during "the past few years."

Since the last statement is demonstrably accurate, it effectively disposes of later Maoist charges, made during the Cultural Revolution and accepted by many foreign analysts, that those of his colleagues who were subsequently branded his opponents forced him to relinquish the chairmanship of the C.P.R. Nor is it likely that Mao gave up the post, or was pressured into giving it up, in order to appease Khrushchev and purchase more aid from him, although it is true that an important increment of Soviet aid—not covered by a long-term credit, however—was promised in March, 1959.

What is virtually certain is that Mao wanted, for reasons of age and health, to spare himself the time and energy consumed by the ceremonial aspects of the chairmanship of the C.P.R.; the writer has seen an unpublished photograph of him dating from this period in which he is badly underweight and obviously convalescing from a serious illness. It therefore made sense for him to "retreat to the second line," as he put it later, and leave cere-monial and administrative duties largely to his colleagues. He had not yet published the fourth volume of his *Selected Works,* cover-ing the years from 1945 to 1949 (the Chinese edition of this volume was published in 1960, and the translations in 1961), and he undoubtedly wanted to have time to collate and edit the docu-ments that were to be included in it. In view of his obsession with "modern revisionism," which at that time was personified in his eyes by Tito, the fact that Tito occupied a post closely analogous to the chairmanship of the C.P.R. may have been an additional consideration. But most important of all, probably, was Mao's evident determination to protect and strengthen his leadership of the Party through his chairmanship of the Central Committee and the Politburo. It is almost certainly significant that it was only after September, 1956, when the title of Honorary Chairman of the Central Committee was created by the new Party constitution, that Mao began to indicate an interest in giving up the chairman-ship of the C.P.R. It is likely that, as Mao indicated in the original version of his February 27, 1957, speech, he wanted Chou En-lai to succeed him in the latter role. But if so, Chou was probably unwilling on the ground that the premiership was a more impor-tant office and one better suited to his tastes and talents. In any case, the statement of December, 1958, announcing Mao's deci-sion not to succeed himself as Chairman of the C.P.R. did not indicate whom the Party would designate to succeed him, and it therefore seems plausible to suppose that the decision was left in suspense.

The spring of 1959 was marked by a flareup of an insurgency that had been going on in Tibet for about four years, by a result-ing sharp deterioration of relations with India, and by the onset of a three-year period of predominantly bad weather that greatly complicated the agricultural course of the Great Leap Forward. It was in this unfavorable atmosphere that, in late April, Liu Shao-ch'i, the second-ranking figure in the Party and the senior patron of the Party apparatus, was nominated and elected by the National People's Congress to succeed Mao as Chairman of the C.P.R. Liu had probably sought the post in the belief that it would provide him with a platform from which—in collaboration with his close colleague Teng Hsiao-p'ing at the head of the Party apparatus and with outgoing Vice Chairman of the C.P.R. Chu Teh, who took over Liu's former state post of Chairman of the

Standing Committee of the National People's Congress—he could act as an effective "nonantagonistic" counterbalance to Mao's radical and erratic tendencies. To some extent, this happened. Chairman Mao and Chairman Liu, as they were called in the press, often appeared together in public thereafter, Mao always being given precedence but Liu clearly being treated as a major figure in his own right and not merely as Mao's second-in-command.

The traumatic events of 1958 had affected not only the countryside but all sectors of Chinese life, including the armed forces (the People's Liberation Army, or PLA). Most of its personnel were of rural origin and were naturally disturbed by the news from home. The PLA was expected to make substantial labor inputs to the Great Leap Forward, the target for 1959 being 40 million man-days. The officer corps can hardly have been pleased by the "officers to the ranks" campaign beginning in 1958, under which they were required to spend at least one month per year as ordinary soldiers. In early 1959, signs began to appear that the Party leadership had decided to increase the power of the public security apparatus. Even if this step was not aimed at the armed forces, it was bound to be viewed with suspicion by the military leadership, which as in any Communist country since Stalin's time has tended to regard the security forces as a rival and a possible threat.

The military viewpoint in this growing controversy was appropriately and forcefully represented by the brusque, professionally oriented Defense Minister, Marshal P'eng Te-huai. He had opposed the Great Leap Forward from the beginning, mainly because in his view it threatened China's long-term economic development, its relations with the Soviet Union, and the morale and efficiency of the PLA. By the end of 1958, there was considerable evidence that he was right on all three counts, and he evidently believed that the problem could and should be met, not by the modifications introduced in late 1958 and combined with intensified police pressures against discontent, but by a virtual abandonment of the Great Leap Forward. As a professional military man, furthermore, he not only opposed Mao's basic domestic strategy of 1958 (the Great Leap Forward) but had serious reservations as well about Mao's parallel external strategy as announced at the military conference of May–July, 1958.

Unlike Mao, P'eng wanted to avoid revolutionary adventures abroad backed by a budding Chinese nuclear-weapons program and concentrate on the modernization of the conventional forces along Soviet lines which he had inaugurated in 1954. He wanted to rely for China's ultimate external security, for the time being at least, on the Soviet nuclear shield rather than on an expensive Chinese nuclear deterrent. For these reasons, he favored close cooperation with the Soviet Union as a means of ensuring aid and protection and deplored the harmful effect on Sino-Soviet relations of the domestic and external strategies that Mao unfolded in 1958. P'eng may also have objected to the demands on the PLA and the damage to its image caused by the revolt in Tibet and the consequent worsening of relations with India, for which his civilian colleagues' policies were largely responsible.

In late April, 1959, by which time it probably appeared to P'eng that no modification of policy adequate to meet his objections was immediately in prospect, he left on a seven-week tour of the Soviet Union and Eastern Europe. A relatively nonpolitical figure, he may have believed naïvely that he could strengthen his case by gathering and citing Soviet support for it; in reality, the exact opposite was closer to the truth. Or he may have intended simply to prepare the strongest possible case and risk his career as a matter of principle. In any event, he had extensive talks with Soviet civilian and military leaders, including Khrushchev, during his trip. On June 20, a week after P'eng's return to China, Khrushchev took a step evidently in keeping with P'eng's views by rejecting a Chinese request for a sample and designs of an atomic weapon and abrogating an agreement of October, 1957, on military nuclear aid to China. It is probably not a coincidence that P'eng made no further public appearances after June 21. On June 23, as though in an effort to avoid completely undermining P'eng's position in the eyes of his colleagues, Khrushchev gave an extraordinary interview to W. Averell Harriman, in which he said that the Soviet Union had sent missiles (type unspecified) to China and would give it active military support when the time came for the "liberation" of Taiwan. The interview was published in *Life* on July 13, and the next day P'eng wrote a circular letter attacking the errors and excesses of the Great Leap Forward and the people's communes in much the same terms as those used by Khrushchev in a speech delivered on July 18. The obvious Soviet sympathy for P'eng's views can only have weakened him in his debate with his colleagues and contributed, together with several other factors, to the sharp worsening of Sino-Soviet relations during the summer of 1959.

At an important meeting of the Party Central Committee, usually known as the Lushan Plenum (August 2–16), P'eng, with the support of Chief of Staff Huang K'o-ch'eng and a few others, launched an attack on the Great Leap Forward, even the modified version that had been agreed on by the mainstream of the Party leadership at the end of 1958. The attack had little chance of success on its merits, and the chance was reduced to zero by P'eng's escalation of it into an assault on Mao's personal leadership and the validity of his "thought." Confronted in effect with the necessity of choosing between Mao and P'eng on a question of confidence, nearly all those present, including the other senior military leaders, chose Mao. P'eng and Huang, along with their relatively few supporters, were purged quietly from all their posts and became the main although unnamed targets of a brief propaganda campaign against "rightist" tendencies that was accompanied by an intensification of the already impressive propaganda cult of Mao Tse-tung and his "thought." P'eng was replaced as Defense Minister by his major rival, Marshal Lin Piao, whom he had outranked in the order of precedence among marshals established in 1955, and Huang K'o-ch'eng was succeeded as Chief of Staff by the former Minister of Public Security, Lo Jui-ch'ing.

Events of the next few years proved even more clearly than before that P'eng Te-huai had been right in his courageous criticisms of the Great Leap Forward and Mao's *personalismo*. P'eng became the improbable hero of a group of more or less dissident intellectuals within and outside the Party, some of whom began in 1961 to write in thinly disguised allegorical fashion in his defense and in criticism of Mao for his "cult of personality," the Great Leap Forward, and the purging of P'eng. Encouraged by this support and by the general trend of the post-Great Leap Forward period, P'eng in 1962 unsuccessfully demanded his own rehabilitation. These rumblings of support for P'eng and attacks on himself were among the considerations that were to lead Mao to launch the Cultural Revolution.

Having disposed of P'eng Te-huai, the Party leadership prepared for the celebration of the C.P.R.'s tenth anniversary (October 1, 1959) by announcing a cut in the claimed harvest for 1958 from 375 million tons to 250 million tons (still somewhat too high) and a corresponding reduction of the targets for 1959. This step had to be taken sooner or later if economic planning was not to be rendered totally impossible. On the industrial front, the leadership's mood was bullish, and large imports of capital equipment

from the Soviet Union were projected for 1960. But the spring
and summer of 1960 saw a further sharp deterioration of Sino-
Soviet relations, mainly on Chinese initiative, and in July, in an act
of excessive and unwise political pressure and reprisal, Khrushchev
abruptly recalled the 1,390 Soviet technicians then in China and
terminated the Soviet aid program of which they had been the
executors. Khrushchev thereby dealt the Chinese industrialization
program a heavy blow, one that he probably timed to coincide
with indications of a poor Chinese harvest for 1960, which came
on the heels of a mediocre one in 1959.

The Chinese economy reeled from these two blows and continued to deteriorate until about the end of 1961. Food shortages of
near-famine proportions, accompanied by some popular unrest and
widespread disillusionment, appeared in 1961. By the late summer
and early autumn of 1960, the Party leadership knew that it must
bring the Great Leap Forward to an end, although as usual without any public admissions that might suggest an acknowledgment
that the policy being terminated had been a mistake from the beginning. The problems officially conceded to have arisen during
the Great Leap Forward were blamed on bad weather, errors by
local cadres, and the withdrawal of Soviet aid.

Thus ended the most traumatic episode in the C.P.R.'s history,
one that necessitated a period of retrenchment to avoid disaster
and achieve recovery and intensified the forces that in a more
mature form were to lead to the Cultural Revolution.

The Retreat from the Leap (1961–65)

In January, 1961, a meeting of the Central Committee inaugurated a program of retrenchment that was to be designed and
supervised largely by the leadership of the Party apparatus while
Mao, who dislikes being associated with retreat except when
necessary in time of war, kept his hands off economic policy for
the time being and gave most of his attention to foreign policy,
notably the burgeoning Sino-Soviet dispute. The meeting announced the re-establishment of regional bureaus of the Party
Central Committee (their predecessors had been abolished in
1954), but unlike the earlier ones, these were created essentially
from above and were not intended to be autonomous. Nevertheless,
they were put under protégés and supporters of General Secretary
Teng Hsiao-p'ing and soon began to take on the attributes of semi-

autonomous "independent kingdoms" (a Chinese Communist term of opprobrium) linked to the center mainly through Teng.

The most urgent task was to increase agricultural production, and the only way to do so appeared to be to reverse the thrust of the Great Leap Forward by restoring at least the minimum necessary material incentives to the peasants. With this in mind, from about the end of 1960 on, the labor discipline and demands for work imposed by the people's communes since 1958 were eased further and the communes considerably decentralized while being decreased in size and therefore increased in number (from 24,000 in 1959 to 74,000 in 1963). Small private plots, on which the peasants were permitted to grow fruits and vegetables as a valuable supplement to the grain grown on the communal land, were restored, and their owners were allowed to sell their produce in the "free" (actually, regulated) market. To improve the food situation and relieve the strain on the transport network connecting the cities with the countryside, the regime began in 1961 to import annually from 1 to 6 million tons of grain, chiefly wheat from Canada and Australia. Heavy industrial expansion was cut back, except for modern (including nuclear) weapons, and the emphasis was shifted to light industry, especially plants serving agriculture (chemical fertilizer factories, for example). In an effort to extract better performance from intellectuals and technicians, there was a limited increase in intellectual freedom through a partial revival of the "blooming and contending" of 1956–57. Apart from grain imports, China's external trade was shifted sharply, although of course not totally, away from the Soviet Union and other Communist countries and toward the developed non-Communist countries (other than the United States, which offered to sell grain to China in 1961 but was rebuffed for political and ideological reasons), mainly the Western European countries and Japan; the prime Chinese interest in these contacts was the acquisition of capital equipment appropriate to the priorities already mentioned and above all of a broad spectrum of technological knowledge.

In spite of more bad weather in 1961, this program achieved remarkably rapid results, mainly because of the restoration of a degree of peasant incentives. By January, 1962, it was clear to the Party leadership that the winter wheat harvest would be a good one and that the bottom of the crisis had probably been rounded, as turned out to be the case. For nearly five years longer, the Party apparatus maintained effective control over economic policy, and China by and large was increasingly well administered and well fed. Although obviously agreeable, this situation constituted an implicit rebuke to the Great Leap Forward and in Mao's eyes to himself, as well as a threat to the outlook for his vaguely defined ideal of "uninterrupted revolution."

In January, 1962, at an important Party "work conference," Liu Shao-ch'i delivered a powerful criticism of the Great Leap Forward, and at least indirectly of Mao, and argued that since the economy had by no means fully recovered, the retrenchment policies currently in effect should be continued. He also advocated a "reversal of verdicts" (that is, rehabilitation) with respect to some "rightists" denounced in earlier years, although not of P'eng Te-huai, as well as more "democracy" and less "centralism" in implementing the Communist organizational principle of "democratic centralism" within the Party. Mao evidently objected, although ineffectively, to Liu's economic position and still more to his political position, and this conference appears to have inaugurated a three-year period during which the "contradiction" between Mao and Liu ceased to be essentially "nonantagonistic" and sharpened until it approached the "antagonistic."

In addition to Mao's attitude, another factor that worked to disrupt the stability desired by the Party apparatus leadership and create an atmosphere within which Mao could promote his plans was a period of crisis in the spring of 1962. As a last overt manifestation of the discontent engendered by the Great Leap Forward, some 100,000 refugees poured into Hong Kong in May before the authorities on the Chinese side succeeded in sealing the border. At about the same time, some 60,000–80,000 Kazakhs and Uighurs fled from Sinkiang into Soviet Central Asia. In June, there was acute tension in the Taiwan Strait area over indications that the Nationalists might be planning an attack on the mainland to take advantage of the conditions existing there; the crisis evaporated after the United States Government made it clear to Peking and Taipei that if any such attack occurred, it would not receive American support. There was also a brief period of tension over Laos, but this eased when an international agreement was signed at Geneva on July 23 purporting to put an end to four years of political crisis in Laos. In July, as its concern over the other aspects of the crisis subsided, Peking turned to the remaining aspect and began to increase its pressures on the Indian Army. The outcome was the famous Sino-Indian border war of October–November, 1962, whose immediate objective on the Chinese side was to push the Indian Army back from the militarily sensitive border area separating Kashmir from western Tibet and western Sinkiang, but which also had the broader purposes of humiliating the Nehru government and helping to unite the Chinese leadership and public on one issue at least.

On August 1 (Army Day) Liu Shao-ch'i, who as Chairman of the C.P.R. was titular Commander-in-Chief of the PLA and may have been trying to increase its loyalty to himself as against Mao, published a revised version of an essay he had written in 1939, *How to Be a Good Communist*. Characteristic of Liu's usually tactful style, the revised version paid more deference to Mao and less to the Soviet Union than had the original; it still constituted, however, a piece of self-assertion of a kind rarely attempted in China since 1949 by anyone but Mao.

By September, 1962, Mao had reinjected himself into the main-stream of Chinese domestic policy-making sufficiently to be able to dominate, partly through packing the hall, a meeting of the Party Central Committee. The main domestic decisions taken at this meeting were to tighten discipline within the Party apparatus (a move in the opposite direction from what Liu had been advocating) and, in line with Mao's current emphasis on "class struggle," to launch a "Socialist Education Campaign" aimed mainly at improving discipline and performance in the Party apparatus, and especially among the local cadres in the rural areas. As the campaign progressed, in a rather erratic fashion marked by one of a series of periodic "downward transfers" (*hsia-fang*) of cadres from higher to lower levels to strengthen the latter that have occurred since 1957, there re-emerged with increasing clarity the difference that had divided Mao from Liu Shao-ch'i and the other Party apparatus leaders in 1956–57: whether the apparatus should clean its own house through such tested devices as "work teams" sent from higher headquarters, as Liu preferred, or whether the "masses" should be mobilized from outside the framework of the Party to "struggle" against erring cadres, as Mao wished. To Mao, this issue had profound ideological and political connotations and was probably responsible in part for a dramatic warning that in July, 1964, when Liu was taking personal charge of the Socialist Education Campaign (or "Four Cleans," *Ssu-Ch'ing*, as it is sometimes called), Mao inserted into an open letter to the Soviet leadership, bearing the uncompromising title "On Khrushchev's Phony Communism and Its Historical Lessons for the World" (also known as the Ninth Letter). Mao warned that "Khrushchev revisionism" might well take root and grow in China at all levels, including that of the Party leadership, unless vigorously combated. In other words, Mao was beginning openly, although as yet implicitly, to link his main domestic and foreign adversaries as jointly guilty of "modern revisionism" in its Khrushchevian variant. The counterstrategy that Mao advocated emphasized the political mobilization of the masses and the cultivation of a revolutionary mentality on the part of the youth. In January, 1965, Mao tried with little success to direct the main thrust of the Socialist Education Campaign, which was to flounder on through 1966 until it was enveloped in the Cultural Revolution, away from local cadres and toward the higher levels of the Party apparatus; no effective mechanism for such a campaign existed as yet. It was also evidently in January, 1965, that Mao decided, presumably without communicating his decision to more than a few people, that he must get rid of Liu Shao-ch'i; the last straw may have been Liu's insistence on being re-elected Chairman of the C.P.R. at a National People's Congress session of December, 1964–January, 1965, perhaps in an effort among other things to maintain some influence over the armed forces.

By contrast with the refractory Party apparatus, the PLA under Mao's "close comrade in arms" Lin Piao must have appeared a paragon of Maoist purity and zeal. Since the fall of P'eng Te-huai, and especially since the end of 1960, Lin and Chief of Staff Lo Jui-ch'ing had moved vigorously and with considerable effect to increase the political indoctrination of the PLA along familiar Maoist lines ("people's war," "men over weapons," and the like), in lieu of the Soviet-style professionalism favored by P'eng Te-huai, to repair the damage to military morale inflicted by the Great Leap Forward. Until the end of 1964, at any rate, an effort was made not to interfere with the professional *esprit* and competence of the officer corps. By the spring of 1963, Mao was sufficiently impressed by the PLA's political progress to have the Party's propaganda machine hold up a series of heroic soldiers, most of them dead and all possibly mythological, for public emulation, and by the beginning of 1964 to launch a campaign exhorting the entire country, but especially the youth, to "learn from the PLA" as a whole. As an organizational counterpart to the latter campaign, political departments modeled on the staff sections of the same name that supervised political indoctrination in the PLA, and usually staffed by recently discharged or even active military personnel, were set up within many public bodies, notably Party committees, government agencies, and economic enterprises, as a means of political education but to some extent also as a means of supervision and control. The staffs of these new political departments included a high percentage of personnel affiliated with the massive political apparatus of the PLA, headed by the General Political Department of the General Staff; it had long been a tendency of Mao's to use such personnel in civilian capacities more normally (in a Communist-controlled area) filled by personnel of the civilian territorial Party apparatus. Early in 1965, in the supposedly appropriate atmosphere of crisis created by the escalation of the war in Vietnam, the campaign by Mao and Lin Piao to "guerrillaize" the PLA was intensified, and in May the abolition of titles and insignia of rank was decreed. It was at this point, and largely although not exclusively for this reason, that Lo Jui-ch'ing, who had increasingly made himself a champion of professionalism within the PLA, found it necessary to go into opposition.

External developments during this period thus interacted significantly with domestic ones. The rapid escalation of the dispute with Khrushchev, the essential ideological aspect of the quarrel being in Mao's eyes the issue of his adversary's alleged "modern revisionism," intensified Mao's suspicions of supposedly revisionist tendencies among his own colleagues, and perhaps the converse was true as well. The overthrow of Khrushchev by his erstwhile subordinates in October, 1964, made no essential change in this issue in Mao's view, since the problem of revisionism at home and in the Soviet Union remained. The escalation of the war in Vietnam probably delayed for several months the intensification of the debate on domestic policy in China. It produced a strategic debate as to the proper course in the light of the crisis to the south. Specifically, the main issues argued were the advisability of Hanoi's current strategy of moving its own regular forces (as contrasted with the local Viet Cong) into South Vietnam for the first time, the desirable degree of Chinese involvement, the chances of an American attack on China and the best method of defending against it if it came, and the proper attitude toward the Soviet Union under current conditions. Lo Jui-ch'ing took an essentially professional and rather hawklike stand in favor of strong Chinese support (short of direct intervention) for Hanoi's strategy and a restoration of practical cooperation with the Soviet Union in military matters in order to get advanced weapons for defense against a possible American strategic attack. He was overborne by the Maoist school, of which Lin Piao made himself the main spokesman, and was purged early in 1966, although more for his opposition to the "guerrillaization" of the PLA than for his views on external affairs. Lin argued for a protracted, "self-reliant," "people's war" in Vietnam, and in China as well should the United States invade it (the type of threat he alleged to be the most likely), for no more than a rather cautious and indirect Chinese involvement (mainly logistical) in Vietnam, and for a continuation of the politico-idelogical conflict with the Soviet Union. During this period, domestic political tensions were also sharpened somewhat by serious setbacks sustained in the Third World, notably the collapse of an Afro-Asian Conference to have been held at Algiers and the overthrow or repression of local Communists and other leftists by the local military in a number of African countries and above all in Indonesia.

Mao's concern for the outlook for "uninterrupted revolution" in China led him, as his conflict with the Party apparatus leadership intensified, to worry increasingly about the (to him) insufficiently revolutionary attitude of the country's youth. The Communist Youth League, controlled by the Party apparatus, was strongly suspect in Mao's eyes and virtually ceased to function in 1964–65. Early in 1964, Mao had the propaganda machine launch a campaign in favor of training a younger generation of "revolutionary successors." There were indications during the next two years that the problem continued to obsess him.

Another problem in Mao's eyes was the inadequate ideological stand of many intellectuals. The worst, to him, were of course those who had been criticizing him in print. But beyond them, the Chinese intelligentsia as a whole teemed with tendencies that Mao found profoundly distasteful. One that was selected for special propaganda attack in 1964 was the conciliatory, anti-"class struggle," line propounded by philosopher Yang Hsien-chen, to the effect that "Two unite into one," as against the dialectical Marxist counterproposition that "One divides into two." Another target that came under attack a little later was the economist Sun Yeh-fang, who advocated the type of "market socialism" known in Soviet discussions of economics as Libermanism. The socialist virtues and achievements of the Tachai people's commune (in Shansi) and the Taching oil field (in Heilungkiang) were publicly praised as models and by way of contrast to the theories of "bourgeois" and "revisionist" intellectuals.

All Mao's efforts from January, 1962, to late 1965 failed to shake seriously the grip of the Party apparatus leadership on the domestic political and economic systems. The PLA was moving in the direction of serving as a Maoist counterweight to the Party apparatus but was not yet in a position to play that role. Given his imperious nature and the importance in terms of his world outlook of the issues at stake, Mao refused to conform to the naïve expectations of his adversaries by accepting continued frustration. Mao, who among other things is an accomplished poet in the classical Chinese tradition, had given a hint of what he yearned to do to his critics and adversaries when he wrote, in 1961, that

The Golden Monkey wrathfully swung his massive cudgel,
And the jadelike firmament was cleared of dust.

FURTHER READINGS

Over-all surveys of the political history of the C.P.R. prior to the Cultural Revolution are very rare. One, of Cultural Revolution vintage and written in China from a strongly Maoist perspective, is "Long Live the Invincible Thought of Mao Tse-tung," in *Current Background*, American Consulate General, Hong Kong, no. 884, July 18, 1969. A good brief summary is Roderick MacFarquhar, "Communist China's Twenty Years: A Periodization," *The China Quarterly*, no. 39 (July–September, 1969), pp. 55–63. A fuller discussion may be found in O. Edmund Clubb, *Twentieth Century China*, New York: Columbia University Press, 1964, Chapter 9. James Pinckney Harrison, *The Long March to Power: A History of the Chinese Communist Party, 1921–72*, New York: Praeger, 1972, covers political history from the perspective of the Party. A recent adddition to this list is Edward E. Rice, *Mao's Way*, Berkeley and Los Angeles: University of California Press, 1972.

Valuable analysis of developments in the early years, written unfortunately without the benefit of an opportunity for first-hand observation, is A. Doak Barnett, *Communist China: The Early Years, 1949–55*, New York: Praeger, 1964, London: Pall Mall Press, 1964. A work including some useful factual information from a strongly anti-Communist perspective is Richard L. Walker, *China under Communism: The First Five Years*, New Haven, Conn.: Yale University Press, 1955, London: George Allen & Unwin, 1956.

The years immediately following those treated in these volumes are covered by an anonymous British diplomat in an invaluable compilation, consisting of major Chinese documents in translation and informative commentaries, Robert R. Bowie and John K. Fairbank (authors of foreword), *Communist China, 1955–1959: Policy Documents with Analysis*, Cambridge, Mass.: Harvard University Press, 1962. The "blooming and contending" episode is perceptively analyzed in Roderick MacFarquhar, *The Hundred Flowers Campaign and the Chinese Intellectuals*, New York: Praeger, 1960, London: Atlantic Books, 1960; and Richard H. Solomon, *Mao's Revolution and the*

Chinese Political Culture, Berkeley and Los Angeles: University of California Press, 1971, Chapter 17. A good discussion of the Great Leap Forward may be found in *ibid.,* Chapter 18.

The P'eng Te-huai affair is dealt with in Philip Bridgham, "Factionalism in the Central Committee," in John Wilson Lewis, ed., *Party Leadership and Revolutionary Power in China,* Cambridge and New York: Cambridge University Press, 1970, pp. 203–35; David A. Charles (pseud.), "The Dismissal of Marshal P'eng Teh-huai," *The China Quarterly,* no. 8 (October–December, 1961), pp. 63–76; J. D. Simmonds, "P'eng Te-huai: A Chronological Re-Examination," *ibid.,* no. 37 (January–March, 1969), pp. 120–38; Franz Michael, "The Struggle for Power," *Problems of Communism,* vol. xvi, no. 3 (May–June, 1967), pp. 12–21; Frederick C. Teiwes, "The Evolution of Leadership Purges in Communist China," *The China Quarterly,* no. 41 (January–March, 1970), pp. 122–35.

For a variety of reasons, most books by foreign travelers in China more recent than Marco Polo have little value to the serious student of Chinese politics. An exception, mainly because of the author's long journalistic acquaintance with the Chinese Communist leaders, is Edgar Snow, *The Other Side of the River: Red China Today,* New York: Random House, 1961, London: Gollancz, 1963, Harmondsworth: Penguin, 1970 (a revised edition was published as *Red China Today,* New York: Vintage, 1970), which is based on a visit lasting from June to November, 1960. Another is Barbara W. Tuchman, *Report from China,* New York: Macmillan, 1972.

The period of retreat from the Great Leap Forward is examined from various angles in H. F. Schurmann, "Peking's Recognition of Crisis," *Problems of Communism,* vol. x, no. 5 (September–October, 1961), pp. 5–14; Arthur A. Cohen and C. F. Steffens, "Disillusionment within the Ranks," *Problems of Communism,* vol. xii, no. 3 (May–June, 1963), pp. 10–17; Charles Neuhauser, "The Chinese Communist Party in the 1960s: Prelude to the Cultural Revolution," *The China Quarterly,* no. 32 (October–December, 1967), pp. 3–36; Richard Baum and Frederick C. Teiwes, *Ssu-Ch'ing: The Socialist Education Movement of 1962–1966,* Berkeley: University of California, Center for Chinese Studies, 1968; Donald Munro, "The Yang Hsien-chen Affair," *The China Quarterly,* no. 22 (April–June, 1965), pp. 75–82. The strategic debate of 1965 is ably analyzed by Uri Ra'anan in "Peking's Foreign Policy 'Debate,' 1965–1966," in Tang Tsou, ed., *China's Policies in Asia and America's Alternatives* (vol. 2 of *China in Crisis,* Ping-ti Ho and Tang Tsou, eds.), Chicago: University of Chicago Press, 1968, pp. 23–71; and from a somewhat different perspective in Harry Harding and Melvin Gurtov, *The Purge of Lo Jui-ch'ing: The Politics of Chinese Strategic Planning,* The Rand Corporation, R-548-PR, February, 1971.

4. The Cultural Revolution and Since

It is a very unusual thing for a national leader to set out to shake up, from top to bottom and at a real risk of anarchy, the political system over which he presides. In fact, the only recent example that comes to mind is Mao Tse-tung's Cultural Revolution in China. The origins of the Cultural Revolution, therefore, can hardly be attributed, as some analysts propose, to basic sociological causes, such as discontent among students and industrial workers over inadequate job opportunities and rule by the Party apparatus; such attitudes are general in developing countries, and yet China is the only one to have had a Cultural Revolution. The inspiration and leadership of the Cultural Revolution were Mao's, and without his initiative there would have been no Cultural Revolution.

The Launching of the Cultural Revolution

By September, 1965, Mao's annoyance at his intellectual critics and his frustration over his inability to galvanize the Party apparatus into genuine compliance with his demand for a regeneration of revolutionary momentum had reached the point at which he felt compelled to take action. Furthermore, he had made a bad guess by predicting (in January, in an interview with Edgar Snow) that the United States would not escalate in Vietnam, had been rather inconspicuous since then, and may have felt that he needed to do something to erase the memory of his error. The time was propitious, since Lin Piao had just written a Maoist interpretation of the struggle in Vietnam (*Long Live the Victory of People's War!*, published on September 3) that played down the American escalation as something only to be expected from that "imperialist" power and as insufficient justification for direct Chinese involvement in the war. It is unlikely that Mao at that time intended to purge the Party apparatus leadership as drastically as he subsequently did, especially since (contrary to later Maoist accusations made during the Cultural Revolution) it does not appear to have been engaged in any coordinated conspiracy against him. More probably, he hoped that with the issue of intellectual criticism as the entering wedge and the escalation in Vietnam for an external backdrop, he could pressure the Party apparatus leadership into falling into line with his wishes to a greater extent than before.

In September–October, 1965, accordingly, at a central work conference (see Chapter 7), consisting in this case of the Politburo Standing Committee and the first secretaries of the regional Party bureaus, Mao urged a "rectification" campaign against "bourgeois reactionary thinking" within the intellectual community and the Party. He encountered considerable resistance to his proposal, some of it probably based on the tensions created by the escalation in Vietnam, and the most he could get was agreement to a rather mild and bureaucratic campaign to be conducted mainly in Peking and under the direction of P'eng Chen, the First Secretary of the Peking Municipal Party Committee and Mayor of the city. Although P'eng had gained considerable favor with Mao by taking an exceptionally strong anti-Soviet line, Mao must have realized, at least by the end of the conference, that P'eng, some of whose colleagues and protégés were among the intended targets of Mao's campaign, had little real enthusiasm for the task he had been assigned. Dissatisfied with this outcome but unable to change it for the time being, probably because he did not command a favorable majority in the Politburo Standing Committee, Mao retreated in November to the Yangtze Valley and South China, where he spent the next six months with some of his closest followers observing developments in Peking and planning his next moves. One of these was an article by his supporter Yao Wen-yuan, originally published on November 10, 1965, attacking Wu Han, one of the leading members of the group of intellectuals who had been criticizing Mao.

The deadlock began to be broken when, on February 12, 1966, P'eng Chen's "Group of Five in Charge of the Cultural Revolution" issued an "Outline Report" that attempted to divert the campaign from the political direction intended by Mao and into historical and aesthetic channels. By making this move, P'eng rendered himself vulnerable to subsequent Maoist charges of unilateral action and "revisionist" ideological tendencies (in effect, lack of political seriousness).

During this period, Mao had the support of Lin Piao and the

PLA's political apparatus. In February, 1966, evidently with some use of force by Lin, Chief of Staff Lo Jui-ch'ing was purged for having allegedly attempted a coup (the "February Coup") whose other participants were later said to have included P'eng Chen, Party propaganda chief Lu Ting-i, and Yang Shang-k'un, a key official of the Party Secretariat.

In March and April, in rather odd circumstances suggesting that he already felt threatened by Mao's maneuvers, Liu Shao-ch'i paid a state visit (as Chairman of the C.P.R.) to Pakistan, Afghanistan, and Burma; he received a very low-level welcome on his return. During his absence, there were two important developments relating to Sino-Soviet relations, a subject on which Liu was less militant than Mao and some of his other colleagues. On March 22, evidently after some debate, the CPC unprecedently rejected an invitation to send a delegation to the forthcoming Soviet Twenty-Third Party Congress. On March 28, Mao vetoed in strong language a proposal for a form of "united action" with the Soviet Union on Vietnam brought by a high-ranking Japanese Communist delegation and apparently favored by several other high CPC leaders, including even P'eng Chen, who seems to have modified his attitude toward the Soviet Union at the end, but probably not including Lin Piao.

In April, the *Liberation Army Daily,* which is controlled by the General Political Department of the PLA General Staff (see Chapter 9) and at that time was controlled indirectly by Lin Piao, launched a propaganda barrage against the intellectuals whom P'eng Chen was trying to protect and in effect against P'eng himself. It is probable that troops loyal to Lin were sent into Peking some time in April to hold themselves in readiness for a move against P'eng if necessary. P'eng did not appear when a high-level Albanian delegation visited Peking at the end of April. A week later, the delegation paid a call on Mao in the Yangtze Valley, and he used the visit as an occasion for having a photograph taken that suggested, correctly in all probability, that he had at last achieved a majority on the Politburo Standing Committee and was therefore in a position to oust P'eng Chen and proceed with the next stage that he was almost certainly already contemplating, the organization of the Red Guards. The swing man who had just come over to his side to make a majority of four on the seven-man Standing Committee was General Secretary Teng Hsiao-p'ing, who evidently relished the prospect of the purge of P'eng Chen, his forceful rival and colleague on the Secretariat; the other members of the group beside Mao were Chou En-lai and Lin Piao. On May 7, the day the photograph was taken of these four men plus the Albanians (it was published on May 11), Mao sent an important directive to Lin Piao to the effect that the PLA and all other sectors of Chinese society should engage not only in their normal occupations but also in "economic construction," "mass work" (political activity), and "criticizing the bourgeoisie" (ideological activity). More than any other single document, perhaps, this one expresses the spirit of the Cultural Revolution as Mao envisaged it. On May 9, China's third nuclear test was conducted, presumably at Lin Piao's direction and in order to help dramatize Mao's impending return from the Yangtze Valley to Peking for the main purpose of purging P'eng Chen.

It is not certain when Mao actually returned to Peking, but it is known that on May 16 his group, speaking in the name of the Party Central Committee, issued a statement denouncing P'eng Chen's "Outline Report," abolishing his "Group of Five," and creating a Cultural Revolution Group under the Politburo Standing Committee (that is, effectively under the dominant four-man faction; later it was said to be under the Central Committee). This new group, whose creation Mao had probably proposed unsuccessfully at the conference held the previous September–October, was headed by Ch'en Po-ta, Mao's longtime favorite propagandist, and had among its other members K'ang Sheng and Chiang Ch'ing (Mme. Mao Tse-tung). The May 16 directive is considered by the CPC to mark the official beginning of the Cultural Revolution.

During the period between May 16 and June 1, evidently with some use of military force (but probably without actual fighting), P'eng Chen was ousted, the Peking Municipal Party Committee purged, and the principal propaganda organs in Peking, including the *People's Daily,* brought under more militant Maoist leadership than before. Direction of the CPC's propaganda program was taken over by First Secretary T'ao Chu of the CPC's Central-South China Bureau, in whose bailiwick Mao had spent part of his time during the preceding six months; T'ao also joined the Party Secretariat (without having been formally elected by the full Central Committee) and appeared to be the most rapidly rising figure in the Party leadership. But P'eng Chen had also appeared in the same light to many people just before the Cultural Revolution, and T'ao was to prove no more able or willing than P'eng and many others to follow Mao through all the stages of the Cultural Revolution as it proceeded to escalate.

The Emergence of the Red Guards

On May 25, 1966, P'eng Chen having fallen or being about to fall, a group of seven faculty members and students at Peking University did something that Mao had apparently been quietly encouraging since the previous September but that had been obstructed by P'eng Chen: they put up a large-character poster (see Chapter 10) attacking the leading officials of the university. On June 1, Mao endorsed the poster and ordered it published. On the strength of this beginning, a purge of university faculties promptly got under way, with some students and Party cadres, however, supporting the individuals whom the Maoists were denouncing. On June 18, a postponement of the enrollment of students for the coming university year was announced, and the effect was to cancel the ensuing academic year and enable high-school and university students to devote full time to political activity. During this period, students began to organize themselves in many places, with some outside help, into units known as Red Guards, the typical Red Guard being fanatically Maoist.

Mao's approval of the emerging Red Guard movement was a most un-Leninist instance of "spontaneity" and therefore must have been basically unacceptable from the beginning to the Party apparatus leaders, even those like Teng Hsiao-p'ing, who had agreed to the purge of P'eng Chen. Probably aware of this attitude but not feeling ready yet to cope with it, Mao again left Peking for the Yangtze Valley on June 2. While he was away, the Party apparatus leadership, Liu Shao-ch'i and Teng Hsiao-p'ing being its senior figures, followed a standard CPC practice of organizing "work teams" that attempted to bring the turbulent students under control but accomplished little beyond antagonizing them further and making them more receptive than ever to future inflammatory appeals from Mao and his personal supporters. According to an interesting Yugoslav account that appears to be at least partially accurate, Liu and Teng and even P'eng Chen, as well as other members of the Party apparatus leadership, maneuvered during June and July to hold a Central Committee Plenary Session, possibly without Mao's presence, that would terminate the Cultural Revolution and remove Mao, who was thought to be under an undesirable degree of influence from Lin Piao, from power. Their support came mainly from the northern and western parts of the country, whereas a large percentage of the Party apparatus leadership in the East China and Central-South China regions supported Mao and Lin.

Meanwhile, Mao was again basing himself mainly in the Shanghai area, which was under the control of his close supporters, and making plans for a triumphal return to Peking when conditions were ripe. On July 16, probably at the suggestion of T'ao Chu, Mao took a widely and rather ludicrously publicized swim (not his first) in the Yangtze River. He returned to Peking on July 19 (according to a later statement by Chou; other sources give other dates) and insisted that a Central Committee Plenary Session could not legitimately be held without his presence. At the same time, Lin Piao appears to have moved additional loyal troops into the Peking area, and probably also into the city itself. Each side then prepared for the coming Plenary Session, Mao having the advantage of Lin Piao's (and almost certainly Chou En-lai's) support and, according to the Yugoslav account, initially Teng Hsiao-p'ing's as well.

The Eleventh Plenary Session got under way on August 1 (Army Day, a probably significant fact in view of the military pressures that were being exerted by the Mao-Lin group). It was apparently attended irregularly by some Maoists who were not Central Committee members. There was a great deal of controversy at the meeting over the Cultural Revolution in general and the Red Guards in particular: Mao was already beginning to urge them publicly to "bombard the headquarters" of his opponents. Mao held a general advantage by virtue of Lin Piao's strong support and tried to dramatize his popular appeal by an unannounced appearance to the "masses" on August 10. A Central Committee decision of August 8 and the communiqué issued on August 12 at the end of the Plenary Session endorsed the Cultural Revolution as a mass movement for revolutionizing Chinese society, but neither named the Red Guards, who apparently still lacked full support within the Party leadership. The August 8 decision promised that scientists, technicians, and administrators who "are patriotic, work energetically, are not against the Party and socialism, and maintain no illicit relations with any foreign country" would not be subjected to the full force of the Cultural Revolution. The Politburo and its Standing Committee were enlarged, rather than being purged, but Lin Piao emerged from the Plenary Session as the sole Vice Chairman of the Central Committee (previously, all members of the Politburo Standing Committee except Teng Hsiao-p'ing had also been Vice Chairmen of the Central Committee) and as Mao's obvious choice, willing or unwilling, as his heir.

By the end of the Plenary Session, Red Guard organizations had been formed among students in most parts of the country. Their political and propaganda guidance came from the Cultural Revolution Group; the PLA provided some training and logistical support and moved about 10 million of them to Peking by rail and truck during the next few months, with highly disruptive effects on the transport network. Their main purpose in going, apart from enjoying themselves, was to proclaim loyalty to Mao and hostility to his opponents, and if possible to see him. This they did at a series of eight gigantic rallies held between August 18 and November 26 at each of which Mao appeared. The main speakers, however, were Lin Piao and Chou En-lai, whose remarks contrasted to the extent that Lin urged the Red Guards to carry the Cultural Revolution into all corners of the land, whereas Chou exhorted them not to disrupt the working of the economy. After November, the rallies ceased to be held, partly to spare Mao the necessity of appearing to the Red Guards in cold weather and partly to decongest Peking by getting most of them out of it and into the provinces, where they could begin the work of attacking the regional and provincial Party apparatuses, for by this time Mao had clearly decided that the apparatus could not be persuaded to reform itself as he wished and must be subjected to forceful pressures from outside. Furthermore, the Red Guards had been creating serious problems in Peking and other cities by attacks on, and indeed atrocities against, foreigners and Chinese to whom they objected for one reason or another. Exhortations from above to use persuasion rather than violence had little effect.

During the rallies, Liu Shao-ch'i and Teng Hsiao-p'ing had shown the opposite of enthusiasm for the proceedings. There were good Leninist reasons for this, and more specific ones as well: by mid-November, Red Guards were making propaganda attacks on them (although they were not yet being denounced in the official press). The central Party apparatus in Peking, which had little real power immediately available to it, collapsed and ceased to function under the impact of Red Guard demonstrations in the last weeks of 1966. A number of hitherto apparently Maoist leaders, such as T'ao Chu, were purged at this time in irregular ways and sometimes subjected to mass (or kangaroo) trials by Red

Guards, evidently because they would not agree to the "remolding" of the Party apparatus by the Red Guards. At the same time, Red Guards began to demonstrate against and put pressure on the Party apparatus leadership at the regional and provincial levels.

Here, however, unlike in Peking, they were attacking adversaries who had real power and who therefore put up what was in many cases a highly effective resistance. Regional and provincial leaders used all their resources and even formed Red Guard units of their own in some instances. The Maoist high command in Peking then tried to supplement the efforts of the Red Guards with a new force known as the "revolutionary rebels" and consisting mostly of workers, but in this case, too, the local Party apparatus leaders were able to respond by forming similar units under their control. In Shanghai, since it was a particularly Maoist area, the "revolutionary" elements succeeded in effecting a "power seizure" from the Party apparatus and proclaiming a commune early in February, 1967. It soon became clear, however, that without the support of local PLA commanders a Maoist "power seizure" could not survive in Shanghai or anywhere else, and it was also clear that the PLA was much more concerned with order and stability than were the Red Guards. Before the end of the month, accordingly, the commune gave way to a revolutionary committee whose components, at least in theory, were representatives of "revolutionary organizations" (Red Guards and "revolutionary rebels"), PLA personnel, and Party cadres who were officially considered (with or without justification) to have deserted the Liu-Teng machine and come over to the Cultural Revolution. The Shanghai Revolutionary Committee based on this "three-way alliance" was declared in Peking to be the model for all of China and, on this basis, by the end of April, 1967, Peking had recognized as legitimate "power seizures" in five other areas (Heilungkiang, Shansi, Shantung, Kweichow, and Peking), where the local military leaders were apparently more than ordinarily sympathetic to the Cultural Revolution. "Power seizures" in a few other areas were rejected by Peking as "false" because "revolutionary" elements were allowed insufficient participation. In most of the country, the Party apparatus, often with some support from local military leaders (the chief political officers of the provincial military districts were generally secretaries of the provincial Party committees as well), was holding its own; the Maoist assault on it was producing not so much "power seizures" as the threat of chaos, at least in the cities.

The Intervention of the Army

Since the Red Guards and the "revolutionary rebels" were generally proving inadequate to overthrow the Party apparatus, Mao decided in late January, 1967, to commit to the struggle the only other force available (or supposedly available) to him, the PLA. Although direct intervention in politics was not a normal role for the PLA, at any rate since 1949, and was probably an unwelcome one to many of its commanders, there is no convincing reason to doubt that the new role was essentially acceptable to Lin Piao. He appears to have supported Mao and the Cultural Revolution strongly from the beginning, for ideological and personal reasons; now that the PLA's new role had made him even more indispensable than before, he probably bargained vigorously with Mao for further assurances regarding his status as heir apparent. The PLA was given a twofold mission, one aspect of which was explicit, the other implicit. The explicit one was to "support the left"; in other words, to oust resisting Party apparatus leaders and install "revolutionary" elements in power in the provinces. The implicit one was to prevent chaos; even though the effective thrust of Mao's policies was toward chaos, he did not want that to be the result and constantly sought to manage the whirlwind that he had unleashed, for example by issuing a series of aphoristic "latest instructions" to all his followers.

Although it became apparent to Mao only gradually that there was a "contradiction" between these two missions, it was obvious to the provincial military district commanders more or less from the start, and they tended to prefer stability to "supporting the left." In many cases, they established military control commissions in the major cities, instituted something resembling martial law, ousted the Party committees as such but worked quietly with many of their individual members who possessed essential administrative skills and knowledge, and suppressed Red Guard turbulence forcefully. Cries of anguish that naturally went up from the Red Guards affected by this "adverse current," as they called it, reached Peking and produced a major controversy within the Party leadership over the question of whether to support or oppose the anti-Red Guard behavior of much of the PLA. An obscure crisis at the end of March, 1967, resulted in the Politburo's and its Standing Committee's ceasing to function. Liu Shao-ch'i began to be attacked in the official press for the first time, although as "China's Khrushchev" rather than in his own name. Lin Piao put increased pressure on PLA commanders to "support the left" rather than repressing it and issued a directive on April 6 to the effect that they should stop using force against "revolutionary" elements.

The resulting easing of military controls and the disappearance of the regular Party leading body, the Politburo, left no effective checks on Red Guard turbulence and on the trumpetings of the Cultural Revolution Group, which kept inciting the Red Guards to "make revolution." Accordingly, there was serious Red Guard violence during this period. Red Guards quarreled with each other over many things, including the allocation of seats on revolutionary committees, and split into innumerable factional groupings that sometimes fought vigorously against each other. Chou En-lai made many trips to trouble spots during this period in an effort to arrange compromises and was also the key person in Peking to whom local organizations sent representatives to request mediation and help in working out the composition of revolutionary committees. Red Guard violence became a problem in Peking in February, 1967, when Red Guards besieged the Soviet Embassy for about two weeks, and there was violence against other foreign diplomats and embassies as well. There had been something close to a temporary takeover of the Portuguese colony of Macao at the beginning of the year. In May, disorders were launched by various Maoist elements in Hong Kong, including Red Guards, and continued through the summer, but without producing much of an effect on the well-entrenched British colonial government. Red Guards and other Maoists (including diplomatic personnel) staged incidents along the Sino-Soviet border and in some foreign capitals, notably Rangoon and London. All this was hardly affected by a joint directive issued on June 6 by the CPC Central Committee (actually Mao), the State Council (actually Chou), the Party's Military Affairs Committee (actually Lin), and the Cultural Revolution Group (actually Chiang Ch'ing), forbidding such violence and authorizing the PLA to prevent it, but not to use force in the process of doing so. Only one provincial revolutionary committee was formed during the summer of 1967, in Tsinghai.

In mid-July, a two-man investigating team from Peking—Hsieh Fu-chih, Minister of Public Security and Chairman of the Peking Revolutionary Committee, and Wang Li, a particularly militant member of the Cultural Revolution Group—arrived at the massive industrial complex of Wuhan on the middle Yangtze River. There had been serious disorder among Red Guard groups there since early in the year, and the powerful Wuhan Military Region commander, Ch'en Tsai-tao, had been repressing the more militant and Maoist of these groups. When Hsieh and Wang indicated support for the Maoist groups, Ch'en connived at their seizure and beating on July 20 by some of his supporters. Lin Piao immediately ordered loyal military units to move toward the city, while Chou En-lai flew to Wuhan. Hsieh and Wang were released the following day and given a hero's welcome on their return to Peking. After a brief period of military movements and operations, apparently short of actual combat, Ch'en Tsai-tao was relieved of his command, but he was not severely punished for his defiance, probably because the other military region commanders felt considerable sympathy for him.

Early August saw a flurry of activity by the militants in Peking aimed at capitalizing on the Wuhan Incident, as Ch'en Tsai-tao's act of defiance is usually called, during which Red Guards were supposed to "drag out" non-Maoist "power holders" from the PLA, especially the military regions and military districts. Nothing of the sort happened, however; the militants had overplayed their hand, and their cause was further harmed by the seizure and burning of the British diplomatic compound by some of them on August 22. The greater part of the army command, almost certainly with the support of Chou En-lai (Lin Piao's attitude is uncertain), opposed any further leftist excesses and succeeded in purging some of the lesser members of the Cultural Revolution Group (including Wang Li), as well as the director of the PLA General Staff's General Political Department, Hsiao Hua, who was considered close to Lin Piao, on the charge of belonging to a vaguely defined ultraleftist movement known as the May 16 Group and used on several occasions since then as a political whipping boy for leftist excesses during the Cultural Revolution. The decision was taken to authorize the PLA to use force defensively (preferably not including the firing of weapons) to protect itself against Red Guard violence, a decision so important that it could be made to seem authoritative only through the explicit endorsement of Mao and Chiang Ch'ing, the two patron deities of the Red Guard movement, which they accordingly gave, however reluctantly, in early September.

With this new mandate, the PLA proceeded more vigorously against Red Guard disorder and a somewhat greater level of stability was achieved in the provinces. A wave of eighteen provincial revolutionary committees was formed, largely under military auspices and with increasingly token representation for "revolutionary" elements, between September, 1967, and the end of May, 1968. The revolutionary committees in effect replaced the pre–Cultural Revolution Party committees and local governments at the provincial level and below.

This ascendancy of the forces of stability provoked a reaction from the extreme Maoists, notably Chiang Ch'ing, who regarded Chou En-lai as the brains behind the objectionable trend. The two sides could agree on purging in March, 1968, Acting Chief of Staff Yang Ch'eng-wu, who had succeeded Lo Jui-ch'ing in 1966, since he had offended both Chiang Ch'ing and certain of the military region commanders, and on replacing him (as full Chief of Staff) with Huang Yung-sheng, who was close to Lin Piao and yet as commander of the Canton Military Region had been active in repressing Red Guard violence in that area and had not given support to the violence in Hong Kong. Apart from that, the spring of 1968 saw a virtually open political offensive by Chiang Ch'ing against Chou En-lai, but it was an offensive that achieved no visible results. Chiang had greater success during the summer of 1968, however, in encouraging an upsurge of Red Guard turbulence comparable, although not quite equal, to the violence of the previous year. Things rapidly got out of hand in some areas, especially in the southern Autonomous Region of Kwangsi, which is especially sensitive because the principal railway to North Vietnam runs through it. Rival Red Guard units raided supply trains bound for North Vietnam and seized weapons with which to fight one another; a series of orders from Peking to stop had little effect. Farther east in Kwangsi, the city of Wuchow suffered heavy damage and casulties in the course of fighting among Red Guards; many dozens of bodies, bound before execution, floated down the Pearl River and were sighted off Hong Kong.

The End of the Cultural Revolution

By the end of July, 1968, Mao had come to the traumatic conclusion that the Red Guards had misunderstood him, were doing more harm than good, and had to be suppressed as an organized political movement. The month of August saw the publication of articles strongly implying that the Red Guards had been guilty of starting a trend toward anarchy and "many centers," that as students they were essentially bourgeois, and that the Cultural Revolution ought to be led by the working class. So-called workers' provost corps, in which the guiding element was the PLA but in which teams of workers and peasants were included as political window dressing, began to break up the Red Guard units, sometimes with a great deal of force. At last, the PLA was given a clear mandate, although not a formal one, to use whatever degree of force was necessary to restore order, and it did exactly that. The five remaining provincial revolutionary committees were established in August and early September, and the conclusion of the process was made the occasion of a major rally in Peking on September 7. The process was probably accelerated somewhat by the sense of alarm generated by the Soviet invasion of Czechoslovakia on August 21, 1968, but that cannot have been the precipitating cause, since Mao's decision to repudiate the Red Guards and authorize their suppression had been taken before the end of July.

Major political movements in the C.P.R. are rarely terminated formally, presumably because to do so might seem to suggest an admission that it had been a mistake to launch them in the first place. Officially, the Cultural Revolution has not ended and is, of course, a huge success; actually, it was largely a failure and was abandoned because it threatened to become a disaster. This is certainly true if one regards concern for the future of the revolution as Mao's major single motive in launching the Cultural Revolution, and the Red Guards as the main symbols and vessels of that concern, as it would be most reasonable to do. The only other sensible alternative to the official view could be that the use of the PLA as an instrument for controlling and revolutionizing Chinese society was the main distinguishing feature of the Cultural Revolution and that, by this criterion, the Cultural Revolution continued well beyond 1968, but this is a less persuasive interpretation than the other, since Mao's basic objective was the rejuvenation rather than the militarization of the revolution and of Chinese society. By that criterion, the Cultural Revolution ended with the suppression of the Red Guards as a political force in the late summer and autumn of 1968.

Somewhat tentatively, it can be concluded that the results of the Cultural Revolution were a mixed bag, but one in which the failures (from the point of view of its sponsors) probably outweighed the successes. To be sure, intellectual dissent has been silenced, and most adherents of Liu Shao-ch'i and Teng Hsiao-p'ing have been purged, although not necessarily permanently in all cases, from the Party apparatus. On the other hand, public morale and confidence in the regime were somewhat impaired, the economy had been damaged although not severely, the educational system had been badly harmed, and the army had been left in control of the provinces to an extent that probably no civilian Party leader had anticipated or desired; about two-thirds of the chairmen of the provincial revolutionary committees had military backgrounds or affiliations (as commanders or political officers, usually of the corresponding military districts), and none was the representative of a "revolutionary" organization. Most serious of all, from the Maoist point of view at any rate, the excesses and (unadmitted) failure of the Cultural Revolution had cast doubt on the validity of Mao Tse-tung's "mass line" approach to politics (see Chapter 6), one of the central themes of his "thought."

Lin Piao's Bid

This last disturbing thought, however, was clearly not accepted by Lin Piao, who emerged from the Cultural Revolution in a seemingly strong position. Although by no means supreme, he had Mao's confidence, or at least the strong presumption of such confidence created by his designation as Mao's heir. He was the senior figure in the PLA, at that time the strongest political force in the country. These were formidable assets but not quite sufficient for his purposes; he needed the legitimacy and security (in view of the fate of Mao's previous heir, Liu Shao-ch'i) that would be conferred by ratification of his position at a Party Congress, which in any event was long overdue. But the congress was repeatedly postponed during 1968, mainly no doubt because of unsettled conditions in the provinces, but also probably because of concern over the strong and obvious Soviet objections to political trends in China and the fear that the Soviet Union might take action as it had against Czechoslovakia, and perhaps because of reservations in some quarters about Lin as Mao's successor.

Nevertheless, there was some movement along lines favorable to Lin, and it is only reasonable to assume that the movement owed something to his initiative and his influence, for the time being, on Mao. Those who had objections to Lin, of whom Chou En-lai as the third-ranking figure in the Party was easily the most important, had to concede him the initiative when he could persuade Mao to let him exercise it. The Twelfth Plenary Session of the Party Central Committee (October 13–31, 1968), at which Lin made an important unpublished speech, dismissed Liu Shao-ch'i from all his Party and state offices, with questionable authority, and, by doing so, further opened the way for Lin to replace him as Mao's successor. The meeting adopted the draft of a new Party constitution, to be submitted to the Ninth Party Congress whenever it met, in which Lin was named as Mao's successor (for further details on this constitution, see Chapter 7). The meeting also apparently decided, probably at Lin's instigation, to sanction certain programs that would proclaim the continued validity of Mao's "mass line" and help to cope with some aftereffects of the Cultural Revolution at the same time. There were two main programs of this kind that went into effect shortly afterward. One was a massive transfer of population, especially former Red Guards, from the cities to the countryside to help relieve crowding and disorder in the cities and to promote rural development by the injection of fresh manpower, much of it skilled. By the time these transfers had virtually ended in the early spring of 1969, they had involved about 30 million people and had apparently generated considerable dislocation and discontent in the rural areas. The other program was a restoration, on a limited scale, and in practice not everywhere, of some of the features of the Great Leap Forward; in some rural areas, private plots and work points (see Chapter 10) were abolished, certainly with adverse effects on peasant incentives and almost certainly on peasant morale.

During this period, Chou En-lai's role seems to have been confined largely to foreign affairs, although only for the time being as it turned out. On November 25, 1968, he proposed a resumption of the ambassadorial talks at Warsaw with the United States; the date he suggested was February 20, 1969, by which time the incoming Nixon Administration would have had time to get its feet on the ground. Chou rationalized this move, which he probably regarded as a desirable if minor form of insurance against possible Soviet pressures, but which was not welcome to the militant Maoists, by citing for domestic consumption the recognized Maoist principle that at times it is permissible and even necessary to negotiate with an adversary. There is some reason to believe that at that time, and until about the middle of January, Mao was either absent on vacation or ill, or both, and that Lin Piao's influence in Peking was thus temporarily in decline. When Mao returned to political activity, Lin was prominently beside him. Following a rally for military personnel on January 25 at which virtually the whole current Party leadership appeared, the press began to build up a strong propaganda case against the Nixon Administration. On February 19, citing the defection to American custody of a

Chinese diplomat two weeks earlier, Peking canceled the scheduled session of the ambassadorial talks with the United States. Lin's influence and his call for a continuation of the "mass line" at home and the dual-adversary strategy (anti-American and anti-Soviet) abroad had proven able to exert more effective influence on Mao at that time than had Chou's more pragmatic and flexible approach.

Lin's reiteration of these Maoist fundamentals was almost certainly motivated in large part by his desire to appear in the most orthodox light possible at the forthcoming Ninth Party Congress, then apparently scheduled for mid-March, 1969. But the logic of the dual-adversary strategy, of which Lin had made himself the most prominent spokesman in 1965 (in *Long Live the Victory of People's War!*), required that the slap just administered to American "imperialism" be paralleled with one at Soviet "revisionism" and "social-imperialism." Accordingly, and on the mistaken assumption that the Soviet Union was too preoccupied with a crisis then in progress over West Berlin to react in any dangerous way, Lin evidently planned a local ambush of Soviet forces on a disputed island in the Ussuri River (between Manchuria and the Soviet Maritime Province) on March 2, a dramatically satisfactory day since it also saw the arrival in India of Soviet Defense Minister Andrei Grechko (Soviet-Indian anti-Chinese collusion had long disturbed Peking). But on March 15 Soviet forces struck back on the same island with superior firepower and devastating effect. For personal reasons and out of blind adherence to the dual-adversary strategy, Lin had created a crisis that contained grave risks for Chinese security.

The Party congress was hurriedly postponed, probably to avoid giving provocation of the kind that had caused the Soviet Union to invade Czechoslovakia in order to pre-empt the Czechoslovak Fourteenth Party Congress. The transfer of population to the countryside and the partial resurrection of the Great Leap Forward came to an abrupt halt.

The Ninth Party Congress opened on April 1, after Peking had received (on March 29) a communication from Moscow indicating a greater interest in talks on the border issue than in further fighting. The 1,500 delegates had apparently been chosen rather informally under the supervision of the revolutionary committees of their provinces. The proceedings appear to have been less orderly and less easily controllable by the Party leadership than is usual for a Communist Party congress, partly because of the method of selecting the delegates, but even more perhaps because of differences among both the representatives of the Party center and the delegates from the provinces over what needed to be done after the unprecedented turmoil of the preceding years. Not until April 14 were Lin Piao's political report (the major document presented to the Congress), which had been delivered on April 1, and the draft Party constitution, which had been drawn up at the Central Committee's Twelfth Plenary Session, approved and adopted. Lin's report was a lengthy rationalization of Mao's "thought" and leadership and of the Cultural Revolution, as well as an implicit statement of his own claim to be Mao's successor. The tone was highly militant, and there were only faint suggestions that "consolidation," and not merely further revolutionary advance, were on the country's agenda. Lin's report had a few features of interest relating to foreign policy. One was an important clarification, for the sake of safety, of the C.P.R.'s position on the Sino-Soviet border dispute: Peking was not seriously demanding the return of territories taken by Russia under the "unequal" treaties (see Chapter 13), and the latter should be "taken as the basis for the settlement of the boundary question." Lin revealed that on March 21, Soviet Premier Alexei Kosygin had tried to telephone Peking to discuss the border crisis. Lin implied that he regarded the Soviet Union as a greater threat than the United States, but his comments on American "imperialism" were strongly hostile, and in essence his report reiterated the dual-adversary strategy. It took another ten days after the adoption of Lin's report and the new Party constitution for the Congress to elect a new Central Committee (for an analysis of its composition, see Chapter 7).

Lin was the sole Vice Chairman of the new Central Committee, and Mao and he stood at the head of the Politburo and its five-man Standing Committee elected by the Central Committee immediately after the close of the Ninth Party Congress, the other members, including Chou En-lai, being listed in "brushstroke order" (the Chinese equivalent of alphabetical order; position is determined in ascending order of the number of brushstrokes in one's family name). To outward appearances, Lin was in a virtually unassailable position, having just been voted the man most likely to succeed. In reality, he had serious problems. He was in poor health and had little political sophistication and little real political prestige apart from what he had gained by having Mao's hands laid on him. By taking advantage of his temporary indispensability during the early stages of the Cultural Revolution to bargain his way into the successor's role and then by insisting that his new status be written into the Party constitution, Lin had apparently antagonized Mao. He by no means had the united support of the PLA leadership. He had committed a major blunder on the Ussuri on March 2. He apparently shared the views on agriculture of radicals like Ch'en Po-ta and favored more stress on heavy industry than planning currently in effect contemplated. Worst of all, perhaps, he stood in the way of a man of much greater political ability than he and with a far better objective claim to be Mao's successor.

Lin Piao's Fall

In the atmosphere of the post-Ninth Party Congress period, Lin's apparent penchant for somewhat mindless revolutionary advance had a few opportunities for expression. One such opportunity was the so-called May 7 schools, institutions formed since 1969 by Party and government agencies as places for subjecting cadres and intellectuals (groups not usually performing manual labor) to prolonged periods of political indoctrination and manual labor. Another was a "war preparedness" campaign that got under way about October, 1969, the month in which the Sino-Soviet border talks began, and consisted of such things as the widespread construction of air-raid shelters and the stockpiling of foodstuffs; the purpose was probably to prepare the country for a "people's war" in case the talks broke down and to provide a less dangerous outlet than provocation of the Soviet Union for the anti-Soviet energies of people sharing the views of Lin Piao and the radical Maoists.

Apart from a few things like these, the dominant trend of the post-Ninth Party Congress period was one toward restabilization, and the high cards, therefore, came more and more into Chou En-lai's hands. Restabilization in domestic affairs was inevitably a slow and difficult process (see the next section). In foreign affairs, on the other hand, it was relatively easy (apart from such major knotty problems as the tension with the Soviet Union) and obviously urgent, inasmuch as during 1969 the Soviet Union built up its forces near the border to overwhelming levels, staged incidents, uttered threats, and on June 13 gave Peking a virtual ultimatum to begin talks on the border issue within two or three months. Since Peking was genuinely worried and was in a military position markedly inferior to the Soviet Union's (see Chapter 9), it was compelled to seek improvement of its diplomatic contacts and relationships with as many other countries as possible in order to build a network of political restraints around the Soviet Union. These relationships had fallen to a low level as a result of the Cultural Revolution, but in most cases they were capable of being rebuilt because of the widespread desire in foreign countries for better relations with the C.P.R. The actual job of rebuilding them, however, demanded skills and prestige possessed by only one man in China, Chou En-lai. In this context, he was probably more indispensable than Lin Piao had been during the Cultural Revolution.

The process began in mid-May, 1969, with the sending of ambassadors to countries with which the C.P.R. maintained diplomatic relations. On May 19, a rally was held for "revolutionary fighters from various parts of China" at which two developments of interest were observable: Chou was listed in the press account as the third-ranking member of the Party leadership (that is, not simply in brushstroke order), and Chou's colleague Ch'en Yi, still formally Foreign Minister, was identified as a (recently appointed) Vice Chairman of Lin Pao's bailiwick, the Military Affairs Committee of the Party Central Committee; in this position Ch'en could presumably present Chou's views and argue against any further provocation of the Russians. Five days later, Chou sent a statement to Moscow, recapitulating the Chinese position on the border issue and evading the Soviet demand for talks; it was this statement that evoked the aforementioned Soviet ultimatum of June 13. On September 11, after further Soviet pressures, Chou talked with Soviet Premier Kosygin, and on October 6, after still more pressures, he communicated to Moscow Peking's agreement to hold border talks. Chou had probably favored such talks from the beginning, but whatever his actual views, it would have been politically impossible—because of the attitude of Lin Piao and the Maoist radicals, and perhaps Mao himself—for him to agree to hold talks except under severe Soviet pressure. The agreement to enter negotiations with the Soviet Union can be regarded as another early stage in the decline of Lin Piao, and the corresponding rise of Chou En-Lai.

Chou's foreign policy at that time was probably the main issue on which his influence and Lin Piao's pulled against one another. Chou's policy of normalizing the C.P.R.'s external relations and soothing the Soviet Union (although no more than necessary to provide reasonable assurance against a Soviet attack) required as a further integral part the establishment of a positive political relationship with the United States, the only possible effective counterweight to the Soviet Union. His policy obviously involved a drastic modification of the dual-adversary strategy, which enjoined defiance to the point of occasional provocation of American "imperialism" and Soviet "revisionism." It is very likely that Lin clung, but unsuccessfully, to the dual-adversary strategy and opposed the talks with the Soviet Union as well as any moves toward the United States. For a year after the beginning of the Sino-Soviet border talks on October 20, 1969, Chou's two major modifications of the dual-adversary strategy were in effect on trial. The border talks were essentially deadlocked, and it was always possible that the Soviet Union might break them off and revert to a strategy of active pressures in spite of Chou's diplomacy. Ambassadorial talks were held with the United States in January and February, 1970, and at the second of these sessions some interest was indicated on the Chinese side in extending to President Nixon the invitation to visit China that he claimed to be eager to receive. But this promising beginning was marred by the Cambodian crisis and a ringing public statement by Mao Tse-tung on May 20, 1970, denouncing American imperialism and all its works.

The atmospherics of the Second Plenary Session of the Ninth Central Committee (August 23–September 6, 1970) suggest that Chou felt himself prepared to do political battle on behalf of stabilization, not yet against Lin Piao, but against the most vulnerable of the leading Maoist radicals. Much as Lin was becoming obsolete with the decline of the dual-adversary strategy, Ch'en Po-ta, even though he had been elected to the Politburo Standing Committee after the Ninth Party Congress, was becoming obsolete by virtue of the marked, although not complete, reduction of the propaganda cult of Mao Tse-tung that had been in progress since mid-1969: Ch'en's career had been built on the promotion of the cult. He was an ideological radical and appears to have favored a continuation of the Great Leap Forward-like policies of 1968–69, including abolition of private plots and of inequalities in peasant incomes; if so, he lost on that issue, since private plots were guaranteed in a draft state constitution (see Chapter 8) adopted at the Plenary Session for future submission to the National People's Congress. He was probably opposed on this issue by a stability-oriented coalition including Chou En-lai and much of the military leadership; it may not be a coincidence that his last recorded public appearance occurred on Army Day (August 1), 1970. In addition, by getting rid of Ch'en, who had headed the Cultural Revolution Group, Chou begin to get control over cultural affairs and propaganda; it is certainly significant that a cultural group under the State Council quietly made its appearance not long after the Second Plenary Session. Mao must have given his support to the purging of Ch'en Po-ta about this time and directed his personal supporters to do the same; during 1971, Chiang Ch'ing publicly denounced Ch'en, although not by name. Ch'en was not formally purged: he simply became inactive and was denounced in the press (although again not by name) as a "sham Marxist." Another member of the five-man Politburo Standing Committee after the Ninth Party Congress to become inactive about the end of 1970 was K'ang Sheng, who had been in charge of relations with foreign Communist Parties and had probably been trying to assume control over the rebuilding of the Party apparatus in the wake of the Cultural Revolution; by easing him out, again with Mao's at least passive approval, Chou gained effective control over these two important functions. Including these two men, about half of the Politburo had become politically inactive by about the end of 1970; various reasons could be speculatively assigned in different cases, but the unifying theme seems to be a streamlining of the formal Party leadership at Chou En-lai's initiative and the informal supplementing of what was left with trusted colleagues of Chou's. (The latter point is developed more fully in the next section and in Chapter 6.)

It should not be thought that Chou had everything his own way at the Second Plenary Session. The draft state constitution approved at the session for submission to the National People's Congress, which was to be convened "at an appropriate time," named Lin Piao as Mao's successor, as the Party constitution of 1969 had done; it is highly probable that, during the following year, Lin was urging and Chou was obstructing the holding of the National People's Congress, which would presumably adopt the constitution and complete the legitimation of the role that Lin desired for himself. On September 11, the anniversary of the critical talks between Chou and Kosygin, the *People's Daily* published a front-page photograph of Mao and Lin, nominally in connection with the public celebration of the conclusion of the Second Plenary Session five days earlier.

During October, the planks of Chou's foreign policy began to fall into place, with inevitably beneficial effects on his domestic political position. On October 10, a high-level Soviet political figure, V. S. Tolstikov, arrived as ambassador; the strategy of soothing the dangerous Russians, without conceding them anything in the nature of principle, appeared to be paying off. Also in October, President Nicolae Ceausescu of Romania paid a visit to Washington that was one of the critical links in a chain of intermediate steps that led to the Nixon trip to China. It was at the time of the Ceausescu visit that President Nixon first used in public the term People's Republic of China, an important signal and concession to Peking; thus Chou's opening toward the United States also appeared to be paying off. It is probably not a pure coincidence that Lin Piao's last public speech was delivered on October 1, 1970; it was, to be sure, not his last public appearance, which occurred on June 3, 1971, during a visit by President Ceausescu to Peking. When Edgar Snow interviewed Mao in December, 1970, Mao said, among other things, that Chou had his complete confidence and made the major operational decisions in domestic and foreign policy, often without consulting Mao; nothing was said about Lin, and Snow apparently got no impression during his last visit to China (August, 1970–February, 1971) that Lin was a genuinely important political figure.

Although not conclusive, the evidence thus suggests that Chou's political stock rose rapidly and Lin's declined after October, 1970. Chou continued the informal purging of the Party leadership already referred to. He undoubtedly bargained privately with members of the PLA leadership against Lin Piao, and, judging by the outcome, he was successful with most of the central military leadership, with the notable exception of Chief of Staff Huang Yung-sheng, whom he may have considered too close to Lin to be safe to approach, and with at least the most politically powerful of the military region commanders, Ch'en Hsi-lien of Shenyang (Mukden) and Hsu Shih-yu of Nanking (both of whom had been elected to the Politburo after the Ninth Party Congress). At some point, probably soon after October, 1970, and at Mao's direct order, the radical Maoists remaining within the top Party leadership began to give Chou at least quiet, and also essential, support in his mounting campaign to get rid of Lin Piao; their willingness to endorse the purging of Ch'en Po-ta, who had been virtually one of themselves, may have been intended in part as a symbol of their willingness to support the purging of Lin as well.

During the summer of 1971, as the opening of the National People's Congress scheduled for late in the year approached, and especially after the announcement on July 15 that Henry Kissinger had just visited Peking and that President Nixon had been invited to do the same, tension within the Chinese leadership mounted. It is known that the Nixon visit remained controversial among the cadres at least until Mao received Nixon in person, and it is very likely that it was controversial within the top leadership during the summer of 1971; Lin Piao almost certainly opposed it. The controversiality in China of the proposed Nixon visit was one of the reasons for the extraordinary secrecy with which the Chinese side, as well as the American (for its own reasons), insisted on surrounding the arrangements for it. To a large extent out of irritation at Peking's opening to the United States, the Soviet Union mounted an extraordinary propaganda and diplomatic offensive, with very threatening overtones for China, that reached its height in August and early September. It could be argued, and very likely was by Chou, that because Lin was especially objectionable in Moscow as Mao's designated heir (and a military man at that), as the major exponent of the dual-adversary strategy and "people's war" (the latter concept being very unpopular in Moscow because of its alleged racist character), and as the author of the first Ussuri clash, Lin was dangerous and must be sacrificed as a soothing gesture to the Soviet Union. Lin's opposition to the opening to the United States, the best available counterweight to the Soviet Union, also contributed to his expendability. There were other likely counts as well in the indictment against him. He was politically incompetent to succeed Mao; he had displayed a tendency toward the "cult of personality" by continuing to build up his own propaganda cult while Mao (since mid-1969) had been cutting his down to pre–Cultural Revolution levels. Lin's domestic policies centered on a more-Maoist-than-Mao faith in the "mass line" combined with a neglect of modern technology except advanced weapons. He appears to have wanted the PLA to remain the major political force in the country and to have opposed the rebuilding of the Party apparatus then in progress (see the next section and Chapter 7) to a level at which it could begin to replace the PLA as the leading political force. All this, plus the fact that he was on Chou's target list, was sufficient reason in the eyes of the top Party leadership for purging him, but not necessarily in the eyes of the Chinese public, the world, and above all his supporters in the PLA; for their benefit, a more damning indictment would have to be drawn up when the time came.

It is possible, but not probable, that Lin was so ill or so politically obtuse that he either did not realize what was happening or was in no position to attempt a countermove. But if so, he certainly had colleagues and supporters who were in such a position. Furthermore, Lin had demonstrated during the Cultural Revolution, in his behavior and in his speeches, an interest in and aptitude for more or less bloodless military coups for political purposes. It is entirely possible, therefore, that as his adversaries were to charge later, he contemplated and even organized some sort of military coup during the late summer of 1971. It is implausible, however, that he aimed this coup directly at Mao, as he was subsequently accused of having done, since to do this would destroy the legitimacy of his political position whether he succeeded or failed; it is much more probable that his coup, whatever it may have amounted to, was directed against Chou En-lai. If so, it appears likely that he and his immediate supporters met the usual fate of a military group in a Communist country if it contemplates or attempts a coup against the civilian Party leadership when (as it normally does) the latter controls the police: they were pre-empted and seized by the Public Security Forces (see Chapter 10).

On September 30, 1971, the Soviet news agency Tass announced that a Chinese (British-built) Trident jet aircraft had crashed in the Mongolian People's Republic on the night of September 12–13. Later Soviet leaks, although not entirely consistent with one another, indicated that there had been nine people aboard and that the bodies were too badly burned to permit precise identification, but that it could be determined that at least some, if not all, had been killed by small arms and that they were all too young for Lin Piao to have been one of them. By that time, stories had already begun to leak from Peking to the effect that Lin had indeed been one of the nine.

Whatever Lin may have been contemplating, Chou's final move against him clearly began on September 11, an interesting day inasmuch as it was the date on which Khrushchev died, the second anniversary of the Chou-Kosygin talks, and the first anniversary of the photograph of Mao and Lin in the *People's Daily*. There is known to have been a high-level meeting, perhaps a central work conference, on the night of September 12–13, probably to ratify an accomplished fact—the arrest of Lin and his immediate supporters, and possibly their execution (their actual fate is uncertain). The principal individuals who disappeared with Lin were members of the PLA General Staff who were evidently his closest supporters: Chief of Staff Huang Yung-sheng, Deputy Chief of Staff Wu Fa-hsien, Director Ch'iu Hui-tso of the General Rear Services Department, and Navy Chief Political Officer Li Tso-p'eng. Although various explanations of the Trident crash can be speculatively advanced, the one that appears the most plausible and in accord with the available evidence is probably that it was staged by Lin's adversaries (with the controls set electronically and with just enough fuel in the tanks to come down outside China) in an effort to prove that Lin, and possibly his colleagues, were trying to defect to the Soviet Union after the failure of a coup against Mao. In earlier years, major figures who had been purged, such as Kao Kang, had been charged, either falsely or with much exaggeration, with being anti-Mao and pro-American (in Kao's case) or anti-Mao and pro-Soviet (in Liu's case); no crimes less heinous than these were apparently considered sufficient to rationalize purges at the highest level. It was nothing new, therefore, for Lin to be charged with anti-Maoism and pro-Sovietism, and the crash was probably "merely corroborative detail intended to lend artistic verisimilitude to an otherwise bald and unconvincing narrative" (*The Mikado*). Civil air flights were grounded for three days (September 13–15) and military flights for an even longer period, probably in order to prevent Lin's supporters in the provinces from coordinating with each other or coming to Peking.

There was a brief upsurge of "war preparedness" measures in September; since they were especially intense in the Canton area, Huang Yung-sheng's base, they may have been intended as a cover for moving troops loyal to Lin and Huang toward Peking. The main events of the National Day (October 1) celebration were canceled, presumably because it would have been embarrassing to hold the observance without Lin's usual presence on the reviewing stand and premature to make a public explanation of his absence. In all these moves, Chou clearly had the support of Mao, Mao's personal supporters (as indicated by Chiang Ch'ing's appearance with Chou more than once during the crisis), and elements of the military (in particular Chou's old friend and colleague Yeh Chien-ying), in some cases probably because Mao had so ordered and/or Chou seemed a lesser evil than the troublesome Lin, rather than from real enthusiasm. By October 5, when it was announced that Dr. Kissinger would visit Peking again before the end of the month, the immediate crisis involving the fall of Lin Piao and his closest supporters was clearly over; the repercussions certainly were not.

During the next few months, closed briefings were held for cadres to rationalize the forthcoming Nixon visit (no easy task) and present the official version of the Lin Piao affair, which was to the effect that he had plotted against Mao, tried three times to assassinate him, and died while trying to defect to the Soviet Union. For the benefit of the outside world, an ambiguous picture was purposely presented, if only because the U.S. Government might justifiably have felt some doubts about the stability of a negotiating partner that admitted to having just purged its Defense Minister. Lin's functions (Vice Chairman of the Central Committee, Chairman of the Military Affairs Committee, and Defense Minister) were not formally filled by anyone else, even on an acting basis, probably in order to help preserve the ambiguity and avoid unnecessarily antagonizing his former supporters. The closest thing to an official admission of Lin's fall was the appearance on February 14, 1972 (the anniversary of the Sino-Soviet treaty of 1950 and one of several indications of Chou's En-lai's strategy of soothing the Soviet Union), of a new foreign-language edition of the Little Red Book minus the preface by Lin that had appeared in the original edition. On the other hand, press articles began to appear using the phrase "swindlers like Liu Shao-ch'i" to refer to Lin Piao, who was accused of various rather implausible failings in an apparent effort to discredit him in the eyes of the PLA specifically, as well as the public in general. Among the charges against him were: opposition to military modernization, poor generalship, contacts with the Soviet Union prior to September, 1971, and the like. It seemed quite possible that he would eventually be accused of having been the real moving spirit behind the elusive May 16 Group. His purged colleagues were not publicly denounced to anything like the same extent, probably in an effort to avoid giving unnecessary and possibly counterproductive offense to the PLA officer corps. The usual May Day celebration was canceled in 1972, and the approach of Army Day (August 1) presented a special problem, since, although the Defense Minister had not appeared on this occasion, it had been customary for the Chief of Staff to deliver a speech, and the Chief of Staff was not available. Accordingly, the official version of Lin's fall, along the lines already indicated, was given out to various foreigners from late June to July by spokesmen in Peking, by the Chinese Embassy in Algiers, and by Mao himself (in interviews with Ceylonese Premier Bandaranaike and French Foreign Minister Maurice Schumann). When Army Day came, Yeh Chien-ying delivered the speech, formally as Vice Chairman of the Military Affairs Committee, informally as Chou En-lai's military colleague and counterpart.

Post–Cultural Revolution Stabilization

In spite of many problems and some challenges, Lin Piao's in particular, the dominant trend since the end of the Cultural Revolution has been in the direction of stabilization, or normalization. Since fairly detailed comments on the major aspects of this process are offered elsewhere (see especially Chapter 7 on the Party, Chapter 8 on the state system, Chapter 9 on the PLA, and Chapter 13 on foreign policy), the account given here will be brief.

Clearly the main architect of stabilization is Chou En-lai. Although accepting certain results of the Cultural Revolution, such as the disappearances of some leaders like Liu Shao-ch'i who had been hopelessly compromised by official public denunciations, he evidently wants to restore something like the political situation that existed just before the Cultural Revolution. He wants to get the army out of politics, emphatically including provincial politics, where the leading role that it gained during the Cultural Revolution obviously contains the potential for a slide into warlordism. He wants to launch the country on a period of sustained, balanced economic growth, facilitated by a higher level of material incentives and external economic contacts than existed during the Cultural Revolution. He wants to modernize the conventional equipment of the armed forces and give them a small but usable nuclear capability, probably for some time to come of less than intercontinental range. He wants to rebuild the Party apparatus, apparently under his own direct control, and make it once more the leading political force in the country, but not to let it become as strong as it was before the Cultural Revolution. The State Council would be relatively more influential and freer of Party apparatus interference. This is an ambitious blueprint, and there are many obstacles to its fulfillment. It has certainly not been fulfilled as yet, although Chou has been making significant progress toward his goal. To help himself do so, he has made skillful use of the Soviet (and to some extent an alleged Japanese) threat, but this is not to say that he does not regard the threat as real.

He is by no means all-powerful. There have been some objections to the purge of Lin Piao, and some refusals to join in the propaganda attacks on him, on the part of a few privincial military leaders. Some of them have been quietly purged, but by no means all of them. It has not been possible, or has not seemed prudent, to announce Lin's fall in the official press, to name formal replacements for him and his colleagues who were purged in September, 1971, or to hold a Central Committee Plenary Session or the National People's Congress. Since the National People's Congress has not met, no state constitution is formally in effect (except in a vestigial sense that of 1954), and the revolutionary committees, which are given permanent status as government bodies in the draft state constitution adopted by the Central Committee in September, 1970, are in a rather uncertain situation. If Chou's object, at some important meetings that were evidently held in May and June, 1972, was to get agreement to an official statement on the Lin Piao affair on the Party anniversary (July 1), he failed.

On the other hand, progress is being made in whittling down Lin Piao's former base, which apparently has no collective future since he has fallen (and is probably dead) and has had no successor. The work of rebuilding the Party apparatus has not been easy, but it has continued. Party committees began to be formed at the *hsien* (district or country) level at the end of 1969, and a year later they began to be formed at the provincial level; the list of provincial Party committees was completed in August, 1971. They were intended to give leadership to the revolutionary committees, and the latter had their functions confined to the government (or administrative) sphere with the emergence of the new Party committees. On the other hand, there is a very high degree of overlap between the leaderships of the provincial Party committees and the corresponding revolutionary committees at the top, although less so as one moves down the hierarchy, and both leaderships are military to a high degree. At lower levels, however, military participation in revolutionary committees appears to have begun to decline. The propaganda campaign to "learn from the PLA" has stopped. The rebuilding of a greatly streamlined government bureaucracy, which is of course Chou En-lai's bailiwick, has been proceeding fairly rapidly. Some high-ranking figures who got into trouble during the Cultural Revolution but are apparently not considered to have been hopelessly compromised—such as Ch'en Yun, an economic planner and a member of the pre-1967 Politburo Standing Committee, and Ch'en Tsai-tao of Wuhan Incident fame

—have reappeared and presumably are being used in some capacity. Chou has put together an informal team of trusted colleagues acceptable to Mao who help him in running the major sectors of the political system: propaganda, the armed forces, the economy, the public security system, and so forth. Chou seems to reserve supervision of the new Party apparatus and of foreign affairs almost exclusively to himself. The public security system is being revived at the center and at the local level—a process that began in 1970. Chou exploited his successful handling of the Nixon visit and Mao's willingness to receive Nixon for his own political benefit. He has been careful to continue cultivating Mao's confidence and support, and these evidently have been as forthcoming since Lin Piao's fall as they were before it; Mao's support automatically carries with it at least the outward cooperation of his personal following, including Chiang Ch'ing. There is no convincing reason to credit the occasional speculation that Mao and the Maoists are preparing to dump Chou; even if they tried, it is by no means certain that they could succeed. The restoration of stability has been helped by the absence, since March, 1969, of any more major mass campaigns.

So far, then, Chou has been making good progress toward his goal against formidable obstacles. It has been perhaps his finest hour. On the other hand, regional military power has by no means been fully eliminated. Whether it will be eliminated or, if it is not, will develop into warlordism free of effective control from the center, remains to be seen; the chances appear to be against the emergence of warlordism.

FURTHER READINGS

Original documents on the Cultural Revolution can be found in *Important Documents on the Great Proletarian Cultural Revolution in China,* Peking: Foreign Language Press, 1970; *The Great Cultural Revolution in China,* Hong Kong: Asia Research Centre, 1967; and *The Great Power Struggle in China,* Hong Kong: Asia Research Centre, 1969.

Among the numerous published analyses of the Cultural Revolution, the following can be specially recommended: Thomas W. Robinson, ed., *The Cultural Revolution in China,* Berkeley: University of California Press, 1971; Richard Baum, ed., *China in Ferment: Perspectives on the Cultural Revolution,* Englewood Cliffs, N.J.: Prentice-Hall, 1971; Tai Sung An, *Mao Tse-tung's Cultural Revolution,* New York: Pegasus, 1972; Philip Bridgham, "Mao's 'Cultural Revolution': Origin and Development," *The China Quarterly,* no. 29 (January–

March, 1967), pp. 1–35, "Mao's Cultural Revolution in 1967: The Struggle To Seize Power," *ibid.*, no. 34 (April–June, 1968), pp. 6–37, and "Mao's Cultural Revolution: The Struggle to Consolidate Power," *ibid.*, no. 41 (January–March, 1970), pp. 1–25; Richard Baum, "China: Year of the Mangoes," *Asian Survey*, vol. ix, no. 1 (January, 1969), pp. 1–17; John Israel, "The Red Guards in Historical Perspective: Continuity and Change in the Chinese Youth Movement," *The China Quarterly*, no. 30 (April–June, 1967), pp. 1–32; Charles Neuhauser, "The Impact of the Cultural Revolution on the Chinese Communist Party Machine," *Asian Survey*, vol. viii, no. 6 (June, 1968), pp. 465–88; Barry Burton, "The Cultural Revolution's Ultraleft Conspiracy: The 'May 16 Group,'" *ibid.*, vol. xi, no. 11 (November, 1971), pp. 1029–63; Harry Gelman, "Mao and the Permanent Purge," *Problems of Communism*, vol. xv, no. 6 (November–December, 1966), pp. 2–14; Ross Terrill, "The Siege Mentality," *ibid.*, vol. xvi, no. 2 (March–April, 1967), pp. 1–10; Gene T. Hsiao, "The Background and Development of 'The Proletarian Cultural Revolution,'" *Asian Survey*, vol. vii, no. 6 (June, 1967), pp. 389–404; Parris H. Chang, "Mao's Great Purge: A Political Balance Sheet," *Problems of Communism*, vol. xviii, no. 2 (March–April, 1969), pp. 1–10; Jürgen Domes, "Some Results of the Cultural Revolution in China," *Asian Survey*, vol. xi, no. 9 (September, 1971), pp. 932–40; and Stanley Karnow, *Mao and China: From Revolution to Revolution*, New York: Viking, 1972.

The episode of Mao and the Japanese Communist delegation is treated in Kikuzo Ito and Minoru Shibata, "The Dilemma of Mao Tse-tung," *The China Quarterly*, no. 35 (July–September, 1968), pp. 58–77. The Yugoslav account referred to in the text is B. Bogunovic, "The Storm in July—the Great Cultural Revolution," American Consulate General, Hong Kong, *Survey of the China Mainland Press*, no. 3855 (January 9, 1967), pp. 1–5.

The "power seizure" in Shanghai is treated analytically in Evelyn Anderson, "Shanghai: The Masses Unleashed," *Problems of Communism*, vol. xvii, no. 1 (January–February, 1968), pp. 12–21; and by an eyewitness in Neale Hunter, *Shanghai Journal: An Eyewitness Account of the Cultural Revolution*, New York: Praeger, 1969, Boston: Beacon, 1971. There is a worthwhile account of the Red Guard movement: Hans Granqvist, *The Red Guard: A Report on Mao's Revolution*, New York: Praeger, 1967, London: Pall Mall Press, 1967. There are two interesting books by foreigners imprisoned in China during the Cultural Revolution: Norman Barrymaine, *The Time Bomb: Today's China from the Inside*, New York: Taplinger, 1971, London: Davies, 1971; and Eric Gordon, *Freedom Is a Word*, New York: Morrow, 1972.

On the post-Cultural Revolution period, there is an excellent analysis by Harry Harding, "Political Trends in China since the Cultural

Revolution," *The Annals,* vol. 402 (July, 1972), pp. 67–82. See also Parris H. Chang, "Decentralization of Power" (pp. 67–75), and Victor C. Falkenheim, "Continuing Central Predominance" (pp. 75–83), both in *Problems of Communism,* vol. xxi, no. 4 (July–August, 1972). On the Soviet aspect, see Harold C. Hinton, *The Bear at the Gate: Chinese Policymaking under Soviet Pressure,* Washington: American Enterprise Institute, and Stanford, Calif.: The Hoover Institution, 1971. There are several valuable personal accounts of post-Cultural Revolution China by foreign visitors: *The New York Times Report from Red China,* New York: Avon, 1972; Committee of Concerned Asian Scholars, *China: Inside the People's Republic,* New York: Bantam, 1972; Ross Terrill, *800,000,000: The Real China,* Boston: Little, Brown, 1972; Klaus Mehnert, *China Returns,* New York: Dutton, 1972 (as *China Today,* London: Thames & Hudson, 1972); and Seymour Topping, *Journey Between Two Chinas,* New York: Harper & Row, 1972.

5. Ideology

The relative importance of the Chinese and the Marxist-Leninist components of Chinese Communist ideology is not easy to determine. Neither of these components is a simple substance whose presence in an ideological compound can be measured as well as identified. It appears that the ratio has been changing over time in favor of the Chinese component, which is by no means wholly traditional in character. The Marxist-Leninist component, however, still appears to be primary, inasmuch as the Chinese Communist leadership remains genuinely committed not only to the concept of political and social revolution but also to the leadership of the Communist Party and to the ultimate attainment of "socialism" and "Communism."

The Marxist-Leninist Foundations and the Soviet Experience

Karl Marx took as the foundation of his philosophy the concept, derived from Greek thought via the writings of his predecessor Hegel, that the universe operates on the principle of the dialectic, whereby one state of affairs (the thesis) is transformed through "contradictions" with its opposite (the antithesis) into a new, higher state of affairs (the synthesis), which in turn is transformed in the same manner. Applying this concept to human history, or rather the history of Western man as he understood it, Marx concluded that there had been a progression from primitive Communism successively through slave societies and feudalism to capitalism, and that in the future there would be one to socialism and ultimately Communism. Since Marx, like many other thinkers of his era, was a materialist, and since furthermore he was intensely concerned with the problems as well as the achievements of the Industrial Revolution as he observed them in the mid-nineteenth century, he believed that the progress of history (that is, of the dialectic in human affairs) was shaped by economic forces. More precisely, he held that the dominant state of technology (the "mode of production") determined economic and social organization ("production relations") and the character of the state, which (except in the case of the two Communist stages, which were considered stateless) he regarded as the dictatorship of one class over the others. Each dominant class or institution (the absolute monarchy under slavery, the feudal aristocracy, and the capitalist class or bourgeoisie) was or would be overthrown by the succeeding dominant class in a revolution on whose nature—necessarily violent or possibly nonviolent—Marx vacillated somewhat. The principal oppressed class under capitalism, the proletariat or industrial working class, would find its sufferings intolerable (the law of increasing misery) and in time would overthrow the bourgeoisie and usher in a "dictatorship of the proletariat" over it. This stage would give way to socialism, a state of affairs in which there would exist only two classes (the working class and the peasantry), and the state would gradually "wither away" through the abolition of the distinction between the two classes as the peasantry was raised to the economic, technical, and cultural level of the working class. Then would appear the ultimate classless and stateless stage of Communism, in which the governing principle would be, "From each according to his ability, to each according to his need." Since they lay in the future, the final stages of socialism and Communism were envisaged only vaguely by Marx, and his scheme had the obvious logical defect that it expected the dialectic somehow to stop functioning when the ultimate stage of Communism had been reached. Nonetheless, as an eloquent protest against the sufferings of the working class and as a vision of a better future, Marxism had in many countries a prompt and great impact on intellectuals, and to a lesser extent on nonintellectual labor leaders, even though by the time of Marx's death (1883) the condition of the working class had tended to improve without the intervention of revolution in Europe and the United States, as a result of union activity and social legislation.

At the beginning of the twentieth century, the most plausible outlook for Marxism as a body of theory and practice was evolution in the direction of "revisionism," or in other words, nonrevolutionary moderation. Specifically, the expectation of proletarian revolution was generally giving way to trust in legal activity as a means of improving the status of the working class within the capitalist order. Some individual Marxists and Marxist groups have continued to think along these lines down to the present. If this view had prevailed, the phenomenon generically described as Communism would not exist. For Marxism to develop a revolutionary, Communist, mainstream in "contradiction" with the evolutionary, "revisionist," trend, World War I was probably a necessary condition, since it weakened the political and social structure of the established, more or less capitalist, regimes of Europe, the absolutist states (Russia, Germany, Austria-Hungary, Turkey) more than the liberal ones (Britain and France, mainly). But even the war was not a sufficient condition for the emergence of Communism. For this, the combination of Russia's peculiar conditions and the unique personality of Vladimir Ilyich Lenin was required.

By virtue of its geographic location on the eastern fringes of Europe, its autocratic tradition, and its turbulent modern history, Russia was politically the most absolutist and socially the most backward of the principal European states that became involved in World War I. Consequently, it was defeated (by Germany) for the third time in a century in a major war; it had lost the Crimean War to Britain, France, and Turkey in 1853–56 and the Russo-Japanese War to Japan in 1904–5, each time with traumatic but not quite revolutionary effects. The strain was too much for the antiquated and discredited Tsarist regime, which collapsed in March, 1917, under the impact of urban riots and the defection of much of its army in the wake of defeats in the field. It was succeeded by a liberal, parliamentary Provisional Government, which tried to keep Russia in the war against Germany and to postpone the solution of such major problems as the land question until a more democratically elected government could be established. This approach might have worked if the Provisional Government had survived until the collapse of Germany on the Western Front in November, 1918. Weakened by its own military efforts against Germany in the meantime, however, the Provisional Government was further weakened by pressures from right-wing generals desiring a dictatorship to the point where it was overthrown with almost ludicrous ease by Lenin's organization, the Bolsheviks, on November 7, 1917 (known as the October Revolution because it occurred on October 25 according to the calendar then in use in Russia).

A man of keen intellect and energetic temperament, Lenin was embittered early in life by the execution of his elder brother for conspiring against Tsar Alexander III. In 1903, Lenin began the process of creating a Bolshevik ("majority") Party from the Russian Social Democratic (Marxist) Party, whose other main faction, the Mensheviks ("minority"), had "revisionist" tendencies. Lenin strongly espoused the revolutionary, as against the evolutionary, version of the Marxist vision and insisted that its realization demanded that the proletariat be led by a tightly disciplined, and typically small, Party of professional revolutionaries who need not be of working-class origin. In effect, Lenin rejected Marx's determinism and feared that in the absence of such leadership the workings of "spontaneity" (unregulated popular activity, a bugbear of Lenin's) would fail to produce the desired revolution. The Party itself must operate according to the principle of "democratic centralism," which means in essence the taking of major decisions by majority vote in the Party's leading body (usually the Political Bureau of the Central Committee) and strict obedience by lower Party bodies and all Party members to these decisions, tempered by a system of indirect elections to Party offices by the Party membership. The thrust of Lenin's organizational principles has been toward centralization of power and authority. Lenin was not quite a dictator, but he effectively if unconsciously paved the way for a successor who was.

Whereas Marx had believed that the predetermined workings of history would produce proletarian revolutions in the most advanced countries (Germany or Britain) earlier than in others, Lenin held that, on the contrary, the revolution could be *made* to happen in the most backward major country within the Western capitalist orbit, namely, Russia. This was not because he was a nationalist—he was not—but because he was more activist than Marx and believed that he and his Party could and should exploit Russia's peculiar position as the weakest link in the chain of capitalism. But even in Russia there must be a revolutionary situation, meaning above all that the masses (especially the proletariat, but also the peasants) must be in a revolutionary mood. After 1905, Lenin came to believe that an alliance of workers and peasants, the former and their Bolshevik "vanguard" exercising "hegemony" over the latter, could and should execute an essentially violent revolution, rather than place any reliance on the rudimentary parliamentary institutions created by Tsar Nicholas II after 1905 in an effort to stave off revolution through reforms. Accordingly, Lenin totally denied any legitimacy to the Provisional Government, which grew out of the Duma (parliament) created by Nicholas. Instead, Lenin insisted successfully that his Party should work with the soviets (representative councils elected informally by workers in factories and by military units after the collapse of the Tsarist regime in March, 1917) to overthrow the Provisional Government. The peasants could not be organized and led very effectively at that time, but they were useful because their rebelliousness weakened the established order in the countryside. Under Lenin's effective leadership, and with their tight organization, the Bolsheviks increased their representation in the principal soviets by championing the redress of popular grievances and by working against certain right-wing generals threatening the Provisional Government. After a virtually bloodless coup against the latter on November 7, power in the capital city of Petrograd (now Leningrad) was in Bolshevik hands, in the name of the soviets throughout Russia and of proletarian dictatorship. The coup was timed to prevent the Provisional Government from transmitting its authority to a democratically elected Constituent Assembly.

While rapidly reducing the soviets and other manifestations of "spontaneity" within the initially limited area under his control to a position of subordination to his Party, Lenin had to fight a civil war (1918–21) against a variety of "White" (anti-Bolshevik) armies, sometimes backed by interventionist contingents of French, British, Japanese, and American troops. Tight discipline, revolutionary enthusiasm, and a central location gave the Bolsheviks the victory over their disunited opponents, but at a fearful cost to a Russia already drained by the war against the Central Powers. The cost was increased by Bolshevik policy in the early years, which was one of "war Communism" (military Communism would be a better translation) and included the forcible requisitioning of grain from the peasants. In March, 1921, a mutiny on the part of an important and previously loyal naval unit convinced Lenin to initiate a more moderate policy, the New Economic Policy (NEP), under which free enterprise was restored except in the "commanding heights" of banking, heavy industry, and communications. At the same time, Lenin characteristically moved to prevent this retreat from becoming a rout by tightening the political grip of the Party on the people and by introducing even stricter discipline within the Party (now known as the Communist Party). Specifically, he had the Party adopt a ban on "factions," a faction being defined as a minority grouping within the Politburo or Central Committee attempting to function collectively in opposition to the dominant majority and its prevailing line. "Factionalism" thus defined, which would of course be regarded in any parliamentary system as a normal and indeed desirable phenomenon, has remained impermissible in all orthodox Marxist-Leninist parties (including the CPC); the imminent lifting of the ban on "factionalism" by the Czechoslovak Party in 1968 was a major cause of the Soviet invasion.

Being internationally minded like Marx, Lenin thought in more or less worldwide terms and never believed that proletarian revolution could succeed and survive in Russia unless it also occurred shortly afterward in other countries, preferably in the advanced capitalist countries of the West. In his view, the latter, as well as Russia itself, had entered by the end of the nineteenth century the "highest" stage of their development, that of "imperialism," an expansionist one in which control of the "colonial and semicolonial areas" enabled the bourgeoisie of the "imperialist" countries to bribe their workers into political passivity with various concessions made possible by exploitation of the colonies. It was the task of the young Communist Parties that emerged in the "imperialist" countries after 1917 to energize and lead the proletariats of their countries in a revolutionary struggle that would have the effect of safeguarding the young Soviet Russian state from attempted annihilation by the "imperialists," a scenario that alternated in Lenin's mind with the possibility of wars within the "imperialist camp," such as he had held World War I to be. Lenin visualized these "proletarian revolutionary" movements in the developed (especially the "imperialist") countries as the more important wing of a worldwide anti-"imperialist" offensive directed from Moscow (to which city the Soviet capital was moved in 1918). The other wing was to be "national revolutionary" movements in the "colonial and semi-colonial" countries, whose detachment through revolution from the "imperialist" countries would, in Lenin's opinion, deal the latter a fatal blow. The national revolutionary movements would, of course, include Communist Parties where these existed, but in view of the weakness or even the absence of a socioeconomic basis for an industrial proletariat in most colonial and semicolonial countries, leadership of these movements would have to rest for the indefinite future with the "national bourgeoisie" (anti-"imperialist" local capitalists). To coordinate the activities of Communist Parties in both categories, Lenin established the Third International (the Communist International, or Comintern) in 1919. By 1921, Lenin was becoming discouraged over the immediate prospects for the proletarian revolutionary movements in the developed countries and had come to feel somewhat higher hopes for the national revolutionary movements in the colonial and semicolonial areas, of which he considered the Kuomintang in China to be one. After Lenin's death in early 1924, Stalin rapidly acquired control over the central machinery of the Comintern and made its alliance with the Kuomintang for a few years into what was probably the main Soviet foreign-policy effort of the mid-1920's, and of course a disastrously unsuccessful one.

Before coming to power, Lenin had visualized the administration of a workers' state, a proletarian dictatorship, as a very simple affair. He soon changed his mind and found it necessary to employ non-Communist specialists in important positions in the bureaucracy, the armed forces, and other sectors of public life. Correspondingly, the Party grew in size and required an increasingly large administrative headquarters, known as the Secretariat of the Central Committee. In 1922, Joseph Vissarionovich Stalin was put in charge of the Secretariat as General Secretary. Although supposedly not a policy-making position, in Stalin's ambitious hands it rapidly became one of great power. Stalin appointed his followers to key positions in the Party apparatus, from which a growing number were elected to the Central Committee and were thus in a position to influence the composition of the Politburo, on which Stalin also sat. Within the Politburo, he skillfully and unscrupulously formed tactical alliances to get rid of his rivals in sequence, the first major one to be ousted being the radical Leon Trotsky and the second the moderate Nikolai Bukharin. Stalin took particular pains to gain and retain control over the Party apparatus within the political police, which grew in size and in its level of activity but without being allowed as yet by the Politburo to take criminal action against high Party leaders.

If only to differentiate himself from the hated Trotsky, who preached the rapid development of the revolution in Russia and its replication abroad as well ("permanent revolution"), Stalin advocated, beginning in 1924, the doctrine of "socialism in one country." The essence of this was that the Soviet Union should build up its strength in every way as a basis (not a substitute) for the later expansion of Communism and Soviet power abroad. The disaster of 1927 in China reinforced the validity of this principle in Stalin's mind, and in 1928 he threw his weight successfully behind a policy of terminating the NEP and launching a program of forced-draft heavy industrialization and collectivization of agriculture, under the rubric of the First Five-Year Plan (1928–32).

Although impressive gains were achieved on the industrial front, the impact on agriculture of Stalin's brutal approach was nearly disastrous: there was widespread famine in the rural regions in the early 1930's. Up to that point, Stalin had carried most of the Party leadership with him, but serious strains developed as it became clear after 1932 that he intended to maintain the pressure on the peasants and to use police terror against Party members who objected. By 1934, a rather vague movement was under way within the Party leadership to curb Stalin's power and perhaps to depose him. The leader, or at least the prospective leader, of this movement, Sergei Kirov, was accordingly murdered at Stalin's instigation late in 1934. Stalin then unleashed a massive blood purge aimed not only at eliminating real or potential opposition in the Party and all other sectors of public life but at cowing the entire population through the use of random terror. Several million people were killed, and a still larger number were imprisoned or sent to forced labor. By 1939, Stalin's position was no longer challenged, although his colleagues intrigued against each other for his favor, and he instituted a "cult of personality" focused on himself and equaled up to that time only by Hitler's.

In addition to the satisfaction of his vanity and the possession of complete domestic control, Stalin wanted the greatest possible freedom of maneuver in his conduct of Soviet foreign policy. After 1934, he realized that Hitler was a menace but hoped to manage him so that he would strike against the Western democracies rather than the Soviet Union. Stalin was not yet fully in control and had to tolerate a brief "popular front" interlude, during which foreign Communist Parties were instructed by the Comintern to cooperate with other antifascist parties. But after 1936, when Stalin's victory at home became virtually irreversible, he rapidly wound up this phase and made vaguely identified "Trotskyites," more than Hitler and his allies, the main international targets of Comintern propaganda. The main exception was in the Far East, where Stalin directed the CPC (in 1935–36) to ally itself with the Kuomintang against Japan, which he had feared since before he had seen reason to feel concerned over the rise of Hitler. These policy shifts rendered the Comintern obsolete in Stalin's eyes, although he did not formally abolish it until 1943, and, from that time on, he dominated the other Communist Parties (with the main and increasing exception of the CPC) more than ever in an essentially bilateral fashion. Stalin and the Western democracies were each trying to buy time to prepare for a likely German attack and to ensure that the other would be the first victim of such an attack. The Western democracies made their deal with Hitler at Munich in 1938 at the expense of Czechoslovakia; Stalin made his a year later, mainly at the expense of Poland. Poland was promptly partitioned through German invasion in the west followed by Soviet occupation in the east. Since Britain was committed to fight for Poland against Germany and did so, Stalin had contributed decisively if indirectly to the outbreak of World War II while avoiding active involvement in it.

But not for long. Conflicts soon arose between Berlin and Moscow over the delimitation of their respective spheres of influence in Eastern Europe, especially the Balkans. Because of his own horror at the idea of a two-front war (in Europe and the Far East), Stalin did not believe that Hitler would attack him while Britain was still unconquered. But Hitler did exactly that in June, 1941, and it was fortunate for Stalin that his neutrality pact with Japan, signed the previous April, and still more the Japanese preoccupation with the impending conquest of Southeast Asia, inhibited Tokyo's armies from complying with Hitler's request that they follow his example. In 1943, the balance of the titanic struggle tipped in favor of the Soviet Union, thanks to German strategic and political errors, a stout Soviet performance including effective leadership by Stalin, and support for the Soviet Union from its Western allies. The latter gave their consent to a Soviet sphere of influence, but not to Soviet domination, in postwar Eastern Europe. But the Soviet victory over Germany in 1945 left Stalin in a position to assert domination and to transform the East European countries into his satellites, a process that he achieved by degrees and completed in 1947–48, by which time all semblance of the wartime alliance with the Western democracies had disappeared. One European regime, that of Tito in Yugoslavia, successfully fended off Soviet domination and was subjected in retaliation to a massive campaign of propaganda and political pressures orchestrated in Moscow.

While conducting his cold war with the West, centering on a political struggle to decide the fate of Germany and a proxy war in Korea, Stalin dashed the hopes of his people for a better life after World War II and fastened a tighter dictatorship than ever on them. Opposition to this policy on the part of some intellectuals, economic planners, and Party leaders, as well as his own growing mental disturbance, led Stalin to decide, by the beginning of 1953, to launch another purge comparable to that of the 1930's.

The early weeks of 1953 saw a tense, almost silent struggle between Stalin and an emerging opposition group for control of the police and the support of the armed forces. By the time of his death —officially announced on March 5, 1953, as of natural causes— Stalin had been defeated in this struggle.

His successors were, of course, those who had defeated him, and they proceeded to eliminate the worst excesses of his police regime. The initially most powerful of them, police boss Lavrenti Beria, overreached himself by seemingly trying to make himself a dictator, and he alienated the military and other hawkish elements of the leadership by advocating an accommodation with the West over Germany; he was accordingly overthrown in late June, 1953, and shot six months later. Georgi Malenkov, the next leader to be "more equal" (George Orwell's phrase) than the others, favored a posture of stabilization in foreign policy and a better deal for the Soviet consumer (see Chapter 3). This line had enough opponents in the Soviet elite to enable Nikita Khrushchev to oust Malenkov from the premiership in 1955 and from the Politburo in 1957. The essence of Khrushchev's domestic policy was an effort to modernize Soviet industrial and agricultural technology somewhat along American lines and to use the Communist Party apparatus, of which he as First Secretary was the head, as the main instrument of this transformation. To rationalize this controversial departure from Soviet tradition, he denounced the memory of Stalin from time to time as a negative symbol of that tradition. He tried to find resources for his domestic program and to facilitate a dynamic foreign policy aimed at competing vigorously but "peacefully" with the United States by emphasizing missile rather than conventional forces. All these planks in his platform, as well as his tendency, especially conspicuous in the case of his attempt to introduce offensive missiles secretly into Cuba (October, 1962), toward a personalized and occasionally adventurous style of leadership, antagonized the semi-Stalinist figures who held most of the other key positions in the Party leadership and apparatus. Among the counts against him was probably the increasing emotionalism and ineffectiveness of his China, or anti-China, policy. For these things, or some combination of them, he was ousted by his colleagues in mid-October, 1964.

The successor leadership was, and is, headed by Leonid Brezhnev as First (later General) Secretary of the Party Central Committee and by Alexei Kosygin as Premier. Their domestic style and policy have represented something of a reaction against

Khrushchev's in a semi-Stalinist direction, although without the restoration of full-fledged police terror. The Party apparatus has essentially been restored to its traditional Leninist role as the overall political directing mechanism, rather than being the economic bureaucracy that Khrushchev tried to make it. Khrushchev's tentative political liberalization has been largely stopped, and indeed partially reversed. Stalin is not praised officially as a rule, but neither is he denounced. While avoiding Khrushchev's occasional adventurism, the Brezhnev-Kosygin leadership has built up the Soviet Union's strategic nuclear forces to a level of approximate parity with the United States and since about 1966 has conducted an increasingly active policy in Europe, the Middle East, and Asia. Like Khrushchev's, it has become increasingly obsessed with its China problem and has come to aim its external activities more against China than against the United States.

Such, in brief, is the body of Marxist-Leninist theory and Soviet practice that the CPC has variously accepted, adapted, rejected, or merely observed. By way of transition to a consideration of the form that Marxism-Leninism has assumed in China, it may be helpful to summarize the theoretical perspective from which the major European prophets of Marxism-Leninism have viewed China.

With uncharacteristic humility, Marx admitted to being rather ignorant of the "Asiatic societies," as he called them, including China. He was therefore uncertain and ambiguous as to whether China was either a feudal society that would follow the same progression as Western societies or a special case marked by a combination of bureaucratic rule and free (nonfeudal) land tenure. More important to him was the hope that the Western capitalist states of his day, through their commercial activities and "gunboat diplomacy," were evoking revolutionary unrest in China that might have profoundly destructive effects on the capitalist order in Europe.

Lenin did little theorizing about China, but he saw clearly that, as the most populous of the "semicolonial" countries, it could play an important part in the struggle against "imperialism." Being sensitive after 1905 to the revolutionary potential of the peasantry in Russia, if given leadership by the proletariat and its "vanguard" the Bolsheviks (later, the Communist Party), he readily believed that the Chinese peasantry could play an important anti-"imperialist" role under "national revolutionary" leadership.

Stalin, who did not care for fine doctrinal distinctions as a rule, swept aside Marx's tentative view that "Asiatic societies," including China, might follow a path of development different from that of Western societies and decreed that China was in its feudal stage. More important, Stalin concluded after the disaster of 1927 that rural guerrilla warfare offered probably the best strategy for the CPC; it does not necessarily follow, however, that the adoption of such a strategy by Mao Tse-tung and other Chinese Communist leaders, beginning in 1928, reflected merely their acceptance of directives from Moscow. Guerrilla warfare is a simple and familiar concept, although difficult of successful execution, and one that must have seemed an obvious possible course to most would-be revolutionary strategists contemplating the Chinese scene in 1928.

The rise of Mao Tse-tung, who departed to some extent in theory and still more in practice from orthodox (that is, European and Soviet) Marxism-Leninism while preserving a surface appearance of orthodoxy, and his increasing claims (since 1949) to theoretical originality, have posed grave doctrinal problems for Soviet leaders and thinkers. Mao rejected, under the rubric "New Democracy," the idea of "national bourgeois" leadership in favor of "proletarian" (that is, Communist) leadership of the Chinese revolution at an earlier time than Lenin's and Stalin's thinking would have indicated. A comparable eagerness by Tito, combined with his rejection of Soviet efforts to treat Yugoslavia as a satellite, produced an open break between him and Stalin in 1948. But Stalin was in no position even to try to dominate China in the same way, because of its vast size, and furthermore he apparently learned from his experience with Tito. Accordingly, once Mao became the chief of a Communist state as well as the leader of a Communist Party, Stalin had his press pay tribute to Mao as a theorist and concede that the revolutionary experience of the CPC was a valid and valuable model for Asia. In late 1951, however, the latter concession was withdrawn, mainly because Peking had been taking advantage of it vigorously in its effort to give leadership to other Asian Communist movements. Since then, the Soviet Union for all practical purposes has rejected, sometimes quietly and sometimes openly, the idea that Mao has "creatively enriched" the "treasury of Marxism-Leninism." In particular, Soviet writers have never conceded that the development of China since 1949 constitutes a valid model for developing countries, or at any rate a model superior to the Soviet Union itself.

The Sinicization of Marxism-Leninism

In 1946, Liu Shao-ch'i told the sympathetic American journalist Anna Louise Strong that Mao Tse-tung's "great accomplishment" was that he had "created a Chinese or Asiatic form of Marxism." Great or not, it is an accomplishment that can indeed be plausibly attributed to Mao.

Even before Mao's time, and indeed from the middle of the nineteenth century, the gradual breakdown of the Confucian state and its Manchu rulers under the impact of domestic and foreign pressures that were significantly different from any that China had experienced before had progressively discredited the Confucian world outlook as well. From the mid-nineteenth century on, accordingly, major antiestablishment Chinese political movements tended to adopt foreign ideologies, which had the advantages of not having been discredited in Chinese experience and of being almost equally new to all sections of society rather than the preserve of some particular sector. Thus, the anti-Manchu Taiping movement (ca. 1850–65) adopted a version of Protestant Christianity as the basis of its ideology, and the Kuomintang based its ideology on aspects of nineteenth-century Western nationalism. But adoption was followed by Sinicization, or adaptation Chinese-style, to a degree that left the result almost unrecognizable, or at any rate unacceptable, in the eyes of the originators of the ideological basis or their contemporary descendants. Thus, Christian missionaries in China disowned Taiping Christianity, and the Western powers necessarily objected to Kuomintang nationalism, especially in the form imparted to it by Chiang Kai-shek, since they were among its principal targets. In fact, they were blamed (in Chiang Kai-shek's *China's Destiny,* published in 1943) for virtually all China's modern problems. So it has been with Marxism-Leninism: first adoption, then after the disaster of 1927 adaptation or Sinicization, under the aegis of Mao Tse-tung, his being the version among the alternative possibilities that prevailed because it was the one that seemed to work best under Chinese conditions.

The changes that Marxism-Leninism has undergone in the process of Sinicization are numerous, but many of them are in the nature of atmospherics or the application of one rather than another theory or policy within the spectrum of Marxism-Leninism because of the demands posed by specific conditions (a legitimate choice in the eyes of an orthodox Leninist). Some of the changes, however, have gone beyond this and involve qualitative transformations exceeding the limits of what Leninist orthodoxy regards as permissible. These transformations can be considered, at least for the sake of convenience of analysis, to center on the dichotomy between class and nation (or "people"). European societies, especially that of Russia, emerged from feudalism only in modern times and have retained a rather rigid class structure into the recent past; accordingly, Western (including Marxist-Leninist) intellectuals have tended to think of classes not merely as abstractions but as concrete, mutually exclusive, and often antagonistic entities. It was therefore natural for the Marxist-Leninist concept of revolution to be built around the clash between exploiting and exploited classes. China, on the other hand, emerged from feudalism two millennia ago, at least with respect to the important matter of land tenure. Social and class distinctions of course persisted, but they were considerably less rigid (that is, hereditarily determined) than in the West, even though Marxist-Leninist (including Chinese Communist) thinkers have generally classified pre-1949 China as essentially feudal.

Modern Chinese intellectuals, accordingly, have talked of China's class structure, partly as a result of the influence of Western ways of thinking, but they have tended to build their ideas more significantly on other concepts. This was one reason that Marxism, in its pre-Leninist form, had very little impact on China. The de-emphasis, in reality if not always in appearance, of class considerations was powerfully stimulated by China's reduction to the status of a "semicolony" by the "imperialist" powers (including Tsarist Russia). The humiliation felt by an increasing number of Chinese, of various classes, tended to strengthen the feeling that what united Chinese (Chineseness, as it were) was more important than what divided them, except for Chinese considered to be cooperating at least objectively with the "imperialist" powers or to be partly responsible for China's weakness and humiliation. This tendency came out clearly at the time of the nationalist, student-led May Fourth Movement of 1919. It was therefore natural that Marxism-Leninism in its Chinese environment should take on a more nationalist and populist coloring than it had possessed in the lands of its origin.

During Stalin's lifetime, the CPC, even when it came under Mao's leadership after 1937, kept these tendencies from becoming so intrusive that Stalin felt it necessary or worthwhile at any given time to take official notice of them, although he made occasional disparaging comments in private. After 1948, and especially as the

CPC showed itself, to Soviet surprise, to be in a position to seize power, both sides were eager not to recapitulate the Stalin-Tito dispute. After Stalin's death, Mao took less and less trouble to conceal his feeling of seniority and superiority tó Stalin's quarreling successors, a posture reinforced by their occasional tendency to pay public deference to Mao for one reason or another. After the mid-1950's, Mao displayed an increasing tendency toward ideological creativity, for domestic reasons and in an effort to one-up the Soviet Union. He acted more and more as though he believed, as he undoubtedly did, that the ideological and political center of the international Communist movement had shifted from "revisionist" Moscow to revolutionary Peking. "Revisionist" or not, Moscow objected increasingly to Mao's successive innovations: the concept of an essentially peaceful "transition to socialism" (a nonviolent class struggle under Communist rule, 1954–55), the concept of Communism by consent (the Hundred Flowers, 1956–57), the concept that the Party can and should be "rectified" from outside its own ranks through the "spontaneous" (induced, actually) action of the masses (in 1957 and in the Cultural Revolution). Increasingly, in recent years, and especially since the Cultural Revolution, Soviet propaganda has accused Mao and his colleagues of having abandoned Marxism-Leninism (whose nature is claimed to be a matter of agreement between the Soviet Party and the rest of the international Communist movement) and gone nationalist; this is true to some extent, but in reality probably to no greater extent than it is true of the Soviet leadership itself. Soviet propaganda also calls China expansionist, which in the sense of a tendency toward military aggression and aggrandizement it has not essentially been; unlike the Soviet Union (and the United States), the C.P.R. does not have large combat forces on foreign soil.

Origins and Theoretical Aspects of Mao's "Thought"

Three main strands can be discerned among the origins of Mao Tse-tung's "thought": the personal, the Chinese, and the Marxist-Leninist.

Mao's is a highly activist personality, although his activism is tempered by a capacity for flexibility and patience. Like Lenin, he implicitly rejects Marx's determinism and abhors "spontaneity" (he did not originally intend the Red Guards to provide an example of "spontaneity" in action during the Cultural Revolution).

He is a voluntarist, a believer in the immense potential of the human will, a tendency that can easily lead to what Communists call "subjectivism" (a state of mind in which objective conditions are ignored or slighted). This potentiality can be inferred easily from the occasional favorable use in Maoist propaganda of the term "revolutionary romanticism."

Although Mao strongly opposes that component of traditional Chinese folk wisdom that counsels adaptation to harsh reality rather than a possibly disastrous struggle against it, he is an intensely Chinese personality. He sees much that is glorious in China's past, shares the Chinese cultural superiority complex toward other peoples, and feels a sense of insecurity toward the outside world arising largely from the humiliating weakness and vulnerability that overtook China in modern times. Mao's concern with China's place in the world classes him as a nationalist; his concern with the lot of the common people, whom he has described approvingly as "poor and blank" (that is, untutored and honest), qualifies him as a populist.

Despite Mao's limited theoretical knowledge of Marxism-Leninism, he has aptly been called a "natural Leninist." He easily found it congenial to think, as Leninists do, in terms of social classes and class struggle, a two-stage revolution ("democratic" and "socialist"), the "democratic centralist" Communist Party as the leading political force in the revolution, and a worldwide revolutionary struggle supported and guided by the Soviet Union against "imperialism."

Official Chinese Communist thinking holds that Marxism-Leninism is a "pure" ideology (*li-lun*) of universal applicability, one that in order to be put into effect must be combined with a practice suitable to the conditions of the country in question, whereupon it becomes a "practical" ideology (or "thought," *szu-hsiang*). Thus, Peking always refers to the "thought" of Mao Tse-tung, not to his ideology or to Maoism. One important consequence of this distinction is that it denies to Soviet practice, or "thought," any degree of universality that might be inconvenient for the CPC. Another is that Mao has been somewhat inhibited from claiming universal applicability for his own "thought," although this inhibition has largely evaporated since about 1964 and was replaced during the Cultural Revolution with a propaganda cult of Mao's "thought" equal to the height of the Soviet cult of Stalin. For political as well as for ideological, and for domestic as well as for external, reasons Mao's "thought" grew increasingly radical from the mid-1950's on under the banner of a campaign against "modern revisionism" at home and abroad (see Chapter 3).

There is no doubt that, at least until recently, Mao has done very little reading of the works of Marx, Engels, and Lenin. Those of Stalin he did not begin to study until 1937, a year when, because of the outbreak of the Sino-Japanese War, Mao began to think of himself as a statesman of national and international stature. Insofar as it has a philosophical aspect, Mao's "thought" is not fully dialectical in spite of its stress on "contradictions." It is largely binary (two-term), whereas the true dialectic is ternary (three-term); in other words, the "contradictions" are often left philosophically unresolved, rather in the manner of the traditional Chinese complementarity (rather than "contradiction") between *yin* (the female principle) and *yang* (the male principle). This tendency may help to explain the widely observed ability of the Chinese Communists, especially in external affairs, to follow seemingly incompatible policies toward a single problem or area simultaneously, without apparently feeling called on to resolve the "contradiction" in a manner satisfying to Western logic. For example, during the spring of 1971, the Chinese sent an ambassador to Rangoon (where there had been none for about four years) and launched on Chinese soil a "liberation radio" for Burma, urging the Burmese to revolt against their government.

The question of Mao's originality within the Marxist-Leninist tradition has been widely debated. The usual question discussed has been whether Lenin and Stalin anticipated and inspired Mao's revolutionary strategy of rurally based guerrilla warfare. The question seems somewhat sterile since it requires no great brilliance to see that in an agrarian country political control of the countryside can be of crucial importance. The difficult problem is how to acquire that control, and Mao's specific techniques for doing so appear to have been largely worked out through trial and error rather than borrowed from Lenin and Stalin. In short, Mao's concept of the peasantry as the main driving (not leading) force in the Chinese revolution does appear to have an element of originality within the Marxist-Leninist tradition. The same can be said of his related concept of a "protracted" revolutionary war as the main path to power for Communists in China and other "colonial and semicolonial" countries. Another "original" contribution by Mao to the "treasury of Marxism-Leninism" is the implicit (more than explicit) proposition that social origins and class status do not necessarily determine a person's political "stand" and role, and that the latter can be rendered correct (revolutionary) through political education (including the intensive version known as thought reform). Mao has also been original, or at any rate unorthodox, in asserting that "nonantagonistic contradictions" between the leaders and the people may exist under socialism and that some undefined "contradictions" may persist even under Communism.

Political Aspects of Mao's "Thought"

Like most other so-called right versions of the Leninist revolutionary strategy, Mao's represents in essence a formula for manipulating the force of nationalism against foreign "imperialism" and that of "class struggle" against indigenous "feudalism" (regional militarism or warlordism, rural landlordism, and so on) and certain "reactionary" strata of the bourgeoisie (for example, "bureaucratic capitalists," or businessmen-officials), but not against the bourgeoisie as a whole, the latter being a target of "left" strategies. Where Maoism differs from the usual "right" version of the Leninist strategy is not in Mao's willingness to form a united front with certain more or less progressive strata of the bourgeoisie (in his case, the national bourgeoisie, or patriotic big businessmen, and the petty bourgeoisie, or small businessmen and intellectuals), but in his general insistence on doing so "from below" (that is, not in alliance with the leadership of parties or other organizations representing these groups and indeed normally in opposition to such leaderships) rather than "from above" (that is, in alliance with such groups), and in his general, although not invariable, insistence on organized violence ("armed struggle," "revolutionary war," "people's war," "protracted war," and the like) as the only really effective path to power.

In the enemy camp, domestic "feudalism" is held to be weaker than and subservient to foreign "imperialism," and the latter is accordingly regarded as the major adversary; this was the case with Japan from about 1932 to 1945, and it came to be true of the United States shortly after 1945. Mao quite correctly considered it fortunate for the cause of Communist revolution in China that the "feudal" forces were divided into regional machines and that the country was not the colony of a single "imperialist" power.

Mao identifies as the first major component of his revolutionary coalition the Communist Party, which must exist before the struggle can begin to take an effective form and which takes leadership over the struggle relatively early in the process (as against the Leninist and Stalinist image of a relatively late assumption of revolutionary leadership by the Communist Party in a "colonial or semicolonial" country). Mao calls the phase of the struggle following the assumption by the Communist Party of revolutionary leadership New Democracy, to distinguish it from "bourgeois" democracy, in which leadership would rest with the national bourgeoisie. The second main component is the Red Army, which fights for revolutionary goals as defined by the Party and under the latter's leadership. The third component is the revolutionary united front, which Mao holds to be composed of four "friendly classes" (actually, two classes and two strata): the proletariat (whose "vanguard" the Communist Party of course is) as the leading element, the peasantry as its only truly reliable ally, the national bourgeoisie, and the petty bourgeoisie. Under Mao's leadership, the CPC claimed to monopolize representation of the proletariat and the peasantry, but it tolerated (and still tolerates) tame parties claiming to represent the two bourgeois strata.

According to Mao, this revolutionary coalition must operate from fixed territorial bases ("soviets," "liberated areas"); in a peasant society like China's these bases must be mainly if not entirely in rural areas, typically in rugged and easily defensible terrain. In this way, a reasonably stable population can be controlled and used as a tax base and a source of civil and military recruits. Good relations with the poorer and more numerous elements of this population must be assured through a judicious (neither excessively violent nor overly moderate) use of class struggle, including land redistribution (land reform, agrarian reform). From these bases, the Red Army (as well as its auxiliaries, the guerrilla and militia units) conducts a "protracted" war against the domestic and foreign enemies of the revolution. Given the Red Army's usual initial inferiority in numbers and equipment, it fights at first a strategic defensive campaign until a state of strategic stalemate is achieved; when it has attained superiority, it goes over to a strategic counteroffensive. For much of the war, it will be necessary for the Red Army to employ a guerrilla strategy (in other words, to fight in small, dispersed, but still carefully coordinated formations); when possible, typically toward the end, it will fight mobile warfare (a war of maneuver fought by large formations), and only at the end will it fight positional warfare (combat involving the capture of fixed enemy positions; in principle, Mao rejects defensive positional warfare). The net effect of a war so conducted is to "encircle the cities from the countryside." Mao insists that the revolutionary struggle must be as "self-reliant" (*tzu-li keng-sheng*) as possible; the base areas should be able to feed themselves, and the Communist Party should not be unduly receptive to foreign (mainly Soviet) influence. The process, still not entirely understood, by which Mao increased the autonomy of his Party with respect to Moscow in proportion as his own influence over the CPC grew and as it came closer to being in power has been aptly termed "emancipation by conspiracy."

From about 1936 on, Mao came increasingly to see the revolutionary strategy that he was developing as a suitable, indeed the best, model or example for other countries in Asia and the Third World. In time, and especially after 1949, his belief in the solidarity of the "revolutionary people of the world" led him to take increasing interest in the prospects for revolution in the developed ("imperialist," "capitalist") countries as well. In 1964, he divided the entire world, except for the United States and the "socialist camp" (the Communist "bloc," including the C.P.R., of course) into two "intermediate zones," the first being the underdeveloped and the second the developed countries. At that time, he clearly expected the major revolutionary developments to occur in the first of these zones. In the second, urban insurrection along the lines of the Paris Commune of 1871 is regarded by Mao in principle as the best revolutionary strategy. Mao has long regarded the CPC and the Chinese "people" as a source of "support" (mainly moral and political, but on occasion material and even military) for revolutions elsewhere, and since about 1959, when he decided that the Soviet Union could no longer be relied on as the main source of such support, as the principal source. But such support must not infringe, at least in principle, on the self-reliance of the revolutionary movement receiving it.

Mao's model for "socialist construction" in post-1949 China, which he evidently considers a suitable one for other "socialist" (Communist-controlled) ones to imitate, although he has not elaborated the point explicitly, is known officially as People's Democratic Dictatorship. The "people" (90–95 per cent of the population) are those who accept the "leadership" of the Communist Party, a relationship that is one of "democracy" (that is, one free in principle of coercion). The people are composed of the "four friendly classes," two of which are the "working classes," the proletariat and the peasantry, and two of which are the "marginal classes" (or in strict Marxist phraseology, strata), the national bourgeoisie and the petty bourgeoisie. The people (or masses) are asserted to be fundamentally socialist by nature. The Party observes the principle of the "mass line" in exercising its "leadership." This central Chinese Communist political concept was given its classic description by Mao Tse-tung in his "Some Questions Concerning Methods of Leadership," published on June 1, 1943:

> In all the practical work of our Party, all correct leadership is necessarily "from the masses, to the masses." This means: take the ideas of the masses (scattered and unsystematic ideas) and concentrate them (through study turn them into concentrated systematic ideas), then go to the masses and propagate and explain these ideas until the masses embrace them as their own, hold fast to them and translate them into action, and test the correctness of these ideas in such action.

The most intensive manifestation of this leadership strategy is the "mass campaign," in which virtually the whole population is mobilized for a specific purpose and a limited time (as in the land-reform campaign of 1950–52, for example). Closely related to the "from the people" principle is Mao's belief in the desirability of eliminating "bureaucratism" from the Party and the state by causing them to be "rectified" by the "masses." For the "reactionaries" (5–10 per cent of the population) there is an admitted dictatorship. In effect, Mao has borrowed, largely unadmittedly and with important modifications, Stalin's formula for building "socialism in one country": the Party-controlled police state (but without Stalin's massive blood purges, generally speaking), the collectivization (socialization, "cooperativization") of agriculture (but without mechanization on the Soviet scale and without the degree of coercion employed by Stalin), and rapid heavy industrialization (with increasing modifications after 1956 designed to fit Chinese conditions). The People's Democratic Dictatorship (equated by the CPC since 1956 with the classic Marxist stage of "proletarian dictatorship," but never with the Soviet concept of "people's democracy"—an incipient proletarian dictatorship—applied to the East European countries) was described by Mao in 1964 as a state of affairs that must last through the stage of "socialism," during which, therefore, there must be no dilution of Communist Party dictatorship such as was attempted by Khrushchev, and into the "transition to Communism." As against Liu Shao-ch'i, who said in 1956 that the struggle between "capitalism" and "socialism" in China had basically been decided, Mao insists that the class struggle persists. Mao nevertheless decided in 1954–55 that this class struggle, and the "transition to socialism," can be basically peaceful. In theory at least, remaining "bourgeois" elements were deprived without violence of their economic base in 1955–56 and of their ideological base in 1957–58; Mao later decided, however, that "bourgeois" ideology had infected elements of the CPC, and these of course became the principal targets of the Cultural Revolution.

As for development strategy, Mao wants ideological and political considerations "in command" over purely economic ones. Similarly, although he does not consider himself anti-technological, he has popularized the slogan "red over expert" (that is, it is better to be ideologically sound than technically competent, although the two are not considered necessarily incompatible). Mao wants balanced growth between city and countryside and among regions, rather than rapid urbanization or rapid development of some regions at the expense of others. He believes in egalitarianism, local initiative, and only the necessary minimum of purely economic (as opposed to ideological or political) incentives. His approach to education, which is heavily development-oriented, stresses manual labor and political training in addition to academic and technical education. As his directive of May 7, 1966, to Lin Piao indicates, he saw the PLA at that time as a "great school" of his own "thought" for the entire country. His ideal is a Maoist version of the Renaissance man, able to do nearly anything useful with at least reasonable proficiency and motivated to "serve the people" in whatever way Mao directs.

For reasons of self-gratification and national unity, Mao has promoted an enormous "cult of personality" around himself, and the second of these considerations has impelled most of his colleagues and subordinates, and indeed most Chinese, to comply with his wishes in this respect to one degree or another. Mao apparently regards himself as a "continuator" (a major prophet) of the Marxist-Leninist tradition (a concept that in the Soviet Union seems to have died with Stalin), although he has never said so flatly and has conceded that his cult grew to excessive proportions during the Cultural Revolution and therefore had to be pruned somewhat afterward. Among all his professed followers, there appears to be a core of genuine belief in his "thought" and leadership. Among the true believers (for example, his wife, Chiang Ch'ing), there is an emotional acceptance ("enthusiasm," in traditional religious parlance) that amounts to an unconscious exaggeration of the level of belief. Among others, who might be considered opportunists, there appears to be a degree of conscious exaggeration of the level of belief for political purposes, one of which no doubt is survival insurance. But open criticism of or opposition to Mao and his "thought" is rare to an almost incredible degree. A major reason for this is undoubtedly a general recollection that the era before Mao's "thought" became China's official ideology was one of chaos, and a fear that repudiation of his "thought" might open the way to another descent into chaos.

FURTHER READINGS

Marxist-Leninist theory is a complex subject with a vast literature. The best introduction is the standard work by R. N. Carew Hunt, *The Theory and Practice of Communism: An Introduction,* 5th ed., rev., Baltimore and Harmondsworth: Penguin Books, 1963.

Some especially valuable books on Soviet political history and Soviet politics are: Leonard Schapiro, *The Communist Party of the Soviet Union,* rev. ed., New York: Random House, 1970, London: Eyre & Spottiswoode, 1970; Wolfgang Leonhard, *The Kremlin Since Stalin,* New York: Praeger, 1962, London: Oxford University Press, 1962; Carl A. Linden, *Khrushchev and the Soviet Leadership, 1957–1964,* Baltimore: Johns Hopkins University Press, 1966; Michel Tatu, *Power in the Kremlin,* New York: Viking, 1968, London: Collins, 1969; Alexander Dallin and Thomas B. Larson, eds., *Soviet Politics Since Khrushchev,* Englewood Cliffs, N.J.: Prentice-Hall, 1968; John W. Strong, ed., *The Soviet Union Under Brezhnev and Kosygin,* New York: Van Nostrand Reinhold, 1971. Some particularly good books on Soviet foreign policy, international Communism, etc., are: Vernon V. Aspaturian, ed., *Process and Power in Soviet Foreign Policy,* Boston: Little, Brown, 1971; Zbigniew Brzezinski, *The Soviet Bloc: Unity and Conflict,* rev. ed., Cambridge, Mass.: Harvard Paperbacks, 1970; David Rees, *The Age of Containment: The Cold War,* London: Macmillan, 1967, New York: St. Martin's Press, 1967; Richard Lowenthal, *World Communism: The Disintegration of a Secular Faith,* London and New York: Oxford University Press, 1964.

The theoretical problems presented to Marxist-Leninist thought by the phenomenon of China are dealt with in Donald M. Lowe, *The Function of "China" in Marx, Lenin, and Mao,* Berkeley: University of California Press, 1966; Karl A. Wittfogel, "The Marxist View of China," *The China Quarterly,* no. 11 (July–September, 1962), pp. 1–20, and no. 12 (October–December, 1962), pp. 154–69; and a good article by Maurice Meisner, "The Despotism of Concepts: Wittfogel and Marx on China," *ibid.,* no. 16 (October–December, 1963), pp. 99–111.

The indigenous aspect of the intellectual environment within which

Chinese Communism emerged is competently described in Chester C. Tan, *Chinese Political Thought in the Twentieth Century*, New York: Anchor Books, 1971.

The standard original source on the "thought" of Mao Tse-tung is of course *Selected Works of Mao Tse-tung*, 4 vols (covering to 1949), Peking: Foreign Languages Press, various editions. A useful one-volume collection, including some post-1949 writings, is *Selected Readings from the Works of Mao Tse-tung*, Peking: Foreign Languages Press, 1967; see also *Selected Military Writings of Mao Tse-tung*, Peking: Foreign Languages Press, 1963. A sampler intended for popular consumption is the famous Little Red Book (*Quotations from Chairman Mao Tse-tung*, Peking: Foreign Languages Press, 1966 and subsequently).

Of the numerous books and articles on Mao's "thought," the best is Stuart R. Schram, *The Political Thought of Mao Tse-tung*, rev. ed., New York: Praeger, 1969, Harmondsworth: Penguin, 1969. Other useful treatments are: Arthur A. Cohen, *The Communism of Mao Tse-tung*, Chicago: University of Chicago Press, 1964; Jerome Ch'en, *Mao*, Englewood Cliffs, N.J.: Prentice-Hall, 1969, and *Mao Papers: Anthology and Bibliography*, London: Oxford University Press, 1970; Arthur A. Cohen, "Maoism," in Milorad M. Drachkovitch, ed., *Marxism in the Modern World*, Stanford, Calif.: The Hoover Institution, 1965; Maurice Meisner, "Leninism and Maoism: Some Populist Perspectives on Marxism-Leninism in China," *The China Quarterly*, no. 45 (January–March, 1971), pp. 2–36; Stuart R. Schram, "Mao Tse-tung and the Theory of the Permanent Revolution," *ibid.*, no. 46 (April–June, 1971), pp. 221–44. The pros and cons of various aspects of Mao's "thought," notably the question of his "originality," are debated rather acrimoniously by Karl A. Wittfogel, "The Legend of 'Maoism,'" *ibid.*, no. 1 (January–March, 1960), pp. 72–86, and no. 2 (April–June, 1960), pp. 16–34, and Benjamin Schwartz, "The Legend of the 'Legend of "Maoism,"'" *ibid.*, pp. 35–42; and by Stuart R. Schram, "The Man and His Doctrine," *Problems of Communism*, vol. xv, no. 5 (September–October, 1966), pp. 1–7, and Arthur A. Cohen, "The Man and His Policies," *ibid.*, pp. 8–16 (see also their exchange in *ibid.*, vol. xvi, no. 2 [March–April, 1967], pp. 95–99).

Some important works on general Chinese Communist ideology are Franz Schurmann, *Ideology and Organization in Communist China*, 2nd ed., Berkeley: University of California Press, 1969; Benjamin I. Schwartz, *Communism and China: Ideology in Flux*, New York: Atheneum, 1970; Michael Lindsay, *China and the Cold War: A Study in International Politics*, Melbourne: Melbourne University Press, 1955; Hélène Carrère d'Encausse and Stuart R. Schram, *Marxism and Asia: An Introduction with Readings*, London: Allen Lane, 1969. An ambitious but not very successful effort is James Chieh Hsiung, *Ideology and Practice: The Evolution of Chinese Communism*, New York: Praeger, 1970.

6. The Leadership

In spite of occasional limited purges, the post-1949 Chinese Communist leadership had the reputation prior to the Cultural Revolution of being one of the world's most stable. In terms of personnel turnover, this was largely true, but it has become clear that there were conflicts of personality, power, and policy beneath this apparently calm surface. That these did not erupt oftener may have been due to the ingrained Chinese dislike of personal confrontations and to Mao's reluctance to look like another Stalin.

Leadership in Theory and Practice

The theoretical key to the proper leading relationship between the masses and the CPC, or more precisely and typically Party Committees within non-Party organizations, is the "mass line" (see Chapter 5).

It is obvious that a dialectical relationship between the Party and the masses would be very difficult to attain and maintain, and that in practice the Party committees will tend to give greater weight to implementing directives received from their superiors. To do this to the point of ignoring the views of the masses is an error known as "commandism," which of course is supposed to be avoided. To a considerable extent in practice as well as in theory, Party committees function as feedback mechanisms; in other words, they tend to implement, to the best of their ability and in the light of local conditions, directives received from above, but then also to report the results (usually in a way not likely to reflect discredit on themselves, it can be assumed) and if necessary request modifications of the directive in the light of its proven impact on the masses. The thrust of Party policy toward the masses is essentially one of mobilizing them and compelling their participation, through exhortations, organization, and if necessary coercion, in the political process as structured by the CPC. Occasionally, large-scale mass campaigns involving intensive propaganda and exceptionally hard work are launched for limited periods and specific purposes ("Resist America, Aid Korea" in 1950–51, for example).

It has often been pointed out that ideology and organization are the main pillars of the Chinese Communist political system. The ideology is of course essentially the "thought" of Mao Tse-tung, as propagated widely and intensively among the masses. To what extent it really moves the masses, thereby legitimating and reinforcing the CPC's "leadership," is difficult to say, but it must be presumed to play some actual role if only because no admittedly different alternative can be presented in public. But organization is probably of greater practical importance. Literally everyone is enrolled, or is supposed to be, in one or more public organizations formed and controlled, directly or indirectly, by the CPC. By virtue of being organized, everyone is also under surveillance. Someone who fails to perform as desired can be subjected to varying degrees of coercion, ranging from reprimand and minor deprivations to imprisonment, forced labor, and execution. At the higher levels of this scale of sanctions, he is of course assumed to have ceased to belong to the "people" and to have become a "reactionary." Organizational controls are employed to ensure that as far as possible everyone, whether within or outside the CPC and no matter what his primary employment, engages for part of his time in two types of activity deemed essential: political study (usually in small groups and normally of Mao's "thought") and manual labor.

Within the Party, leadership is theoretically exercised according to the Leninist principle of democratic centralism (see Chapter 7). As with the masses, there is a tendency to emphasize faithful implementation of directives received from above over the theoretical "democratic" features of the system. Also as with the masses, ideology and organization are the major keys. Within the Party, and to a considerable extent outside it, "rectification" campaigns involving intensified ideological study, "criticism and self-criticism," and the like are employed for purposes of reform and renewal, in preference to mass expulsions or blood purges of the Stalinist type. Prior to the Cultural Revolution at any rate, there was a kind of dialectical interaction between the principles represented by Mao Tse-tung (ideology) and Liu Shao-ch'i (organization), and as long as this process functioned effectively, the Party as a whole continued to perform its self-appointed (its members would say historically ordained) leading role. When the Cultural Revolution upset the balance in favor of ideology, there was an almost inevitable reaction; organization had to be brought back, but it reappeared in most un-Marxist-Leninist guise, in military uniform.

Edgar Snow was told by a high-ranking CPC member in 1960 that, for practical purposes, China was being run by a group of about 800 Party leaders, this being the number that had survived from the Party's earliest years and had moved to the top of the hierarchy. Indeed, they had already been at the top for more than a decade, so that it was already a fairly old leadership. The picture since the Cultural Revolution is not entirely clear, since less is known both of the structure of the leading Party and state bodies and of the backgrounds of the individuals composing them. But if anything, the important decisions are taken by an even smaller group of leaders than was the case before the Cultural Revolution.

The Eighth Central Committee

Until 1956, the CPC was led by a Central Committee elected at the Seventh Party Congress (1945) and a Politburo with a somewhat fluctuating membership of about a dozen.

The first CPC Central Committee to be elected after the Party's seizure of power was the Eighth, so called because it was elected by the Eighth Party Congress (in September, 1956). Like other such Communist bodies, it contained both regular (voting) and alternate (nonvoting) members. The ninety-seven regulars and seventy-three alternates (the number changed somewhat as a result of later developments, notably the election of twenty-five additional alternates in May, 1958) were listed as was customary in descending order of the number of votes received, beginning of course with Mao Tse-tung. Rather interestingly and with unusual frankness, it was revealed that the method of electing this Central Committee had been to begin with "free" nominations from the various delegations to the Congress, which were then screened by the outgoing Politburo. This list was then subjected to a preliminary secret ballot of the entire membership of the Congress. The Congress leadership, or Presidium, then suggested ninety-seven as the desirable number of regular members and seventy-three as the number of alternates, and those numbers of candidates receiving the most votes in a second secret ballot were declared elected. This procedure was presumably congenial to the Party apparatus leadership, which had generally dominated the Congress.

The Central Committee elected in this way included nearly all members of the Seventh Central Committee (thirty-six out of forty-four regulars, twenty-six out of thirty-three alternates), nearly all of whom were elected to regular membership. Although the Seventh Party Congress had been strongly Maoist in tone and the Central Committee elected by it appeared superficially to be a Maoist group, such was to prove not to be the case: during the years following 1956, Mao's principal opponents as well as his major supporters were to emerge from the ranks of those who had been elected to the Central Committee in 1945 and re-elected in 1956. The average age of this group in 1956 was about fifty-five; that of the new faces on the Central Committee (as of 1956) was about three years less. The older group (those elected to the Central Committee in 1945, not necessarily for the first time) was rather strongly Central and South Chinese in origin, as an obvious result of the Party's having made its main bases in those regions during its early years; the younger group (those elected to the Central Committee for the first time in 1956) were predominantly North Chinese, again for obvious historical reasons. About three-fourths of both groups had had some form of college-level education or training. Only eight were women. Again for historical reasons, the older members of the Eighth Central Committee were much more likely than the younger to have received some training abroad (usually in the Soviet Union or France); the percentage in the case of the 1945 regulars was 60, in the case of the 1956 alternates only 12. The percentages of these groups that had traveled abroad (usually to the Soviet Union) for purposes other than study were similarly greater at the higher than at the lower age levels. Only a handful of the senior Central Committee members, notably Chou En-lai, had traveled extensively outside the Communist bloc since 1949; only a very few had ever been in the United States. Although almost all the regulars and many alternates had held a military rank of some sort (either as unit commanders or political officers) at some time in the past, many of those had concentrated on civilian work since 1949. By 1956, slightly under half of the entire Central Committee membership (regulars and alternates combined) were specializing in Party (mainly apparatus) work, the remainder being divided about equally between governmental and military assignments (some men with military backgrounds were engaged in essentially civilian work).

Immediately after its election, the Eighth Central Committee elected a seventeen-man Politburo plus six alternates (three regular members were added in 1958). At its head stood a six-man Standing Committee, whose senior member, Mao Tse-tung, was also Chairman of the Central Committee; its junior member, Teng Hsiao-p'ing, had just been elected General Secretary of the Central Committee, and its other four members (Liu Shao-ch'i, Chou En-lai, Chu Teh, and Ch'en Yun, in that order) were also designated Vice Chairmen of the Central Committee. The membership of this Politburo, including alternates, correspond rather closely with the membership during the period preceding the Eighth Party Congress, one of the differences of course being the dropping of Kao Kang. It is worth noting that the relative ranking of Politburo members, as determined by the number of votes received from the Central Committee, did not always correspond with the relative rank on the Central Committee as determined by the votes received at the Eighth Party Congress. Chou En-lai, for example, ranked only sixth on the Eighth Central Committee, but third on the Politburo. The reasons for these differences might well vary from case to case. The four main functional constituencies within the Party leadership—Mao Tse-tung's ideologists and propagandists (for example, Ch'en Po-ta, Lu Ting-i), Liu Shao-ch'i and his Party apparatus men (for example, Teng Hsiao-p'ing, P'eng Chen), Chou En-lai and his governmental administrators (for example, Li Hsien-nien, Po I-po), and the military (for example, P'eng Te-huai, Lin Piao)—were all well represented on the new Politburo (including alternates). The Secretariat elected at the same time was by definition manned by Party apparatus men.

Prior to the Cultural Revolution, the composition of the 1956 Politburo was altered only to the extent of two deaths, the purging of P'eng Te-huai (1959), and the election of Lin Piao to the Standing Committee and of Li Ching-ch'üan and T'an Chen-lin (both Party apparatus men) to regular membership in May, 1958.

Leading Bodies During the Cultural Revolution

There is evidence, notably an important photograph published in rather dramatic circumstances in early May, 1966, to indicate that the Cultural Revolution, or more specifically the stage involving the purge of P'eng Chen and his supporters in Peking, was launched by a bare majority of four men out of the seven on the Standing Committee of the Politburo: Mao Tse-tung, Chou En-lai, Lin Piao, and Teng Hsiao-p'ing, who as the latest recruit to the group was the swing man.

At the Eleventh Plenary Session of the Central Committee in August, 1966, Lin Piao became the sole Vice Chairman of the Central Committee. Three men (P'eng Chen, the supposedly pro-Soviet Chang Wen-t'ien, and the now disgraced propaganda chief Lu Ting-i) were dropped from the Politburo and six new members were added (the Party apparatus men T'ao Chu and Li Hsueh-feng; the senior military figures Hsu Hsiang-ch'ien, Nieh Jung-chen, and Yeh Chien-ying; and the public security specialist Hsieh Fu-chih). The Politburo Standing Committee had its rank order reshuffled somewhat and was enlarged to eleven men by the addition of T'ao Chu, Ch'en Po-ta (a favorite propagandist of Mao's), K'ang Sheng, and Li Fu-ch'un (the top economic planner); it should be noted that no one on the preceding seven-man Standing Committee was dropped at that time. The Secretariat lost at least five members (notably P'eng Chen, Wang Chia-hsiang, Lu Ting-i, former Chief of Staff Lo Jui-ch'ing, and Mao's former confidential secretary, Yang Shang-k'un), and gained at least three members (T'ao Chu, who appeared to be on his way to becoming the General Secretary in lieu of Teng Hsiao-p'ing, Yeh Chien-ying, and the specialist in relations with foreign leftist organizations Liu Ning-i). All this was done without the usual formal announcement. The net effect was to give Mao and his supporters a stronger majority on both the Politburo and the Secretariat.

After the Eleventh Plenary Session, the top leadership of the Party rested in effect in the hands of Mao, Lin Piao, and Chou En-lai, Lin serving as Mao's deputy and heir presumptive, and Chou standing somewhat apart and on a slightly lower level but doing most of the practical work of running the Cultural Revolution while trying to maintain some degree of order.

The Party Secretariat collapsed in late 1966 under the impact of the Red Guards. The Politburo, or at least the Standing Committee, continued to function after a fashion until about the end of March, 1967, when in the course of a dispute over how much support to give to the army in its efforts to cope with Red Guard disorders the Standing Committee in effect ceased to operate. This meant that more than ever the Red Guards were under the control of no one at the top except to some extent the Cultural Revolution Group (supposedly "under the Central Committee" but actually led by Ch'en Po-ta and still more by Chiang Ch'ing) and to some extent Mao himself. This situation led to a wave of Red Guard disorders, followed by a reaction from the army (see Chapter 4).

An effort was made to remedy this obviously unsatisfactory situation and fill the virtual organizational vacuum at the top. Beginning on May 20, 1968, a new, informal, leading body sometimes referred to as the "proletarian headquarters" emerged to replace in effect the Standing Committee of the Politburo; it soon stabilized at fourteen members. These were seemingly divided into a senior seven (Mao, Lin, Chou, Ch'en Po-ta, K'ang Sheng, Li Fu-ch'un, and Chiang Ch'ing) and a junior seven (ideologists Chang Ch'un-ch'iao and Yao Wen-yuan, Hsieh Fu-chih, Chief of Staff Huang Yung-sheng, Deputy Chief of Staff Wu Fa-hsien, Lin Piao's wife, Yeh Ch'ün, and public security specialist Wang Tung-hsing). It will be noted that the Party apparatus, which was represented only by K'ang Sheng, lost heavily, to the corresponding gain of the other three major functional constituencies. It is not at all clear how this body operated, or even if it actually met and deliberated collectively, but in any event it is unlikely to have functioned by majority vote, as had normally been the case for the Standing Committee of the Politburo before the Cultural Revolution. The Party leadership remained in this rather amorphous state until the Ninth Party Congress, with Mao, Lin, and Chou continuing to stand on a pinnacle all their own.

The Ninth Central Committee

The Ninth Party Congress (April, 1969) was able to elect a Central Committee only after considerable debate. It was a large body (170 regulars, 109 alternates). About 40 per cent of its members had military backgrounds, as against about 30 per cent for the Eighth Central Committee, a trend obviously reflecting the enhanced political role of the PLA resulting from the Cultural Revolution. Of the other major functional constituencies, the Maoists and the administrators were both well represented, the pre–Cultural Revolution Party apparatus much less so. The chairmen of all twenty-nine of the top-level revolutionary committees were elected to the Central Committee, all but three of them as regular members. The percentage of women roughly doubled (from 5 on the Eighth Central Committee to 10 on the Ninth, approximately), but few, apart perhaps from Chiang Ch'ing, appeared to wield much influence. The regulars and alternates (except for Mao and Lin Piao, whose names were given first) were named in two lists in brushstroke order, rather than in order of the number of votes received. This procedure was in keeping with the more "revolutionary" atmosphere of the time, to be sure, but the main purpose was probably to disguise the low number of votes received by some of the more obscure Maoists (notably the "model" workers and peasants included for purely ideological and propaganda reasons). The new Central Committee included only 53 out of 173 living regular and alternate members of the Eighth Central Committee. In spite of some spectacular purges at the top, like that of Liu Shao-ch'i, the heaviest casualties were among the lower-ranking half of the Eighth Central Committee and therefore disproportionately among northerners. Less is known about many of the new members elected to the Central Committee at the Ninth Party Congress, but, apart from the token Maoists (again notably the "model" workers and peasants), it appears likely that they were not very different from those they replaced, except probably for being more evenly distributed with respect to geographic origins. At the top, Central and South China continued to predominate, although other leaders from those regions had been among those purged during the Cultural Revolution.

On April 28, 1969, immediately after the close of the Ninth Party Congress, the new Central Committee met and elected a Politburo of twenty-one regulars and four alternates. As with the Central Committee, Mao and Lin were listed first, followed by the others in brushstroke order. The same method of listing was employed for the Politburo Standing Committee, composed of Mao, Lin Piao, Ch'en Po-ta, Chou En-lai, and K'ang Sheng. After the Ninth Party Congress the growing influence of Chou En-lai paralleled and probably was largely responsible for the striking fact that about half the membership of the Politburo became inactive for one reason or another. In the case of the Standing Committee, Ch'en Po-ta and K'ang Sheng virtually disappeared in late 1970, and Lin Piao was purged in September, 1971. Thus, a new central leadership, largely dominated by Chou with some collaboration from the leading Maoists (including Mao) and some of the military, emerged in lieu of the one elected by the Ninth Party Congress. Because this leadership situation has not been formalized, however, analysis of it is presented in Chapter 4 rather than here.

Groupings and Alignments

There appear to be six significant categories in which politically important individuals can be grouped: functional constituencies, geographic associations, age groups, shared experiences, personal allegiance, and community of interest or viewpoint. These are not mutually exclusive: an individual can be classified in more than one category.

It has already been indicated that there are four major functional constituencies: the Maoists (mainly ideologists and propagandists), the Party apparatus men, the governmental administrators, and the military. Enough has probably been said, or will be later, about all but one, the governmental administrators. This large and complex category includes individuals working more or less under the jurisdiction of the State Council in areas like economic planning and administration, internal security, and foreign affairs. It also includes by extension, or at least has close affinities with, many types of intellectuals and specialists not necessarily under the direct jurisdiction of the State Council (journalists, writers, artists, engineers, and the like), some of them non-Communists. Premier Chou En-lai is clearly both the effective head and the symbolic patron of this constituency. In spite of this powerful leadership, the constituency as a whole is not (or not yet) so highly developed, cohesive, or self-conscious as in the older and more bureaucratic society of the Soviet Union.

The geographic category includes areas of origin and of service. Provincial origins have long been important in Chinese politics, although they have recently appeared to be growing less so under the Communist regime. There has long been a disproportionately large group of men from Hunan and Hupeh in the upper ranks of the CPC, not because these are the native provinces of Mao and Lin Piao respectively and therefore favored by them, but because in recent decades these provinces have been proverbially rebellious and politically active. There has long been an important group of Party figures from the huge southwestern province of Szechwan. Some of the senior members of this group (such as Chu Teh) appear to have had serious differences with Mao Tse-tung during the Long March—over its destination, in particular—and never to have fully restored their relations with him; the Szechwan group suffered heavily during the Cultural Revolution. "Areas of service" refers mainly to the various base areas (soviets, liberated areas, border regions, and so forth) controlled by the CPC at various times since about 1930. For compelling and obvious historical reasons, these were located mainly in Central and South China until the Long March, and thereafter mainly in North and Northwest China.

The major age groups within the leadership are political "generations," each distinguished mainly by its date (or approximate date) of joining the Party, which date in turn is often correlated with some important historical event (the outbreak of war with Japan, for example). On the military side, there is a similar concept of the "military generation," which has been defined by a leading specialist, William W. Whitson, as "a group of men, regardless of age, who entered the military during a particular period characterized by a crisis of professional feast or professional famine." These observations do not fully apply to the special cases of a small and shrinking group of "aged comrades," elderly figures like Chu Teh, Tung Pi-wu, Liu Po-ch'eng, who joined the CPC when no longer young. Even if they are discounted, however, the fact remains that the top Party leadership is comparatively old. This has produced a partial blockage at the lower levels. This has obviously been less true since the Cultural Revolution, but it is still a problem.

"Shared experiences" covers such phenomena as participation in the Long March, service in the "white" (Kuomintang- or Japanese-controlled) areas during the decade after the Long March, membership in the "December Ninth" group (students involved in an anti-Japanese demonstration, allegedly under Liu Shao-ch'i's leadership, in 1935; there appears to have been an abortive effort in 1965 to exploit the anniversary of this demonstration to enhance Liu's waning political position), service in one or another of the PLA's field armies or in the Korean War, or recent service of some kind (for example, Lo Jui-ch'ing's six years of service as PLA Chief of Staff appear to have modified his outlook from that of an army political officer and a public security specialist to that of at least a passable imitation of a professional military man).

The category of personal allegiance includes two subcategories. The broader one is based on genuine "charisma," and the classic example is of course Mao Tse-tung's widespread personal appeal within the CPC and among the non-Communist public. The narrower one is the clique or faction, based normally on the familiar foundation of patronage; Teng Hsiao-p'ing, as effective head of the Party apparatus from about the end of 1952 on, was able to build up an impressive personal following in this way.

"Community of interest or viewpoint" appears largely self-explanatory. By way of illustration, it is difficult to explain the rapid growth of Chou En-lai's influence during and still more since the Cultural Revolution unless one assigns great weight to the probability that his relatively pragmatic, sophisticated, and nationally oriented viewpoint has commanded widespread agreement and support, especially but by no means exclusively among the government administrators and the military.

Two Leading Personalities

Politics everywhere is an intensely personal process, and without the personal element, the study of politics is in danger of losing touch with reality. Accordingly, there follow brief sketches of four carefully selected prominent figures, two of them winners (to date at least) and two of them losers in the political struggles of recent years. It is not an accident that each is primarily associated with a different one of the four major functional constituencies within the Chinese political system.

Inevitably, the first is Mao Tse-tung. Born of peasant stock on December 26, 1893, in Hunan, Mao possessed in full the activist, rebellious temperament traditionally associated with the natives of that province. A profoundly Chinese and China-centered personality, he has traveled outside China only twice, both times to the Soviet Union (December, 1949–February, 1950 and November, 1957). He has been aptly called a revolutionary romantic (by Stuart Schram) and has repeatedly been carried away with the assumed correctness of whatever line he was pursuing at the time.

Mao was a founding member of the CPC, mainly as a result of his contacts in Peking, around 1920, with its two main early leaders, Ch'en Tu-hsiu and Li Ta-chao. After the formation of the alliance with the Kuomintang, Mao worked at a high level for a few years, and apparently with enthusiasm, within its apparatus in organizational and labor affairs. After 1925, still working within the Kuomintang, he became involved primarily in peasant affairs and was probably the first prominent CPC member to grasp the revolutionary potential of social unrest in the countryside. Neither his own Party leadership nor the Left Kuomintang, with which the CPC was then still cooperating, however, was willing to go as far in approving and organizing rural revolt against the landlord class as Mao advocated in a famous and passionate report written in March, 1927. Later that year, following his Party's break with the Left Kuomintang as well as with Chiang Kai-shek, Mao organized an unsuccessful revolt, the Autumn Harvest Uprising, in Hunan. Then he retreated to the rugged terrain on the Hunan-Kiangsi border and, like several other leading Communists in other areas but more effectively, begain painfully to build a rural base or soviet. This task required seeking peasant support through land and other reforms and creating a government structure and a military force on this basis. By Communist standards, Mao was rather moderate in his approach to land reform, and in this as well as in other respects, he showed himself capable, when he thought it necessary, of displaying a remarkable patience and flexibility that formed a striking contrast with his dominant activist streak.

So successful was Mao that his soviet, centering in Kiangsi, became the most flourishing one in China, and it was accordingly to Kiangsi that the Party Central Committee began to transfer its headquarters in 1931, when its base in Shanghai came under Kuomintang police pressure. Led by Chou En-lai, the new arrivals challenged Mao's position, and in particular his guerrilla-oriented military strategy and his addiction to using Party cadres from the army as well as from the territorial Party apparatus for major political and administrative tasks. There apparently emerged a situation in which there were two parallel, and somewhat rival, military policy-making bodies: one within the government mechanism of the Central Soviet Republic (created in November, 1931, with nominal authority over all soviets in China), effectively headed by Mao Tse-tung and generally oriented toward guerrilla warfare; the other under the Party Central Committee, effectively headed by Chou En-lai and strongly inclined toward conventional strategy. In 1934, the balance shifted in favor of the latter, perhaps because of the increased participation in it of the only Comintern representative in Kiangsi, Otto Braun (usually known by his Chinese name, Li T'e). There was thus a tendency toward a conventional strategy and, whether for that reason or not, the outcome was disaster and the survivors had to escape annihilation by embarking on the Long March in October, 1934. The fiasco enabled Mao to pin the blame for the loss of the Kiangsi base on his rivals and enhanced the credibility of his alternative of guerrilla warfare, distasteful though it was to many of the Red Army commanders. In January, 1935, at an irregular Politburo conference at Tsuni in Kweichow, Mao gained effective control over the Red Army's political mechanism, as well as a considerable influence over its strategy. It is not clear whether he was formally elected to any new Party office, but this is not a crucial point, since in any case the Party's development until 1949 depended largely on its military achievements, so that Mao's military ascendancy inevitably conveyed great and increasing political influence as well.

After 1935, his political leadership was incomplete and largely informal, and it needed to be filled out through a demonstration of mastery of political as well as military strategy at the national level. Mao's basic shrewdness equipped him well for this task. In 1936, for example, he predicted to Edgar Snow with astonishing accuracy not only the Japanese attack on China that began in 1937 but also the outbreak and course of World War II in the Pacific. Once the war with Japan had begun, Mao clearly opted for an independent role for the CPC, a largely nominal united front with the Kuomintang decorated for the moment with strongly pro-Kuomintang propaganda, and in reality a simultaneous politico-military struggle against the Japanese and the Kuomintang. He got acceptance for this strategy as against alternatives proposed by various colleagues, and in the process enhanced his position in the Politburo and the Party to the point of virtual unchallengeability by 1938. He was probably greatly helped by the fact that by then Stalin had indicated privately to the Party leadership that he favored a strategy resembling Mao's—indeed, Mao's earlier stress on guerrilla warfare had been explicitly approved by the Comintern as early as 1928—and by the fact that in 1938 the major Soviet encyclopedia unqualifiedly referred to Mao as the leader of the CPC.

In a manner with which Moscow was to become even more familiar, Mao repaid this support with an increasingly independent line, which has been described as "emancipation by conspiracy." He took advantage for this purpose of Stalin's overwhelming preoccupation after June, 1941, with the war against Germany. He also made some use of Stalinist writings and techniques, although not of bloody mass purges, in further building up his own leadership over the CPC. These trends, as well as a growing cult of Mao, were given a vigorous push by an important "rectification" campaign within the Party that he launched early in 1942. Stalin's dissolution of the Comintern in May, 1953, provided a seeming justification and an enhanced opportunity for Mao's independent line, and also removed the last major disincentive to his assumption of formal in addition to effective leadership of the Party. Had he assumed formal leadership within the Comintern framework, he might have been forced to choose between bowing to Stalin and defying him openly, as Tito was to do five years later. In June, 1943, accordingly, Mao had himself "elected" to a new post, that of Chairman of the Central Committee, which carried with it *ex officio* the effective leadership of the Politburo and the Secretariat (on these bodies, see Chapter 7). He signaled this event in somewhat Stalinist fashion by writing a tract explaining his concepts of political leadership and the "mass line" and by inaugurating a rewriting of Party history in order to date his full ascendancy from January, 1935, and make it appear inevitable as well as desirable, and to blacken the reputations of previous major Party leaders (notably Ch'en Tu-hsiu, Li Li-san, and Wang Ming). These policies of Mao's and his domination of the Party leadership were ratified at the Seventh Party Congress in the spring of 1945.

Mao then had to steer the Party through the period of great dangers and opportunities presented by the Soviet invasion of Manchuria, the end of the war with Japan, an American military presence in China south of the Great Wall, American and Soviet efforts to prevent an outbreak of civil war in China by arranging a political settlement between the CPC and the Kuomintang, and the actual outbreak of civil war following the failure of this effort. Mao's formula was essentially the same as in the preceding stages, and it prospered as before, thanks to good luck and the ineptness of the opposition as well as to Mao's shrewdness and his Party's strenuous efforts. The formula was essentially one of political struggle, and military struggle to the extent necessary, against all the other actors, paralleled for a time by much propaganda about national unity and indeed by a willingness to accept a political settlement on Communist terms (in effect, freedom of political action for the CPC in the Nationalist areas, no such freedom for the Kuomintang in the Communist areas). The CPC benefited considerably from the Soviet invasion of Manchuria, for example through the acquisition from the Soviet Army of stocks of captured Japanese weapons, and yet managed to evade the accompanying danger of satellitization and Stalin's wish for Communist acceptance of Chiang Kai-shek's political leadership as a preferable alternative to civil war. For a number of reasons—of which the most important were probably a desire to get American arms as Tito had done, or at least discourage American military intervention on behalf of the Kuomintang, and a felt need for an alternate source of possible support in case his relations with the Soviet Union became impossible—Mao for a time took a friendly line toward the United States, showing for example an interest in American economic aid and in visiting Washington in January, 1945. Nothing came of these overtures or of the American effort to stave off civil war through mediation and a political settlement. The Kuomintang was outmaneuvered at virtually every turn, politically and militarily.

Mao entered the period after the "liberation" of 1949 with enormous prestige, which his colleagues conceded should be promoted within limits as a source of national unity and stability. The promotion was especially strenuous in the school system, with effects that were to appear later in the frenzied Mao-worship of the Red Guards. But like many other historic figures, Mao found the tasks of a statesman in power more difficult, and probably less exciting, than those of a revolutionary leader. Especially after his serious illness at the beginning of 1954, the impatient strand in his nature came to the fore and was reinforced by intimations of immortality. In spite of such occasional feats as his reported swim of July, 1966, in the Yangtze, Mao grew gradually less vigorous physically, and doubles were sometimes employed to spare him the fatigue of public appearances. There are reasons to believe that he may have developed Parkinson's Disease, and possibly throat cancer (he has been a heavy smoker most of his life). All this not only did not prevent, but actually contributed to, a growing radicalism and bursts of political activity, punctuated by spells of inconspicuousness probably coinciding with bouts of illness. After about 1957, when Mao sustained a major political setback in the shape of the fiasco suffered by his Hundred Flowers campaign for free speech, the dominant theme of his political career became his drive against "revisionism," or "modern revisionism" as he often called it, at home and abroad. (The course and results of this drive are traced in Chapters 3 and 4.)

During the Cultural Revolution, the cult of Mao ballooned to fantastic proportions, and it is impossible not to believe that Mao regarded this phenomenon as necessary if not entirely desirable. Yet he told Edgar Snow in December, 1970, that by the end of the Cultural Revolution he had become disgusted with the lengths to which his cult had been carried, and it is certain that after the Ninth Party Congress, and especially from July, 1969, on, there occurred a noticeable although by no means complete de-escalation of the cult in domestic and foreign propaganda. A curious footnote to this period is that, from the time of the Ninth Party Congress on, his name began to be spelled officially as Mao Tsetung, so that the phrase "Marxism-Leninism-Mao Tsetung Thought" could be used (in Western language propaganda) without the encumbrance of a third hyphen.

Mao is no Stalin, especially in the sense that he has not used police to terrorize and execute his colleagues, although during the Cultural Revolution he allowed some of them to be branded as hostile to him and subjected to mob action by the Red Guards. He has, however, a determination, which he shares with Stalin without necessarily having derived it from him, that he must always appear right and his actual or alleged adversaries wrong. Thus, when he has decided to break, or make public a previous break, with an opponent (or merely a predecessor who might otherwise appear as a rival for prestige), he has launched a propaganda campaign vilifying the entire career of the individual in question; even the most naïve reader must be left wondering how such an obvious rascal could have deceived the rest of the Party and Mao himself for so long. There is a strong family resemblance among these campaigns, including the recent one against Liu Shao-ch'i. The Maoist version of the CPC's history portrays it as culminating inevitably and gloriously, after a period of vicissitudes under the direction of a series of incompetent scoundrels, in Mao's ever-correct leadership.

Some observations can be made that, while perhaps not of great importance, shed some interesting light on Mao's personality, private and public. He is a fine poet in the classical tradition. He prefers to work mainly at night. His personal likes and dislikes undoubtedly influence his political attitudes; his wife, Chiang Ch'ing, reportedly once told a visitor that her husband's main objections to Khrushchev were that he had bad table manners and smelled when excited. When asked by a Japanese interviewer whether he thought he had ever made a mistake, Mao admitted to one: having called his regime the People's Republic of China rather than simply the Republic of China; probably he meant that the latter designation would have made it easier for foreign governments to maintain diplomatic relations with Peking rather than with Taipei. In recent years, Mao has apparently devoted much of his time to reading and presumably to writing some kind of political testament, yet to be published and sometimes irreverently referred to as his Second Thoughts; Edgar Snow (December, 1970) and President Nixon (February, 1972) found him in a booklined study. In a rather surprising turn of phrase, he told Snow in January, 1965, that he was "soon going to see God."

Sometimes, at least since the Cultural Revolution, he seems to feel that China and the world have misunderstood him and are not worthy of the simple wisdom, summarized in the phrase "uninterrupted revolution," that he claims to offer; he described himself rather charmingly to Snow, in December, 1970, as a "lone monk walking the world with a leaky umbrella."

Abundant reasons are given elsewhere (see especially Chapter 4) as to why the other leading personality to be sketched should be Chou En-lai. Additional authority for this choice is lent by the following passage, written by former CPC leader Chang Kuo-t'ao, which appears far less surprising now than it did when it was published in 1953:

> So far as I know, there are only two major factions in the Party—Mao's and Chou's. But the two men are working together even though they are diametrically opposite in temperament and can never be in really complete harmony.

Chang goes on to list as leading members of Mao's faction Liu Shao-ch'i, Lin Piao, and Kao Kang; as members of Chou's, Generals Chu Teh, Nieh Jung-chen, and Liu Po-ch'eng, economic planner Ch'en Yun, and former CPC leader Li Li-san (now dead).

Chou is a man of brilliant intelligence, keen memory, and extraordinary practical competence. He has a "charismatic" personality that tends to dominate any gathering, and yet he is acutely sensitive to the feelings of those around him. He is an extremely effective bargainer and negotiator, tough on essentials but flexible on incidentals, a statement whose credibility is enhanced if we recall that as a young man he was an accomplished amateur actor.

Although no less typically Chinese than Mao, inasmuch as he was born in 1898 into a family of officials under the Manchu dynasty, Chou is far more cosmopolitan than Mao and indeed than the vast majority of his colleagues. He nominally studied, but actually devoted most of his time to political agitation among fellow Chinese, in Western Europe in the early 1920's, at which time he joined the CPC. Returning to China, he held high posts in the CPC, in which he has been a Politburo member continuously since 1927, and in the Kuomintang; probably the most important was the effective directorship of the Political Department of the Kuomintang's Whampoa Academy for army cadets, where he built up useful contacts with future leaders of the Red Army.

Chou's ability and flexibility enabled him not only to survive the successive changes in Party leadership after the disastrous break of 1927 with the Kuomintang but to enhance his own influence as well. He was probably also helped by the fact that, from the time he first visited Moscow in 1928, he made a strongly favorable impression on Stalin and other Soviet leaders. During this period, he concentrated on military affairs, especially on their political aspect. This interest, which Mao Tse-tung of course shared, and the fact that Chou favored regular organization and strategies and opposed the use of military political personnel outside the armed forces, tended to bring the two men into conflict after Chou moved to Kiangsi in 1931. After being displaced by Mao as the effective head of the Red Army's political apparatus during the Long March, Chou seems to have reached a *modus vivendi* with Mao. He stopped trying to threaten Mao's growing political position, but without ceasing to disagree with him on policy issues as before, and concentrated increasingly on managing with brilliant success the Party's relations with the Kuomintang, the Soviet Union, and the United States. During the Sino-Japanese War, he spent much of his time as the CPC's representative in the Nationalists' wartime capital of Chungking, where he projected a good image of himself and his Party to Chinese (apart from Kuomintang diehards) and foreigners alike. In the later wartime and early postwar years, he was the CPC's main delegate to the important negotiations with the Kuomintang and with American representatives on a possible political and military settlement.

His proven diplomatic talents were recognized in 1949, when he was put in charge of the new government's Foreign Ministry. As if this were not enough for one man, he also became Premier (Chairman of the Government Administration Council, renamed the State Council in 1954). He was, of course, concurrently a senior Central Committee and Politburo member in the CPC, third-ranking after Mao and Liu Shao-ch'i. To fulfill these heavy responsibilities, he had to work unusually long hours, as indeed he had done for many years. When he turned over the Foreign Ministry to his friend Ch'en Yi in February, 1958, he probably did so mainly in order to give himself time to devote to his domestic responsibilities, which were becoming more burdensome with the approach of the Great Leap Forward: he retained his ultimate authority over the implementation of foreign policy, however, and was an important voice in its formulation.

Until the Cultural Revolution, it was fashionable among foreign analysts to think of Chou, for all his brilliance, as an administrator without a personal power base. As the quotation from Chang Kuo-t'ao suggests, this was a serious error. Whatever his real views and ambitions, Chou has cultivated, at least since the mid-1930's, the image of a man who has no interest in the dangerous honor of being the Party's top leader. Recent events have shown that he has no objection to exercising great personal power, however, but he cares less about the trappings of power than Mao does and works well with people whom he respects without insisting on the deference that Mao receives. As Premier, he has had much personal exposure since 1949 and has acquired a public standing second only to Mao's. He has in fact had a power base, a composite of his administrators within the State Council, the security services, and elements of the PLA leadership (notably senior professionally minded soldiers like Yeh Chien-ying, and important figures in the pre-1954 Second and Third Field Armies).

Another source of Chou's influence has been his relationship of mutual respect and substantial, although not complete, cooperation with Mao Tse-tung. Chou apparently regards Mao as a towering figure who has accomplished great things for China as well as for himself, although prone to errors of judgment. In Chou's view, evidently, Mao is essential as a source and symbol of national unity and in any case is too strong and determined to be directly opposed on major issues with any hope of success. For his part, Mao apparently shares the general respect for Chou's ability and achievements and regards him as virtually indispensable. Given the two men's complementary qualities, and the fact that Chou has largely adjusted his working schedule to Mao's nocturnal one, this relationship has proven remarkably close and effective. In his original, unpublished, speech of February 27, 1957 (see Chapter 3), Mao expressed high regard for Chou and intimated that he would like to see Chou as his successor (probably in the state rather than the Party). During the Great Leap Forward and still more during the Cultural Revolution, Chou's strategy was basically to support Mao in general but to try to moderate his excesses and counteract their effects as tactfully as possible, rather than to oppose him directly as Liu Shao-ch'i came increasingly to do. During the Cultural Revolution, this approach helped greatly to stave off anarchy and brought Chou even greater prestige and influence as he mediated incessantly among quarreling factions and hammered out the compromises that made possible the emergence of provincial revolutionary committees acceptable locally and in Peking and to the PLA and the Maoists.

Chou can hardly have been happy, for personal reasons, that in spite of his brilliant performance, it was not he but Lin Piao who emerged from the Cultural Revolution as Mao's proclaimed "close comrade-in-arms and successor." In addition, Chou must have felt that a soldier of very limited political sophistication who had taken advantage of the temporary indispensability of his support to bargain his way into the role of heir apparent was hardly a suitable figure to direct the destiny of China after Mao's death. Chou apparently began to maneuver at about the time of the Ninth Party Congress to build on his enhanced prestige and strengthen his power position, for example by forming alliances within the army (with military region commanders Ch'en Hsi-lien and Hsu Shih-yu among others, it seems). When Lin blundered, in unwisely provoking the Soviet Union by staging a border incident on March 2, 1969, Chou was the only person qualified to cope diplomatically with the dangerously aroused Russians, and he moved to enhance his position at Lin's expense. This was not simply a power struggle, since genuine and important differences of domestic and foreign policy were also involved (see Chapter 4). The critical month was probably October, 1970, when the success of Chou's Soviet policy was validated by the arrival of Soviet Ambassador Tolstikov, a close colleague of the previously detested and seemingly highly anti-Chinese Brezhnev, in lieu of the originally designated ambassador, who had been rejected by Peking as being of inadequate political stature. It was in that same month that a reasonably definite invitation was conveyed to President Nixon, secretly of course and via an intermediary from a third country, to visit China as he was admittedly eager to do. It was probably at about that time that Chou began to have the active support, perhaps at Mao's direct order, of the still important Maoist faction within the Party leadership, including Chiang Ch'ing, who had previously been sniping at Chou. The Maoists also resented Lin Piao's pushfulness and his tendency to promote his own "cult" while Mao's was declining somewhat. In this masterly way, Chou appears to have prepared Lin's downfall well before it finally occurred in September, 1971. The purge, of which this was only the most striking aspect, has been conducted with a deftness and outward appearance of ambiguity that are or can be hallmarks of Chou's political "style." The result is that it is very hard to be sure, from the outside, what has actually happened. Lin's fall has not been formally announced in the press, and many of Chou's *de facto* collaborators have not been officially named as even acting in the capacities in which they are actually functioning. To Chou, the substance is everything and the appearance very little, except when it reinforces the reality of power, and nothing when as in this instance it might complicate the exercise of power. He needs to consolidate his position while Mao is still alive and supporting him; afterward, he presumably hopes to function as *primus inter pares* in an effective "collective leadership" composed largely of men who share his essentially pragmatic views.

Two Prominent Losers

Liu Shao-ch'i and Lin Piao were purged after waging unsuccessful power struggles—one mainly against Mao Tse-tung and the other mainly against Chou En-lai—that as usual within Communist movements were accompanied by important policy differences.

Of the two main types of CPC member during the Party's early history, the ideologist and the labor organizer, Liu Shao-ch'i clearly belonged to the second. (Mao had affinities with both, a fact that helps to explain his success.) Born in 1898 in Hunan, Liu had already begun to specialize in the practical, as against the agitational, aspects of labor organization before he went to Moscow for a brief period of study in 1920–21. On his return to China, he plunged more deeply than before into this type of work in several areas, including Mao's Kiangsi soviet. From these early years on, he displayed the qualities of caution, hard work, fairness, and administrative ability that were to carry him to the top of the Party hierarchy, but also rather colorless and self-effacing characteristics that were to prevent him from building up a positive public image and handicap him in his final efforts to contain Mao.

After the Long March, Liu began to engage mainly in the dangerous task of Party organization in the "white" (mainly Japanese-occupied) areas of North China. He apparently played an important role in the anti-Japanese student demonstrations of December 9, 1935, in Peking. In mid-1937, he went to Yenan and shocked the Party leadership with a report criticizing it for its earlier adventurous tendencies, particularly for not protecting itself sufficiently against the Kuomintang, and for an inadequate effort to take the political lead in a nationwide Japanese struggle. Mao was impressed by the boldness of his fellow Hunanese, or perhaps he felt that Liu would be a useful ally against his rivals; in any event, he formed a close relationship with Liu, who received increasingly important assignments. In early 1941, for example, he was given the task of putting the CPC's New Fourth Army back on its feet after it had been attacked and hurt by Nationalist forces north of the Yangtze River.

During this period, Liu specialized increasingly in Party organization and the indoctrination of Party members. In 1939, for example, he published an important work, *How to Be a Good Communist,* in which he stressed the concept (essentially Confucian in origin) of "self-cultivation," rather than the alternative later favored by Mao of being "remolded" through "criticism" from outside the Party by the "masses." In 1945, at the Seventh Party Congress, Liu delivered a major report on the New Party constitution and effectively emerged the second-ranking figure in the CPC, a position he strengthened through conscientious hard work during the next several years. On the rare occasions when Mao was away (in Chungking in the summer of 1945, in Moscow in 1949–50 and 1957), Liu was in charge of Party affairs. In the autumn of 1948, he took on the important task in *On Internationalism and Nationalism* of presenting the CPC's position on the Stalin-Tito dispute, a position of basic support for Stalin qualified by some overtones critical of his high-handed ways with other Communist Parties. Liu went out of his way during these days to praise Mao for major innovations in the adaptation of Marxism-Leninism to Asian conditions, especially in revolutionary warfare, and notably in a famous interview with Anna Louise Strong in 1946 and in a speech delivered in Peking in November, 1949, to a meeting of the World Federation of Trade Unions.

The obvious temperamental differences between Mao and Liu, however, were increasingly accentuated by policy differences during the mid-1950's. Liu tended to emphasize the advantages of centrally directed administrative procedures, rather than the ideologically inspired local initiative dear to Mao. In the crucial area of agriculture, Liu seems to have favored a slower rate of collectivization and to have placed more stress on mechanization than Mao.

Still more important, Liu evidently grew more and more distressed at Mao's increasingly arbitrary behavior, which probably represented in part an effort to escape being kicked upstairs to the post of Honorary Chairman of the Central Committee (created by the 1956 Party constitution) to which Liu may have wanted to retire him. Liu almost certainly took over the post of Chairman of the C.P.R. in the spring of 1959, in succession to Mao, in the hope of being able to balance Mao if not contain him. The tension between them increased when Liu, about the beginning of 1961, took charge of the economic retreat from the Great Leap Forward. As late as October, 1961, however, Mao told Field Marshal Viscount Bernard Montgomery that he still regarded Liu as his successor. Liu's position as Chief of State, titular Commander-in-Chief of the PLA (effectively led, however, by Mao's supporter Lin Piao after 1959), and second-ranking figure in the Party proved inadequate to enable him to cope with Mao. Liu was apparently an object of rivalry on the part of K'ang Sheng, who probably aspired to succeed him as the senior patron of the Party apparatus. According to Liu's 1967 "confession," it was K'ang who suggested to him that he republish *How to Be a Good Communist*, which accordingly appeared on August 1, 1962, and who made some revisions in it, including the insertion of laudatory references to Mao. In spite of this, K'ang may have intended to tempt Liu into a piece of self-assertion that could later be used against him, as actually it was. That it proceeded to outsell Mao's *Selected Works* must have counted against it in Maoist eyes.

Liu was often accused by Westerners of being slavishly pro-Soviet, but this was untrue: he preserved a balanced attitude toward the Soviet Union as he did toward most things. He led the CPC's delegation to the important Moscow conference of November–December, 1960, at which Sino-Soviet differences were aired before the representatives of most of the world's Communist Parties, but it was Teng Hsiao-p'ing who did most of the work of presenting the CPC's case. It is virtually certain that Liu disapproved of the lengths to which Mao was prepared to go in his campaign against Soviet "revisionism," especially in the early post-Khrushchev period. His last public statement (July 22, 1966) was the only one of four issued on that occasion that did not denounce the Soviet Union.

It appears to have been in January, 1965, at the conclusion of a prolonged disagreement over the conduct of the Socialist Education Campaign, that Mao decided to purge Liu (see Chapter 3). It is not certain when Liu became aware of this decision, but he must have been at least partially alerted by the further disagreement, later in 1965, over the launching of the Cultural Revolution, by Mao's retreat to the Yangtze Valley in November, and by the clear indications that P'eng Chen and some others were in deep political trouble. In March–April, 1966, probably to remind his colleagues and the world of his role as Chief of State and thus reinforce his political position if possible, Liu visited several Asian countries; he also appears to have held talks with potential supporters in Northwest and Southwest China, as Teng Hsiao-p'ing reportedly also did during the same period. Liu was given a very low-level welcome on his return to Peking, a sure sign of trouble.

Liu's obvious lack of enthusiasm for the Red Guards enabled Mao to use them against him with decisive effect. As early as mid-November, 1966, Liu began to be denounced in their propaganda, although not yet in the official press. Still formally a member of the Politburo Standing Committee, he apparently became increasingly inactive after the beginning of 1967. Accordingly, as someone no longer a real factor in the power situation, he became a target whom the Maoists and the military, otherwise in sharp disagreement over the PLA's proper role in the Cultural Revolution, could agree on denouncing. After the end of March, 1967, when the Politburo and its Standing Committee ceased to function, Liu promptly became the target of attacks in the official press, not yet by name, however, but rather as "China's Khrushchev." By this time, Liu had begun to make a series of rather dignified oral and written "confessions" in which he admitted to having disagreed with Mao on various issues but little more; these were of course rejected by the Maoists (including the Red Guards) as inadequate. His wife, the attractive Wang Kuang-mei, was outrageously treated at a mass "trial" held by Red Guards on April 10, 1967. They were prevented somehow from "dragging out" Liu himself and subjecting him to similar indignities, but on August 5, a delegation of them managed to "criticize" Liu, as well as Teng Hsiao-p'ing and T'ao Chu, in their homes. Liu's reported behavior on that occasion was considerably more dignified than Teng's, and one suspects that there is a residue of quiet respect and passive sympathy for him among at least some of his former colleagues. The inauguration of the practice, in mid-October, 1968, of using his name in official statements attacking him appears to have intentionally put him beyond the hope of a political comeback, but there is no convincing reason to doubt that he is still alive.

The same cannot be said of the other prominent loser, Lin Piao. Lin was born in Hupeh in 1907, and, like many other CPC members, he became involved in revolutionary activity while a student. In 1925, he became a cadet at the Kuomintang's Whampoa

Academy and joined the CPC. After the split of 1927, he rose rapidly in the young Red Army by virtue of his outstanding military ability, and soon attached himself to the political leadership of Mao Tse-tung. He played an increasingly prominent combat role during the Nationalist Annihilation Campaigns against the soviet areas (1931–34) and the Long March. In 1937, he assumed command of one of the three divisions into which the Eighth Route Army, as the Red Army in North China was then called, was divided. He won a local victory over a Japanese force at P'ing-hsingkuan in Shansi in September, 1937, which CPC propaganda then inflated to major proportions. The strain of the war, plus possibly wounds and what appears to have been chronic tuberculosis, evidently weakened him, and he did not spend the entire war in combat assignments. There is a strong possibility that he spent some time in the Soviet Union, for medical treatment, advanced military training, or both. He joined Chou En-lai for unsuccessful negotiations with the Kuomintang in 1942–43. At the time of the Japanese surrender, Lin was given command of the Communist forces in the important Manchurian theater, where he performed brilliantly. After "liberating" it in late 1948, he took a major part in the campaign for North China and then, from the mid-spring of 1949, commanded the Fourth Field Army in the "liberation" of South China. During this period, he conveyed the impression of being not only a brilliant field commander but also a vigorous and decisive personality. He was rewarded with the leading positions in the Party, governmental, and military hierarchies of the newly established Central-South Region.

He soon began to spend much of his time away from the region. It is very likely that he commanded the "Chinese People's Volunteers" when they initially intervened in Korea (in October–November, 1950). If so, he was soon replaced by P'eng Te-huai, perhaps because of wounds, illness, his chronic rivalry with P'eng, defeats suffered beginning in January, 1951, or some combination of these.

In spite of spells of inactivity caused by ill health, Lin rose rapidly in the Party hierarchy during the 1950's. One probable reason was a desire on the part of Mao Tse-tung, whom Lin was careful to continue cultivating, to use him to balance the equally meteoric rise of the Party apparatus man Teng Hsiao-p'ing. Another was Lin's role in keeping the military leadership loyal to Mao, Liu Shao-ch'i, and Chou En-lai during the Kao Kang crisis of early 1954. Lin was elected to the Politburo in March, 1955, at the same time as Teng, and to its Standing Committee in May, 1958.

Lin's greatest political prize was probably the Defense Ministry, which he was given in August, 1959, following the purge of his rival, P'eng Te-huai; this post also carried with it the effective chairmanship of the Party's important Military Affairs Committee. Lin used his new position as China's most powerful soldier to increase the level of indoctrination within the PLA in politics and the "thought" of Mao Tse-tung, without however going to such lengths as to interfere with the technical proficiency of the officer corps at least down to the outbreak of the Cultural Revolution. His success was, or seemed, great enough so that in 1963 the PLA began to be held up in Maoist propaganda as a model for the entire nation to emulate. Together with his colleague Hsiao Hua, who headed the PLA General Staff's powerful General Political Department after 1964, Lin also began to use PLA political personnel to run newly created political departments in Party bodies, government agencies, and economic enterprises, evidently as part of Mao's plan for reinjecting revolutionary momentum into the political system.

In retrospect, the crucial aspect of Lin's career was his relationship to the Cultural Revolution, a complex subject. The reconstruction offered here is based on Lin's known statements dating from the period, on the seemingly most authoritative secondary analyses, and above all on his own actions and those of others evidently under his control or influence.

According to a well-informed Chinese diplomat who defected in 1966, Lin then had the reputation of being even more of an ideologue and political extremist than Mao. It appears that this reputation was justified; certainly, Lin was much less sophisticated politically than Mao or Chou En-lai, although more so militarily.

Lin's frequently professed devotion to Mao and his "thought" appears to have been genuine, as well as uncritical and extreme. As is shown by the editorial line of the General Political Department's organ, *Liberation Army Daily*, in late 1965 and early 1966, Lin and Hsiao Hua were basically favorable to the successive stages of the Cultural Revolution as unfolded by Mao Tse-tung, for example in Mao's letter of May 7, 1966, to Lin, to the effect that the PLA should be a "great school" of correct political activity and of Mao's "thought." Lin evidently supported the Maoist assault on "bourgeois ideology" in cultural and academic circles, the offensive against P'eng Chen, and the mobilization and unleashing of the Red Guards. As an extension of the earlier use of personnel under the General Political Department on missions outside the PLA, such personnel began to work quietly on Chinese academic campuses from September, 1965, on. Lin probably not only approved of the formation of the Red Guard units but also assured Mao that the PLA could and would support and manage them—as it did initially by providing logistical support and transportation and some training.

The image of the PLA as a "great school" and as a main promoter and ultimately the would-be manager of the Cultural Revolution (the "main pillar of the proletarian dictatorship") fitted well with, and reinforced, Lin's highly politicized view of the PLA's role. It was "guerrillaized" to a considerable degree in 1965–66, for example through the abolition of formal titles and insignia of rank (spring, 1965) and through emphasis on close combat in training exercises, an approach that produced a clash with the more professionally oriented Chief of Staff, Lo Jui-ch'ing. Lin's outlook also included a keen appreciation of the potential for the use of armed force in political coups, whether in the cause of "revolution" or of "counterrevolution." There is reasonably persuasive evidence that he executed coups of some sort against Lo Jui-ch'ing (February–March, 1966) and P'eng Chen (April–May, 1966).

Maoist political strategy has long viewed external tension as a valuable if not indispensable atmosphere for domestic campaigns. As he indicated to a Japanese Communist delegation on March 28, 1966, however, Mao seems to have been genuinely afraid that the United States and the Soviet Union might actually attack China in the near future. Presumably, he had in mind the tension over Vietnam, the probable American response to which he had badly underestimated in an interview with Edgar Snow a year earlier, the reinforcement of Soviet troops in the Mongolian People's Republic then getting under way, and the purge of Lo Jui-ch'ing a few weeks earlier. With a keener appreciation of military realities, including the state of mutual deterrence between the United States and the Soviet Union, Lin appears to have felt greater confidence that the United States was moving away from rather than toward a confrontation with China and that any likely threat could be deterred through China's nuclear-weapons program and loudly publicized nuclear tests (one was held on May 9, 1966). If deterrence should fail, Lin believed (as he said in *Long Live the Victory of People's War!*, published on September 3,

1965) that the Chinese armed forces and people could win in a "people's war."

Given this rather primitive view, Lin saw no reason to modify the established Maoist dual-adversary strategy, of which his work just cited is in fact a classic expression, especially since the tension with the United States and the Soviet Union would provide an appropriate backdrop for the Cultural Revolution and help to justify an important political role for the PLA and himself. There was to be a considerable difference in practice between the methods applied to American "imperialism" and Soviet "revisionism," however. The United States had proven itself militarily dangerous if provoked, in Korea, in the Taiwan Strait, and now in Vietnam; accordingly, apart from a great deal of relatively meaningless propaganda, it was not to be actually provoked this time. There was never more than the faintest hint of a threat to send Red Guards to Vietnam, for example, a logical ploy given the theoretical premises of the Cultural Revolution. When Maoists demonstrated and rioted in Hong Kong in 1967, they never threatened the American Consulate General or American citizens. On the other hand, if the militarily dangerous United States was considered to be a political "paper tiger," as Mao had been saying since 1946, it could and should be disposed of by the "revolutionary people of the world" through "people's wars," without China's having to confront it directly on the battlefield. The Soviet Union, however, had not yet proven itself militarily dangerous to China. Politically, of course, it was a major nuisance and an object of intense dislike; among the reasons for this well-known Maoist attitude was an anti-Chinese "secret letter" that Moscow circulated to friendly Communist Parties early in 1966. But the "Khrushchev revisionists" ruling in Moscow were thought to be disliked by their own people and therefore would be vulnerable to revolt if the Soviet people could be galvanized through propaganda (pro-Stalin, rather than pro-Mao) and demonstrations of Chinese anti-"revisionist" determination. Accordingly, almost certainly with Lin's approval and very probably under his active direction, a conscious policy of defying and provoking the "Khrushchev revisionists" was adopted. Their demand for "united action" on Vietnam was loudly and repeatedly rejected. For about a year beginning in the winter of 1965–66, Chinese soldiers, peasants, and students staged highly provocative border incidents along the Sino-Soviet frontier, mainly its Manchurian sector (such incidents had been occurring from time to time since 1960, according to Soviet sources). On April 19, 1966, Peking promulgated a new set of highly arbitrary regulations governing foreign shipping on border rivers (the Amur and the Ussuri). On March 22, 1966, after nearly a month of delay and probably after some indecision and debate, Peking rather abusively rejected an invitation to send a delegation to the Soviet Party's forthcoming Twenty-third Party Congress. After the fall of Lo Jui-ch'ing in early 1966, Soviet rail shipments of military equipment for North Vietnam began to be obstructed while crossing China.

Lin's fundamentalism and militancy were clearly accompanied by a strong dose of opportunism and careerism. He had been the third-ranking member of the list of marshals created in 1955. Peng Te-huai, the man immediately above him and his rival of long standing, had been eliminated in 1959. During the Cultural Revolution, Lin was to criticize caustically the senior man on the list, the venerable and popular Chu Teh, although Chu's prestige spared him from being purged. Of the former marshals ("former" because of the abolition of ranks in 1965), all had varying degrees of political trouble with the Red Guards during the Cultural Revolution, or least found it advisable to be as inconspicuous as possible for a time. The most politically powerful of them, the formidable Ho Lung, who was briefly prominent as a patron of the Red Guard movement, disappeared in rather obscure circumstances about the end of 1966. At a slightly lower level of prestige but not of actual military power, Lin succeeded in having a close colleague, Huang Yung-sheng, named as PLA Chief of Staff in March, 1968, after his predecessor, Yang Ch'eng-wu (who held only the title of Acting Chief of Staff), had succeeded in antagonizing the Maoists and certain powerful military region commanders. Meanwhile, Lin had already bargained himself, beginning at about the time of the Eleventh Central Committee Plenary Session in August, 1966, into the position of Mao's announced successor in exchange for his support. After that Lin worked fairly hard to consolidate his position, by means that included (especially after the Ninth Party Congress) the promotion of a "cult of personality" for himself similar to Mao's, although less obtrusive.

Lin apparently had three main sources of leverage in his campaign, beginning in 1965, to promote his political objectives and career. The first was his vociferous loyalty to Mao. The second was his presumed control over, and ability to "deliver," the PLA. The third was his presumed competence to protect the country's security against external threats without suspending the promotion of Maoist foreign policy objectives. In time, however, these assets or qualities proved to be illusory, and this became a source of vulnerability for him. The PLA's initial patronage of the Red Guards did not suffice to prevent them from committing excesses that showed that they did not really understand the "latest instructions" rained on them by Mao during the Cultural Revolution. After its intervention in January, 1967, the PLA proved to be neither fully controllable nor ideologically reliable from the Maoist point of view. Brash provocation of the Soviet Union turned out to be highly unsafe after the invasion of Czechoslovakia and the clashes of March 1969, on the Ussuri River, the first of which Lin appears to have organized, at least in part, for his own political purposes. His obvious careerism evidently alienated some of his leading military colleagues and, more important, Mao himself. A major manifestation of his careerism was his insistence on being formally named as Mao's successor in the Party constitution adopted at the Ninth Party Congress in April, 1969, and in the draft state constitution to have been adopted at the Fourth National People's Congress (originally scheduled for late 1970.)

Lin's basic political ineptitude, as well as his poor health, prevented him from comprehending his vulnerabilities and from taking effective steps to protect himself from their consequences. His political fate was sealed when Chou En-lai, at about the time of the Ninth Party Congress and with Mao's at least passive approval, undertook to bring about Lin's downfall. In the face of this threat, he seems to have remained fairly inactive, apart from promoting his own cult, pushing for the National People's Congress to meet and legitimate his position as Mao's successor in the state, and indulging in a few irritating gestures, such as arranging for a photograph of Mao and himself to be printed on the front page of the *People's Daily* on September 11, 1970, the first anniversary of Chou En-lai's crucial talks with Soviet Premier Kosygin (see Chapter 4). During his last stay in China (August, 1970–February, 1971), Edgar Snow evidently did not form the impression that Lin was politically active or truly influential, although Cambodian Prince Norodom Sihanouk, in exile in Peking, continued to insist for the benefit of foreign visitors (and misleadingly, if this analysis is correct), at least until the summer of 1971, that Chou was continuing to consult with Lin on important policy questions. Lin evidently clung to his preference for a more or less "guerrillaized" PLA, with its political apparatus (which had not been extensively purged during the Cultural Revolution) deeply involved in provincial politics, reliance mainly on China's nuclear program (publicity for which had been prudently reduced since the Soviet invasion of Czechoslovakia) for deterrence of possible external attack, and maintenance of the dual-adversary strategy. In the post-Czechoslovakia context, this meant continued defiance of the Soviet Union (by loudly publicized preparations for a "people's war," for example) and rejection of Chou En-lai's argument that a positive relationship with the United States was necessary in order to cope with the Soviet threat.

Against a menacing background of Soviet diplomatic moves and Soviet propaganda statements with a strongly anti-Chinese flavor, Chou made his move against Lin on September 11–12, 1971. The details are obscure, but it seems likely that Lin is dead. Conceivably, he was dying of natural causes when he was overthrown, or he may actually have died in the famous airplane crash of September 12 in Mongolia as claimed in the more or less official version given by Mao to foreign visitors in the summer of 1972. The political case made against him—not in the press, as yet— has concentrated on the two charges necessary to blacken his reputation in the circumstances: he was allegedly opposed to Mao and even tried to kill him, and he was allegedly pro-Soviet (the crash may have been staged to show that Lin was trying to defect to the Soviet Union). Neither charge appears to be true, any more than many of the charges made against high Party members purged in earlier years appear credible. For many months, the nearest thing to a public announcement of his fall was the placing on sale in Peking on February 14, 1972, of a new edition of the Little Red Book in several foreign languages, including English, with Lin Piao's preface deleted.

The Succession

Predictions about the succession to the highest office in any political system are notoriously hazardous, even for those with inside information. We have seen that Mao referred to Liu Shao-ch'i as his successor as late as October, 1961, only three months before the beginning of their disagreement that led after three more years to Mao's decision to dump him. It is a curious coincidence—and probably nothing more—that three prominent Chinese (Lo Jui-ch'ing, Lin Piao, and Huang Yung-sheng) were purged shortly after the appearance of studies of them by Western analysts describing them as political comers. One also recalls that Marshal Georgi Zhukov was purged in October, 1957, only a few months after Allen Dulles, in a highly unusual statement, had referred to him as the likely future leader of the Soviet Union.

In the autumn of 1972, Chou En-lai was the obvious man to succeed Mao as head of the Party and state, but there is a theory, especially on Taiwan, that he is vulnerable to being dumped by Mao at the instigation of the Maoists, notably Chiang Ch'ing. It must be admitted that in the past several years analysts on Taiwan have been ahead of those in the West in perceiving power conflicts in Peking, but they have also tended to overstress these and overlook the elements of strength and cohesion in the Communist system. Chou's current position rests not only on his personal power and Mao's favor but on his program as well. Furthermore, Mao is probably too old and feeble to be capable of the enormous effort required to purge Chou, even if he should wish to do so; it is true, of course, that similar things were said about Mao before the Cultural Revolution. It seems most unlikely that Mao would decide to try to get rid of Chou, thereby losing the advantage of his skill and experience. As his performance during Mao's interview with President Nixon shows, Chou has cultivated in the best Chinese tradition an attitude of respectful obedience to his superior, much as Chiang Kai-shek's elder son and probable political heir, Chiang Ching-kuo, has done with his father. Chou has been careful not to push himself formally into the shoes of the deposed Lin Piao, even on a formally acting basis, or to do the same for the other members of his "team" with respect to the purged members of Lin's. To do so irregularly would be to risk the displeasure of Mao and (probably less important) of the Maoists. To do so in a formal manner, for example via a Party Congress and a National People's Congress, is probably unnecessary at present and, as the experience of Liu Shao-ch'i and Lin Piao shows, is by no means a guarantee of tenure. It is more useful, and more in keeping with Chou's "style," to act at least for the time being as *de facto* chairman of the board of the new "collective leadership" that has emerged from the Cultural Revolution and the constituencies that it represents: the Maoists, the new Party apparatus, the streamlined state and government hierarchies, the armed forces being progressively purged of Lin's supporters, and the revived security services. The Maoists probably continue to dislike Chou but are restrained from opposing him actively, not only by the strength of his position but also by Mao's orders (note for example that Chiang Ch'ing was hostess to Mrs. Nixon during a state dinner in Peking, with whatever feelings) and by the fact that they are somewhat compromised by having supported Chou against Lin Piao.

The probability, then, is that, assuming his survival, Chou will make it as Mao's successor, in essential respects at least. But his leadership "style" is likely to be much more "collective," much less flamboyant, than Mao's. He will probably further reduce the dimensions of the Mao cult and deny infallibility to Mao's "thought," without however abandoning it as the ideological basis of the political system, if only because there is no viable alternative. The official ideology may possibly be labeled as Marxism-Leninism rather than as the "thought" of Mao Tse-tung, but it is likely to retain a Maoist flavor. A more serious problem for Chou, in addition to his age (he was born in 1898), is likely to be that of countering the centrifugal forces unleashed by the Cultural Revolution and the disruption of the Party apparatus. (The uncertain outlook on this crucial point is discussed in Chapter 15.)

FURTHER READINGS

Any work on Chinese Communist leadership must come promptly to grips with the important, rather theoretical output of John Wilson Lewis. His major effort on this subject is *Leadership in Communist China*, Ithaca, N.Y.: Cornell University Press, 1963. Other relevant writings of his, somewhat more digestible because shorter, are *Chinese Communist Party Leadership and the Succession to Mao Tse-tung: An Appraisal of Tensions*, Washington, D.C.: U.S. Department of State, 1964; "Revolutionary Struggle and the Second Generation in Communist China," *The China Quarterly*, no. 21 (January–March, 1965), pp. 126–47; "Leader, Commissar, and Bureaucrat: The Chinese Political System in the Last Days of the Revolution," in Ping-ti Ho and Tang Tsou, eds., *China in Crisis*, vol. 1, book 2, Chicago: University of Chicago Press, 1968, pp. 449–81. On more specific aspects of leadership, see Michel C. Oksenberg, "Local Leaders in Rural China, 1962–65: Individual Attributes, Bureaucratic Positions, and Political Recruitment," in A. Doak Barnett, ed., *Chinese Communist Politics in Action*, Seattle: University of Washington Press, 1969, pp. 155–215; Ying-mao Kau, "The Urban Bureaucratic Elite in Communist China: A Case Study of Wuhan, 1949–65," *ibid.*, pp. 216–67; G. William Skinner and Edwin A. Winckler, "Compliance Succession in Rural Communist China: A Cyclical Theory," in Amitai Etzioni, ed., *A Sociological Reader on Complex Organizations*, 2nd ed., New York: Holt, Rinehart & Winston, 1969, pp. 410–38. The reference to

Edgar Snow's comments on the post-1949 Chinese leadership is to his *The Other Side of the River: Red China Today*, New York: Random House, 1961, London: Gollancz, 1963, Harmondsworth: Penguin, 1970, Chapter 44.

On the Eighth and Ninth Central Committees, see Donald W. Klein, "The 'Next Generation' of Chinese Communist Leaders," *The China Quarterly*, no. 12 (October–December, 1962), pp. 57–74; Donald W. Klein and Lois B. Hager, "The Ninth Central Committee," *ibid.*, no. 45 (January–March, 1971), pp. 37–56; Franklin W. Houn, "The Eighth Central Committee of the Chinese Communist Party: A Study of an Elite," *The American Political Science Review*, vol. 51, no. 2 (June, 1957), pp. 392–404.

On various types of groupings within the CPC leadership, see John Israel, "The December 9th Movement: A Case Study in Chinese Communist Historiography," *The China Quarterly*, no. 23 (July–September, 1965), pp. 140–69; Ralph L. Powell, "The Increasing Power of Lin Piao and the Party-Soldiers 1959–1966," *ibid.*, no. 34 (April–June, 1968), pp. 38–65; William W. Whitson, "The Concept of Military Generation: The Chinese Communist Case," *Asian Survey*, vol. viii, no. 11 (November, 1968), pp. 921–47, and "The Field Army in Chinese Communist Military Politics," *The China Quarterly*, no. 37 (January–March, 1969), pp. 1–30. The limited foreign experience of the CPC leadership is documented in Donald W. Klein, "Peking's Leaders: A Study in Isolation," *ibid.*, no. 7 (July–September, 1961), pp. 35–43.

The best general source for biographical information is Donald W. Klein and Anne B. Clark, *Biographic Dictionary of Chinese Communism, 1921–1965*, 2 vols., Cambridge, Mass.: Harvard University Press, 1971. A pioneering elite study is Robert C. North, *Kuomintang and Chinese Communist Elites*, Stanford, Calif.: The Hoover Institution, 1952.

Of the enormous literature on Mao Tse-tung in a variety of languages, only a small fraction can be mentioned here. The best general biography is Stuart Schram, *Mao Tse-tung*, Harmondsworth and Baltimore: Penguin, 1968. Other useful works include three by Jerome Ch'en, *Mao and the Chinese Revolution*, London and New York: Oxford University Press, 1967; *Mao*, Englewood Cliffs, N.J.: Prentice-Hall, 1969; and *Mao Papers: Anthology and Bibliography*, London and New York: Oxford University Press, 1970. Mao's autobiography is contained in various editions of Edgar Snow's *Red Star Over China*. There are two important recent interviews with Mao by Snow: "Interview with Mao," *The New Republic*, February 27, 1965, pp. 17–23, and "A Conversation with Mao Tse-tung," *Life*, April 30, 1971, pp. 46–48. A valuable sketch (from which the quotation regarding Chou En-lai is drawn) is Chang Kuo-t'ao, "Mao—A New Portrait by an Old Colleague," *The New York Times Magazine*, August 2, 1953.

Some important recent information on Mao's political career during the Kiangsi and Long March periods is contained in a series of articles in *The China Quarterly, nos.* 40, 42, 43, and 46. On a significant aspect of Mao's rise to power, see William F. Dorrill, "Transfer of Legitimacy in the Chinese Communist Party: Origins of the Maoist Myth," *ibid.,* no. 36 (October–December, 1968), pp. 45–60.

Some statements by Mao not included in his *Selected Works* are in American Consulate General, Hong Kong, *Current Background,* nos. 819, 830, 863, 885, 891, 892, and 897; Joint Publications Research Service, "Selections from Chairman Mao," *Translations on Communist China,* no. 90 (February 12, 1970).

There is much less on Chou En-lai. There is an anecdotal, superficial biography in English: Kai-yu Hsu, *Chou En-lai: China's Gray Eminence,* New York: Doubleday, 1969. A small collection of his public statements has been assembled in *Quotations from Chou En-lai,* Melbourne: Paul Flesch, 1969. There are two useful studies by Thomas W. Robinson: "Chou En-lai's Political Style: Comparisons with Mao Tse-tung and Lin Piao," *Asian Survey,* vol. x, no. 12 (December, 1970), pp. 1101–16; "Chou En-lai and the Cultural Revolution in China," in Thomas W. Robinson, ed., *The Cultural Revolution in China,* Berkeley: University of California Press, 1971, pp. 165–312. See also Ting Wang and Hsu I-fan, "Chou Rising from Turmoil," *Courrier d'Extrême-Orient* (Brussels), September, 1968, pp. 323–28.

On Liu Shao-ch'i, see *Collected Works of Liu Shao-ch'i,* 2 vols, Hong Kong: Union Research Institute, 1968, 1969 (note the introduction by Chang Kuo-t'ao); *Quotations from President Liu Shao-ch'i,* New York and Tokyo: Walker and Weatherhill, 1968; Howard L. Boorman, "Liu Shao-ch'i: A Political Profile," *The China Quarterly,* no. 10 (April–June, 1962), pp. 1–22; Howard L. Boorman, *"How To Be a Good Communist:* The Political Ethics of Liu Shao-ch'i," *Asian Survey,* vol. xxiii, no. 8 (August, 1963), pp. 372–83; Peter Cheng, "Liu Shao-ch'i and the Cultural Revolution," *ibid.,* vol. xi, no. 10 (October, 1971), pp. 943–57.

On the conflict between Mao and Liu, see Stuart Schram, "Mao Tse-tung and Liu Shao-ch'i, 1939–1969," *Asian Survey,* vol. xii, no. 4 (April, 1972), pp. 275–93; Parris H. Chang, "Struggle Between the Two Roads in China's Countryside," *Current Scene* (Hong Kong), vol. vi, no. 3 (February 15, 1968); The Editor, "The Conflict Between Mao Tse-tung and Liu Shao-ch'i over Agricultural Mechanization in Communist China," *ibid.,* no. 17 (October 1, 1968); The Editor, "The Mao-Liu Controversy over Rural Public Health," *ibid.,* vol. vii, no. 12 (June 15, 1969). The interview with Mao Tse-tung in which he named Liu as his successor is reported in Field Marshal Viscount Montgomery, "China on the Move," *The Sunday Times* (London), October 15, 1961. Documents relating to the Cultural Revolution campaign against Liu and his wife may be found in American Consulate General, Hong Kong, *Current Background,* nos. 827, 836, 848; *Selections from China Mainland Magazines,* nos. 619, 651, 652, 653. The "confessions" and "trial" of Liu were reported in the Japanese press on the basis of wall posters (especially the Tokyo Papers, *Mainichi,* January 28 and 29, 1967; April 6, 1967; August 3, 1967; *Asahi,* July 30, 1967; *Sankei,* August 2, 1967; *Tokyo Shimbun,* August 16, 1967).

The major study of Lin Piao is Thomas W. Robinson, *A Politico-Military Biography of Lin Piao,* 2 vols, Santa Monica, Calif.: The Rand Corporation, 1971, 1972. Other useful studies by the same author are *Lin Piao as an Elite Type,* Santa Monica, Calif.: The Rand Corporation, July, 1971; "Lin Piao: A Chinese Military Politician," in William W. Whitson, ed., *The Military and Political Power in China in the 1970's,* New York: Praeger, 1972, pp. 73–92. Also useful are The Editor, "Lin Piao: A Political Profile," *Current Scene,* vol. vii, no. 5 (March 10, 1969); The Editor, "Lin Piao and the Cultural Revolution," *ibid.,* vol. viii, no. 14 (August 1, 1970). Lin's important tract, *Long Live the Victory of People's War!,* is reprinted in Samuel B. Griffith, ed., *Peking and People's Wars,* New York: Praeger, 1966, London: Pall Mall Press, 1966. Some of his statements during the Cultural Revolution appear in *The Great Cultural Revolution in China,* Hong Kong: Asia Research Centre, 1967; *The Great Power Struggle in China,* Hong Kong: Asia Research Centre, 1969. Soviet evidence on border incidents is reported by Hugo Portisch in Vienna *Kurier,* June 15, 1967. There is an essentially journalistic biography of Lin by Martin Ebon, *Lin Piao: The Life and Writings of China's New Ruler,* New York: Stein & Day, 1970.

On Lo Jui-ch'ing, see Sterling Seagrave and Robert A. Jones, "From China, with Love," *Esquire,* January, 1966, pp. 42–45, 47, 112, 114–15. On Huang Yung-sheng, Jürgen Domes, "Generals and Red Guards," *Asia Quarterly* (Brussels), 1971/1, pp. 3–31; 1971/2, pp. 123–59. In the case of Lin Piao, the reference is to Robinson's study *(supra).* A brief pre–Cultural Revolution discussion of the succession question is Harold C. Hinton, "The Succession Problem in Communist China," *Current Scene,* vol. i, no. 7 (July 19, 1961).

An important addition to the literature on leadership is Robert A. Scalapino, ed., *Elites in the People's Republic of China,* Seattle and London: University of Washington Press, 1972.

7. The Party

The CPC's "leadership" over the country is the centerpiece of Communist Chinese politics, at least in theory. The first section of the famous Little Red Book deals with the Communist Party. There is nothing surprising in this unless one shares the common misapprehension that the Cultural Revolution was intended as an assault on the Party. The Cultural Revolution was actually directed, at least in Mao's eyes, against "revisionist" elements of the Party apparatus (internal administrative bureaucracy), not against the Party as a whole, of which Mao considers himself the symbol as well as the leader. For purposes of analysis, it is important to keep in mind the formal distinction between the Party and its apparatus, as well as the distinction between the Party and other structures normally controlled by it, such as the state.

The Leninist Model

The CPC was formed in 1921 under the auspices of, and in affiliation with, the Comintern, which was already dominated by the Soviet Communist Party. Naturally, therefore, the CPC was modeled from the beginning on the Leninist concept of what a Communist Party should be.

This concept begins with the relatively small, "narrow," Party of committed and disciplined activists, rather than a larger, "open," Party of mere sympathizers. Membership can be secret, and the Party as a whole can be an underground one if necessary; any Party not in power should be prepared to go underground and rely on covert operations if the situation requires. The typical sanction for breaches of Party discipline or for insufficient activism is expulsion. Expulsions on a fairly wide scale, known as purges, are considered more or less a sign of health, rather than of disease; more accurately, they supposedly prevent the onset of disease by cleansing the Party's ranks of deadwood. Sometimes a purge is conducted by calling in all or most Party cards and issuing new cards only to individuals approved by higher authority for continuation as members.

The organizational and operational principle animating an orthodox Leninist Communist Party is known officially as democratic centralism. The authoritative definition of this term, as given in numerous Soviet sources, is as follows:

> All the leading Party bodies from top to bottom are elected.
> Regular accounts are rendered by Party bodies to their Party organizations.
> Strict Party discipline and subordination of the minority to the majority are observed.
> Decisions of the higher Party bodies are absolutely binding on all lower bodies.

These statements are not fully self-explanatory and become intelligible to a non-Communist reader only if the context of their actual operational significance is defined.

The Party is organized in a series of hierarchically arranged pyramids of two main types. One is territorial; in other words, its structure corresponds to the administrative geography of the country in question. The other is functional; it exists within some non-Party body such as the armed forces or a mass organization (labor unions, women's organizations, and the like). The "primary" organization in each type of pyramid is usually called the branch. At each level, executive authority rests with a Party committee, known at the highest level as the Central Committee. It is theoretically elected by a Party congress representing, via indirect elections except at the lowest level, the membership of the organization as a whole. In reality, the membership of the Party committee is largely determined in advance of the "election" by the *de facto* leadership (at the central level, normally the Politburo). At the center, each newly "elected" Central Committee "elects" a largely predetermined smaller group of its own members to the Politburo, the Party's highest policy-making body. In theory, all Politburo members are equal and decisions are taken by majority vote. The Central Committee also "elects" some other high Party bodies, of which the most important next to the Politburo is usually the Secretariat. The latter is supposedly an administrative rather than a policymaking body, and it therefore does not take formal votes and its members are or may be ranked (first secretary, second secretary, and so on). The Secretariat's great influence over the Party's internal administration (including promotion of Party members) and over the Party's relations with non-Party bodies, however, even though in theory exercised purely in implementation of Central Committee and Politburo directives, in practice can become or approach complete control in the hands of a dictatorial leader like Stalin. The Secretariat presides over a large Party bureaucracy comparable to that of the state (in the case of a Communist Party in power), which in turn controls and administers the entire Party apparatus in addition to other duties. The apparatus consists in effect of those Party members—very roughly one-fifth of the total Party membership—who devote full time to work within the Party under the ultimate direction of the Secretariat, rather than in some other capacity (in the armed forces, for example).

Perhaps the most thoroughly totalitarian aspect of an orthodox Communist Party is the ban on "factionalism" that was imposed on the Soviet Party at Lenin's insistence in 1921 and has been adopted by the others since then. In theory at least, free debate is allowed and even encouraged within a decision-making body like the Politburo down to the taking of the vote on a given issue. At that point, not only must the debate stop, but the minority must wholeheartedly support the majority, in order to present a front of unanimity to the outside world, and must not work for the reconsideration or reversal of the decision (unless reversal somehow becomes the wish of the majority). For a minority to organize and agitate against the majority on any issue, and still more on a question of power, is to be guilty of the heinous sin of "factionalism." The trend toward abolition of the ban on "factionalism" within the Czechoslovak Party in 1968, with the aim of introducing an essentially un-Leninist measure of democracy, was one of the major causes of the Soviet invasion.

It is obvious that in practice the principle of "centralism" outweighs that of "democracy" in an orthodox Leninist Party, and that a strongly elitist tendency is at work through the ability of leading bodies once constituted to entrench and perpetuate themselves to a considerable extent by co-opting acceptable new members. Early in the twentieth century, Trotsky saw that this would be one of the effects of Leninist organizational principles and even predicted the emergence of a dictator. In due course, he appeared, in the person of Stalin. His dictatorship arose from the increasing domination of the Party apparatus over the Party as a whole, and of the Secretariat (of which he was General Secretary after 1922) over the Party apparatus. He consolidated and strengthened his position through the extensive use of police terror within as well as outside the Party and created through propaganda an over-powering "cult of personality" focused on himself. Since his death, the usual Communist position is that in these respects Stalin was guilty of distorting Leninist Party principles, and a case can certainly be made for this contention. On the other hand, it can be argued with at least equal plausibility that the potential for such distortions was already present in the Leninist model of Party organization and functioning.

In a country controlled by a Leninist Communist Party, whether one with Stalinist distortions or not, the whole of public life is dominated by the Party in a manner paralleling the totalitarian tendencies of the Party's internal organization and functioning. In theory at least, no private organizational initiative having an even remotely political flavor is permitted. All public organizations must be created and controlled by the Party, directly or indirectly. Party control over non-Party bodies is achieved, apart from ulti-mate police sanctions, in three main ways: a Party organization within the body in question, the monopolization of major posts by Party members, and intensive propaganda and indoctrination stressing the leadership of the Party. The net effect is that, al-though it is possible to have a successful nonpolitical career in a Communist-controlled country, as a technician or artist of some kind for example, it is not possible to have a political career or exert political influence without joining the Party and rising in its ranks through conformity to its requirements, which are normally based on the Leninist model.

The CPC as a Leninist Party (1945–55)

Until the spring of 1955, the CPC was clearly within the per-missible limits for a Party of the Leninist type, even though it was being increasingly Sinicized by its environment and by the leader-ship and "thought" of Mao Tse-tung.

The CPC entered the post-1949 period under a leadership that had been formalized, and a constitution that had been adopted, at its Seventh Party Congress (April–June, 1945). The main political themes of the Congress and the constitution, the latter being largely the work of Liu Shao-ch'i, were praise of Mao's leadership and "thought," reiteration of his concept of New Democracy (see

Chapter 5), and the demand that the Kuomintang take the CPC and various minor parties into a "democratic coalition government." The new constitution, which replaced one adopted in 1928, created the post of Chairman of the Central Committee and specified that the main "leading bodies" of the Party, apart from the Central Committee, should as usual be the Politburo and the Secretariat. Since the Party had been functioning under rather decentralized wartime conditions, the composition of the new Central Committee emerged from an informal compromise between the central Party leadership and its local counterparts in the various "liberated areas" and reflected the increasingly northern origins of the Party membership since the Long March.

The new Central Committee promptly elected Mao Tse-tung as its Chairman and that of the Politburo. In addition, he chaired a powerful Secretariat that soon afterward came to be headed by the five senior figures in the Party leadership (Mao, Liu Shao-ch'i, Chou En-lai, Chu Teh, and Ch'en Yun). After 1952, when the regional bureaus of the Central Committee began to be abolished (see Chapter 3) and many of their personnel were transferred to Peking, the fastest-rising figures in the Party leadership were probably Teng Hsiao-p'ing, the former head of the Southwest Bureau and increasingly a specialist in Party apparatus affairs, and Lin Piao, a military hero and favorite of Mao's. Teng and Lin, representing respectively the two main tendencies within the Party, the essentially orthodox Leninist apparatus and the Maoist group, were elected to the Politburo at a Central Committee meeting in April, 1955.

The enormous growth of the CPC's responsibilities after 1949 necessarily led to a rapid expansion of Party membership (from 1.2 million in 1945 to 6.5 million in 1954). Most of these were cadres (administrative personnel either within the Party or in a public body outside it; not all cadres working outside the CPC are Party members).

There are two significant indications, among others, that, in spite of Mao Tse-tung's unchallenged personal ascendancy, the CPC during the decade under review deserved to be considered an orthodox Leninist Party. One is a number of Chinese statements after Stalin's death and even during his lifetime (for example, Liu Shao-ch'i's important report, "On the Party," to the Seventh Party Congress) saying or implying that Stalin had violated Leninist Party norms by imposing a rigid bureaucratic reign of terror on the Party. Another is that, although the CPC leadership convened numerous conferences during the early years after 1949, these were used to explain policy rather than to make it; important policies were decided on by the Politburo, apparently by majority vote. In one respect, however, the CPC differed significantly from the Soviet and other Western Communist Parties: for purposes of maintaining discipline and effectiveness, less stress was (and is) placed on administrative control and outright coercion and more on thought control via intensive indoctrination in various ways, notably at small meetings.

Leninism Under Stress (1955–65)

What amounted to a challenge to Leninism within the CPC by Mao Tse-tung and his personal supporters began in the spring of 1955 in connection with an agricultural crisis and a debate over the rate of collectivization (see Chapter 3). That Mao was faced with an adverse majority in the Politburo and the Central Committee and refused to bow to it in normal Leninist fashion created an extremely difficult situation. Liu Shao-ch'i, the senior figure on the majority side, tried to find a way out by initiating in May a type of meeting known from then on as the central work conference, at which policy questions could be discussed and in effect decided in a somewhat less formal fashion (the conference was larger in membership than the Politburo and lacked the constitutional standing of the Central Committee), without the embarrassment of a direct vote adverse to Mao as in the Politburo. Mao retaliated in late July by creating an informal forum, a conference of provincial Party secretaries, before which he stated his radical position on agriculture at intervals over the next three years.

Mao managed to get his way, but his opponents took advantage of the favorable atmosphere created by Khrushchev's attack on Stalin in February, 1956, to move against him, always with the fewest possible elements of direct confrontation. This move was made mainly at the Eighth Party Congress (September 15–27, 1956; see Chapter 3). From the Party standpoint, probably its most important aspect was that Mao was deprived of direct control over the Party Secretariat, and hence over the apparatus; that function, together with the newly revived title of General Secretary, was bestowed on Teng Hsiao-p'ing.

The preamble to the new Party constitution adopted at the Eighth Party Congress placed heavy ideological emphasis on Marxism-Leninism rather than on the "thought" of Mao Tse-tung —an important distinction in the context of the leadership dispute

Chart 1

The Communist Party of China
Prior to the Cultural Revolution (simplified)

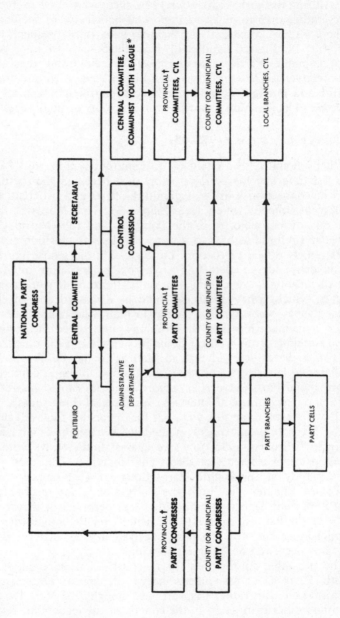

* The Communist Youth League has a system of congresses similar to that of the Communist Party of China.
† Or Special Municipality or Autonomous Region.

Reprinted from Major Governments of Asia, 2d ed., edited by George McTurnan Kahin.
© 1958 and 1963 by Cornell University. Used by permission of Cornell University Press.

then in progress and a striking change from the 1945 constitution. The preamble also strongly reaffirmed allegiance to democratic centralism and other orthodox Leninist principles, to a degree that appeared to constitute an implicit criticism of Mao. The provisions regarding Party membership were slightly more liberal, from the standpoint of the individual member, than those in the 1945 constitution. The National Party Congress was to meet annually during its term of five years. The Central Committee, also elected for a five-year term, was normally to meet twice a year. A new body, the Standing Committee of the Politburo, was created and subsequently manned by the same big five who made up the outgoing Secretariat (Mao, Liu, Chou En-lai, Chu Teh, and Ch'en Yun), plus Teng Hsiao-p'ing. A new title, Honorary Chairman of the Central Committee, was created in the obvious although only implied expectation that it would be given to Mao when the Party leadership "deems it necessary." In his authoritative report to the Congress on the constitution, Teng Hsiao-p'ing said significantly that "our Party . . . posts guards against deification of individuals" and placed heavy emphasis on democratic centralism (by implication, in contrast to Mao's personal leadership), and yet, in a way characteristic of the opposition to Mao in those years, he also stressed the principle that the Party's relationship with the public must be conducted in accordance with the Maoist principle of the "mass line" ("from the masses, to the masses").

The setback to Mao administered at the Eighth Party Congress was insufficient to prevent him from continuing to launch, through such means as his personal ascendancy over the Party's propaganda machine, a series of personal political initiatives. The willingness of the opposition to acquiesce to them, for the time being at least, was probably influenced by the example of the unsettling effects in Eastern Europe, in late 1956, of Khrushchev's denunciation of Stalin. Given the increasing demands on the Party, notably those stemming from the need to launch and control the Great Leap Forward, as well as the normal operation of Parkinson's Law, Party membership continued to expand rapidly (to 17 million by 1961).

When the Party apparatus was given, in late 1960, the difficult mission of supervising the retreat from the Great Leap Forward, it promptly revived the regional bureaus of the Central Committee that had existed prior to 1954. The new bureaus, however, were staffed at the top largely by colleagues and followers of General Secretary Teng Hsiao-p'ing, rather than by independently powerful Party leaders as in the earlier period. These circumstances were seemingly favorable to a restoration of normal Leninist Party functioning, but a number of problems and anomalies combined to inhibit the full working out of such a tendency. Mao began, in January, 1962, to press again for more radical policies. Because of intra-Party conflicts and preoccupation with economic recovery, it proved impossible to hold the Ninth Party Congress in 1961, as should have been done according to the Party constitution, and indeed for eight years thereafter. The fortieth anniversary of the foundation of the CPC (July 1, 1961), which might have been expected to be used by the Party apparatus to dramatize its temporary ascendancy, was actually celebrated in a fairly subdued way.

This situation probably reflected a decision by the Party apparatus leadership to assume a low-key, almost passive, public posture in its bizarre contest with Mao Tse-tung, while continuing to strengthen its organization and hopefully its powers of resistance. Accordingly, at the important Tenth Plenary Session of the Central Committee (late September, 1962) the general political tone was strongly Maoist. The Party apparatus apparently gained in strength, however, through a decision to tighten Party discipline by reinforcing the network of Party control commissions and through the election to the Secretariat of three new members: propaganda chief Lu Ting-i, Party organization and intelligence specialist K'ang Sheng, and PLA Chief of Staff Lo Jui-ch'ing. The other members of the Secretariat were General Secretary Teng Hsiao-p'ing, P'eng Chen, Wang Chia-hsiang, T'an Chen-lin, Li Hsueh-feng, Li Fu-ch'un, and Li Hsien-nien, and alternates Liu Lan-t'ao, Yang Shang-k'un, and Hu Ch'iao-mu. The problem of growing "bureaucratism" within the Party apparatus, a matter of particular concern to Mao, was to be dealt with by the limited measure of moving personnel more frequently from one assignment to another.

During the years following the Tenth Plenary Session, the Party apparatus was successful on the whole in confining to an internal "rectification" movement within the Party the Socialist Education Campaign it had decided on, as against the Maoist desire for criticism of the apparatus from outside, by the "masses." Leninism and democratic centralism, Chinese style, were proving too strong to be shaken by Maoist charges of "revisionism" or by anything short of a massive and carefully prepared assault from outside.

This assault came, of course, under the name of the Cultural Revolution.

The Impact of the Cultural Revolution

Starting in September, 1965, when Mao began his effort to launch the Cultural Revolution, the Party apparatus leadership (principally Liu Shao-ch'i and Teng Hsiao-p'ing) fought a delaying action while trying to oppose Mao no more than was strictly necessary. At first, until May, 1966, they agreed in effect to sacrifice one of their own number, P'eng Chen, in the hope of satisfying Mao as well as ridding themselves of a rival. Then they tried to manage the Red Guards without opposing them outright, although they basically objected to the Red Guards as a form of "spontaneity" not initiated or controlled by the Party apparatus. The virtual annihilation of the central Party apparatus by the Red Guards in the last months of 1966 alerted the Party committees at the regional, provincial, and local levels to the seriousness of the threat. Their resistance to the Red Guards and "revolutionary rebels" was terminated, in many instances, after the army intervened, beginning in late January, 1967.

After that, the military made use of many Party cadres in administrative positions, but the former territorial Party committees at the regional and provincial levels, and to a lesser extent below that, ceased to function as coherent entities. The functional Party committees also became largely inactive, with one important nearly complete exception—those in the armed forces. Many prominent cadres were denounced and disgraced and vanished from public life. Others—a much larger number in fact, since only about 1 per cent of the total Party membership was purged during the Cultural Revolution—worked on or under the gradually growing number of revolutionary committees formed, largely under military auspices, at and below the provincial level.

The Ninth Party Congress (April, 1969) registered the severe impact of the Cultural Revolution on the upper ranks of the CPC; a rough indicator was that only 30 per cent of the Eighth Central Committee (elected in 1956) were re-elected to the Ninth. The delegates to the Congress were evidently selected mainly by the revolutionary committees, rather than elected by Party organizations in the normal way. The new Central Committee was large, cumbersome, and included a number of obscure Maoists obviously lacking in real influence. The Politburo and its five-man Standing Committee (Mao, Lin Piao, Chou En-lai, Ch'en Po-ta, K'ang Sheng) were dominated by the tripartite coalition that had emerged more or less victorious from the Cultural Revolution: the Maoists, the military, and Chou En-lai's administrators.

The new Party constitution adopted at the Congress differed from the draft that had been circulating for about six months in that the final version dropped all references to the possibility of future Cultural Revolutions, specified that the Party should exercise leadership over the armed forces as well as over other sectors of society, and gave higher Party bodies control over the convening of congresses by lower bodies. Apart from these features, the constitution naturally acclaimed Mao Tse-tung as the Party's leader, implicitly for life, and his "thought" as the Party's ideological basis. In a unique and even more un-Leninist passage, Lin Piao was described as Mao's "close comrade-in-arms and successor." The Party's leading bodies, including the Central Committee, are described as being elected through "democratic consultation," a vague formula that appears to leave even more freedom than before for manipulation and domination of the process by the top leadership. There is no mention of a Party Secretariat or regional bureaus. It was made easier than before for new members to enter the Party by abolishing the requirement of a period of probation, a provision presumably designed originally to facilitate the mass entry of Red Guards and ex-Red Guards into the Party (which in fact has not occurred). In order to prevent the Party apparatus from re-entrenching itself and from blocking direct contact between Mao and individual Party members or criticism of the apparatus by the latter, Party members in disagreement with their superiors are authorized to make their views known directly to the Central Committee or even to Mao.

Rebuilding the Party Since the Cultural Revolution

After the Ninth Party Congress, the necessary task of rebuilding the Party apparatus, by restoring many pre–Cultural Revolution cadres to important posts, among other things, got gradually under way. It was done with little publicity, because of the bad image the apparatus had acquired during the Cultural Revolution.

This was especially true at the central level. The departments of the Central Committee, which had been under the control of the Secretariat, were revived cautiously; the United Front Work

Department, handling relations with non-Party bodies, was mentioned publicly in May, 1970, and the International Liaison Department, handling relations with foreign Communist Parties, in March, 1971. Other departments were referred to without being named, but there was no public reference to the Secretariat, which presumably no longer existed as a formal body (it had not been mentioned in the constitution adopted at the Ninth Party Congress), or at any rate was not functioning in anything like the pre–Cultural Revolution manner. The Communist Youth League, which had ceased to function in 1965 and been replaced in effect by the Red Guards, was cautiously revived; Maoist radicals evidently made an effort to revive the Red Guard organizations under the label Communist Youth League, but with little success. As during the Cultural Revolution, many cadres were sent for periods at May 7 schools (so called after a 1966 directive from Mao to Lin Piao), where the emphasis was on the study of Mao's "thought" and on often grueling manual labor.

Although the Central Committee's regional bureaus were not formally revived, some of their functions were apparently performed informally by the military regions of the PLA. Similarly, in addition to dominating the revolutionary committees, the military at the provincial level (meaning mainly the commands of the provincial military districts) played an important role in reviving the territorial Party committees. This was a slow process, however, perhaps because the military felt little enthusiasm for it and preferred the existing situation in which their control over local administration was more direct. The process began in more than a token way only after the military was prodded by a resolution of the Second Plenary Session of the Ninth Central Committee (August 23–September 6, 1970), at which there was admitted to have been "fierce debate" over this and other issues. The process of forming Party committees at the provincial and lower levels, more or less simultaneously rather than beginning at the bottom, then got under way in earnest. The first provincial-level Party Committee (for Hunan, Mao's native province) was established in December, 1970. The provincial-level Party committees, which emerged in an order clearly reflecting political considerations including the current status of Party leaders (Lin Piao's native province, Hupeh, was only sixteenth on the list of twenty-nine), were supposed to be completed by July 1, 1971, the Party's fiftieth anniversary, but the last ones were not actually formed until August, 1971. The first secretary of a provincial Party committee was always the chairman of the corresponding revolutionary committee as well, and in the great majority of instances he was a military man. In theory at least, the Party committees were entitled to give directives to the revolutionary committees, which were essentially governmental or administrative bodies, whose permanency furthermore was not assured in the absence of formal adoption of a new draft constitution for the state that the Party Central Committee approved in September, 1970 (see Chapter 8).

The rising influence of Chou En-lai and the decline and fall of Lin Piao paralleled, and probably contributed significantly to, a process of gradual demilitarization of the revolutionary committees, beginning at the local level, and apparently of the Party committees as well. It appeared that Chou En-lai had taken personal charge, since late 1970, of the crucial process of rebuilding the Party apparatus according to a new model whose outlines were not entirely clear. For that purpose, he appeared to have effectively displaced the ailing K'ang Sheng, who had been the fifth-ranking figure in the Party leadership since about May, 1968, and had been confirmed in that position at the Ninth Party Congress. There has been a noticeable tendency since the Congress, and still more since the overthrow of Lin Piao, to de-emphasize in propaganda pronouncements Mao's personal leadership of the Party in favor of the principle of "collective leadership" by the Central Committee, of which Chou En-lai seems to be the effective head.

FURTHER READINGS

Good analyses of the structure and functioning of the Leninist model of a Communist Party are scarce; a recent official Soviet one may be found in *Fundamentals of Marxism-Leninism*, rev. ed., Moscow: Foreign Languages Publishing House, 1963, Chapter 13, from which the quotation on democratic centralism is taken.

Two important, although rather abstract and difficult, works dealing among other things with the CPC as a Party are John Wilson Lewis, *Leadership in Communist China*, Ithaca, N.Y.: Cornell University Press, 1963; and Franz Schurmann, *Ideology and Organization in Communist China*, 2nd ed., Berkeley: University of California Press, 1969. Considerable detail on Party functioning may be found in A. Doak Barnett, *Cadres, Bureaucracy, and Political Power in Communist China*, New York: Columbia University Press, 1967. Valuable essays on various aspects of the Party are collected in John Wilson Lewis, ed., *Party Leadership and Revolutionary Power in China*, Cambridge: Cambridge University Press, 1970.

The 1945 Party constitution, together with Liu Shao-ch'i's commentary, "On the Party," can be found in *Collected Works of Liu Shao-ch'i, 1945–1957*, Hong Kong: Union Research Institute, 1969. The standard study of the emergence of the central work conference is Parris H. Chang's important "Research Notes on the Changing Loci of Decision in the CCP," *The China Quarterly*, no. 44 (October–December, 1970), pp. 169–94. The text of the 1956 Party constitution can be found in vol. ii of Peter S. H. Tang, *Communist China Today*, 2 vols, London: Thames & Hudson, 1957, New York: Praeger, 1958. The text of Teng Hsiao-p'ing's commentary on it at the Eighth Party Congress was released on September 18, 1956, but is not readily available in English except in American Consulate General, Hong Kong, *Current Background*, no. 417 (October 10, 1956).

An aspect of the CPC during the following decade is covered in Frederick C. Teiwes, *Provincial Party Personnel in Mainland China, 1956–1966*, New York: Columbia University East Asian Institute, 1967. Major developments in the years preceding the Cultural Revolution are treated in two important studies: Richard Baum and Frederick C. Teiwes, *Ssu-Ch'ing: The Socialist Movement of 1962–1966*, Berkeley: University of California Center for Chinese Studies, 1968; and Charles Neuhauser, "The Chinese Communist Party in the 1960's: Prelude to the Cultural Revolution," *The China Quarterly*, no. 32 (October–December, 1967), pp. 3–36. The effects of the Cultural Revolution are well covered in Charles Neuhauser, "The Impact of the Cultural Revolution on the Chinese Communist Party Machine," *Asian Survey*, vol. viii, no. 6 (June, 1968), pp. 465–88.

The documents relating to the Ninth Party Congress, including the new constitution, are available in American Consulate General, Hong Kong, *Current Background*, no. 880 (May 9, 1969); and *The Ninth National Congress of the Communist Party of China (Documents)*, Peking: Foreign Languages Press, 1969.

8. The State

As Marxist-Leninists, the Chinese Communists have always (except during the Cultural Revolution) stressed the need for a strong Communist Party; as Chinese, they have also attached much importance (again except for the Cultural Revolution period) to a state system elaborate and formal enough to render credible the Party's claim to legitimacy and authority, and effective enough to relieve the Party of many administrative responsibilities. "State" will be used here to refer in the broadest sense to the formal aspects of the political system (apart from the Party); "government" will be used in a narrow, European, sense to refer to what in the United States is called the Executive branch, in particular the Cabinet.

The Pre-1954 Situation

Since about 1930, whenever the CPC controlled a significant piece of territory (a base area, soviet, border region, or liberated area), it established some sort of government for it, under Party control of course. Probably the most ambitious and advanced of these prior to the formal establishment of the C.P.R. on October 1, 1949, were the North and Northeast China Regional Governments, created very shortly before. In this, as in many other ways, the CPC gained detailed experience that was to be invaluable after 1949. But from the Long March until 1949, there was no single state or government claiming jurisdiction over all the Communist-controlled areas in China.

The creation of such a state began in the spring of 1949, after the capture of Peking, with the formation of a large, essentially consultative body known as the Chinese People's Political Consultative Conference. It was considered to represent the increasingly comprehensive "united front" that the CPC claimed to be leading.

It included many non-Communists, all receptive to the CPC's leadership, but also many Communists, and it was unquestionably under the CPC's full control. It held its First Plenary Session in Peking at the end of September, 1949. In addition to hearing and approving reports by various Communist leaders, the session elected the principal officials of the new state and government, passed an Organic Law prescribing the organizing of the latter, and adopted a Common Program setting forth the general principles on which the new China, as it was then widely called, would formally be run. The Common Program was essentially a document designed to mobilize popular support by stressing the CPC's interim, or "democratic," goals, rather than its ultimate, or "socialist," ones, although the latter were in no way repudiated or concealed. After this session, the Chinese People's Political Consultative Conference continued to exist and even acquired local branches and otherwise proliferated, but it became increasingly unimportant now that its main function of legitimating the establishment of Communist rule had been performed. Like many other institutions, it entered a state of suspended animation during the Cultural Revolution.

The Organic Law did not mention the CPC, but it clearly implied Communist control over the new state by saying that the latter would be based on the classic Leninist organizational principle of democratic centralism (see Chapter 7). An All-China (later known as National) People's Congress was to be set up in due time through universal suffrage, as well as people's congresses at lower levels (principally province, municipality, and rural district).

The highest executive body of the state was the Central People's Government Council, chaired by Mao Tse-tung and endowed with sweeping powers of legislation, supervision, appointment, and so forth, over the entire state and government; its membership included almost all members of the CPC's ruling body, the Politburo.

The most important body supervised by the Central People's Government Council was the Government Administration Council (cabinet), headed by Chou En-lai as Chairman (or Premier). The latter body was designed and empowered to perform normal governmental functions, most of them of course administrative, through a fluctuating but always sizable number of subordinate ministries and commissions. Another such body was the People's Revolutionary Military Council, which was manned by major military as well as civilian figures and had charge over military policy and military affairs; this arrangement gave Mao Tse-tung, who chaired the People's Revolutionary Military Council as well as the Central People's Government Council, rather than Chou En-lai, formal authority over the armed forces. Similarly, when a powerfully staffed State Planning Committee was created under the chairmanship of Kao Kang in November, 1952, to draw up and implement the First Five-Year Plan, it came under the Central People's Government Council, rather than under the Government Administration Council. The Organic Law also specified as subordinate to the Central People's Government Council the Supreme People's Court and the Supreme People's Procuratorate (or public prosecutor), each with a network of subordinate bodies at lower levels.

There stood between the center and the provinces a group of powerful regional governments (for the Northeast, North China, Northwest China, East China, Southwest China, and Central-South China), which, by force of circumstances and like the corresponding regional bureaus of the CPC Central Committee, initially were to a considerable extent under military influence (see Chapter 3). In late 1952, mainly as another preliminary to centralized economic planning, the powers of the regional governments were reduced. In June, 1954, after the purge of Kao Kang (see Chapter 3) and as part of the preparation for the introduction of a formal constitution, the regional governments were abolished. Thus, the central government was brought into direct contact with the next lower territorial units—the provinces (decreasing in number through consolidation during this period), the special municipalities (Peking, Shanghai, and, after 1967, Tientsin) and the autonomous regions (for major national minorities).

The 1954 Constitution and Its Application

These institutions were designed to be essentially transitional; the process of "building socialism," which began in 1953, seemed to require new, more permanent ones. At the beginning of 1953, accordingly, the Central People's Government Council set up a committee headed by Mao Tse-tung to draft a permanent state constitution and set in motion machinery, including an electoral law, for holding elections to a National People's Congress, which was to ratify the constitution, elect the major officials to serve under it, and approve the First Five-Year Plan. A number of difficulties combined to delay the convening of the National

Chart 2

State System of the People's Republic of China, 1954 to the Cultural Revolution (simplified)

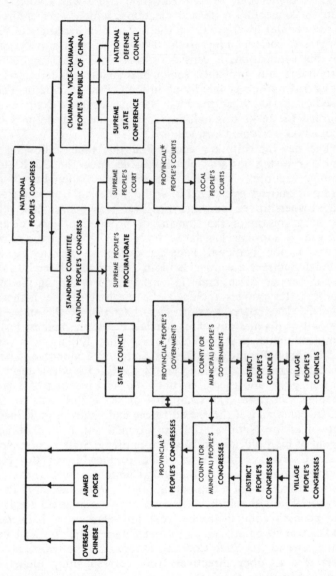

* Or Special Municipality or Autonomous Region (under each of which the names of the subordinate units are somewhat different from those shown on the chart).

Reprinted from Major Governments of Asia, 2d ed., edited by George McTurnan Kahin.
© 1958 and 1963 by Cornell University. Used by permission of Cornell University Press.

People's Congress from late 1953, when it was originally scheduled, to September, 1954. Meanwhile, there was a voter registra-
tion in connection with the elections, which were indirect and
at the popular level produced the lowest of a hierarchy of people's
congresses corresponding to the layers of administrative geography.
In this connection, a census of sorts was also conducted, the
astounding but probably somewhat underestimated total result
being 583 million people living in the C.P.R. (excluding Taiwan).
Needless to say, when the First National People's Congress met, it
fulfilled the tasks originally given it by the now defunct Central
People's Government Council.

The new constitution adopted at this time, following a preamble stressing socialist objectives, declared the C.P.R. to be a
unitary republic, in which the various "nationalities" (ethnic
groups) enjoyed equality, but without the right of secession. Private ownership of personal property was guaranteed, although
the socialization of the "means of production" was clearly envisaged. A supreme legislative body (the "highest organ of state
power"), the National People's Congress, was to be formed
through indirect elections held in the principal territorial units
and the armed forces and (at least in theory) among the overseas
Chinese. Its powers included the election of the highest state
officials. The power to supervise the work of the state, and to
appoint or dismiss any of its officials below the highest level (the
main individual thus protected being Chou En-lai), was vested in
the National People's Congress's Standing Committee. The Chief
of State would be the Chairman of the C.P.R., whose term was to
be four years and thereafter until the next meeting of a National
People's Congress. The Chairman of the C.P.R. was to exercise
titular command of the armed forces and chair an undefined body
known as the National Defense Council and a kind of personal
forum of high officials entitled the Supreme State Conference. The
State Council, which was to be responsible to the National
People's Congress and its Standing Committee, was to exercise the
normal functions of a cabinet. Similarly, it was declared that each
territorial unit should have its own people's congress (legislature)
and people's council (executive); the relationship between these
bodies was to be analogous to that between the National People's
Congress and the State Council, except that the people's councils
were also to obey directives from corresponding higher bodies
(and, ultimately, the State Council). A hierarchy of courts and
procuratorates corresponding to the territorial levels of the state

was established. The civil rights and social welfare of private citizens were guaranteed in great detail; no provision was made for suspending these rights through executive or legislative action.

The operation of the 1954 state constitution prior to the Cultural Revolution, a complex subject many of whose details are unknown outside China, can be considered under four headings: the National People's Congress and its Standing Committee, the Chairmanship of the C.P.R., the State Council, and local government.

The National People's Congress met approximately annually until the Cultural Revolution, for a total of ten sessions (1954–60, 1962, 1963, and 1964–65). There are officially considered to have been three National People's Congresses, because its membership was elected three times (1953–54, 1959, 1964). It performed essentially the same rubber-stamp functions as the Soviet Union's Supreme Soviet or analogous bodies in other Communist countries: hearing reports by high officials and "electing" some of them (in reality, approving their previous selection at the highest level in the CPC). The agendas and all other aspects of the National People's Congress were highly sensitive to general political developments; for example, the number of deputies attending sessions of the First and Second National People's Congresses declined steadily after each election, a probable reflection of purges and other manifestations of political tension, as well as natural attrition; in a genuine parliamentary system, these vacancies would of course have been filled through by-elections or some other means. The Third National People's Congress, which met only once (December, 1964–January, 1965), had more than twice as many deputies as the first two (roughly 2,800 as against 1,200). On two occasions (in 1957 and 1962), the National People's Congress met in closed session prior to the beginning of its formal public session in order to facilitate orientation and control by the Standing Committee and ultimately by the Party leadership. In addition to its domestic public-relations function of creating a façade of domestic and parliamentary government, the National People's Congress sometimes performed an external function as well: delegations representing it visited friendly foreign countries at intervals between 1956 and 1965.

Given the largely theoretical character of the National People's Congress's authority, its Standing Committee possessed little authority. This was not the result of any failure to meet. The First Standing Committee met 109 times, the Second 137 times, and the

Third 32 times. The Chairman of the First, Liu Shao-ch'i, drew his undoubted influence from his second-ranking position in the Party hierarchy; he apparently never succeeded, in spite of his obvious liking for constitutional formalities, in making the Standing Committee into much more than a figurehead body. This may have been partly due, as in the Soviet Union, to the relatively greater prestige and influence of the State Council (in the Soviet Union, Council of Ministers), which was the main body supposedly supervised by the Standing Committee, since it and the National People's Congress had no real authority over the people's congresses at lower levels. When Liu gave up the chairmanship of the Standing Committee in 1959 to become Chairman of the C.P.R. in succession to Mao Tse-tung, his former state office passed to Marshal Chu Teh, a venerable but somewhat obsolete figure who had previously been Vice Chairman of the C.P.R. and who obviously was in no position to enhance the limited role of the Standing Committee.

Although the 1954 constitution left open the possibility that the Chairman of the C.P.R. (an office for which no analogue exists in the Soviet Union) might be intended to be a figurehead, the fact that the first Chairman was Mao Tse-tung indicates that such was not exactly the case. For one thing, Mao convened the Supreme State Conference, whose composition he was entitled to determine, sixteen times during his tenure as Chairman of the C.P.R. (1954–59) and, on certain of those occasions (notably February 27, 1957), made important personal policy statements to it. Indeed, apart from prestige, the power to convene the Supreme State Conference was probably the most important feature of the chairmanship. It can be demonstrated that Mao had decided by early 1958 to give up the chairmanship of the C.P.R., and this decision can be correlated with high plausibility with his political feud with the "revisionist" Tito, who held an analogous title and post.

Liu Shao-ch'i, on the other hand, sent a message of greeting to Tito on every Yugoslav National Day (November 28) that fell during his effective tenure as Chairman of the C.P.R. (1959–65). Liu had not one Vice Chairman, as had been true under Mao, but two: the elderly Communist Tung Pi-wu and the non-Communist Sung Ch'ing-ling (Mme. Sun Yat-sen). Liu clearly made a serious effort to enhance the dignity and power of the chairmanship of the C.P.R. (although he is known to have convened the Supreme State Conference on only five occasions) and to use it as one of the bases for his gradually escalating power struggle with Mao. It is equally clear that in both respects he essentially failed. The main reason was his own shortage of "charisma" and Mao's vastly greater prestige within the Party and throughout the country. Even when the two men (each referred to as Chairman) appeared together on state occasions after 1959, Mao was always listed first in press accounts. The main area in which Liu exploited publicly the potential of the chairmanship of the C.P.R. was diplomacy. Mao traveled abroad while Chairman of the C.P.R. only once (to the Soviet Union, in 1957), and even then he went in his Party rather than in his state capacity. Liu, on the other hand, visited Communist and friendly non-Communist countries in 1963 and 1966 in his state capacity, and on at least one occasion conducted important negotiations. This performance was counted strongly against him during the Cultural Revolution by Red Guard critics, who presumably reflected, if in exaggerated degree, Mao's own antiformalistic tendencies and sense of rivalry. It is possible that Liu tried to capitalize on his titular command of the armed forces to check the efforts of Mao and Lin Piao, after the fall of P'eng Te-huai, to politicize the army further, and use it for partisan purposes, but if so, he obviously failed.

Whatever various Chinese leaders may have thought about the state system, none could dispute the need for an effective State Council. Its role was essentially administrative and had as few ideological and political overtones as it is possible for any aspect of the political system in a Communist country to have. It left policy-making to the Party, along with the launching of mass campaigns and the supervision of the apparatus, cadres, and mass organizations. The leader of the State Council, Chou En-lai, was exceedingly capable and prestigious. In Parkinsonian fashion, the number of ministries and commissions under the State Council, most of them concerned with economic affairs, grew steadily to about fifty. The meetings of the State Council were more frequent (about one a month from 1954 to 1966) and more businesslike than those of any other body within the state system. Correspondingly, there was a somewhat lower turnover of leading personnel than elsewhere in the state system. Some of the C.P.R.'s most prestigious figures, nearly all of them CPC members, served under Chou En-lai as vice premiers, ministers, and chairmen of commissions, often in addition to other duties. One of the ways in which Party control over the State Council was assured, apart from the obvious fact that Premier Chou sat on the Politburo, was through the continuous presence of General Secretary Teng Hsiao-p'ing, the effective head of the Party apparatus, as a senior Vice Premier. He was named Acting Premier during some of Chou's early (but not later) absences abroad, and there are reasons for believing that he antagonized Chou by trying to play too active a role within the State Council. He may also have tried to assert a stronger role for the Party committees within bodies under the State Council than Chou was willing to accept.

The bodies under the State Council, as well as the lower-level analogues they supervised, were grouped somewhat vaguely into approximately ten functional "systems" (*hsi-t'ung*) dealing with political and legal affairs, propaganda and education, finance and trade, and the like. At any of the local levels, as at the center, bodies under the People's Council were subject to close supervision in various forms by the corresponding Party organs. The principal personnel of the People's Council were "elected" by the People's Congress after being selected by the appropriate local Party committee. Thus, the local people's councils and their subordinate agencies were supervised from above by the State Council and horizontally by the corresponding local Party committees. It was seemingly a cumbersome system, but in practice it generally worked well. The major reason for this relative efficiency was probably that no one, except perhaps Chou En-lai with respect to his own operations, disputed the primacy in practice of the Party (including its apparatus) over the state system (including the government), a logical view since all key state officials were Party members when they assumed their state offices.

The Impact of the Cultural Revolution

From a power-political point of view, the Cultural Revolution can be regarded essentially as an offensive by the ideologists (under Mao Tse-tung), the army (under Lin Piao), and the government bureaucracy (under Chou En-lai) against the Party apparatus. As a leading member of the victorious coalition, and given Chou En-lai's great and growing personal prestige and influence, the bureaucracy succeeded in maintaining a reasonable level of operating efficiency during the Cultural Revolution. Chou set himself from the beginning to extract concessions from his allies, especially Mao, for his constituency as an explicit or implicit price for his participation in the Cultural Revolution. It is highly probable that Chou was mainly responsible for the promise made at the time of the Eleventh Central Committee Plenary Session (August, 1966) that specialists with needed skills would not be treated as targets of the Cultural Revolution as long as they did their work well and maintained no ties with foreign powers.

Although Chou was active during the ensuing months in publicly urging the Red Guards not to disrupt the economy, which was one of the State Council's responsibilities, the pledge was by no means fully kept. Chou was occasionally criticized by Red Guards, and, to a much greater extent, several of his vice premiers (notably Foreign Minister Ch'en Yi) were also criticized. Chou succeeded in saving from actual purging only six of his fifteen vice premiers, including Ch'en Yi and Lin Piao (who did not need saving); needless to say, Teng Hsiao-p'ing was not one of those saved. About half the ministers disappeared and must be presumed purged. Some of the ministries, notably the Foreign Ministry, from August 19 to 22, 1967, experienced physical "power seizures" by Red Guards and other militants. Chou's general approach was to try to manage the turbulence, to safeguard essentials by appearing to cooperate cheerfully with the unavoidable minimum amount of disruptive activity. He succeeded in preventing the establishment of revolutionary committees within agencies under the State Council; if they had been set up, "three-way alliances" would have been necessary, with the result that the army would have been brought in and probably would have become dominant. The State Council ceased to hold formal plenary meetings after March, 1966. Nevertheless, essential administrative and economic functions, with the major exceptions of the police and the rail system, continued to operate during the Cultural Revolution with reasonable efficiency.

The other elements of the state system, being associated to one degree or another with Liu Shao-ch'i, suffered much more severely than did the State Council. During 1965 and the first half of 1966, as Maoist pressures to launch the Cultural Revolution intensified, Liu became increasingly inactive as Chairman of the C.P.R., and after mid-1966 the office itself became a dead letter. By the same token, the National People's Congress, its Standing Committee, the Supreme State Conference, and the National Defense Council ceased to meet after early 1965. The hierarchies of people's Courts and people's procuratorates became virtually inoperative; their functions were apparently performed by the revolutionary committees.

At the three levels below the center, the people's congresses and people's councils ceased to function during the Cultural Revolution. Their functions, or a more informal version of them, were assumed by the corresponding revolutionary committees, those at the provincial level being probably the most important. The major revolutionary committees were essentially controlled in every case except probably one (Shanghai) by their military components (see Chapter 4). A varying but significant degree of continuity and effectiveness was ensured, except for a few areas unusually prone to violence, by the military's practice of retaining or taking back in key administrative posts as many of the pre–Cultural Revolution Party and government cadres as had not been formally denounced as anti-Maoist to the point of being hopelessly compromised. The Red Guards frequently complained about this practice, which however contributed greatly to efficiency and stability.

Rebuilding the State System After the Cultural Revolution

During the Cultural Revolution and into 1970, the State Council and its subordinate agencies underwent a massive shrinkage, due partly to purging and partly to reductions in force for other reasons. The number of ministries, commissions, and other agencies at the center declined, mainly through mergers, from 90 to 26; the number of personnel fell from roughly 60,000 to about 10,000. There was an increase, although not a sharp one, in the number of cabinet posts held by military men; this trend probably represented an effort by Chou En-lai to keep on good terms with elements of the military, and quite possibly to split them from Lin Piao. At its new, lower level, the State Council began to stabilize. It even began—thanks partly to the importance of its functions, partly to Chou En-lai's increasing influence, and partly to the virtual annihilation of the other major components of the state system during the Cultural Revolution—to take on greater significance than before. The public security bureaus began to revive in 1970. A major innovation was the unannounced creation, probably late in 1960 or early in 1970, of a so-called Cultural Group under the State Council which almost certainly took over the functions of the once-important Cultural Revolution Group, headed by Ch'en Po-ta, which had been nominally under the Party Central Committee. The transfer of the function of cultural control from Party to state auspices may have been one of the issues leading to Ch'en Po-ta's fall during 1970.

The status of Liu Shao-ch'i, as Chairman of the C.P.R. and in his other capacities, remained obscure until it was announced in mid-October, 1968, that he had "long ago" been deprived "of all power and positions both within the Party and outside it." The lack of a Chief of State became a serious embarrassment the following year, as the C.P.R. began to normalize its foreign relations. Accordingly, Vice Chairman Tung Pi-wu began to perform the protocol functions of the chairmanship, without however being given the title of Acting Chairman until the beginning of 1972.

The main reason for this delay was likely the obvious indecision, and probable disagreement, within the leadership over what to do about the broader and more important problems of drafting a new, post–Cultural Revolution state constitution paralleling the one adopted for the Party at the Ninth Congress in April, 1969, and of convening another National People's Congress to ratify the new constitution. The draft of a new state constitution was adopted, probably after considerable debate, at the Second Plenary Session of the Ninth Central Committee (August 23–September 6, 1970) and was then circulated without being formally published. Far briefer and less formal than the 1954 constitution, it also differed from its predecessor not only in praising Mao Tse-tung but (like the new Party constitution) in naming Lin Piao as his successor. The office of Chairman of the C.P.R. was abolished, and there was in effect to be no formal Chief of State. The National People's Congress and its Standing Committee, the Supreme People's Court, and the State Council were continued, although their functions were left somewhat vaguer than before. The National People's Congress appeared to lose its power to elect the leading officials. The Supreme People's Procuratorate was abolished. It is very likely that Lin Piao was eager to have the National People's Congress meet and adopt this constitution, thereby formalizing his role in the state, vague though it would be, as the Ninth Party Congress had done in the Party. It is equally likely that his opponents, led by Chou En-lai, objected and that the issue was one of those leading to Lin's fall in September, 1971. After that, various difficulties, including presumably the problem of what to do about the draft constitution, continued to delay the convening of the National People's Congress.

At the local level, the permanency of the revolutionary committees as government bodies was specified in the draft constitution, whereas previously they had generally been spoken of as temporary bodies. Permanent or not, the revolutionary committees tended to yield priority to new, post–Cultural Revolution Party committees after the latter began to be formed in 1970. "Revolutionary" elements like the Red Guards tended to be squeezed out of the revolutionary committees. Many military personnel were withdrawn from local revolutionary committees in 1971, although apparently not from those at the provincial level. Perhaps in an effort to mask these shifts, the "three-way alliances" began to be spoken of as consisting of "old, middle-aged, and young people." The dubious status in 1972 of the draft state constitution appears to leave the future of the revolutionary committees also in doubt.

FURTHER READINGS

As is true of other Communist countries, there are relatively few good published studies of the Chinese state and government, as contrasted with the Party. For the early period, S. B. Thomas, *Government and Administration in Communist China*, rev. ed., New York: Institute of Pacific Relations, 1953, is detailed and objective. Much information on a typical central ministry and local government, based on interviews with refugee cadres, is presented in A. Doak Barnett, *Cadres, Bureaucracy, and Political Power in Communist China*, New York: Columbia University Press, 1967.

Some aspects of the fate of the state and government during the Cultural Revolution, with emphasis on the State Council, are treated in Thomas W. Robinson, *The Cultural Revolution in China*, Berkeley: University of California Press, 1971, pp. 165–312; and Donald W. Klein, "The State Council and the Cultural Revolution," *The China Quarterly*, no. 35 (July–September, 1968), pp. 78–95.

The information presented on the period since the Cultural Revolution is based mainly on original Chinese sources. The figures on the reduction of State Council agencies and personnel were given by Chou En-lai to Edgar Snow and appear in "Talks with Chou En-lai: The Open Door," *The New Republic*, March 27, 1971, p. 21).

9. The Armed Forces

The performance of the PLA in the post-"liberation" period, especially in the first years after 1949, was heavily conditioned by its earlier history. There is no space here for even a summary of that history, but it is worth noting the main reasons the PLA had emerged victorious from the civil war, despite the fact that, for about two years after 1945, the Nationalists had a clear superiority in number of troops, equipment, and level of foreign aid and support. Nevertheless, the effects of the war against Japan told far more heavily on the Nationalists than on the CPC, although those effects were much more pronounced on the Nationalists' home front than on their armed forces. The advantage in political leadership, policy-making, and the viability of the home front lay heavily on the side of the CPC and had an important influence on the war efforts of both sides. This was equally true of strictly military leadership, strategy, and tactics; the CPC had a significant positional advantage because it controlled the key areas of North China from which conquests of the country had traditionally originated. The Nationalists' tactical mobility was if anything hampered by their inadequately maintained American motorized equipment, whereas the largely foot-slogging PLA could manage forty miles a day when necessary. The PLA, partly because its commanders were far less corrupt, was much more successful than the Nationalists in ensuring the adequate feeding and logistical support of its troops, at a modest but viable level. These advantages, reinforced by more intensive political control and indoctrination, produced a marked superiority of morale for the PLA. From these ingredients came victory.

Post-"Liberation" Missions

Like any military establishment, the PLA fulfills some of its current missions simply by existing and without being employed in combat. This has ordinarily been true of its first mission, that of serving as the ultimate guarantor of domestic control and public order. In other words, the regime's normal political controls have generally been sufficient for this purpose, but the PLA has, of course, been available as a supplement or replacement if needed. The most consistent need for military intervention to cope with popular unrest has occurred in the national minority areas, especially Tibet (see Chapter 12). Prior to the Cultural Revolution, once the post–civil war mopping-up was completed, there was seldom any need to use the PLA for this purpose, except in the non–Han-inhabited border areas; the main exceptions occurred just after the end of the Great Leap Forward in the traditionally turbulent provinces of the central Yangtze Valley. During and immediately after the Cultural Revolution, and especially in the autumns of 1967 and 1968, the PLA was used extensively to restore and maintain order, because the breakdown of the normal civil mechanisms had rendered them incapable of doing so.

Like the armies of many other developing countries, the PLA has been used consciously and systematically by its political leadership as an effective instrument of economic development. The PLA has contributed to this end by such measures as growing some of its own food, constructing public works (roads, bridges, and the like), operating factories to help meet its own needs, and helping in the agricultural operations of the peasants. Although not quantifiable, the PLA's contribution to the Chinese economy has obviously been substantial.

Prior to 1949, the PLA helped to mobilize the populace of the Communist areas in support of the CPC's programs. This task was performed in particular by personnel of the PLA's political apparatus, in spite of the disapproval of many of the commanders and apparently of some civilian Party leaders, including Chou En-lai. After 1949, as the Party's civilian membership expanded and the PLA confined itself increasingly to a purely military role, this practice largely ceased, except that the adoption of conscription in 1955 gave the PLA an opportunity to give political indoctrination as well as military training to a substantial fraction of the country's young manpower. After Lin Piao became Defense Minister in 1959 and still more as the Cultural Revolution approached, PLA political personnel again began to be used outside the armed forces in ways that are described below.

The PLA is expected to provide border security to whatever extent may be necessary, a concept that includes the prevention as far as possible of unauthorized movement across the frontiers. It also includes on occasion the conduct of political activity amounting to propaganda among minority peoples invited from across the border, as for example the Sino-Burmese border in the mid-1950's. For a variety of reasons that appear to include promotion of border security and gaining of leverage on adjacent countries, the PLA has engaged since the mid-1950's in road-building on territory belonging to or at least claimed by a neighboring state, and in linking these roads with the Chinese road network. This has occurred along China's entire southern border, with varying degrees of consent from the other countries concerned. Probably the most important of these roads are those leading into Pakistani-held Kashmir, the Aksai Chin area (claimed by India as the northeast corner of Kashmir), Nepal (to Katmandu), and northwestern Laos.

The PLA is, of course, China's military deterrent (there are political deterrents as well) to a possible attack by a foreign adversary, meaning primarily the United States at first and the Soviet Union in recent years. At the conventional level, deterrence is achieved not only by offering the adversary the prospect of an exceedingly tough fight if he should—as is unlikely—try to invade China, but also by threatening retaliation on the ground against the enemy's territory or allies for any kind of attack (a "war without boundaries" was the phrase used in this context in 1965, the time of the escalation of the war in Vietnam). The C.P.R. has been creating a nuclear deterrent force since about 1956 (see below).

If deterrence is thought to be failing, or likely to fail, the PLA has been known to try what amounted to pre-emption, or a spoiling attack, in order to prevent an actually or supposedly hostile army from installing itself next to China's frontiers and perhaps becoming emboldened to put pressure on China. The two main instances of this sort have been the Chinese intervention in the Korean War (1950) and the attack on the Indian Army (1962). A much less spectacular example was the intrusion by a small Chinese force into the Kachin State, in northern Burma, in 1956, apparently for the main purpose of putting pressure on the Burmese Government to ensure that no arms moved through the area to the Khamba guerrillas in eastern Tibet (see Chapter 12). Although the PLA and its civilian leadership have displayed excessive (but perhaps understandable) sensitivity regarding the security of China's borders and border regions, they are also capable of showing restraint for military or political reasons. Since the Soviet Union is not only a genuine (that is, territorial) Asian power but also a very strong, as well as a formerly friendly, one, the C.P.R. has necessarily tolerated a Soviet military presence next to the Chinese border as it would not tolerate an American presence in 1950. The PLA has generally refrained from taking punitive action across the border against Khambas who have taken refuge in northern Nepal since 1959 and have been raiding Tibet, presumably because to take such action would tend to push Nepal undesirably and unnecessarily close to India.

The PLA provides military aid (arms, with or without training) to carefully selected friendly foreign governments. The most substantial of its military aid programs are those in North Korea, North Vietnam, Pakistan, Tanzania, and Albania. The PLA also provides arms, and sometimes training as well, to guerrilla movements or "people's wars" regarded in Peking as politically useful. Probably the main current examples of this are the programs for the Communist guerrilla movements in South Vietnam, Laos, Cambodia, Malaysia, and the Philippines; the tribal insurrections in northern Burma and northern Thailand; the Arab guerrilla movements in the Palestine area and along the Persian Gulf; and assorted tribal insurgencies and guerrilla movements in sub-Saharan Africa, especially those aimed at the "White Redoubt" countries (South Africa, Rhodesia, Angola, and Mozambique).

In the improbable contingency of a major attack on China, the PLA would, of course, be called on to conduct defensive operations, whose nature would vary according to the nature of the attack. Against an air attack, active (air defense) and passive (civil defense) measures would presumably be employed. An invasion, assuming a technically superior invader, would probably be met with a somewhat decentralized defense in depth supplemented by a "people's war" waged by the militia and the populace.

The PLA has an obvious, although rather complex, relationship to the CPC's goal of "liberating" Taiwan. The PLA was actually preparing for an amphibious invasion of the island in early 1950 until stopped not only by the intrinsic difficulties of the operation but also by the outbreak of war in Korea and the simultaneous extension of American protection to Taiwan (June 27, 1950). Since then, the PLA has been unable to pose a credible threat to, much less mount an actual attack on, Taiwan. It has maintained a superiority over the Nationalist armed forces, however, sufficient to deny any credibility to the central Nationalist myth of a "return to the mainland." Communist military superiority is one reason that if unification occurs, it will obviously have to be largely, although not necessarily entirely, on the mainland's terms.

To date, the PLA has not engaged in overt military action on or against foreign territory primarily for aggressive purposes or for the promotion of revolution. Any such action has been taken for reasons of national security and has been, at least in Peking's eyes, essentially defensive in nature. On the basis of this record, it is certainly fair to conclude that the CPC leadership does not regard overt military action across frontiers for either aggressive or revolutionary purposes as one of the PLA's missions. The record was compiled, however, during a period when the C.P.R. would have been prevented from taking such action even had it wished to do so because it was subject to unilateral nuclear deterrence by the United States and the Soviet Union. The time is approaching, however, although how soon it would be difficult to say, when the C.P.R. will possess at least a minimum nuclear deterrent of its own; in other words, it will be able to inflict "unacceptable" nuclear damage in retaliation for a possible nuclear first strike against itself by another power. In theory at least, the C.P.R. will then be able to hold a "nuclear umbrella" over itself, and perhaps over its allies, and neutralize the superior nuclear striking power of its adversaries. Since this will be an unprecedented situation for China, it is impossible to predict with any certainty what its behavior in those conditions would be. China might begin to practice "nuclear blackmail" or apply conventional military pressures against its non-nuclear neighbors. But such a course would still be militarily risky and would create serious political drawbacks in addition to some possible political gains. The probabilities, therefore, seem to be against aggressive Chinese behavior under cover of a minimum (or better) nuclear deterrent, but the possibility cannot logically be entirely excluded. The Maoist propaganda assertion that China is incapable of acting aggressively toward its neighbors because its foreign policy is a projection of its domestic policy and because the latter is good (by definition) hardly rises, to adapt a famous American judicial quotation, to the dignity of argument.

Organization, Controls, Capabilities

Since 1930, the CPC Central Committee appears to have had under one name or another a Military Affairs Committee composed largely of military men that served as the Party's highest body for the formulation of military policy in the broadest sense. From 1949 to 1954, it was paralleled in the state system by the People's Revolutionary Military Council, a powerful body chaired by Mao Tse-tung *ex officio* (as Chairman of the Central People's Government Council) but one that was not under the jurisdiction of Chou En-lai's Government Administration Council (or cabinet), a situation that must not have been entirely satisfactory to Chou. In September, 1954, the new state constitution named the Chairman of the C.P.R. Commander-in-Chief of the armed forces, abolished the People's Revolutionary Military Council, and replaced it with a much weaker, largely honorary body, the National Defense Council. At the same time, there was created a Ministry of National Defense (or Defense Ministry) under the State Council (the new name for the cabinet). A number of the other ministries are concerned mainly with the production of military equipment. The first Defense Minister was P'eng Te-huai; he also served as effective Chairman of the Military Affairs Committee, although Mao Tse-tung appears to have been its formal Chairman since 1935. The Defense Ministry is essentially, although informally, subordinate to the Military Affairs Committee, but the relationship has been at once eased and obscured by putting the same individual in effective charge of both. Under the Defense Ministry since 1954 stands, also rather informally, the PLA General Staff. At the time of P'eng Te-huai's replacement by Lin Piao in 1959, Lo Jui-ch'ing (until then Minister of Public Security) replaced Huang K'o-ch'eng as Chief of Staff, and the departments under the General Staff were consolidated to three: the General Staff Department (controlling the combat arms), the General Rear Services Department (for logistics), and the General Political Department (for political control and indoctrination). For the purposes of this book, the last of these is clearly the most important.

Also for the purposes of this discussion, the navy and air force may be largely ignored, since their political role has generally been minor compared with that of the army (or ground forces). Below the central level, the ground forces are divided into two major components: the main forces (the principal combat forces from army corps downward, responsible to the Military Affairs Committee through the General Staff) and the regional forces (territorial units responsible to the Defense Ministry). The regional forces are grouped under eleven military regions (thirteen before 1969–70, when Inner Mongolia and Tibet were downgraded to military districts), each designated by the name of the city where its head-

Chart 3

The People's Liberation Army, 1971

(simplified)

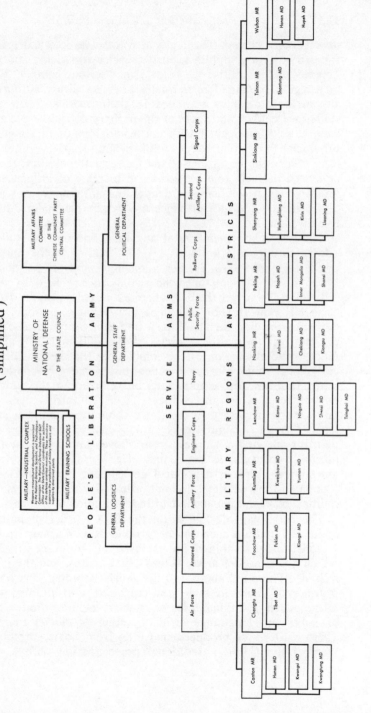

quarters are located. The regional forces are designed principally for garrison duty, public security, service functions, and training (mainly of the militia; see below), not serious combat. The military region commanders normally have no direct authority over any main force units stationed in their regions. Their political staffs (see below) and those of the military districts have normally been closely interlocked with the leaderships of the regional and provincial Party committees (until the Cultural Revolution, at any rate). Since the beginning of the Cultural Revolution, the army's enhanced political role has led to an increase of influence for the military region commanders. Under the military regions are military districts, one to a province or comparable major administrative division.

The two senior members of any PLA line unit or staff section (down through the battalion level), whether in the main forces or the regional forces, are the commander and the political officer ("commissar"). Sometimes the two posts are held by the same individual, who can then be assumed to be especially trusted or especially powerful, or both. The institution of political officer is derived from the Soviet military tradition. A political officer has control over the political affairs of the unit and can, at least in theory, veto any action by the commander that he considers politically undesirable, but not a tactical order issued in combat conditions. Disputes are supposed to be referred to the unit's Party committee, of which the political officer ordinarily serves as secretary, and if necessary to the Party committee at the next higher level. The Party committee, again in theory, decides on the best plan for carrying out orders from above; implementation is then normally entrusted to the commander. For large units (regiment and above), there is a political department that ranks as a staff section and whose director is not ordinarily the same person as the political officer; it is in charge of indoctrination of troops.

The best available figures on the PLA's order of battle show about 2.5 million men in the ground forces (main forces and regional forces combined, but exclusive of public security forces—which guard border areas, forced labor camps, and the like—and militia). There are about 140 divisions, including 2 airborne and 5 armored. These units are well equipped with infantry weapons, all produced in China. Heavy equipment includes limited numbers of tanks and long-range artillery, either of Soviet manufacture (before 1960) or produced in China from Soviet prototypes. In view of the C.P.R.'s traditional preoccupation with a (real or assumed) American and Nationalist threat, the major concentrations of ground forces are in southern Manchuria and along the eastern coast, especially opposite Taiwan. There is also a substantial concentration near Wuhan, presumably as a strategic reserve. Probably for logistical reasons, there have not been large concentrations along China's southern border (including the Indochina sector), nor along the Sino-Soviet border (for the same reason plus the normal Chinese Communist preference for defense in depth against superior opponents). There are indications, however, that in 1972 the forces near the Sino-Soviet border, especially in Manchuria, began to be reinforced.

The navy controls about 30 submarines of Soviet design or manufacture and a few hundred motor torpedo boats, and of course has access to thousands of motorized junks capable of carrying troops or equipment. It is not a navy capable of operating, even defensively, far from the China coast, and certainly not beyond the edge of the continental shelf.

The air force has about 3,000 combat aircraft of Soviet type, including a few MIG-21 fighters. Most of these are obsolescent, and probably in poor condition. The pilots have little combat experience. The C.P.R. is beginning to manufacture some medium bombers of its own.

The C.P.R. has been involved in a nuclear-weapons program since 1957 and has been testing nuclear warheads since 1964. By late 1972, it had succeeded in deploying between 20 and 40 surface-to-surface nuclear-capable missiles of up to 1,000-mile range, presumably liquid-fueled and vulnerable to a hostile first strike; their location and targeting are not a matter of public record. Contrary to many predictions, the C.P.R. has not yet tested a missile of intercontinental range, except in connection with the orbiting of its two earth satellites (April, 1970, and March, 1971).

The PLA's current strategic capabilities can be assessed, somewhat impressionistically, as follows. It is approaching the acquisition of a minimum nuclear deterrent (regional rather than intercontinental) against the two nuclear "superpowers," in the case of the United States mainly through the ability to treat U.S. Asian allies as hostages. It is modernizing its conventional capabilities, especially in armored warfare and air defense. The PLA has already proven itself capable of pre-empting, on a limited front, a presumed threat to the security of China's frontiers, provided of course that such an act does not seem to create an unacceptable risk of "massive retaliation." If necessary, the PLA appears fully capable of waging an effective defense on its own territory; presumably it would be a defense in depth, supplemented by a "people's war" waged by the militia and much of the population. As for operations outside China, it is clear that the PLA has the capability to conduct essentially nonmilitary activities (such as road-building) in nearby areas and to give aid and training to friendly governments and approved revolutionary movements. Major offensive operations on foreign soil are another story. The PLA's "strategic reach" (long-distance mobility by land, sea, and air) and its firepower (as compared with that of the American and Soviet forces) are limited, although they are slowly improving. China is surrounded by difficult terrain barriers and wide expanses of open water. These considerations, plus of course the risks of retaliation, appear to place severe limitations, at least in the near future as in the past, on the PLA's ability as well as on its probable willingness to attempt major offensive operations on foreign soil, except perhaps in immediately adjacent areas.

The Field Army System

As in any military establishment, the military and political behavior of any Chinese officer can be plausibly assumed, although not proved, to be the result of various factors, including geographic origins, civilian education, personal associations, and simple accident. In practice, perhaps the most important influence on a man's outlook is the requirements of the position he currently holds. His "military style," or professional outlook, has been defined as consisting of his views on three questions: the role of the military in society, the proper authority of a commander over his unit, and the appropriate criteria for promotion. Another perspective that can be employed in appraising outlook, performance, and associations is that of the "military generation" to which a given officer belongs—that is, the time (not age) and circumstances in which he began his military career. One authority has distinguished eleven "military generations" in the PLA (the last emerging after 1967).

The concept of "military style" can be applied to the prevailing character of an entire military establishment; in that case, one would try to evaluate the nature and effectiveness of its organization, its prevailing strategic concepts, and its battlefield tactics. In the PLA, "military style" is an outgrowth to a high degree of what may be called the field army system.

Since about 1930, the Chinese Red Army (renamed the People's Liberation Army in 1948) has been largely a collection of regional armies, which were reorganized under new names several times during the next two decades. In February, 1949, the major forces were regrouped into five field armies. The First began as the Second Front Army under Ho Lung and, under a different name, came under the command of P'eng Te-huai toward the end of the civil war; before the Long March, it operated mainly in the central Yangtze Valley, and thereafter mainly in Northwest China. Its leadership suffered a weakening of military position and political influence as a result of the purging of P'eng in 1959, but it was the only field army to be affected in this way. The Second Field Army began as the Fourth Front Army, first under Hsu Hsiang-ch'ien (Chang Kuo-t'ao, a rival of Mao's who left the CPC in 1938, was its political officer) and later under the highly competent professional Liu Po-ch'eng; before the Long March, it operated mainly in the eastern Yangtze Valley, then, under a different title, in North China during the war against Japan, and finally in Central and Southwest China during the last stage of the civil war. Its leadership appears to have been somewhat out of favor with Mao because of its association with Chang Kuo-t'ao and because of Liu Po-ch'eng's outspoken disdain for Mao's "guerrilla mentality," but it has not been subjected to much actual purging. The Third Field Army began as the New Fourth Army (or Corps), which remained behind in the lower Yangtze Valley during the Long March and fought in that area during the war against Japan; its men operated in East China under Ch'en Yi during the final stage of the civil war. The Fourth Field Army began as the First Front Army in Mao's Kiangsi soviet; while known as the 115th Division and under Lin Piao's initial command, its men fought mainly in North China during the war against Japan, then (again under Lin) against the Nationalists successively in Manchuria, North China, and through Central China to Canton. It was the largest, strongest, and most successful of the field armies. The North China Field Army (sometimes known as the Fifth Field Army) existed briefly under that name in 1949, as the successor to a group of units under the competent Nieh Jung-chen which had emerged from the Fourth Field Army system during the war against Japan by virtue of operating in a geographically separate area from the rest. The relatively brief life of this organization probably reflects the traditional Chinese dislike of having a strong military organization not fully under central control in the vicinity of the capital. From the standpoint of geographic origins of most of the personnel, not from that of current location, the First, Second, and Third Field Armies can be regarded as South Chinese, the Fourth and Fifth as North Chinese.

After 1949, the field armies constituted not an active threat to the center, but a cumbersome, decentralized phenomenon that tended to impede not only military modernization but also effective political and economic control by the center over the provinces. The Korean War gave Peking an excellent pretext and opportunity, as well as an urgent incentive, for draining off the best combat units from each field army and sending them to the front. In this way, the center acquired effective control over what became the main force units, those left in the regions generally becoming the regional forces. Nevertheless, field army officers and units transferred to the main forces certainly carried with them many ties and loyalties derived from their previous service; the same obviously applies to the regional forces. The field armies were abolished as such in 1954 and replaced by the smaller military regions controlling only the regional forces.

To a great extent, however, the latter are still structured along the lines of the five field armies. Since 1949, former First Field Army units have predominated in Northwest China, Second Field Army units in Southwest China, Third Field Army units in East China, Fourth Field Army units in Manchuria and the Canton region, and Fifth Field Army units in North China. There are continuing personal bonds among officers who served in a given field army, whether they now serve in the original region, in another region, or at the center. There has been considerable stability among the regional military leaderships; comparatively few were purged during the Cultural Revolution, although a few senior officers formerly with Lin Piao's Fourth Field Army assumed high military and political posts in regions other than those associated with that unit. There is in effect a balance of power, probably consciously maintained, among the field armies. Former field army connections are evidently often considered by Peking when making appointments to military posts at the center. Each field army, as we have seen, has a region or regions where it (or its descendants) predominates, but each region also normally contains a few units from each of the other field armies; from the center's point of view, this system acts as a partial check on what might otherwise be excessive regionalism or decentralization. Other important checks are the gradual (rather than rapid) growth of national consciousness and desire for national unity on the part of the military as well as other elites, and the control by the center over the main forces and the major arsenals, which are located in various regions. Even so, the system embodies a substantial measure of decentralization and strong regional tendencies.

Policy Problems: "Red" Versus "Expert"

As in other aspects of the Chinese Communist system, and as in other Communist armies, the "contradiction" between the "red" (ideological and political considerations) and the "expert" (professional and technical considerations) is an old one in the PLA. There is a myth that in the history of the PLA there have been few conflicts between commanders and political officers and between the systems they represent; such conflicts have not been so severe and obvious as in the Soviet Army, but they have occurred nevertheless. The Party center has always held a balance of one sort or another between commanders and political officers; if it had not, the PLA would probably have ceased to be Communist or ceased to be an army. The "expert" term of the "contradiction" needs little elaboration, except to say that most commanders in the PLA have been no different from commanders in any other army in attaching primary importance to whatever seemed likely to increase the combat effectiveness of their units. "Red" refers mainly to the emphasis placed by the political officers, and under their guidance by the Party committees and political departments, on Party control over the PLA ("The Party commands the gun, and the gun must never be allowed to command the Party," wrote Mao in a famous passage in 1938), and usually also on the "thought" of Mao Tse-tung, especially its military aspects. In addition to the principle just cited, Mao has generally preached that of "man over weapons" (another form of "red over expert") and the idea that the atomic bomb (like American "imperialism," which first produced it) is a "paper tiger." Although these famous slogans convey a rather primitive and oversimplified impression of Mao's military thinking, which concedes the importance of modernization as long as it does not take priority over ideological and political considerations, they do indicate the way in which his thinking has generally been presented to the Chinese people, the PLA, and the world. One of the secrets of Lin Piao's rapid rise, prior to his even more rapid fall, was probably that, while he was professionally competent to an outstanding degree, he also took care to give priority, outwardly at least, to Maoist ideological and political considerations; neither side of his military personality would probably have sufficed without the other.

The Korean War, fought as it was against a technologically superior opponent, gave a powerful stimulus to the "expert" as against the "red" tendency, especially since the latter proved powerless to prevent about 70 per cent of the Chinese prisoners taken by the United Nations Forces from refusing repatriation. A closely related further stimulus was the receipt of significant quantities of Soviet military aid, which was sent in connection with the Chinese role in the Korean War. The first organizational indication of the shifting balance between "red" and "expert" was the creation of the Defense Ministry in 1954 and the appointment of the professionally oriented P'eng Te-huai, who had commanded the "Chinese People's Volunteers" in Korea, to head it. He was by no means slavishly pro-Soviet, but he did favor adaptation of Soviet military professionalism to Chinese conditions, with only a modest admixture of "redness." He was the Chinese equivalent of Marshal Zhukov. In 1955, under his influence, some major innovations were introduced into the PLA. A system of conscription (actually selective service, since only a fraction of the annual crop of eighteen-year-olds was actually inducted) was instituted in place of the previous highly informal method of recruitment; since the conscripts served for only a few years, the new system had as one of its advantages the gradual creation of a trained reserve. At the same time, a hierarchy of formal military ranks, culminating in a galaxy of ten marshals, was introduced, as was a series of decorations for previous service. Soviet-style uniforms were adopted. Work was begun on a nuclear-weapons program (see below). There is no question that these innovations tended to enhance the prestige and influence of "expertness" or that the Party saw and tried to slow this tendency; a major campaign of ideological and political indoctrination was inaugurated within the PLA in 1956.

In 1957, in connection with a leftward shift of political outlook and strategy (see Chapter 3), Mao and the Party leadership began to tip the balance energetically in favor of the "red" principle. The tipping process was intensified in 1958 in conjunction with the Great Leap Forward and the recent realization that the acquisition of nuclear weapons would be a lengthy and largely "self-reliant" process (that is, with Soviet technical but not financial assistance, and without an outright transfer of operational Soviet nuclear weapons and delivery systems). In addition to intensified indoctrination, the Great Leap Forward had several major repercussions within the PLA, all of a "red" character. One was massive inputs of labor by the PLA (40 million man-days were planned for 1959), with an inevitably disruptive effect on training schedules. Another was a program of "officers to the ranks," meaning that every officer was required to spend one month per year serving as an enlisted man. Third, there was a huge expansion, at least on paper and under the slogan "Every one a soldier," of the militia, a force useful mainly for political mobilization and labor but of very little military value except in conjunction with a "people's war." The militia has traditionally been despised and resented by the main forces and has received its training and weapons from the regional forces. It was mainly because of his objections to these trends, as well as to the Great Leap Forward in general, that P'eng Te-huai was purged in the summer of 1959 and replaced by the much more nearly "red" Lin Piao.

The shift from the "expert" principle was intensified for the time being by the 1959–60 decision of the Soviet Union, which shared P'eng's objections to the Great Leap Forward, to cut off military aid to the C.P.R. In the long run, to be sure, the Soviet Union, by forcing the C.P.R. to become "self-reliant" in military technology, while accepting a rapid deterioration of much of its Soviet equipment, may have helped the cause of "expertness."

Under Lin Piao and Chief of Staff Lo Jui-ch'ing, political control and indoctrination within the PLA were greatly intensified, beginning about the end of 1960. The purpose was not only to correct for P'eng Te-huai's allegedly excessive professionalism but to hold the PLA politically steady under the difficult conditions surrounding the collapse of the Great Leap Forward and the process of recovery. Success, or seeming success, in this program opened the way after 1962 to an additional mission, the essentially Maoist one of serving as an example and a political energizer for the civil population (see below). The ultimate since 1955 in politicizing or "reddening" the PLA occurred in the spring of 1965, when the titles and other indications of ranks (including differing uniforms) introduced ten years earlier were abolished, and officers and men began to be referred to, as in the Yenan days, as commanders and fighters. It was this "guerrillaization" of the PLA that brought on the conflict between Lin Piao and Lo Jui-ch'ing that led to the purging of Lo early in 1966.

There must have been many in the PLA who shared the view

of the politicization campaign implied by an air force "fighter" who reportedly asked, at a forum, "What kind of air force is it if the planes cannot fly?"

The PLA in Combat

It has been estimated that PLA units have crossed the Chinese frontier in connection with nine separate operations since 1949, a count that evidently includes the Sino-Indian border war of 1962 even though the PLA operated entirely on soil claimed by China (but also by India). For reasons of security, Chinese propaganda ignored all but the two largest of these operations, the Korean War and the Sino-Indian border war, and surrounded even these with clouds of ambiguity: the troops operating in Korea were called "volunteers" and those along the Indian frontier "border guards."

Chinese intervention in the Korean War began in October, 1950, during a process of partial demobilization that reduced the PLA from a strength of 5 million, swollen through the incorporation of Nationalist units, to a figure about half that size. The shrinking process left many former Nationalist soldiers in the PLA and accordingly also in the Chinese People's Volunteers in Korea. More than a million Chinese "volunteers" fought in Korea at one time or another; casualties were very heavy (perhaps half a million) because of superior United Nations firepower, so heavy in fact that the PLA has never again engaged in combat with American forces.

The initial phase of the Chinese intervention (October–December, 1950) was highly successful because Lin Piao, who apparently commanded the Chinese People's Volunteers at that time, used infiltration and surprise effectively against the badly extended United Nations Forces near the Manchurian border. Sometimes "human sea" tactics, involving the throwing of troops into frontal attacks regardless of casualties, were employed. The Chinese People's Volunteers had rather touchy relations with the battered but fiercely proud North Korean Army and enjoyed little support from the population in North Korea and none at all in South Korea.

As Chinese lines lengthened and United Nations lines shortened near the 38th Parallel, United Nations firepower stabilized the front in the early months of 1951 and then began to roll it back somewhat. P'eng Te-huai took over command of the Chinese People's Volunteers at this point and began to fight a more regular (or conventional) war. Modern weapons and other equipment began to arrive in large quantities from the Soviet Union. Communist aircraft operating from the "privileged sanctuary" (Gen. Douglas MacArthur's phrase) in Manchuria, some of them flown by Soviet pilots, were not used offensively (that is, against United Nations forces on the ground or against targets in South Korea) but contested the United Nations air and sea operations against North Korea with growing effect.

P'eng Te-huai launched two major offensives, in April and May, 1951, evidently in an effort to disrupt the trend toward an armistice along the line near the 38th Parallel. Both were disastrously unsuccessful, and he and the North Korean command had to agree to armistice talks beginning in July. From June, 1951, on, a second wave of Chinese units arrived in Korea. The front largely stabilized and the Chinese People's Volunteers dug themselves into huge underground fortifications. The armistice negotiations at Panmunjom, conducted on the Communist side with a maximum of invective and delaying tactics, helped to deter the United Nations side from launching such major offensive operations as an amphibious landing while the Communist front was being strengthened.

The Chinese People's Volunteers lost far fewer prisoners than did the North Koreans, but whereas only one-third of the latter ultimately refused repatriation, more than two-thirds of the Chinese prisoners refused to go home. This was partly because the Chinese forces included a substantial number of former Nationalist soldiers and were not subjected to the same degree of pressure for repatriation as the Koreans, whose potential nonreturners were the targets of organized intimidation and violence within the prisoner compounds. This figure was so high and so humiliating that Peking chose to make a major issue of it and would probably have continued the war, even in the face of growing American pressures after late 1952, in an effort to ensure the return of all or nearly all of its prisoners, had the death of Stalin early in 1953 not deprived it of effective Soviet support. It accordingly had to sign an armistice (on July 27, 1953) that incorporated the principle of voluntary repatriation of prisoners.

The PLA's next major combat operation was against the Indian Army. It was so brief (October–November, 1962) and so one-sided that there is little information on its performance, although there is a good deal on the Indian debacle. As in the first stage of its Korean intervention, the PLA exploited its initiative, surprise, mobility, and automatic infantry weapons to infiltrate and rout an overextended and poorly prepared opponent. With the painful lessons of Korea probably in mind, in addition to other considerations, such as possible American and Soviet pressures, the PLA then broke off combat operations while still clearly victorious. The next few years saw a rapid buildup of the Indian Army, as well as increasing evidence that the Soviet Union might support India in the event of another Sino-Indian conflict, and accordingly the PLA prudently refrained from intervening in the Indo-Pakistani wars of 1965 and 1971, even though China's informal ally, Pakistan, suffered a setback in the first of these and a disaster in the second.

The Sino-Soviet border clashes of 1969 (see Chapter 4), although politically sensational, were small-scale affairs, and because of the absence of impartial observers, it is difficult to penetrate the propaganda barrages unleased by both sides in order to arrive at a clear picture of the military performance of either side. It is clear, however, that the Soviet Union began a massive buildup of its forces near the Sino-Soviet border and in the Mongolian People's Republic that brought them to an estimated level of forty-four divisions (nearly 1 million men) by 1971, and that in every department, except perhaps number of troops and infantry weapons, the Soviet forces are far superior quantitatively and qualitatively to their potential Chinese adversaries. This applies to nuclear missiles, strategic and tactical aircraft, air defense, naval units in Far Eastern waters, artillery, armor, communications equipment, and transport vehicles, as well as to the respective industrial bases, of course. China could not hope to win a Sino-Soviet war, only to wear the adversary down through a defensive strategy and a "people's war."

The PLA in Politics

Prior to 1949, the political and military leadership of the Chinese Communist movement were so interlocked that it was hard to tell where one began and the other left off. Because many men served in both hierarchies, it is hard to classify their careers as primarily military or civilian. The following figures on military representation on the Party Politburo and Central Committee should be regarded as only approximate.

Of the forty-four regular members of the Seventh Central Committee (elected in 1945), about twenty had military backgrounds; of the thirteen members of the Politburo elected by that Central

Committee (as constituted in the years immediately preceding the Eighth National Party Congress in 1956), however, only three had military backgrounds. The Eighth Central Committee (elected in 1956) had ninety-seven regular members, of whom about forty had military backgrounds; the figures for the corresponding Politburo were eleven out of seventeen (and two out of seven on the Politburo Standing Committee as constituted after May, 1958). This obvious growth in military participation in the upper-level leadership of the CPC, far greater than anything to be found in the Soviet Party, led some observers to conclude that it had become a "military Party," but such was not the case. What actually had happened was that, as of 1949, the PLA officer corps represented the biggest single reservoir of trained talent readily available to the Party leadership; the end of the civil war and the ensuing partial demobilization made it possible to transfer many men with wholly or predominantly military backgrounds to important civilian posts. The PLA became less politically important after 1949, not more so. At least this rapidly became true as the field armies sent their best troops (as well as other less effective ones) to the Korean front and their leading figures to posts in Peking, where they could no longer exert as much influence in their regions; they were abolished as functioning entities in 1954. In short, prior to the Cultural Revolution, the PLA's political power was never such that it could really be exerted coherently and independently at the national level, but only at the regional level or in close cooperation with the civilian Party leadership. This was made clear by P'eng Te-huai's hopeless effort in 1959 to bring about an abandonment of the Great Leap Forward.

The civilian and military elites shared an interest in improving the relations between the PLA and the populace, and particularly the PLA's public image; in traditional China, soldiering had been regarded as one of the very lowest callings. Every year at the time of the spring festival (as the Lunar New Year has been called in China since 1949), the people have been exhorted in official propaganda to "love" the PLA and take good care of military dependents, and the PLA has been exhorted to "serve" the people. Measures like this, as well as the adoption of conscription, seem to have had a considerable effect in encouraging a reasonably favorable popular attitude toward the armed forces. This situation rendered it logical and relatively effective for Mao Tse-tung, after 1962, to have the PLA held up in official propaganda ("Learn from the PLA") as a disciplined and ideologically motivated model for Chinese society as a whole. As we have seen, this model began to send organizational offshoots into the civilian sector in 1963–64, when political departments modeled on those in the PLA and sometimes staffed by personnel from its General Political Department were set up in departments under the Party Central Committee, in government agencies, and in economic enterprises. By 1965, as it became "guerrillaized" and therefore more acceptable to Mao than ever, the PLA began to be described in official statements as the "main pillar of the proletarian dictatorship."

Sino-Soviet Military Relations

After concluding its alliance with the Soviet Union in February, 1950, Peking depended on Moscow as its deterrent or shield against American aggression, which was considered likely, and against a possible Japanese military resurgence. Even though it had begun to acquire nuclear weapons in 1949, however, the Soviet Union proved most reluctant to face the strategically superior United States, even on behalf of its own interests, and much more so on account of China's. If this was true of the Soviet attitude toward Moscow's admitted defensive obligations to the C.P.R., as it was, it was truer still of the Soviet reaction to the demands that Peking began to make after the end of the Korean War for more active Soviet aid and support in connection with the prospective "liberation" of Taiwan. After the Taiwan Strait crisis of 1958, during which Moscow confined its support for Peking to propaganda, the Chinese leadership's growing ideological and political differences with Moscow began to be reinforced by serious doubts about the value of the Sino-Soviet alliance. Although the alliance, which runs until 1980, has never been abrogated, it may be considered to have died for all practical purposes by its tenth birthday, February 14, 1960, which Khrushchev spent in New Delhi, the capital of what was then the C.P.R.'s main Asian rival. It is probably still true, to be sure, that the Soviet Union would take a dim view, or at least would be assumed by the United States to do so, of any American military action against China that came close to the Soviet border or threatened to upset the Asian balance by destroying China as a functioning state, but these are highly improbable contingencies. In the same general connection, it is interesting that since 1949, Peking has displayed remarkably little overt hostility to Australia, in spite of the latter's generally anti-Communist foreign policy and its recognition of the Nationalist government on Taiwan; Australia is also the only area where the United States could realistically—speaking solely in terms of physical geography and population concentrations—emplace intercontinental ballistic missiles that could hit China without overflying the Soviet Union. It is a reasonable inference that Peking does not want to be threatened in this way and therefore refrains from unnecessarily antagonizing Australia. Under existing conditions, the Soviet Union would tend to feel involved, and would perhaps become involved, if the United States threatened China with intercontinental ballistic missiles, and reluctance to risk Soviet involvement could be assumed to operate as a restraint—not the only one —on any such possible threat.

In 1950, initially in connection with the Korean War, the Soviet Union began to provide the C.P.R. with substantial reimbursable conventional military aid in the form of weapons and training in their use, in addition to training given Chinese military and civilian personnel sent to the Soviet Union for long-term study. Beginning in 1955, the Soviet Union transferred to China the industrial capacity to produce a wide range of similar weapons for itself. Both these types of aid—weapons and productive capacity—stopped short, however, of such major offensive weapons systems as heavy bombers or aircraft carriers. Whether the C.P.R. asked for such strategic weapons systems, and what it would have done with them if it had gotten them, is unknown; if it was asked to transfer them, the Soviet Union declined.

In October, 1954, the Soviet Union agreed to give Chinese scientists training in nuclear physics in the Soviet Union. The Chinese decision to acquire nuclear weapons, however, was probably not taken until 1956 and probably because of the decreased sense of Moscow's resoluteness and reliability generated by the Soviet Twentieth Party Congress. In April, 1956, Moscow agreed to begin providing China with nuclear reactors, the first of which were for research purposes. By October, 1957, however, Chinese pressures and wheedling (see Chapter 3) had induced Khrushchev to agree to give the C.P.R. large-scale technical assistance, such as the Soviet Union has never given to any other country, in the development of nuclear warheads (through the building of a gaseous diffusion plant) and surface-to-surface missiles.

At the end of January, 1958, the United States introduced tactical nuclear weapons into South Korea. As nearly as the ensuing developments can be reconstructed, Peking promptly asked Moscow for equivalent operational weapons and delivery systems.

Moscow declined unless this were done within a "joint" (actually Soviet) command over the Soviet and Chinese armed forces, or at least their major components. Such an arrangement would have been wholly unacceptable to Peking, which accordingly dropped its request and withdrew its "volunteers" from Korea. The program of Soviet aid to the Chinese nuclear weapons program remained in effect until June, 1959, when Khrushchev, irritated and alarmed by growing Chinese bumptiousness and increasingly anxious to improve his relations with the United States, canceled it without any public announcement. Soviet conventional military aid to China was terminated soon afterward (apparently in 1960).

Soviet perception of China as a threat, rather than merely as a major nuisance, appears to date from 1965–66. Over and above the sources of Sino-Soviet political friction operative at that time, such as policy disagreements over the escalated war in Vietnam, there were two important military considerations. One was that in 1965 the C.P.R. began to construct a facility for testing intercontinental ballistic missiles. The other was that in August, 1965, Japanese Premier Eisaku Sato began to indicate a determination to press the United States for the return of Okinawa to Japan, an event that would greatly diminish the island's utility as the keystone of American military containment of China. An increase in the level of Soviet forces in the border region (including the Mongolian People's Republic) began about that time; presumably, if American containment of China was beginning to become doubtful, the Soviet Union considered it necessary to fill the gap in order to ensure that no military moves in its direction or any other were made by China.

Chinese perception of this Soviet posture as a threat was blurred by the frenzy of the Cultural Revolution. The perception became clear only with the invasion of Czechoslovakia, which in Peking's eyes showed that the Soviet Union was able and willing to use armed force against Communist states whose policies it disliked, as it certainly disliked those operating in China. The perception was, of course, intensified by the border clashes and the accelerated Soviet military buildup of 1969, and has remained at a high level ever since.

Evolution of Strategic Thinking

The PLA entered the post-1949 period under an official strategic doctrine that was strongly Maoist. It was that of revolutionary "people's war" and emphasized, in a common Chinese Communist phrase, strategic boldness and tactical caution. The CPC still officially considers that the strategy has wide applicability to other countries, and to China if it should be invaded (see Chapter 5). By 1949, the PLA had also acquired considerable experience in conventional warfare, which although it has a place in the Maoist strategy was mainly the preserve of professional commanders.

In theory, the PLA after 1949 had a choice as to which of the two approaches should receive the major emphasis, and the choice was bound to have profound effects on its structure and development. A purely Maoist choice, however, would have inhibited the PLA's technological development by orienting it toward defense, rather than deterrence or offense. A purely conventional emphasis would have produced intolerable political strains by breaking with Maoist tradition. The actual tendency, therefore, has been toward a "mix," with the Maoist approach predominating in theory and the development of a major conventional (including nuclear) capability receiving the major emphasis in practice.

An increasing stress on conventional strategy received a strong stimulus from the Korean War, from the trend toward modernization that followed it, and from the beginning in 1955 of open debate in the Soviet Union on strategic questions including problems relating to nuclear war. At that time, high-ranking military figures in China also gave public expression to their views on questions of military policy. Two main schools emerged. One, consisting of professionally oriented officers in the General Staff, claimed to see a grave danger of an American attack (from such indications as the signing of a treaty of alliance between the United States and Nationalist China), and urged a crash program to acquire modern (including presumably nuclear) weapons, partly through purchase from the Soviet Union. The other school, which included P'eng Te-huai and some prominent civilians, held that an American attack could be avoided through cautious behavior or, if necessary, deterred by the Sino-Soviet alliance; emphasis should be on long-term economic development rather than on heavy expenditures on modern weapons. A compromise, leaning toward the second view but allowing for the development of a Chinese nuclear capability, was reached in 1956 and was embodied in an important speech delivered by Mao (in April, but unpublished at the time) on the "ten great relationships."

During this period, Mao and some other Chinese leaders occasionally ridiculed nuclear weapons and spoke lightheartedly of nuclear war as something that would be a good thing on balance because it would destroy "imperialism" and open the way to a better, more revolutionary world; it was even suggested that China with its huge population would be in a better position than any other country to survive such a war. This primitive view should not be taken at face value as an expression of Mao's "thought" on this subject; he probably meant to discourage excessive emphasis on the Chinese nuclear weapons program and to combat discouragement, in China and the Soviet Union, in the face of American nuclear superiority. Nevertheless, Mao's views were widely taken at face value and horrified many foreigners, including the Soviet leadership.

Another strategic debate broke out in late 1958. P'eng Te-huai believed that the Great Leap Forward and its accompanying radical foreign policy were giving the PLA the worst of both political worlds. Its own military capabilities were being impaired, for example by the requirement to contribute large inputs of labor to the civilian economy, and the Soviet strategic shield was being threatened by the strains that were developing in Sino-Soviet relations. P'eng's argument was rejected and he was purged, but his successor, Lin Piao, aided by the abandonment of the Great Leap Forward and spurred by the virtual collapse of the Sino-Soviet alliance, made some changes that went far to meet P'eng's objections on the domestic front. The militia and civilian labor by the PLA were de-emphasized, and the development of modern (including nuclear) weapons was accelerated.

This posture was soon affected by Mao's insistence, after 1962, on giving the PLA a prominent political role, thereby tending to hamper its development as a modern combat force. In 1965, after the escalation in Vietnam, Chief of Staff Lo Jui-ch'ing challenged the Maoist approach and, in effect, reverted to the emphasis on military modernization and preparation against a strategic attack favored by the General Staff ten years earlier; he also favored an improvement of relations with the Soviet Union, at least on the military plane. Lin Piao rebutted him, supported the Maoist insistence on politicizing the PLA, even in the new conditions created by the war in Vietnam, denounced any idea of cooperating with the Soviet Union, and insisted that the C.P.R. could deter attack with its own nuclear weapons or cope with it via "people's war" if deterrence failed.

Lo's argument was officially rejected, and he was purged, but the modernization of the conventional forces was in fact accelerated, as he had evidently advocated, and the development of strategic and tactical nuclear weapons continued. These trends were slowed, but by no means stopped, by the Cultural Revolution.

This survey of Chinese strategic thinking must be rounded out by a summary of Peking's views on arms control and disarmament. The CPC has always officially opposed any sort of agreement on conventional disarmament, because it would impair Peking's defensive high card (its conventional forces) and might hamper "people's wars" elsewhere. As for nuclear disarmament, Peking has loudly opposed any agreements that it has seen either as representing compromises in principle with "imperialism" or as limiting China's freedom to create its nuclear deterrent while the two "superpowers" retained the ability to strike China with nuclear weapons. Thus, Peking has denounced, on one or both of these grounds, the Nuclear Test Ban Treaty of 1963, the Nonproliferation Treaty (although Peking's support for the proliferation of nuclear weapons among presently non-nuclear powers is a matter of propaganda rather than practice), and the SALT negotiations. Its alternative is complete nuclear disarmament, to be achieved through a conference of all heads of government in the world, and, in the meantime, a pledge by each nuclear power that it will never be the first to use nuclear weapons in any future conflict. This is obviously a highly propagandistic position, under cover of which Peking continues to create its nuclear deterrent force. On the other hand, Peking would gain greatly if its proposals were accepted, since it would be freed of the fear of nuclear destruction and would enhance the security and influence conferred by its possession of large conventional forces. Implicit in Peking's position to date, as just summarized, is a belief in the stability of the "balance of terror" between the United States and the Soviet Union. Recently, however, Peking has shown signs of fearing that the balance is being upset in favor of the Soviet Union, so that Moscow might feel freer to turn its military attention more fully to China without fear of an American response.

The PLA in the Cultural Revolution

Lin Piao and the PLA General Staff's General Political Department, led by Hsiao Hua, were apparently in favor of the Cultural Revolution from the beginning. Limited movements by main force units, as well as firm statements by Lin, contributed heavily to the overthrow of Peking leader P'eng Chen in May, 1966, and to the defeat of the Party apparatus leadership at the Eleventh Central Committee Plenary Session in August, 1966 (see Chapter 4). In return, the PLA was to conduct its own Cultural Revolution within its ranks, rather than being purged from outside by the Maoists like the Party apparatus, and at some point (probably August, 1966) an understanding was reached that Lin Piao was to be Mao's successor. Personnel of the General Political Department were heavily involved in organizing and supporting the Red Guards.

When the Red Guards failed to overthrow the Party apparatus leadership at the regional and provincial levels, Mao and Lin ordered the PLA (actually, the regional forces under the military regions and military districts) to intervene to "support the left." Since the local military commanders were stability-oriented, however, and had close ties with the beleaguered provincial Party apparatuses, they generally tended to suppress activity by the Red Guards rather than support it. Accordingly, in April, 1967, Lin Piao packed the Party's Military Affairs Committee with his supporters, ordered the regional force commanders to stop repressing the Red Guards, and began to use main force units to "support the left." For this purpose, there were some movements of troops between provinces, it being probably the first time since 1949 when such movements were made with little or no regard for field army affiliation.

Continuing confrontations between regional force commanders and Red Guards flared up in the Wuhan Incident of July, 1967 (see Chapter 4). The extreme Maoists wanted to use this affair as a pretext for turning the Red Guards loose on the regional forces' leadership, whom they compared to P'eng Te-huai. But the decision of the Party high command (effectively, Mao, Lin, and Chou En-lai) was against this, and the regional force commanders themselves were of course strongly opposed to any such step. Instead, Hsiao Hua and some of the most extreme members of the Cultural Revolution Group, the main patron of the Red Guards, were purged. Main force units continued to be injected into the more troublesome military regions and military districts, and in September, 1967, permission was publicly given by Mao and Chiang Ch'ing (as it had to be; no lesser authority would have sufficed) to all PLA personnel to use force if attacked by Red Guards.

Under this new mandate, the great majority of the provincial revolutionary committees was formed during the following year. All of them were under strong military influence from a varying mixture of local main force and regional force commanders, a sizable minority of whom had assumed their current posts during the Cultural Revolution in response to Lin Piao's policy. About three-fourths of the revolutionary committees were chaired by the current commander or political officer of the corresponding military district, or sometimes of the military region when its headquarters happened to be located in that particular province.

The PLA Since the Cultural Revolution

As compared with the Eighth Central Committee and its Politburo (elected in 1956), the corresponding bodies elected at and after the Ninth Party Congress in 1969 showed no significant increase in military representation (about 70 out of 170 regular members of the Central Committee had military backgrounds and 11 out of 21 regular members of the Politburo).

During the period after the Ninth Party Congress, Lin Piao moved to the best of his ability to consolidate his position as Mao's successor. He continued the injection of main force units into the provinces, some of the leading positions in the provincial military districts and revolutionary committees being taken over by main force unit commanders. Because the main political agenda item was the elimination of the Red Guards (although the Cultural Revolution continued to operate in theory), the PLA was employed for this purpose.

Chou En-lai began promptly to maneuver against Lin, however. Shortly after the Ninth Party Congress, he succeeded in getting at least one senior military man congenial to him (Ch'en Yi) on the Military Affairs Committee. He brought increasing numbers of military men into administrative positions under the State Council. He appealed for support for himself and his program, to the regional force leaders and evidently succeeded with at least two of the most important of them—Ch'en Hsi-lien, commander of the Mukden Military Region, and Hsu Shih-yu, commander of the Nanking Military Region; they were the only military region commanders to have been elected to the Politburo after the Ninth Party Congress. Chou failed with Huang Yung-sheng, who had commanded the Canton Military Region before becoming Chief of Staff in March, 1968, apparently because Huang was too close to Lin Piao. The General Staff Department and the General Rear

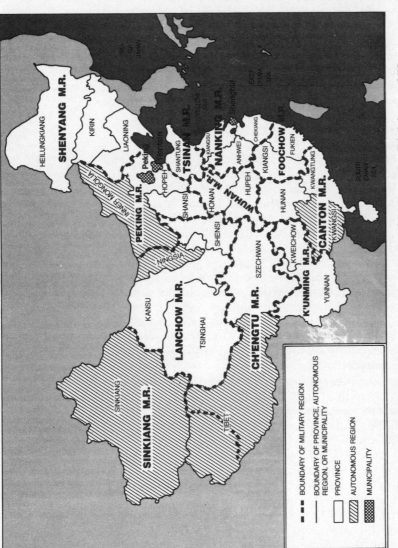

Map 2. Military Regions and Province-Level Administrative Divisions, 1972

This map is based on information compiled by Parris Chang during the course of research for a forthcoming book on the intervention of the People's Liberation Army in Chinese politics. *Reprinted, by permission of the publisher, from Parris Chang, "Decentralization of Power,"* Problems of Communism (July–August, 1972), p. 69.

Services Department of the PLA General Staff continued to be dominated by men loyal to Lin. The General Political Department, however, which had been more or less dormant since the summer of 1967, was revived in late 1969 under a general, Li Te-sheng, who appeared to be oriented toward Mao and Chou rather than toward Lin. By 1970, main force units were beginning to be withdrawn from political duties and to revert to military roles, a probable sign that Chou's influence was beginning to gain ascendancy over Lin's.

Since Lin's fall in September, 1971, Chou has used the prestigious ex-Marshal Yeh Chien-ying as his military deputy. Yeh has presided informally over the Military Affairs Committee and the Defense Ministry and has almost certainly helped greatly in ensuring the loyalty of the main force commanders to Chou's leadership. Chou has exploited the crisis atmosphere arising from the actual Soviet threat and the alleged Japanese threat to make more credible his claim to the support of the main forces and the regional forces, and thereby to combat the potential for regional warlordism that undoubtedly exists.

Under Chou's and Yeh's influence, the PLA is proceeding with its conventional modernization program. Since late 1968, the nuclear weapons program has been conducted with much less publicity than before, presumably for fear of provoking the Soviet Union. On the other hand, an intermediate-range-ballistic-missile testing site went into operation in 1970, without publicity. Chou obviously intends that China should have at least a minimum nuclear deterrent, as well as modern conventional forces, within the limits of its economic and technological capabilities as he understands them.

FURTHER READINGS

There is a large literature on the PLA. Valuable general treatments are John Gittings, *The Role of the Chinese Army,* London and New York: Oxford University Press, 1967; William W. Whitson, ed., *The Military and Political Power in China in the 1970's,* New York: Praeger, 1972; William W. Whitson, with Chen-hsia Huang, *The Chinese High Command: A History of Communist Military Politics, 1927–1971,* New York: Praeger, 1972; and several articles in *The China Quarterly,* no. 18 (April–June, 1964).

On organization, control, and capabilities, see John Gittings, "Military Control and Leadership, 1954–1964," *The China Quarterly,* no. 26 (April–June, 1966), pp. 82–101; Ralph L. Powell, "The Military Affairs Committee and Party Control of the Military in China,"

Asian Survey, vol. iii, no. 7 (July, 1963), pp. 347–56; Samuel B. Griffith II, "Communist China's Capacity to Make War," *Foreign Affairs,* vol. 43, no. 2 (January, 1965), pp. 217–36; International Institute for Strategic Studies (London), *The Military Balance* (annual).

On the Field Army system and related matters, see the chapters on "The Field Army in Chinese Communist Military Politics" and "Military Generations in Communist China," in William W. Whitson, with Chen-hsia Huang, *The Chinese High Command,* pp. 498–517 and 416–35, respectively.

The "red" versus "expert" problem is treated in Ellis Joffe, *Party and Army: Professionalism and Political Control in the Chinese Officer Corps, 1949–1964,* Cambridge, Mass.: Harvard University Press, East Asian Monographs, 1965; J. Chester Cheng, ed., *The Politics of the Chinese Red Army: A Translation of the Bulletin of Activities of the People's Liberation Army,* Stanford, Calif.: The Hoover Institution, 1966.

Various aspects of the PLA's operations in the Korean War are covered in Alexander L. George, *The Chinese Communist Army in Action: The Korean War and Its Aftermath,* New York: Columbia University Press, 1969; and William C. Bradbury, *Mass Behavior in Battle and Captivity: The Communist Soldier in the Korean War,* Samuel M. Meyers and Albert D. Biderman, eds., Chicago: University of Chicago Press, 1968. There is little on the Chinese operations against India in 1962; the best book on the war is written (very critically) from the Indian side: Neville Maxwell, *India's China War,* London: Cape, 1970, New York: Anchor Books, 1972, Harmondsworth: Penguin, 1972. The Sino-Soviet military confrontation is well summarized in *The Military Balance, 1970–1971,* pp. 99–101.

On the political role of the PLA before the Cultural Revolution, see Ellis Joffe, "The Chinese Army Under Lin Piao: Prelude to Political Intervention," in John M. Lindbeck, ed., *China: Management of a Revolutionary Society,* Seattle: University of Washington Press, 1971, pp. 343–74; Chalmers Johnson, "Lin Piao's Army and Its Role in Chinese Society," *Current Scene* (Hong Kong), vol. iv, nos. 13 and 14 (July 1 and 15, 1966).

Various aspects of Sino-Soviet military relations are treated in Raymond L. Garthoff, ed., *Sino-Soviet Military Relations,* New York: Praeger, 1966; Morton H. Halperin, ed., *Sino-Soviet Relations and Arms Control,* Cambridge, Mass.: The MIT Press, 1967; Walter C. Clemens, Jr., *The Arms Race and Sino-Soviet Relations,* Stanford, Calif.: The Hoover Institution, 1968.

Only the most important of the rather numerous writings on Chinese military doctrine and nuclear weapons can be listed here. Good general treatments are Davis B. Bobrow, "Peking's Military Calculus," *World Politics,* vol. xvi, no. 2 (June, 1964), pp. 287–301; Ralph L.

Powell, "Maoist Military Doctrines," *Asian Survey,* vol. viii, no. 4 (April, 1968), pp. 239–62; Alice Langley Hsieh, *Communist China's Strategy in the Nuclear Era,* Englewood Cliffs, N.J.: Prentice-Hall, 1962; William W. Whitson, with Chen-hsia Huang, *The Chinese High Command* (see Chapter 11, "Strategy and Tactics"); Allen S. Whiting, "The Use of Force in Foreign Policy by the People's Republic of China," *The Annals,* vol. cdii (July, 1972), pp. 55–66. On the nuclear aspect specifically, see especially Morton H. Halperin, *China and the Bomb,* New York: Praeger, and London: Pall Mall Press, 1965; Charles H. Murphy, "Mainland China's Evolving Nuclear Deterrent," *Bulletin of the Atomic Scientists,* January, 1972, pp. 28–35. On Chinese attitudes, etc., toward arms control, there are Morton H. Halperin and Dwight H. Perkins, eds., *Communist China and Arms Control,* Cambridge, Mass.: Harvard University East Asian Research Center and Center for International Affairs, 1965; Harry G. Gelber, "Strategic Arms Limitations and the Sino-Soviet Relationship," *Asian Survey,* vol. x, no. 4 (April, 1970), pp. 265–89, and "China and SALT," *Survival,* vol. xii, no. 4 (April, 1970), pp. 122–26.

The role of the PLA during and since the Cultural Revolution is treated in Ralph L. Powell, "The Party, the Government and the Gun," *Asian Survey,* vol. x, no. 6 (June, 1970), pp. 441–71; Jürgen Domes, "The Cultural Revolution and the Army," *ibid.,* vol. viii, no. 5 (May, 1968), pp. 349–63, and "The Role of the Military in the Formation of Revolutionary Committees, 1967–68," *The China Quarterly,* no. 44 (October–December, 1970), pp. 112–45; and William W. Whitson, with Chen-hsia Huang, *The Chinese High Command* (see Chapters 7 and 8 on "The Role of the Military in the Cultural Revolution"). On the Wuhan Incident, see Thomas W. Robinson, "The Wuhan Incident: Local Strife and Provincial Rebellion during the Cultural Revolution," *The China Quarterly,* no. 47 (July–September, 1971), pp. 413–38.

10. *Some Techniques of Political Action*

This chapter is not intended to deal with all the topics that might be considered under its title, since a number of them are covered elsewhere—for example, ideology in Chapter 5, various aspects of organization in Chapters 6 and 7, mass mobilization and education in Chapter 12. This chapter tries to treat four important topics that are not adequately dealt with elsewhere: propaganda, police controls, law, and material incentives.

Propaganda

Probably the most obtrusive aspect of the Chinese Communist political system is its propaganda, which is everywhere at home and surprisingly widespread abroad. For domestic audiences, there are three basic themes or messages: hard work and sacrifice (often in emulation of some particular "model" individual or enterprise), the "thought" of Mao Tse-tung, and rationalization of whatever domestic and foreign policies the regime is pursuing at the moment. For foreign audiences, the first of these is partially omitted, leaving the second and third, although the difference is less than might be expected. Since the beginning of the Cultural Revolution, perhaps the main single message conveyed to the Chinese people as a whole is the exhortation to wipe out the "four olds"—old things, old ideas, old customs, and old habits.

All news and artistic media in the C.P.R. are saturated with official propaganda. Over-all propaganda policy before the Cultural Revolution was coordinated, and to some extent determined, by the Propaganda Department under the CPC Central Committee. This department has not been formally revived since the Cultural Revolution, and it seems likely that many of its functions have been transferred to the State Council's new Cultural Group. In any case, propaganda via media other than cultural (the latter term being intended to cover such things as the drama) is conducted to a large extent by the New China News Agency, which is also under the State Council. It has about thirty bureaus in China and about fifty (including local stringers) in foreign countries. At home and abroad, it releases under its own imprint and also provides to others (newspapers in China and foreign subscribers, for example) news dispatches, editorials and statements of its own, photographs, radio broadcasts, and the texts of official statements and editorials from the Chinese press. Like those of nearly all such bodies in China, its leadership was partially purged during the Cultural Revolution. Since then, it has been regarded as faithfully voicing the current official line; for this reason, when there has been trouble and confusion in a given province during or since the Cultural Revolution, the provincial radio has often stopped airing broadcasts of local origin and confined itself to rebroadcasting material from the New China News Agency.

It is, of course, not possible or necessary to describe all the newspapers and periodicals published in the C.P.R., even the national ones (there are provincial and local ones, most of which have not been allowed to be exported or even sold to foreigners in China since before the Cultural Revolution), but a few deserve mention. The most important newspaper, the Chinese equivalent of *Pravda,* is the *People's Daily* (*Jen-min Jih-pao*), which is considered to be the official organ of the CPC Central Committee. Among its most important contents are editorials signed Observer, evidently a pseudonym for some high-ranking Party member or members. There is no precise Chinese equivalent of *Izvestia,* the newspaper published under the auspices of the Soviet Union's Council of Ministers (corresponding to the State Council). The CPC's main theoretical ("propaganda" would be more accurate) journal is *Red Flag* (*Hung Ch'i*), which normally appears twice a month, although there have been occasional major variations in this schedule since the beginning of the Cultural Revolution. One of the more interesting magazines is (or was, until its suspension in 1966) the semimonthly published by the Communist Youth League, *Chung-kuo Ch'ing-nien* (*China Youth*); its editorials and the letters to the editor provided considerable insight into the trend toward nonrevolutionary attitudes on the part of many of the youth that it was one of the purposes of the Cultural Revolution to correct. For foreign consumption, the most important periodical is the semimonthly *Peking Review*, which appears in several languages, the English edition being the most significant.

Avowedly political and propagandistic books and pamphlets play a very important role in the CPC's over-all propaganda effort, although it must be remembered that by no means the entire population of China is literate. This is too big a subject to be discussed fully here. It is enough to say that the content of political publications in the C.P.R. has always included not only a great deal of propaganda but an increasingly heavy dose of the "thought" of Mao Tse-tung as well. During the Cultural Revolution, this trend assumed overpowering proportions: from the summer of 1966 to October, 1968, for example, no fewer than 740 million copies of the Little Red Book were printed in various languages, as well as more than 2 billion copies of other writings by Mao. Since the Cultural Revolution, the situation has reverted roughly to the pre-1966 level, meaning that there is still a lot of Mao and a lot of general political propaganda, but to a less overwhelming extent than during the Cultural Revolution.

Literature and the arts play an important propaganda as well as cultural role in China. Again, this is a big subject, but it can be pointed out that the film and the drama are especially important in this context because they reach a far larger number of people much oftener than does printed literature; there are 4 billion film attendances in China per year. Perhaps the most important and interesting aspect of this question is the "revolutionary opera" (actually, ballet in many cases). This phenomenon goes back to 1963, when Chiang Ch'ing, after years of personal inconspicuousness and comparative, although not total, political inactivity, began to emerge and to "revolutionize" Peking opera. Actually, Peking opera was virtually abolished as an officially favored art form and replaced by eight (later eleven) "revolutionary operas," which are constantly performed live and presented on film. The plots and propaganda themes are mostly taken from the early history of the CPC, especially the period of the Sino-Japanese War, and the contrast is drawn as sharply as possible between the revolutionary heroism of Red Army men, peasants, and others, and the unrelieved villainy of Kuomintang or local "reactionaries" and Japanese "imperialists." Although it is not explicit, the moral is easily transferable to the present: the people should follow the CPC's leadership in struggling against adversity and domestic and foreign enemies as the Party identifies them. The choreography and music are much more Western than traditionally Chinese, although there is some use of Chinese acrobatic dancing. Chiang Ch'ing has recently popularized the piano as an acceptable instrument for accompanying performances of "revolutionary opera."

Sports and public spectacles of various kinds, including the huge (essentially nonmilitary) parades on May 1 and October 1 in Peking and other major cities, play an important propaganda role. The main theme, of course, is joyful loyalty to the Party, its leadership, and its programs. Sometimes huge crowds are trained to use colored flags with great precision to present, when seen from a distance, a succession of pictures, of Mao for example. Sports faded into the background during the Cultural Revolution, mainly because the youth were otherwise engaged, but also because the bureaucracy directing organized athletics had been headed by ex-Marshal Ho Lung and suffered when he was purged at the end of 1966. Since the Cultural Revolution, organized sports have made a strong comeback. In foreign competition, China prefers to stress the sport in which it is unquestionably the best, meaning of course table tennis. Parades were not held on the usual scale on October 1, 1971, and May 1, 1972, allegedly for reasons of economy, but actually because it would have been embarrassing for Mao to appear without Lin Piao, since Lin's fall had not yet been officially announced.

Posters of various kinds, displayed almost anywhere, are another aspect of Chinese Communist propaganda. Normally, their content is simple and highly political: Oppose American Imperialism, Liberate Taiwan, and the like. There is a more or less unofficial variety of poster, known as the large-character poster (*ta-tzu pao*), which is much favored by the CPC, provided of course that only acceptable messages are conveyed. Theoretically, these are put up by private individuals to demonstrate their enthusiasm for the regime. The large-character posters had a tremendous vogue during the Cultural Revolution, when Red Guards put them up in huge numbers and sometimes included in them important and otherwise unpublished pieces of history and news that were passed to them from above (from the Cultural Revolution Group in most cases, probably) or seized by them from the files of Party and government organizations. The Red Guards' large-character posters, often called wall posters, also included much consciously or unconsciously false and absurd propaganda, and it is not easy to separate what is true from what is not in their output. Japanese correspondents had a major advantage over other foreign correspondents, since they could read the posters and pass at least briefly as Chinese while taking notes or making copies; accordingly, the Japanese press became a major source of information on the often exciting content of the wall posters. After a time, they were forbidden to read the posters, and some of them were subjected to violence by Red Guards. Since the end of the Cultural Revolution, spontaneous posters have more or less disappeared.

Meetings of various kinds and sizes are an important means by which the CPC's line is propagated. Probably the most significant type of meeting is a fairly small one at which a Party cadre presents a message (possibly a summary of the *People's Daily*) and then leads a discussion. Meetings of this kind are very frequent and take up a great deal of time. It is obvious, therefore, that the CPC considers them a highly effective method of getting its message across.

Police Controls

Despite hostile (often Nationalist) propaganda statements to the contrary, the C.P.R. is not a full-blown police state. One reason is that ingenious and usually effective organizational, social, and psychological controls have been developed that reduce the need for a massive police apparatus. Another reason, or probable reason, is that the dreadful "negative example" of Stalinist Russia has been duly noted. Never has the CPC created a single police empire under a single boss directly controlled by the senior Party leader and used by him to exterminate his opponents, or possible opponents, within the Party as well as outside it to anything like the degree that was normal under Stalin after the mid-1930's. In this respect, as in most others, Mao is no Stalin. Even today, the Soviet Union retains many of the unappetizing features of a police state to a much greater extent than does the C.P.R.

On the other hand, it would be a mistake to jump to the conclusion that police controls are of little or no importance in the Chinese political system. They form a significant, even if not overpowering, part of the total picture. One indication of this is the extreme sensitivity of the subject: the CPC publishes less information on it than on almost anything else, except perhaps its military production and dispositions. Security within the Party and the state is very tight; classified documents are carefully guarded; and it is known that the staffs of Chinese diplomatic missions abroad are closely watched.

Prior to 1949, security and police affairs were the concern

almost exclusively of the Party apparatus. Under the Central Committee, there were a Social Affairs Department, which apparently handled counterintelligence; a Liaison Bureau, for intelligence operations against the Kuomintang until 1945; an Enemy Bureau, for intelligence operations against the Japanese until 1945, and thereafter against the Kuomintang; and a Public Security Headquarters, which took care of overt policing.

As the CPC approached the point at which it would be in a position to create a nationwide state, it became clear that more systematic thought would have to be given to police mechanisms as well as to many other things. In *On the People's Democratic Dictatorship* (1949), Mao Tse-tung said that "Our present task is to strengthen the people's state apparatus—mainly the people's army, the people's police and the people's courts—in order to consolidate national defense and protect the people's interests."

After "liberation" and until the Cultural Revolution, control over police operations was divided between the Party and the government. Certain intelligence and counterintelligence functions were performed, under the Central Committee, by the Military Affairs Committee, the United Front Work Department, the Social Affairs Department (whose continued existence during that period is probable although not certain), and the Investigation Bureau. It is likely that at least after September, 1962, when he was elected to the Secretariat, the shadowy but evidently powerful K'ang Sheng supervised intelligence and police activities under the Central Committee.

The rapidly expanding responsibility for overt policing was transferred to the Ministry of Public Security, whose head (Lo Jui-ch'ing, 1949–59; Hsieh Fu-chih, 1959–67?) also directed the State Council's Political and Legal Affairs Bureau (renamed the Internal Affairs Office in 1963), which coordinated the work of several government agencies. One of the probable signs of an intent not to form a police empire was that the Minister of Public Security never served simultaneously on the Party Politburo or Secretariat. The Ministry of Public Security was a large and elaborate organization, whose functions included control of the public security forces (a paramilitary force of several hundred thousand charged with guarding frontiers and forced labor camps and other tasks), investigation of political crimes, and the like.

The various levels of government below the center were also involved in police work, but, in terms of impact on the populace, the most important level was undoubtedly the *hsien* (rural district or county). Interviews with refugee cadres from a not necessarily typical coastal *hsien* of about half a million population have shown that the *hsien* public security bureau included 147 "state cadres" (classified civil servants) and controlled a force of only 96 uniformed policemen. In this instance, as in other *hsien*, any movement (especially a change of residence) between *hsien* required the approval of the public security bureaus concerned, and all citizens were encouraged to inform the police about any violators of laws and regulations, including their own relatives. Indeed, some refugees point to fear of the unknown informer as perhaps the most important single factor producing popular compliance.

A few high points of the public security situation from 1949 to the Cultural Revolution deserve mention. In June, 1951, the regime legally restricted possession of firearms to military personnel (including organized militia units) and authorized civil officials (including, of course, police). The great anti-"counter-revolutionary" campaigns of 1951–52 and 1955 were conducted against targets who were largely unarmed. Where there was armed resistance, as in the minority areas from time to time, the PLA was generally employed. These campaigns, as well as the normal workings of criminal law, yielded a substantial crop of individuals sentenced to forced labor ("labor reform"), as well as to other fates. In spite of some propaganda to the contrary (usually of Nationalist origin), neither from the political nor from the economic point of view did forced labor play as important a part in the C.P.R. as it did in the Soviet Union under Stalin; it is unlikely that the number of forced laborers in China has exceeded 2 million at any one time. Forced labor must not be confused with unpaid labor often performed compulsorily, but without prejudice, by the general population, especially peasants during the agricultural slack season, on dams, roads, and similar projects.

When the Cultural Revolution began, the police apparatus was considered logically enough by the Maoists as part of the Party and government establishment, and it therefore came under heavy attack. The public security forces appear to have been neutralized by the PLA. The Ministry of Public Security seems to have lost most of its authority outside Peking, although Hsieh Fu-chih survived under the protecting wing of Chou En-lai and even chaired the Peking Revolutionary Committee (formed in 1967) and entered the top Party leadership in 1968 (he died in March, 1972). The public security bureaus at the *hsien* level were largely swept away in areas where there was serious disorder; in others, they seem to have survived but to have yielded most of their functions to the PLA.

Immediately after the end of the Cultural Revolution, local police functions, and especially the key one of suppressing the Red Guards as an organized political movement, were performed by the so-called workers' provost corps, in which the PLA played the main role with some help from teams of workers and peasants. Widespread public disorder was a serious problem during this period.

One of the aspects of the trend toward political normalization since the end of the Cultural Revolution has been a rebuilding of the security apparatus. As in most such cases, the details are obscure and are probably consciously kept so. It is likely, however, that the process has the full approval of Chou En-lai and that the immediate responsibility for it belongs, somewhat informally, to Wang Tung-hsing, a longtime personal assistant to Mao Tse-tung in security matters, and an alternate Politburo member since the Ninth Party Congress.

Law

Laws and regulations designed to implement general policies are dealt with elsewhere; this section focuses on civil and criminal law and such closely related topics as the court system. Even this is a complex subject, as in any other society, one requiring much specialized knowledge for a full understanding. The discussion here will be brief and, no doubt unavoidably, inadequate.

There is no "rule of law" in the C.P.R., even in theory. Everything, including the law and the courts, must be subject to the will of the CPC, meaning in practice the shifting decisions of the Party leadership. As in other Communist countries, the Party has not tried to dispense with laws and courts, but it has tried to retain the advantages of having them while accepting only the minimum of concomitant drawbacks, restraints, and the like.

Somewhat parallel with the traditional Chinese distinction between *li* (ethics and rituals) and *fa* (laws and regulations), one authority distinguishes between "internal" (essentially informal and educational) and "external" (formal) "models" of law, with special reference to China. The "internal model" in the C.P.R. includes propaganda efforts to ensure popular compliance with the Party's wishes and directives, as well as an array of informal sanctions, such as occasional mass trials of offenders before mobs manipulated by Party cadres.

For several years after 1949, and especially after the adoption of the 1954 state constitution, the progress of the "external model" was noticeable, although far from spectacular, mainly because legal procedures evolved, although without the compilation and publication of a civil or a criminal code, and because a hierarchy of People's Courts functioned. There were many problems, at least from a Western viewpoint, although not all of them were seen as such by the CPC. Most of the personnel involved in the legal and judicial systems were poorly trained by any standard. Politics reigned more or less supreme; the courts had almost no judicial independence and were under Party control, and political offenses were normally punished more severely than criminal ones. In the civil field, as in pre-1949 China, there was a preference for informal (and usually highly political) mediation and arbitration over formal adjudication. In the criminal field, the law defined offenses in elastic language so that there were few effective restraints on the police, and there was a presumption of guilt on the part of the accused: confessions were expected and were usually obtained, by one means or another. Foreign visitors have not been allowed, then or since, to observe the courts in action.

In the increasingly politicized atmosphere of the post-1957 years, the system just summarily described came under even greater pressure from the Party leadership to operate according to political rather than legal criteria and therefore began to break down. One sign of this trend was the abolition in 1959 of the Ministry of Justice, which seems to have concerned itself mainly with legal education, the supervision of the legal professions, and propaganda on behalf of the Party's laws and policies.

During the Cultural Revolution, the legal and judicial systems were regarded by the Maoists, allegedly with Mao's sanction, as a part of the Establishment to be "bombarded." Accordingly, they virtually ceased to function, at any rate in anything resembling a normal way. The Red Guards often set up kangaroo courts and conducted mass trials, but this practice was repeatedly forbidden by the Mao-Lin-Chou leadership. The bizarre mood of the period was dramatically illustrated by a mass trial held in June, 1966, and presided over by Yang Hsiu-feng, the President of the Supreme People's Court. The accused had committed violence against foreign diplomats, and even though he was conceded to be insane, he was sentenced to death and executed immediately, obviously for the deterrent effect on others. Yang lost his post in 1967 and committed suicide early in 1968.

Since the end of the Cultural Revolution, the courts have been re-emerging under the wing of the revolutionary committees. Mass trials have been used fairly widely to help cope with the violence that is one of the Cultural Revolution's main legacies.

Material Incentives

The CPC has always realized that, human nature being what it it, the population must not only be allowed to live at a subsistence level but must also be permitted to improve its economic condition as an incentive for doing things that the regime wants done. There are basically two things that the CPC tries to extract from the populace through, among other means, material incentives: ideological and political compliance, or if possible enthusiasm, and increased economic productivity, which is of only indirect political relevance. In practice, the regime has designed its incentive system so that it rewards and encourages good performance in both departments simultaneously; for example, acceptable participation in political study and meetings is regarded as an integral part of the individual's job. There are narrow limits, narrower than in the Soviet Union, on the extent to which the regime is able and willing to use material incentives. One obvious reason for this is ideological: Maoism does not deny the legitimacy of material incentives but it insists that they not give rise to major income inequalities or inflation, and that they be subordinated to such ideological considerations as "serving the people." Another reason is, of course, that the Chinese economy is poor in relation to the size of the population it must support.

There are two main headings under which material incentives can usefully be considered: wages and the prices and availability of consumer goods and services.

In the first years after 1949, as earlier in areas under Communist control, workers often received payment in kind ("free supply") according to no very clearly fixed schedule. In 1950, however, Manchuria, the most advanced region in the country, adopted an eight-grade scale of industrial wages based on a Soviet model; this practice soon began to spread to other regions. A worker was paid according to the skill and level of effort considered to be demanded by his job; the lowest grade was paid 35 yuan per month (2.4 yuan = U.S.$1, approximately), the highest only 105 yuan, and only very slight increases in these rates were allowed over the next several years. This system became the basis of a comprehensive nationwide wage reform introduced in 1956. The following year, some wage rates were reduced, mainly for unskilled labor and in order to discourage peasants from migrating to the cities. The rates were based on an approximate assumed output norm or quota; output above that level was rewarded by bonuses, and below-norm output could be penalized.

The 1956 reform had envisaged an increase in the differentials among the various wage grades, but like many other ideas of that period, it soon fell victim to the Great Leap Forward. To a considerable extent, payment in kind was resumed, on the basis of assumed need. This step was ideologically motivated, the aim being to bolster the claim that China was "building Communism." To some extent, straight money wages were paid in addition. The effect was anti-material incentive, since the relationship between output and reward became less direct. The system lapsed with the end of the Great Leap Forward. In 1963, in a curious compromise, the pay of certain grades was reduced, but this was balanced by the promotion of some 10 million workers to higher grades.

Before the Great Leap Forward, a typical rural family owned a small private plot and was allowed to dispose of the produce as it chose, by eating it or selling it on a regulated "free" market. The family also received compensation for whatever land, tools, and animals it had contributed, in theory voluntarily, to the cooperative. The working members of the family also earned work points in the cooperative sector that were evaluated at the end of the season when the various obligations to the state and to the cooperative had been met. During the Great Leap Forward, all these were abolished in favor of the same combination as in industry: "free supply" and hourly wage payments. After the Great Leap Forward, the earlier system was essentially restored.

During the Cultural Revolution, the wage systems in industry and agriculture were tinkered with in order to stress relative equality of material reward and ideological incentives. Bonuses were abolished.

After the end of the Cultural Revolution, economic administration was very decentralized at first and there was considerable variation in wage systems, but there was still a heavy emphasis on ideology and equality. Beginning in early 1972, material incentives and greater wage differentials began to be restored as a stimulus to greater productivity.

As for the prices and availability of consumer goods and services, the cost of necessities (notably food) is kept low; they are generally in adequate supply, and there has been very little inflation. Luxuries (including consumer durables), on the other hand, are deliberately kept expensive, for ideological reasons and as a form of rationing, and with this qualification are in reasonably adequate supply. An important and related type of material incentive is the various fringe benefits and social services. There are contributory (for the worker) social security, sickness, disability, and other benefits for the industrial worker. Most medical care is free. Maternity leave is given with pay for fifty-six days.

In effect, the CPC has generally kept living standards somewhat above subsistence, has improved them gradually (particularly in the sense of reducing income inequalities), and, at the minimum, has prevented economic dissatisfactions from assuming proportions serious enough to constitute a political threat. For a country as poor as China, and until 1949 as chaotic, that represents rather effective use of material incentives and an impressive achievement.

FURTHER READINGS

A good general study of propaganda in the C.P.R. is Franklin W. Houn, *To Change a Nation: Propaganda and Indoctrination in Communist China*, Glencoe, Ill.: The Free Press, 1961. On propaganda addressed to youth, see James R. Townsend, "Revolutionizing Chinese Youth: A Study of *Chung-kuo Ch'ing-mien*," in A. Doak Barnett, ed., *Chinese Communist Politics in Action*, Seattle: University of Washington Press, 1969, pp. 447–76. An important aspect of propaganda is dealt with in John H. Weakland, "Chinese Film Images of Invasion and Resistance," *The China Quarterly*, no. 47 (July–September, 1971), pp. 439–70. *The China Quarterly*, no. 13 (January–March, 1963), devoted to contemporary Chinese literature, was reprinted in book form as Cyril Birch, ed., *Chinese Communist Literature*, New York: Praeger, 1963. The phenomenal escalation of propaganda during the Cultural Revolution is treated in Alan P. L. Liu, "Mass Media in the Cultural Revolution: Problems of Mass Mobilization in Communist China," *Current Scene* (Hong Kong), vol. vii, no. 8 (April 20, 1969). There is a unique and timely study by Jonathan Kolatch, *Sports, Politics and Ideology in China*, New York: Jonathan David, 1972.

Because of the secrecy surrounding the subject, little has been published on Chinese police controls. A fairly useful general article is

Ko-wang Mei, "Police System Under the Chinese Communist Regime," *Issues and Studies* (Taipei), vol. ii, no. 2 (November, 1965), pp. 31–41. Useful information on police operations at the local level can be found in A. Doak Barnett, *Cadres, Bureaucracy, and Political Power in Communist China,* New York: Columbia University Press, 1967.

On law, the following articles can be recommended: Luke T. Lee, "Chinese Communist Law: Its Background and Development," in George P. Jan, ed., *Government in Communist China,* San Francisco: Chandler, 1969, pp. 308–40; Victor H. Li, "The Role of Law in Communist China," *The China Quarterly,* no. 44 (October–December, 1970), pp. 66–111, and "The Evolution and Development of the Chinese Legal System," in John M. Lindbeck, ed., *China: Management of a Revolutionary Society,* Seattle: University of Washington Press, 1971, pp. 221–55; Jerome Alan Cohen, "The Party and the Courts, 1949–1959," *The China Quarterly,* no. 38 (April–June, 1969), pp. 120–57; Allan Spitz, "Maoism and the People's Courts," *Asian Survey,* vol. ix, no. 4 (April, 1969), pp. 255–63; Hsia Tao-tai, "Justice in Peking," *Current Scene,* vol. v, no. 1 (January 16, 1967). See also the following books edited by Jerome Alan Cohen: *The Criminal Process in the People's Republic of China, 1949–1963: An Introduction,* Cambridge, Mass.: Harvard University Press, 1968; *Contemporary Chinese Law: Research Problems and Perspectives,* Cambridge, Mass.: Harvard University Press, 1970; *China's Practice of International Law,* Cambridge, Mass.: Harvard University Press, 1972.

Material incentives and living standards must be studied largely from press sources. A good account of the pre–Cultural Revolution situation is Charles Hoffman, "Work Incentives in Chinese Industry and Agriculture," in Joint Economic Committee of the U.S. Congress, *An Economic Profile of Mainland China,* New York: Praeger, 1968, pp. 471–98.

11. Development and Transformation

The CPC has proclaimed economic development and social justice as two of its highest goals. Many foreign sympathizers hold that progress on these fronts more than justifies the low level of political and intellectual freedom in China, the latter condition being something the CPC itself would not concede. Many leaders of Third World countries have wondered whether the Chinese "model" of economic development has been as successful as its proponents claim, and if so, whether it might be suitable for adaptation to their countries. An evaluation of these views would be a difficult and subjective exercise beyond the scope of this book, but it is clear that the progress of China's economic development under Communist rule raises some questions of profound political significance.

The Chinese Economy

In 1949, the CPC inherited what was actually three economies, the traditional, the modern, and the Manchurian.

The traditional economy, by far the largest, included the vast rural hinterland. It was characterized by heavy population pressure on the land and on other agricultural resources, small land-holdings, and high yields by all but the most modern standards. The peasant lived at the subsistence level, with little opportunity to accumulate savings for investment or innovation. A poor transportation network led to small marketing areas and local self-reliance.

The modern economy, urban and centered on the treaty ports created by foreign trade during the nineteenth century, was rapidly growing but small relative to the traditional economy and very imperfectly integrated with it. American wheat could be bought in Shanghai, for example, more cheaply and easily than wheat from the interior of China; and only the rural areas nearest to them felt the effects of the goods and light industrial activities generated in the treaty ports.

After 1931, Japanese capital and management developed a major heavy industrial system in Manchuria, based on the region's large coal and iron reserves and an efficient rail network.

If the three economies are regarded as a whole, China was less well endowed, relative to its size, with capital and economic skills than any of the countries (Japan and the more advanced Western ones) that have so far achieved a high level of economic development. In 1949, furthermore, all three economies were in a badly battered state as the result of decades of civil and foreign war. By about 1952, nevertheless, the numerous (but nonrepetitive) gains accruing from the cessation of warfare had largely repaired the damage and put the economy into a position where those in charge of it could begin to develop and transform it in accordance with their desires.

The Changing Blueprint

In 1950, Mao Tse-tung announced his regime's timetable for development: after three years of recovery (1950–52) and three Five-Year Plans (1953–67), China would attain a balanced and essentially self-sufficient industrial system, and by the end of the twentieth century, it would become a major industrial power. He cannot accurately be accused, therefore, of not being interested in economics and economic development. But to him, economic development in China can be successful in the long run only if it avoids producing serious social cleavages and inequalities, especially between the cities and the countryside. More positively, the peasants must be motivated and organized to take an active interest and role in economic development, without demanding or getting bureaucratic controls or large investments from some remote center. Mao wants agricultural investment (reclamation, irrigation, and similar activities) to be made and agricultural technology to be mechanized, but he wants the peasants to make the investments (mainly in labor) and to pay for and operate the machinery themselves. Obviously, this can be done only on a collective, not a family farm, basis, and this is a major reason Mao favors so strongly collective organization and activity in the countryside, among his other reasons being an ideological determination to prevent the emergence of either a "rich peasant" economy or a bureaucratic "new class" of elitist managers.

These ideas, while consistent with Mao's long-standing views on peasant problems, were not the ones that dominated the First Five-Year Plan (1953–57). Even Mao had conceived an admiration for Soviet industrial technology, and the Plan was based largely on Soviet models and Soviet aid. Emphasis was to be on heavy industry; it was hoped that gradual collectivization of agriculture, without the brutal methods employed by Stalin, would provide the initial funds needed for industrial investment and repayment of Soviet credits, until the industrial sector could begin to draw its funds largely from the sale of light industrial products to the people rather than direct levies on agriculture. No sooner was the Plan put into "final" form in early 1955, after a shaky start, than a food supply crisis arose. Contrary to a majority of his colleagues, Mao insisted that this crisis could be met, and agriculture enabled to play its assigned role in the Plan, only if the rate of collectivization was accelerated. He argued that the peasants' natural enthusiasm for socialism would make this radical approach work. He won, in the sense that he got his way, and the collectivization process was virtually completed during the winter of 1955–56. But in the process, he not only created serious political strains within the Party leadership, he also produced a situation in which it was virtually impossible to continue following the Soviet developmental model or receiving Soviet credits; the Second Five-Year Plan was swallowed up in the Great Leap Forward, and no more Soviet credits were received after 1957.

Mao probed his way through a variety of intermediate stages before arriving at the Great Leap Forward, and above all the "people's communes" that were its most important feature, as the supposedly best alternative for China to the Soviet developmental model. A vague and sloganeering Twelve-Year Plan for agriculture, announced in January, 1956, listed as the major desirable objectives the elimination of pests, the reclamation of much land, and the mechanization of agriculture, all to be achieved by the collective action of the peasants. Given its vagueness, little more was heard of this plan.

More important, in April, 1956, Mao made an important speech (not published until the Cultural Revolution) on what he called "the ten great relationships." Of these, the first four were economic in nature, Mao's key slogan being "more, faster, better, and more economically." The first were the relationships between industry and agriculture and between heavy and light industry: he conceded that heavy industry must continue to get the lion's share of state investment funds but insisted that the proportion allocated to light industry and agriculture should nevertheless be increased. The second was the relationship between coastal and inland industries: he conceded the correctness of the existing policy of locating most new industry in the interior (for strategic as well as economic reasons) but warned against neglecting coastal industry. The third was the relationship between defense and "economic construction": he urged that the existing level of defense expenditures (one third of the central budget during the First Five-Year Plan) be reduced somewhat in favor of nonmilitary spending, in the long-term interest not only of a sounder economy but of stronger defenses (including ultimately nuclear weapons). The fourth was the relationship among the state, the local collectives (the factory or agricultural cooperative), and the individual worker or peasant: the essence of his argument was that, for economic purposes, the most important of the three was the collective. The economic portions of this important statement are little more than platitudinous common sense applied to socialist economic planning under Chinese conditions; they were not specific enough to be of much help—or harm.

By the spring of 1958, after considerable debate and experimentation, Mao and his colleagues reached agreement on what was to be the Chinese alternative to the Soviet model, or, in other words, on the first phase of the Great Leap Forward. Labor was to be mobilized to a degree never before achieved in order to maximize the output of heavy industry, light industry, and agriculture. The major new investments were to be made in the second and third of these sectors, by peasant labor organized and mobilized through the new "people's communes." Specifically, the "people's communes" were to establish and operate light industrial enterprises in addition to reclaiming land, using more labor-intensive methods in agriculture, and so forth. This approach was labeled "walking on two legs" (that is, combining modern technology and local, initially unskilled, labor). By the summer of 1958, sufficient momentum had been gained so that the Party leadership decided that the communes should also operate heavy industrial enterprises, notably the famous "backyard furnaces" for making steel. These enterprises turned out for the most part to be disastrously unsuccessful—they diverted resources from other, more appropriate tasks and produced a very inferior product—and most of them were accordingly abandoned in the autumn of 1958 (see Chapter 3).

In spite of these and some other modifications, the strains generated by the Great Leap Forward, compounded by three years of bad weather (1959–61), as well as the withdrawal of Soviet technicians and the halt of Soviet-aided construction (1960), brought the economy to the brink of disaster by the end of 1960. An energetic program aimed at recovery was promptly adopted under the leadership of the Party apparatus, while Mao retreated temporarily to the background. Heavy industry was de-emphasized (except for strategic weapons), and the major stress was placed on agriculture and light industry. A reasonable level of incentives was restored to the peasants. Grain imports were inaugurated to help feed the coastal cities. This program had great success in preventing a collapse of consumption, in the rural areas and in the cities; indeed, consumption levels began to improve in 1962. In 1963, when the Third Five-Year Plan should have gone into effect but did not because of the priority being given to recovery from the Great Leap Forward, heavy industrial expansion was resumed to a limited degree. The Third Five-Year Plan nominally began in 1966, with some talk of a "new upsurge," but its nature is unclear, and, in any case, it was promptly swallowed up by the Cultural Revolution as the Second had been by the Great Leap Forward.

From 1962 on, the Party apparatus leadership's economic recovery program was under attack from Mao as "revisionist." In public, his offensive was focused on Sun Yeh-fang, an economist who advocated a version of "market socialism" in which resources should be allocated in accordance with profitability, rather than political or ideological considerations, or the criterion of gross output regardless of cost. In reality, of course, Mao was debating the Party apparatus leadership, as well as the Politburo Standing Committee member and economic planner Ch'en Yun. Mao also found the public polemic with the Soviet Union a convenient forum for getting his views on domestic issues into print. In his so-called Ninth Letter (July 14, 1964) to and against the Soviet leadership, Mao (or his anonymous spokesman, probably Deputy Foreign Minister Ch'iao Kuan-hua) listed fifteen points as "the main contents of the theories and policies advanced by Comrade Mao Tse-tung." These were more heavily ideological and political than the "ten great relationships" of 1956, but several had important economic implications. For example, it was insisted that the "people's commune . . . is a suitable form of organization for the solution of the question of this transition," meaning the transition from "collective ownership" to "ownership by the whole people" (that is Communism). The Maoist principles of manual labor for students and cadres, and increasing equality of personal incomes, were reaffirmed. Above all, the "restoration of capitalism" in a society once embarked on the "transition to socialism" must be prevented. This document can be considered Mao's first public statement of his program for what was to become the Cultural Revolution.

The essence of Mao's economic program for the Cultural Revolution is contained in a letter he wrote to Lin Piao on May 7, 1966. In this, he said in effect that each sector of society (he mentioned specifically the armed forces, the industrial workers, the peasants, students, workers in service trades, and Party and government cadres) should of course emphasize its own specialty but should also engage, to the extent possible, in other types of "economic construction," in "mass work," and in "criticizing the bourgeoisie." This close intermixture of economic and noneconomic considerations is typical of Mao's "thought."

During the Cultural Revolution, the population was exhorted with much propaganda to "learn from" and emulate two models: the poor but successful Tachai production brigade (in Shansi), and the large new Taching oil field (in Heilungkiang). In both the emphasis was on hard work, small income differentials, and largely ideological incentives.

One of the effects of the outbreak of the Cultural Revolution was to transfer the source of economic directives for the State Council and its subordinate agencies from the Party apparatus leadership to Mao and his personal following, notably Ch'en Po-ta. Chou En-lai's basic response to this shift was to pay lip service to the new militancy in the economic sphere, and more than lip service in the ideological and political spheres, but in practice to limit the Cultural Revolution's impact on the economy and to keep the latter functioning as efficiently as possible. For example, he publicly urged the Red Guards to avoid interfering with industrial and agricultural production. This advice was not fully heeded, but the economic impact of the Cultural Revolution and the Red Guards was actually fairly limited. For one thing, unlike the Great Leap Forward, the Cultural Revolution was predominantly an urban movement. Even in the industrial sector, the effect of Red Guard disorders, purges of administrators and managers, and the like, had little economic effect until 1967 and even then produced only about a 15-per-cent drop in industrial output, a serious but far from disastrous situation and an injury far less severe than had been inflicted by the Great Leap Forward. Agriculture was scarcely affected, in marked contrast to the situation produced by the Great Leap Forward.

It was not primarily for economic reasons, therefore, that the Cultural Revolution was brought to an end in the summer and autumn of 1968. Nor were these the main considerations behind a partial reversion to the Great Leap Forward (abolition of private plots and of differential pay through the termination of the work point system in some areas), as well as massive transfers of people (perhaps 30 million) from the cities to the countryside that occurred in late 1968 and early 1969, probably under the influence of Lin Piao and Ch'en Po-ta. The motives were essentially political.

In 1969–70, a more normal and rational economic policy emerged, apparently under the influence of Chou En-lai, and it has continued in effect since the purge of Lin Piao in September, 1971. The Fourth Five-Year Plan went nominally into effect in 1971, but no details were announced, other than claimed percentage increases in production over undisclosed base figures. In industry, the situation resembled the one that had existed from 1963 to 1965: there was a modest long-term expansion of investment and output in the heavy industrial sector, but the emphasis was on transport (including aircraft and trucks), light industry, and in particular on support of agriculture (through fertilizers and farm machinery). In agriculture, Chou's political need for Maoist support dictated a stress on small projects, local initiatives, and the like, but nothing remotely resembling the Great Leap Forward. Peasants appear to have been tacitly guaranteed the retention of their private plots (the point was included in the draft state constitution, which was adopted by the Central Committee in September, 1970, but is not yet formally in effect). Consumption, except temporarily in disaster areas, was maintained at tolerable levels.

The future of China's economic development is very difficult to predict. It appears to depend, as in many if not all other countries, on such imponderables as the shifting relationship between population and food (as well as other natural resources), the pace of industrialization, and its impact on an already hard-pressed ecological base. It is clear, however, that the Chinese economy is capable of generating a modern sector that is impressive in absolute terms. As for the prospects for modernization of the economy and society as a whole, it appears that China has neither the best nor the worst chances among the developing countries, and that it is likely to experience neither a spectacular breakthrough nor a disastrous collapse, at any rate in what is laughingly called the foreseeable future.

The Economic Record

It is impossible to form an exact picture of China's economic performance except during the second half of the First Five-Year Plan. At other times, data have not been adequately available to the regime, have not been published, or have been published in distorted form for propaganda effect (during the Great Leap Forward, the situation was a combination of the first and third). All statements by outsiders, including trained economists, are therefore essentially estimates. The following discussion of various aspects of China's economic performance since 1949 is offered tentatively, with these considerations in mind, and with a minimum of statistics that draw on a range of Western, Soviet, and Chinese sources and are at best approximate or dubious. Foreign trade, on which the C.P.R. publishes no comprehensive statistics, is discussed in the next section.

As a rough quantitative indicator of over-all economic progress to date, it may be noted that Chou En-lai has estimated (to Edgar Snow) China's gross national product for 1970 at $120 billion (three-quarters of it from industry, one-quarter from agriculture), a figure between two and three times the size of the corresponding one for the period around the beginning of the industrialization drive in 1953, and indicating an impressive rate of long-term growth in industry but a much lower one in agriculture.

Much has been done in China since 1949 toward reshaping nature, mainly through mass labor projects, in man's supposed economic interest. There has been substantial reclamation of unused land, although what has been reclaimed is slight in comparison with the existing cultivated area, and much of it appears to be marginal or even submarginal. Water conservancy, especially flood control and irrigation, has been carried out on a large scale. Here, as in all other respects, the record is a mixed one of successes and failures, or at least incomplete successes. Floods have not been eliminated. The dry soil of North China appears to have been overirrigated in some areas (from the Yellow River and its tributaries), with a resulting tendency toward salinization (upward movement from the subsoil of alkaline salts harmful to plants). Afforestation has been conducted on a large scale in North China and Manchuria, but many of the trees have evidently died.

China since 1949 has been the only major country building railways on a substantial scale: the pre-1949 network (including narrow-gauge lines) has been roughly doubled (to about 24,000 miles). Highways and truck traffic have been relatively neglected until recently, but this situation is improving. The same holds for the merchant marine; until now, most of China's foreign trade, including exports, has been carried in chartered bottoms. Until recently, China's civil air transport has been poorly developed at home, and there have been international flights in Chinese aircraft only to immediately adjacent countries, but again this situation is beginning to improve.

As for social infrastructure, there has been a substantial expansion of the educational system, although one that is remarkable more for quantity than quality (see Chapter 12). Public health has been improved by such measures as better sanitation, the curbing of drug consumption and other abuses, and increased availability of simple medical facilities; thousands of laymen ("barefoot doctors") have been trained to give basic medical care to large numbers of people. Traditional Chinese medicine (including acupuncture) is used in addition to Western medicine, and it is beginning to be realized in the West that there are valid reasons for this other than considerations of cost.

Under the impact of the first census (1953–54) and the beginning of economic planning, the CPC gradually abandoned its doctrinaire Marxist disinterest in population control. The subject again fell into official disfavor during the Great Leap Forward, however. During the retreat from the Great Leap Forward, a serious population control campaign was launched. But it necessarily had its main impact in the cities, rather than in the countryside, where about 80 per cent of the people lived. Since then, there has been another such cycle: confusion and lack of progress (during the Cultural Revolution), and the resumption of population control, again with emphasis on the cities, since the end of the Cultural Revolution. China's population in 1972 is probably in the neighborhood of 800 million, and it is unlikely that the growth rate is much less than 2 per cent per year. For purposes of economic development and social stability, the growth rate ought to be halved, but this appears unlikely in the near future.

China reaps the largest harvests of any country in the world. The grain harvest for 1957 was 175 million tons according to the probably accurate official figure, probably about 190–200 million tons for 1958 and 150–160 million tons for 1961, and (according to Chou En-lai) 240 million tons for 1970. In addition to grain, other foodstuffs (vegetables and poultry, for example) are of course produced, to a large extent on the private plots, and make up an important part of the total diet, but there are no figures available on them. In view of population growth, there has been little increase in per-capita food availability, but the total supply is distributed more evenly than before 1949, among regions and among social classes. As in most Communist countries, a large percentage of the grain and industrial crops produced by the peasants is bought compulsorily by the state, at prices fixed somewhat below the free-market price.

There was clearly underinvestment in light industry during the First Five-Year Plan, after which this began to be corrected, but with a greater orientation toward increasing agricultural output than toward producing more consumer goods. In 1970, 14 million tons of chemical fertilizer were produced. Consumer goods, especially textiles and food, have generally been in adequate, but only barely adequate, supply. The prices of necessities, some of them rationed, are kept low; the prices of nonessential goods are high. Roughly speaking, the Chinese population, except in the more remote areas, is in the stage of rural electrification, the bicycle, the ballpoint pen, and the transistor radio; it is not yet at the stage of the motorcycle and the television set.

Heavy industry (including mining, fuels, power, and defense) received the major emphasis during the First Five-Year Plan and therefore grew rapidly during that period, at about 14 per cent per year. There was a further surge of growth rates during the early phase of the Great Leap Forward, followed by a decline, then by a slow recovery until the Cultural Revolution. Since the Cultural Revolution, growth has apparently attained a respectable rate because of the coming into production of previously constructed plants. Steel production seems to have reached 18 million tons in 1970 and 21 million tons in 1971. The military budget, on which virtually nothing is published, is probably about $10 billion per year.

Like that of heavy industry, the progress of science and technology has been very sensitive to political trends. Progress has not been sufficient to produce a nationwide "industrial revolution," but accomplishments at the leading edge have been impressive. There have been considerable achievements in electronics, including computers. China has orbited two earth satellites (April, 1970; March, 1971), in addition to carrying on the development of military missiles and nuclear warheads.

Foreign Economic Relations

For most of the period since 1949, China's foreign trade has totaled only about $4 billion per year (imports plus exports). For the first decade, about two-thirds of that trade was conducted with the Communist countries (roughly 40 per cent of the total with the Soviet Union); the rest was divided about equally between the developing countries and the developed non-Communist countries (other than the United States, which maintained a total embargo on trade with mainland China). There was a slight import surplus until 1955, then an export surplus as China began to repay the credits received from the Soviet Union, a process that took ten years. Since 1965, China has contracted no further long-term external debt. The main single source of hard-currency foreign exchange came to be (in the 1950's) and has remained Hong Kong, from which China buys very little and to which it exports about $500 million worth of food and water per year.

After 1960, trade with the Soviet Union fell off very sharply. The former Soviet share was diverted, for practical purposes, to Japan (which became China's leading trading partner in 1965) and Western Europe (especially West Germany).

The Cultural Revolution had a fairly minor impact on China's foreign trade, mainly in the form of delay in signing contracts. Probably the most important development since the Cultural Revolution is the fairly clear sign that Peking has become concerned, for political and economic reasons, over the growing role of Japan in China's foreign trade, and would like at least to hold down the rate of growth of its trade with Japan and increase the proportional share of the major competitors. (It is too early to predict the effect of the coming into office of the relatively pro-Peking Japanese Government of Premier Kakuei Tanaka in July, 1972, except that Tanaka is clearly anxious to promote Sino-Japanese trade rather than see it level off; he may therefore be disposed to make major political concessions to Peking.) The major beneficiaries of this tendency are likely to be the Common Market countries (especially West Germany), the Soviet Union (whose trade with China has begun to pick up since 1970), and the United States. The United States opened up at least the possibility of benefiting from the trend by abolishing most restrictions on nonstrategic trade with China in 1971. Since then, China has begun to buy a few high-technology items (such as satellite communications equipment and aircraft) from the United States. In many areas, however, American prices are not competitive with those of other major industrial countries, and the growth of Sino-American trade is therefore likely to be slow. Furthermore, although Peking has not appeared since 1960 to pick its trading partners mainly for political reasons, it has certainly tried to extract political as well as commercial advantages from its trade when possible. For example, the hunger of the major Japanese firms for expanded trade with China has been exploited to build up pressure on the Japanese Government for a break of diplomatic and economic relations with Taiwan. A similar approach is likely to be adopted toward the United States.

China's imports have consisted mainly of capital equipment, technological knowledge in various forms, industrial raw materials (copper and rubber, for example), and about 5 million tons of grain (mainly wheat) annually since 1961 (Canada and Australia being the major suppliers). It has exported mainly primary products (pig's bristles and such minerals as tin, for example), foodstuffs, consumer goods (including textiles badly needed at home), and more recently, some capital equipment. From April 15 to May 15 and October 15 to November 15 a trade fair is held at Canton, mainly for signing export contracts with interested foreign buyers; import contracts are normally signed in Peking, after protracted negotiations.

During the decade after 1950, China received a large amount of aid, worth about $2 billion, from the Soviet Union in the heavy industrial (including military) field. This included blueprints, capital equipment, and technical services. Only about one-quarter was covered by known long-term development credits from the Soviet Union; the rest was paid for largely by Chinese exports on a fairly current basis and could therefore be considered simply as trade. Peking does not appear likely to want any further long-term credits from abroad, at least as long as Mao Tse-tung, with his insistence on "self-reliance" reinforced by the decade of difficulties with the Soviet Union, is alive.

Since the mid-1950's, China has become a source of foreign aid, providing it, sometimes as grants and sometimes as credits (more commonly low-interest than interest-free), to some smaller Communist countries (North Korea, North Vietnam, Albania, and apparently Romania) and to a fairly large number of non-Communist Afro-Asian countries. The recipients have been selected by highly political criteria, to reward and encourage friendly governments or to achieve a regional or worldwide propaganda effect, to compete with the United States and/or the Soviet Union, or some combination of these. One of the most interesting and important cases is Tanzania, where Peking is financing and constructing the long and difficult Tan-Zam (Tanzania-Zambia) Railway. In most cases, Chinese economic aid has been connected with light industrial projects (textile mills and cement plants, for example). Chinese military aid has gone mainly to North Korea, North Vietnam, Albania, Pakistan, and Tanzania, as well as a variety of revolutionary movements. To date the C.P.R. has committed itself to about $5 billion in economic and military aid, of which about $3 billion has actually been drawn by the recipient countries. China's commitments to new economic aid programs during 1971 exceeded those of the Soviet Union during the same year.

It seems very likely that, if it is to increase its industrial growth rate significantly, China will have to modify its preference for "self-reliance" to the extent of larger imports of capital equipment and technological knowledge. It is not at all clear, however, where the funds to pay for such an increase would come from, unless Peking also modified its reluctance to accept foreign credits. The outlook, therefore, is for a steady but not spectacular process of industrial growth, matched by a similar growth of foreign trade. China does not seem to have the potential for an economic miracle, in per-capita terms, of the Japanese variety, or for growth in absolute terms to the levels of the United States and the Soviet Union. Nor does it appear likely that China's pattern of economic development will be imitated, successfully or otherwise, by many of the developing countries.

FURTHER READINGS

Three competent general analyses of the Chinese economy can be recommended: Yuan-li Wu, *The Economy of Communist China: An*

Introduction, New York: Praeger, and London: Pall Mall Press, 1965; Audrey Donnithorne, *China's Economic System*, New York: Praeger, and London: George Allen & Unwin, 1967; and Jan S. Prybyla, *The Political Economy of Communist China*, Scranton, Pa.: International Textbook Company, 1970. Two detailed studies by American Government economists have been sponsored by the Joint Economic Committee of the U.S. Congress: *An Economic Profile of Mainland China*, New York: Praeger, 1968; and *The People's Republic of China: An Economic Assessment*, Washington, D.C.: U.S. Government Printing Office, 1972.

There are two good analyses of the First Five-Year Plan and the Great Leap Forward, respectively: Choh-ming Li, *Economic Development of Communist China: An Appraisal of the First Five Years of Industrialization*, Berkeley: University of California Press, 1959; and Richard Moorsteen, "Economic Prospects for Communist China," *World Politics*, vol. ix, no. 2 (January, 1959), pp. 192–220 (overly bullish, but still valuable).

Three interesting, sympathetic analyses of the Maoist economic strategy are available: Jack Gray, "The Economics of Maoism," *Bulletin of the Atomic Scientists*, February, 1969, pp. 42–51; Nicolas Spulber, "Contrasting Economic Patterns: Chinese and Soviet Development Strategies," *Soviet Studies*, vol. xv. no. 1 (July, 1963), pp. 1–16; and Carl Riskin, "Small Industry and the Chinese Model of Development," *The China Quarterly*, no. 46 (April–June, 1971), pp. 245–73. A comprehensive analysis is presented in J. Simmonds, "Mass Modernization—Aspects of the Chinese Experience," *Asia Quarterly* (Brussels), 1972/1, pp. 3–78.

An interesting analysis of the economic policy debate of 1958 is Roderick MacFarquhar, "Communist China's Intra-Party Dispute," *Pacific Affairs*, vol. xxxi, no. 4 (December, 1958), pp. 323–35.

The text of the Twelve-Year Plan can be found in American Consulate General, Hong Kong, *Current Background*, no. 781 (February 14, 1966); that of Mao's "ten great relationships" speech in Jerome Ch'en, *Mao*, Englewood Cliffs, N.J.: Prentice-Hall, 1969, pp. 65–85; and that of Mao's letter of May 7, 1966, to Lin Piao in *Current Background*, no. 891 (October 8, 1969). On Sun Yeh-fang, see *ibid.*, no. 905 (April 29, 1970).

Two books focused on China's external economic relations can be recommended: Alexander Eckstein, *Communist China's Economic Growth and Foreign Trade*, New York: McGraw-Hill, 1966; and Alexander Eckstein, ed., *China Trade Prospects and U. S. Policy*, New York: Praeger, 1971.

12. The People

It is of course much easier to study the CPC's policies toward its people than to know what the actual effects of those policies are. There is no public opinion in China in the Western sense, in view of the Party's tight control over legal political activity and the media. There are no public-opinion polls. Meaningful surveys by outside observers are virtually impossible; as the more perceptive and honest of them concede, their travels and contacts are supervised to varying degrees, and (more important) any Chinese who tried to express discontent or disaffection to a foreigner would run the risk of being discovered and getting into serious trouble. This chapter was written, and should be read, with these limitations in mind.

Participation and Mobilization

As its concept of the "mass line" (see Chapter 6) indicates, the CPC not only will not tolerate even peaceful opposition, it will also not accept mere passive compliance with its directives. It runs what is sometimes called a mobilization regime; its ambitious developmental objectives require the active understanding, support, and collaboration of as many people as possible. In the political sphere, this necessitates a high level of popular participation in the political process.

The high level of participation demanded of the people by the regime takes several forms. The individual's basic economic role (as peasant, industrial worker, and so on) must of course be fulfilled at least adequately. The individual must cheerfully allow himself to be submerged in the stream of propaganda that pours from the regime via radio, newspapers, posters, political meetings, and other means. He must belong to, and take an active part in, one or more of the organizations approved and controlled by the

CPC (see below, under Mass Organizations). He must study in order to raise his ideological consciousness along officially approved lines. If a white-collar worker, he must engage for the same purpose in periods of manual labor. He must vote for the official candidates (the only ones available) at elections, mainly as an expression of his support for the regime. When called on, he must participate in the regime's mass campaigns.

Of these types of activity, the only one that appears to require elaboration here is the last, which is also the only one that could be considered abnormal by Communist standards. A mass campaign (sometimes called a mass movement) is simply a temporary intensification, at the CPC's initiative, of the usual level of propaganda and political activity among the population for some particular purpose. The CPC made use of the mass campaign, like many of its other post-"liberation" techniques, before 1949. Since then, there have been approximately ten such campaigns (it is not always possible to say when one ends and another begins). Prior to 1956, the purposes of the mass campaigns (land reform, "Resist America, Aid Korea," anti-"counterrevolutionaries," cooperativization of agriculture, and others) were mainly consolidation of the CPC's control over the population and promotion of the type of socioeconomic development the Party desired. Beginning in 1956, the effects of the Soviet Twentieth Party Congress and the related increase in tension between Mao and the Party apparatus leadership led to the addition of a highly ideological component to the mass campaigns (the Hundred Flowers campaign, the "rectification" movement of 1957–58, the Great Leap Forward), then to the suspension of mass campaigns as the Party apparatus moved to promote recovery from the Leap (1961–62), then to a resumption of highly ideological but rather ineffective mass campaigns (the Socialist Education Movement in particular) as Mao tried with little cooperation from the Party apparatus to reinject revolutionary momentum into the country (1963–65), then to the Cultural Revolution (1966–68, which in some of its aspects was a mass campaign), and finally the brief campaign (see Chapter 4) to transfer people from the cities to the countryside and reactivate some features of the Great Leap Forward (1968–69).

After the decision has been taken in Peking to initiate a campaign, it has usually spread outward so that the last provinces to take it up have been those along the inland frontiers. Each province, or possibly region, starts some experiments or pilot projects.

The center observes these, selects the one to its liking, and holds it up as the model for the country as a whole. At this point, the campaign assumes nationwide proportions and goes into high gear. The campaign is called off (usually informally, rather than formally) when the center judges that it has passed the point of diminishing returns, or sometimes (as with the Great Leap Forward) not until after it has actually become counterproductive. For reasons of the regime's self-image, if for no other reason, it can never be admitted officially that a given mass campaign should not have been launched in the first place, still less that there might be something wrong with the belief in the essential unity between the Party and the masses that forms the rationale for the mass campaign.

Mass Organizations

Mass organizations are those with large memberships whose main function is to serve as "transmission belts" in the implementation of the regime's "mass line." Broadly speaking, there are two types: those formed on a local basis (in the cities or rural areas), mainly to facilitate local control, administration, and mobilization, and without a national organization; and those with national organizations and functional rather than geographic criteria for membership. Both types are invariably led, at least indirectly and usually directly, by CPC members.

The first type contains two subtypes, one for urban and one for rural areas. The former is the residents' (or street) committee, the regulations governing which date from 1954, and which seemed in 1960 to be on its way to being brought within the framework of urban people's communes until the latter idea was dropped. Essentially, the members of the residents' committees work without special pay to support the local governments and help mobilize the residents for various purposes; they mediate disputes, encourage attendance at meetings, and so on.

The equivalent organization in the countryside is the production team, which since 1959 has been the lowest of three administrative tiers within the people's commune, the intermediate one being the production brigade and the highest one the commune itself. The basic unit of work and of accounting within the commune, the team has considerable autonomy, at least in theory. The membership of the team normally corresponds to the population of the rural village or hamlet, and in effect its leadership (theoretically elected) is the government of the village.

The second type of mass organization can be divided into three subtypes: large functional or occupational organizations, those concerned with foreign affairs, and those of a professional or scholarly character. All three subtypes, in addition to being led by CPC members, as are all mass organizations (the minor parties are not considered mass organizations for the purpose of this analysis), are organized and function like the CPC itself on the basis of "democratic centralism" (see Chapter 7) and have a hierarchy of local organizations as well as a national headquarters.

The category of large functional or occupational organizations includes the Students' Federation and the Women's Federation. The two most important and interesting in this category, however, as well as the two that have had the greatest political difficulties, are probably the All-China Federation of Trade Unions and the Communist Youth League. In the first, there were repeated conflicts even before the Cultural Revolution between the Federation leadership and the Party leadership, because the former tended to act as a spokesman for the interests of the workers and resist the demands of the Party center for keeping wages down and production quotas up. The main problem of the Communist Youth League, whose principal function was probably its role as a recruiting ground for the CPC, was that its leadership was an integral part of the Party apparatus, and that its outlook and much of the membership's were suspected by the Maoists of being insufficiently revolutionary. Accordingly, the Federation and the League came under severe Maoist pressure in 1965 and virtually ceased to function as coherent national organizations. The League was replaced for practical purposes by the Red Guards, but it has begun to be revived quietly since the end of the Cultural Revolution, as an aspect of the gradual rebuilding of the Party apparatus.

Except for the defunct Sino-Soviet Friendship Association, which had (or claimed) a large membership, the organizations of the second type, such as the Chinese People's Institute of Foreign Affairs, are relatively small. They are devoted almost entirely to nominally unofficial (actually, semiofficial) contacts with unofficial non-Communist foreigners, usually but not always those from countries with which the C.P.R. maintains diplomatic relations. Their primary purpose is to give their foreign contacts the best possible impression of the C.P.R.; in this, they are generally rather successful, not only because of their personnel, organization, and experience, but also because most prospective visitors unlikely to be impressed as desired are not admitted to the country.

The third subtype performs some collective functions for its members (writers, artists, and intellectuals), but its main purpose is to facilitate the regime's control over them and their output. It is virtually impossible for a writer or artist, for example, to function except as a member in good standing of one of these organizations and in accordance with its policies, or to express publicly any ideas disapproved of by the regime without serious risk. A well-known case in point is the harmless leftist writer Hu Feng, who got into trouble in 1955 because he objected to the crude, deadening system of controls that the CPC had fastened on the country's literary life.

Social Conditions and "Human Cost"

It can be said fairly safely, and it has been confirmed recently by perceptive foreign visitors, that on the average the individual Chinese lives (except in occasional periods of disorder) at a higher economic level and under tighter social control, and hence in less freedom, than under any previous regime. There is a high level of public order but also a shortage of intellectual curiosity and initiative, because a display of the latter qualities in areas of political sensitivity is not likely to be useful and may even be dangerous. Privacy and private personal relations, including their unattractive aspect of nepotism, are very much at a discount. "Comradeship," meaning in practice the obligation to encourage conformity to public policy and inform on and criticize (perhaps in public meetings) even close friends and relatives who appear to be deviating or slackening their efforts, is exalted instead. Beneath the surface of social life, which can be cheerful, there is usually an undercurrent of tension, partly because the official requirements imposed on the individual are not only strict but, on the basis of the record, liable to change with little or no advance notice. Uniformity of dress, as well as of attitude and behavior, was demanded during the Cultural Revolution; since its termination, more colorful clothing has been permitted, but mainly for children rather than adults.

These generalizations refer to the average Chinese who is not considered an enemy by the regime. But many Chinese have been considered and treated as enemies of the regime, either with good reason or simply as examples. A reasonable estimate of the number of people executed by, or at the instigation of, the regime since 1949 would be 1 million. (Mao gave a figure of 800,000 in 1957.) In addition, a much larger number of people have been sentenced to forced labor or less demanding forms of confinement, have lost their jobs or property, have suffered in their social standing, or undergone other sanctions. There is obviously no way to measure this human cost, nor is it necessarily true that it outweighs the regime's positive achievements, but it ought to be borne in mind as part of a balanced appraisal. It is all too easy for the foreigner to ignore the problem of human cost, because the regime that has exacted it is obviously "there" and likely to remain, because he may wish to visit the country or return to it, because Communist Parties have long experience in cultivating the goodwill of foreign intellectuals, because he is not bearing any of the human cost himself, because the result is not a direct threat or cause of harm to him, and because in any case there is nothing he can do about it.

Religion Under Pressure

Although the 1954 state constitution and the unpublished 1970 draft (see Chapter 8) proclaim freedom of religious belief and observance, the basic incompatibility between traditional religion in all forms and the secular religion calling itself Marxism-Leninism (including its Maoist variant) has rendered this freedom largely illusory in practice. The CPC's basic approach has been to use organizational manipulation, hostile propaganda, and occasional coercion to control, restrict, and ultimately eliminate religion. Proselytism by religious bodies has been practically prohibited. The degree of success achieved, although by no means complete, is impressive.

By the mid-twentieth century, the hold on the Chinese of Confucianism, which is more of an ethical system than a religion, had declined to the level of a residue of attitudes and social practices without an organizational framework. The Communist campaign against it has therefore been confined largely to propaganda. Connected with various popular cults and secret societies, Taoism presented more of a problem. It was subjected to severe persecution during the two major campaigns against "counterrevolutionaries" (1951–52, 1955), and at the end of 1956, was brought under the supervision of a CPC-controlled China Taoist Association. Popular religion (such as "ancestor worship" and various superstitious practices) was left relatively untouched, apart from the considerable impact on the family of such innovations as the Marriage Reform Law of 1950 (see Chapter 3), until the Great Leap Forward. At that time, an extraordinarily violent attack was launched against it, including the desecration of gravesites and the consolidation of burial plots, not only in the name of greater efficiency and productivity but also for the purpose of changing the peasants' outlook. The campaign was largely dropped, along with the Great Leap Forward itself, apparently with inconclusive results.

Like Taoism, Buddhism in China was subjected to severe persecution during the early 1950's. The China Buddhist Association was established in 1953 with jurisdiction over all of the main forms of Buddhism in China (Mahayana or northern Buddhism, Theravada or southern Buddhism, and Lamaism in Tibet and Inner Mongolia). Unlike Taoism, Chinese Buddhism is fortunate in having a large number of coreligionists elsewhere in Asia. Mainly in order to make a good impression on the latter, the CPC eased its persecution of Buddhism after 1955 and accorded it the appearance of greater freedom. The main exception was Tibetan Lamaism, which was closely connected with a growing anti-Chinese revolt in Tibet that began about 1955. The most spectacular evidence of this tension was the flight of the Dalai Lama, the head of the Lamaist hierarchy, to India in March 1959. The Panchen Lama, the second figure in the hierarchy and considered relatively pro-Chinese, was purged in 1964, disappeared during the Cultural Revolution, and was reported by Tibetan refugees to have been killed.

Islam in China has three main schools: the traditionalists (adherents of the Chinese variant of Islam), the reformists (partisans of original, Koranic, Islam), and the modernists (advocates of the introduction of some Western science and philosophy). Regardless of these differences, the China Islamic Association was set up over all three in 1953. Like Buddhism, Islam was protected to a degree, but more in appearance than in reality, by the existence of coreligionists in other countries.

Chinese Christianity obviously has many coreligionists abroad, but unlike Buddhism and Islam, it is considered by the CPC to have close historic connections with foreign "imperialism." At the time of "liberation," the Protestant churches were receiving financial support from sources within the "imperialist" countries (especially the United States), and the Catholic Church had of course acknowledged the spiritual authority of the Holy See. Christians, especially foreign missionaries, thus were persecuted rather severely in the 1950's, in the course of the great campaigns against "counterrevolutionaries." The CPC demanded that all the Christians accept the "three autonomies": "self-administration" (no more control by foreigners), "self-support" (no more foreign financial aid), and "self-propagation" (no more foreign missionaries).

For a variety of reasons, the Protestant churches went rather far toward accepting and implementing the "three autonomies." However reluctantly, they necessarily accepted the regime's seizure of their hospitals, schools, and other institutions, and the imposition in 1950 of a CPC-controlled National Committee of Protestant Churches in China for Self-Administration.

Because of their greater organizational and doctrinal unity, the Catholics resisted the "three autonomies" (except in the matter of finances) more vigorously and more successfully, in spite of considerable persecution. In 1957–58, as one manifestation of the militancy associated with the Great Leap Forward, the regime began to move toward cutting the ties between Chinese Catholicism and the Holy See. This was accomplished with great skill, in a way that has also been used in some East European countries, by coercing certain bishops into consecrating new bishops whose orders were valid under Catholic canon law, but who were sympathetic to the CPC and therefore unacceptable to the Holy See and in schism with it.

As its degree of actual control over the Christian churches in China increased, the regime began to try increasingly to impress Western visitors with the allegedly free and flourishing condition of Christianity under the CPC's "leadership" by permitting carefully controlled contacts with selected representatives of various denominations.

During the retreat from the Great Leap Forward, pressures on religion eased considerably, apparently in part as a reflection of an attitude on the part of the Party apparatus leadership that was more tolerant, although not necessarily more favorable, than that of the true believing Maoists. This phase came to an abrupt end in 1966 under the impact of the Cultural Revolution and the Red Guards. The latter were militantly hostile to any manifestation of religion (other than their own) as a "reactionary" phenomenon and, in the case of Christianity, an "imperialist" one as well. There was considerable violence against "religious followers," damage to and desecration of places of worship, and the like. This behavior tapered off with the suppression of the Red Guards, and the current situation (on which there is little evidence) probably resembles the one that existed during the retreat from the Great Leap Forward.

Education

Like other developing countries, the C.P.R. has placed much emphasis in recent years on mass education and mass literacy. That it appears to have made less progress from the starting point (1949 in this case) than some others (Indonesia since 1945, for example) is due, though only in part, to the difficulty of the Chinese written language, even as somewhat simplified by the regime. Another major problem has been ideological dominance and political interference which at several periods have been extreme by the standard of developing or of Communist countries.

In the early years after 1949, the emphasis was on spare-time literacy courses for adults and on the introduction into the regular educational system of Soviet textbooks and methods, plus indoctrination in the "thought" of Mao Tse-tung. The First Five-Year Plan tended to draw funds away from educational expansion and into economic development, and the former process failed to increase the supply of available jobs as fast as the growing size of the relevant age groups demanded. School hours had to be shortened and political controls tightened. Children of workers and peasants were given preference for admission to middle (secondary) schools and institutions of higher learning, but they had great difficulty in competing for good academic records and good jobs after graduation with children from more culturally advantaged backgrounds. Degrees were not awarded; students were seldom allowed to choose the schools they attended or the jobs they took after graduation; and educational standards were generally low (by advanced foreign standards), except in a handful of advanced research institutions. On the other hand, the system produced a sizable number (in absolute terms, not in relation to the size of the population) of specialized middle-level technicians, a commodity that in most countries is in short supply.

The brief "blooming and contending" period in the Hundred Flowers campaign in the spring of 1957 produced ample evidence of discontent on university campuses with Party controls, Soviet methods, limitations on academic freedom, and the like. The regime took these signs of disaffection on the part of the upcoming generation very seriously; the only known executions in this connection were of three adult ringleaders of middle-school demonstrations. In 1957–58, in reaction to this experience and also as an aspect of the Great Leap Forward, there began to be increased emphasis for students on production, or at any rate on manual labor, as well as on political indoctrination. The result was almost as much exhaustion among the students as among the peasants. There was a brief relaxation of pressure in 1961–62, followed by another increase beginning in 1963. More than ever, students were told that it was more important to be "red" than "expert," and "redness" of course included political consciousness and manual labor.

The educational system was bound to be affected by the Cultural Revolution, because it had implications for the political issues that were debated within the leadership. But there was an even more obvious and direct reason: the Red Guard movement inevitably drew nearly all its recruits from middle-school and university students, usually the children of worker and peasant families who had not been doing well academically and could now blame their problems on the "revisionist" Party apparatus representatives in charge of the educational system. The entire school system was closed down in June, 1966, to permit a policy review in light of the new situation and to facilitate the enrollment of the students as Red Guards. Proposed reforms were announced in January, 1967, with emphasis on increased preference for workers' and peasants' children, shorter curricula, even greater politicization of textbooks and curricula, military training, and even more time to be spent in manual labor; entrance and course examinations were to be abolished. Beginning in March, 1967, efforts were made to get middle-school and university students back to their classrooms (primary schools appear to have reopened in the autumn of 1966), but with little success: many students were reluctant and many teachers were afraid to return. The 1968–69 academic year was greatly complicated by the transfer of millions of ex-Red Guards to the countryside, where facilities had to be provided for them to resume some form of education and make a contribution to the local economy. It was only in 1970–71 that a semblance of normality returned to the regular educational system, for the benefit of those students who remained in the cities. There, and also to a lesser extent in the rural schools, greater stress began to be quietly placed on academic criteria (including examinations once more), although within the framework of the overriding Maoist requirement for political study, manual labor, and military training, in addition to academic work.

The Intellectuals

The CPC uses "intellectual" to designate virtually anyone with a secondary education or higher and some special skill that is not primarily manual or political in character. But intellectuals are obviously as necessary to the C.P.R. as to any other state, and the CPC is well aware of this. It regards them, however, with profound distrust as fundamentally "bourgeois," ideologically and politically unreliable, if only because they like to think for themselves, and susceptible to foreign (including American and Soviet) influence. The CPC's policy toward the intellectuals has oscillated in practice between primary emphasis on its need for their services and primary emphasis on punishing and correcting their actual (and their even greater alleged) unreliability. This applies about equally to intellectuals who are members of the CPC and to intellectuals who are not.

In 1951–52, a number of prominent intellectuals were forced by the CPC to publish "confessions" of alleged errors in thought and deed. Against the background of the tensions associated with the socialization drive of the mid-1950's, there was a massive propaganda campaign against Hu Feng, who has not reappeared. In January, 1956, Chou En-lai publicly conceded that intellectuals should be given more appropriate employment and better working conditions in order to increase their efficiency, but he insisted that they needed to improve their political outlook and said nothing about freedom of thought and expression. The spring of 1956 saw the launching, under the patronage of Mao Tse-tung, of the Hundred Flowers campaign for supposedly free public discussion, with special reference to literature and intellectuals (see Chapter 3). After much persuasion, and after Mao had repeated the invitation to free discussion in his speech of February 27, 1957, on "contradictions," intellectuals and others at last began to "bloom and contend." Many of them soon proved to be "poisonous weeds" in the CPC's eyes by criticizing, among other things, its heavyhanded controls over intellectual life. There followed a massive "antirightist struggle" that soon extracted public "confessions" from some of the critics.

In this as in other respects, the fiasco had a profound effect on the CPC's attitude, and on Mao's in particular. The general nature of the effect was a considerably enhanced distrust of "bourgeois" intellectuals at home and abroad, where of course some exercised political power, and a conviction that even the leftists among them had "revisionist" tendencies. This suspicion was reinforced by the growth of the Sino-Soviet dispute, which led to further pressures on Chinese intellectuals to repudiate "revisionism." There was a brief interlude of relaxation (1961–62) due to the need to recover from the Great Leap Forward; the Party apparatus, which at that time dominated domestic policy, allowed the intellectuals professional freedom (that is, the right not necessarily to be "red" as long as one was "expert"). In practice, although unadmittedly, it also tolerated and may even have quietly encouraged a considerable degree of freedom of thought and expression, under cover of which some writers, such as Wu Han and Teng T'o, went so far as to criticize Maoist domestic and foreign policies. This interlude began to come to an end in September, 1962, when Mao went back on the political warpath at the Tenth Central Committee Plenary Session. In October, 1963, Chou Yang, the Party's watchdog over the intellectuals' ideological affairs, made an important statement (published on December 26, Mao's birthday) urging them to avoid and denounce "revisionism," of which he cited Khrushchev as the horrible example. In 1964, many intellectuals found themselves compelled to do increasing amounts of manual labor, often in the countryside. By that time Chiang Ch'ing had launched her campaign to overhaul drama and the opera and give them a purely Maoist and "revolutionary" content.

The first stage of the Cultural Revolution was a resentful determination on Mao's part to eliminate "bourgeois" tendencies from the intellectual community. The relatively young Yao Wen-yuan, who is sometimes reported to be Mao's son-in-law or nephew, made his political name by leading the charge, beginning with an important article of November, 1965, attacking Wu Han. In the spring of 1966, this exploded into a furious propaganda assault on the "black gang" of "freaks and monsters" of which Wu was considered a leading figure, with the *Liberation Army Daily* leading the charge this time. During the next few months, which saw the emergence of the Red Guard movement, the lengthening list of political victims included the Party's propaganda chief, Lu Ting-i, and Chou Yang, both of whom evidently could not accept the new extremism. The Eleventh Central Committee Plenary Session (August, 1966) promised immunity from the full effects of the Cultural Revolution to "scientists, technicians and ordinary members of working staffs," as long as they did their work, did not oppose the CPC, and had no sympathies or connections with foreign countries, but this concession was of little help to less obviously useful members of the intelligentsia. The latter felt the full fury of the Cultural Revolution and the Red Guards, and many have not re-emerged into public view. It can be assumed that some have been performing manual labor, possibly at May 7 schools (see Chapter 4).

Pressures on intellectuals began to ease somewhat after the end of the Cultural Revolution, although they were still expected to preserve ideological orthodoxy. The fall of Lin Piao and the ascendancy of Chou En-lai, and in particular the increasing contacts with other countries and with foreign visitors, appear to have accelerated the thaw markedly. In mid-February, 1972, Peking bookstores suddenly began to carry certain books that had been banned since the beginning of the Cultural Revolution, notably certain ancient and modern Western classics (for example, Montesquieu) and some Chinese literary and historical classics. A few days afterward, at the time of the Nixon visit, a few prominent non-Communist intellectuals appeared and took part in the public proceedings.

But even now it is clear that Chinese intellectuals, however necessary they may be, have no dependable protection against the effects of ideological and political shifts within the Party leadership. Given the CPC's nature and aims, this is not surprising. What is perhaps surprising is that a political system in which there is so little intellectual freedom should be the object of intense admiration on the part of a sizable number of foreign intellectuals.

The Minor Parties

Chinese Communist political theory holds that the political system rests on an alliance or united front of "four friendly classes." Of these, the CPC monopolizes the right to represent and lead not only the working class (or proletariat) but the peasantry as well; it can hardly claim to play this role, however, with respect to the two bourgeois classes (technically, strata), the national and the petty bourgeoisie. Accordingly, it feels bound by logic to permit the existence of minor parties supposedly representing these two groups (but not the working class or the peasantry). In Chinese Communist parlance, these parties are often referred to collectively as the democratic parties. There is a slight inconsistency here, since the CPC also claims to be democratic, but when used without qualification, the term nearly always means the minor parties, much as "the Party," when used without qualification, refers to the CPC.

The leaderships of all the minor parties announced their support for the CPC before 1949. Even so, three of them were quietly dissolved shortly after "liberation," presumably because the CPC found them objectionable or redundant. Since then, there have been eight parties, each claiming to represent some segment of the national or petty bourgeoisie (businessmen, "patriotic" and "revolutionary" Kuomintang members, intellectuals, and so on). The existence and composition of these parties are intended to lend at least a semblance of reality to the theory of the united front in China, not only at home but on Taiwan and elsewhere. Members of the minor parties serve as delegates to the National People's Congress and in various other public capacities, but it can safely be said that none has ever been allowed to hold a position of real political power. Similarly, "nonparty democrats" are also allowed to fill public positions devoid of any real power. Very few favored members of these groups have been allowed to join the CPC, where they could hope for at least a partial escape from futility.

The minor parties were compelled after 1949 to organize themselves along "democratic centralist" lines, but unlike the CPC, they were virtually prohibited from recruiting new members. They became even more nervous than before about the prospects for their continued existence in 1956, when the CPC began to speak of China's attaining full "socialism" within three years. Under this new dispensation, the bourgeoisie and parties claiming to represent it could be expected to become expendable. But the CPC, then in its Hundred Flowers phase, not only promised publicly and authoritatively that the minor parties would be allowed to exist as long as the CPC itself, it also allowed them to expand their memberships for a time.

Understandably misled, many of the minor party leaders began to presume, and in the spring of 1957 they were prominent among those who spoke out in criticism of the CPC. Like the others, they were punished for their temerity by being made the targets of a massive "antirightist struggle" that took the form of propaganda attacks, loss of public positions at least for a time, and the like. Recruiting of new members was of course stopped. The theory was that, although the bourgeoisie's economic base had been liquidated through the socialization drive of 1955–56, its ideological base had just been shown still to require elimination through ideological "remoulding." Accordingly, in late 1957 and early 1958, the leaders of the minor parties made a great show, in public statements and at meetings, of "giving their hearts to the Party" (the CPC).

After that, the minor parties survived, but little more. Even that seemed to be in doubt during the Cultural Revolution, whose main announced target was "bourgeois" ideology, and whose Red Guards sometimes demanded the abolition of the minor parties. Like a number of other extreme Red Guard demands, this one never became the official policy of the Party leadership, which on the contrary made a quiet but firm decision, possibly after some debate, that the minor parties were not to be eliminated. In effect, the minor parties hid while the storm blew over their heads, and they have remained sensibly inconspicuous since the end of the Cultural Revolution.

The National Minorities

Even more perhaps than ideological differences, ethnic differences and the cultural cleavages associated with them are probably the greatest nontechnological problem facing the world today. The C.P.R. displays that problem in a fairly acute form. Approximately 95 per cent of its population consists of Han (ethnic Chinese), but the other 5 per cent, consisting mainly of peoples of Mongolian, Turkish, Tibetan, and Thai stock living at a lower cultural level than the huge Han majority, fear and tend to dislike the Han, have martial traditions, and in most cases live thinly scattered over vast and strategic regions along China's inland frontiers. They have therefore been a serious problem for the CPC, which has been a serious problem for them, for one thing because their sparse population, strategic location, and the frequent mineralogical wealth of their habitats have tempted it irresistibly to move Han settlers in. On the whole, the CPC has a worse record in dealing with its national minorities than the Soviet Party has. One perhaps indirect indication of this is the fact that the Mongolian People's Republic is kept tied to the Soviet Union as a virtual satellite, not only by the presence of Soviet troops but also by its leaders' vast preference for their current status over the fate of their kinsmen in the almost de-Mongolized

Inner Mongolia Autonomous Region, where the Han outnumber the Mongols severalfold.

Before 1949, the CPC promised freedom to the national minorities, with whom it had had almost no contact prior to the Long March, including the right to secede. Somewhat paradoxically, Mao Tse-tung predicted to Edgar Snow in 1936 that the Mongolian People's Republic would voluntarily federate with revolutionary China, as would the Muslim and Tibetan minorities. In 1949, this easygoing attitude, including any illusions about the likelihood of the Mongolian People's Republic's doing anything but remain under Soviet tutelage, disappeared. The minorities were promised, and received, only Stalinist-style "autonomy" with no right to secede. This has meant that certain large areas—each populated mainly by a single important minority—have been declared autonomous regions directly under the central government, rather than a province. There are five of these: the Inner Mongolia Autonomous Region, the Sinkiang Uighur Autonomous Region, the Kwangsi Chuang Autonomous Region, the Ningsia Hui Autonomous Region, and the Tibet Autonomous Region. Smaller minority groups generally live in "autonomous" areas under the jurisdiction of one of the provinces. To these minorities, happiness has always been the absence of Han officials and settlers. Under the CPC's version of autonomy, this satisfaction is generally denied them. At least until the Cultural Revolution, there was a tendency to give the highest political position in one of the autonomous regions to a member of the national minority in question. But for reasons including the sensitivity of these areas in the CPC's eyes, its basic distrust of the minorities, and the relative backwardness of the minorities in providing recruits for the CPC as in other respects, "autonomy" has been more of a theory than a fact. Han cadres in dominant positions, Han troops, and a large inflow of Han colonists (especially into Inner Mongolia, Sinkiang, and Tibet) have reduced "autonomy" to little more than a few cultural freedoms, including the important right to use the minority languages. Apart from nominal "autonomy" within the state structure, there is no effective autonomy or federal status for the minorities within the other power structures that run China (the Party, the PLA, the propaganda machine, the police, and the economic planning mechanism), all of which are essentially centralized and controlled from Peking; the limited exceptions to this rule do not include effective control by leaders of minority nationalities over their regions.

There can be little doubt that the CPC's long-term policy toward the minorities is one of assimilation. It is assumed that eventually the development process will merge them in a single socialist culture with a strong Han flavor. Like governments of other developing countries, the one in Peking dislikes nomadism, because it is difficult to control. Accordingly, strenuous and sometimes forcible efforts have been made to collectivize the nomadic herdsmen of Inner Mongolia and Sinkiang in such a way as to have them grow fodder for their likestock rather than continue to range. Land reform in the Han areas was paralleled by the abolition of "feudal" privileges for tribal chiefs and the like in the minority areas. More socialist measures, including collectivization, have been applied since about the time of the Great Leap Forward. In 1962, in line with Mao Tse-tung's growing emphasis on class struggle, and still more during the Cultural Revolution, ideological and political pressures on the minorities were increased. The story can best be told through a discussion of developments in the three most important and interesting of the minority areas—Inner Mongolia, Sinkiang, and Tibet.

To a greater degree than in the other two areas, Inner Mongolia had the advantage of being under the leadership of a member of the local minority, the Mongol Ulanfu (a Sinicized Mongol, to be sure). He did his best to protect the interests of his fellow Mongols, who were heavily outnumbered by Han after the merger of Suiyuan with the Inner Mongolia Autonomous Region in 1954. He tried to prevent further colonization of grazing lands by Han settlers and the slaughter of livestock in the process of collectivization. This policy, presumably approved by the Party apparatus leadership in Peking, was at its height during the retreat from the Great Leap Forward. This relatively relaxed situation ended abruptly in the spring of 1967, when the Cultural Revolution in the form of "Han chauvinist" Red Guards descended on Inner Mongolia and, supported by military intervention from outside the region, overthrew Ulanfu. In 1969, Inner Mongolia lost much of its territory to neighboring provinces, apparently in order to reshape political control and military command in the area in such a way as to facilitate defense in depth in the event of a Soviet invasion.

Peking pays close attention to Sinkiang because of its distance from and poor communications with China proper, its tendency toward secessionist movements, and its history of Russian and Soviet pressures. For five years (1950–55), Soviet-controlled "joint" companies virtually dominated parts of western Sinkiang, until they were dissolved and Peking's control extended throughout the region. There has been repeated trouble with local ethnic groups, especially the nomadic and warlike Kazakhs, since shortly after "liberation." The trouble has been aggravated by Peking's program of compelling them to shift from the Arabic alphabet, first to the Cyrillic (Russian) and later to the Latin. In the mid-1950's, Peking began to promote Han immigration on a substantial scale, although it has still not progressed to the point of creating a Han majority in the region. Semimilitary "production and construction" units were formed to promote the security and the development of the region. These pressures, reinforced by a socialization drive during the Great Leap Forward, produced serious upsurges of "local nationalism," including movements for secession, in 1958 and again in 1962. In the latter instance, Soviet consular authorities in Sinkiang apparently encouraged to some extent the flight of some 60,000 Uighurs and Kazakhs across the border into Soviet Central Asia. Peking closed all Soviet consulates in China in retaliation. Attempts by Red Guards to cause trouble for the Party apparatus, headed by First Secretary Wang En-mao, and the national minorities of Sinkiang were fairly firmly contained in the early months of the Cultural Revolution, but disorder mounted in 1967. In mid-1968, General Lung Shu-chin was sent in from Hunan to take control of the region, with the result that Wang was ousted by degrees during the ensuing months. By that time, Sinkiang was tenser than ever because of the Soviet invasion of Czechoslovakia, and during 1969, there was even more tension as occasional armed clashes occurred along the border.

Of all the minority areas ruled from Peking, Tibet has the best claim to be an independent state, even though no foreign country, even India, recognizes it as such. (The Indian position on Tibet has been that Peking has violated its 1951 promise of genuine autonomy for the Tibetans, in addition to claiming a boundary with India that New Delhi cannot accept.) Prior to 1949, Tibet had not been effectively controlled from China for many years. Like the Kuomintang before it, the CPC has divided the Tibetan homeland among various jurisdictions, in an effort to make control easier. Tibet proper (with Lhasa as its capital) has been left under "autonomous" (in the sense already indicated) Tibetan rule; the Nationalist-created province of Tsinghai (in the northeast) has been kept separate, but Sikang (in the southeast) has been divided between Szechwan and Tibet proper. In spite of its formal promise (in May, 1951), following military "liberation," to grant Tibet autonomy and to tolerate Lamaism, the CPC soon began to apply pressures that included Han immigration into the region's eastern sections. Peking's promise in 1955 that Tibet would be made into an autonomous region did not prevent, and may even have helped precipitate, revolts that broke out among the warlike Goloks and Khambas in eastern Tibet soon afterward and gradually evoked increasing sympathy from the more peaceable people of the Lhasa region, including the Dalai Lama. Lamaseries in eastern Tibet served as foci of resistance and sometimes became targets of action by the PLA. The situation became so serious that, in 1957, in line with its general swing toward moderation in the first half of that year, Peking thought it wise to postpone indefinitely the introduction of "democratic" reforms (redistribution of lamasery land and flocks, for example) into Tibet and to withdraw most of the Han cadres, although not the PLA garrison. The pledge lost most of its meaning during the Great Leap Forward, and the revolt continued. By the spring of 1959, Khamba guerrillas had been pushed into the vicinity of Lhasa, which thus became directly involved in the struggle. The result was the spectacular flight of the Dalai Lama to India and of thousands of Khambas to India and Nepal, from which some have continued to carry on armed raids into Tibet, so that a sharp escalation of the previously simmering Sino-Indian border dispute inevitably occurred. The PLA then engaged over the next few years in a program of brutal repression that seems to have reduced the level of resistance considerably. The pledge of 1957 was formally repudiated, and Tibet was subjected to accelerated socialization. It was finally proclaimed an autonomous region in 1965, the unusual delay being a good index to the exceptional difficulty of the CPC's political problems in the region.

During the Cultural Revolution, Red Guards entered Tibet and, with at least some support from Peking, engaged in political violence and outright struggle against the regional leadership under the powerful military figure Chang Kuo-hua, the Tibetans, and even one another. The disorder continued after, and perhaps partly because, Chang was transferred in the spring of 1967 to the even more important, and scarcely less turbulent, province of Szechwan. Violence continued after the end of the Cultural Revolution to an even greater extent than in China proper. Chang Kuo-hua regained some authority over Tibet until his death in February, 1972, when it was downgraded to a province-level military district and placed for purposes of military administration under the Chengtu Military Region, of which Chang was chief political officer.

FURTHER READINGS

A competent general treatment of political participation in the C.P.R., including mass organizations and minor parties, is James R. Townsend, *Political Participation in Communist China,* Berkeley: University of California Press, 1969.

On the complex question of social conditions, Ezra F. Vogel has written a valuable analysis of the psychological climate desired by the regime in "From Friendship to Comradeship: The Change in Personal Relations in Communist China," *The China Quarterly,* no. 21 (January–March, 1965), pp. 46–60. John Wilson Lewis, ed., *The City in Communist China,* Stanford, Calif.: Stanford University Press, 1971, is a detailed study of urban life. On the rural sector, see G. William Skinner, "Marketing and Social Structure in Rural China," *Journal of Asian Studies,* vol. xxiv, nos 1–3 (November, 1964–May, 1965). Richard L. Walker has written an interesting but highly subjective study on *The Human Cost of Communism in China,* Washington, D.C.: U.S. Government Printing Office, 1971; his estimates of "casualties to Communism" in China since 1949 range up to about 60 million.

The best recently published general study on religion is Donald E. MacInnis, *Religious Policy and Practice in Communist China: A Documentary History,* Clement Alexandre, ed., New York: Macmillan, 1971. See also the articles on Chinese Buddhism by Holmes Welch, "Buddhism under the Communists," *The China Quarterly,* no. 6 (April–June, 1961), pp. 1–14; "The Reinterpretation of Chinese Buddhism," *ibid.,* no. 22 (April–June, 1965), pp. 143–53; "Buddhism since the Cultural Revolution," *ibid.,* no. 40 (October–December, 1969), pp. 127–36.

There is a sizable literature on education in the C.P.R., only a small part of which can be cited here. There is a comprehensive study edited by Stewart Fraser, *Chinese Communist Education: Records of the First Decade,* Nashville, Tenn.: Vanderbilt University Press, 1965. Leo A. Orleans, *Professional Manpower and Education in Communist China,* Washington, D.C.: National Science Foundation, 1961, is very useful. A brief sympathetic treatment is Suzanne Pepper, "Education and Political Development in Communist China," *Studies in Comparative Communism,* vol. iii, nos 3–4 (July–October, 1970), pp. 198–223. René Goldman has written an interesting eyewitness account, "The Rectification Campaign at Peking University: May–June, 1957," *The China Quarterly,* no. 12 (October–December, 1962), pp. 138–53. There is a similar one on a later period by Diana Lary, "Teaching

English in China," *ibid.*, no. 24 (October–December, 1965), pp. 1–14. Two good studies by leading specialists are Robert D. Barendsen, "The Agricultural Middle School in Communist China," *ibid.*, no. 8 (October–December, 1961), pp. 106–34; and Donald J. Munro, "Maxims and Realities in China's Educational Policy: The Half-Work, Half-Study Model," *Asian Survey*, vol. vii, no. 4 (April, 1967), pp. 254–72. There are three valuable recent articles on educational realities by the editor of *Current Scene* (Hong Kong): "Educational Crisis in China," vol. v, no. 10 (June 30, 1967), "Educational Reform in Rural China," vol. vii, no. 3 (February 8, 1969), "Recent Developments in Chinese Education," vol. x, no. 7 (July, 1972), pp. 1–6.

Most published analysis of the intellectuals in China has concentrated on literary figures. There are a number of valuable studies of this kind, notably Merle Goldman, *Literary Dissent in Communist China*, Cambridge, Mass.: Harvard University Press, 1967; Roderick MacFarquhar, *The Hundred Flowers Campaign and the Chinese Intellectuals*, New York: Praeger, 1960, London: Atlantic Books, 1960; Dennis Doolin, "The Revival of the 'Hundred Flowers' Campaign: 1961," *The China Quarterly*, no. 8 (October–December, 1961), pp. 34–41; Merle Goldman, "The Unique 'Blooming and Contending' of 1961–62," *ibid.*, no. 37 (January–March, 1969), pp. 54–83; Donald J. Munro, "The Yang Hsien-chen Affair," *ibid.*, no. 22 (April–June, 1965), pp. 75–82; Theodore H. E. Chen, *Thought Reform of the Chinese Intellectuals*, Hong Kong: Hong Kong University Press, 1960; Robert J. Lifton, *Thought Reform and the Psychology of Totalism: A Study of "Brainwashing" in China*, New York: W. W. Norton, and London: Gollancz, 1961; Mu Fu-sheng (pseud.), *The Wilting of the Hundred Flowers: The Chinese Intelligentsia Under Mao*, London: Heinemann, 1962, New York: Praeger, 1963; Joseph Simon, "Ferment Among Intellectuals," *Problems of Communism*, vol. xiii, no. 5 (September–October, 1964), pp. 29–37; Donald J. Munro, "Dissent in Communist China: The Current Anti-Intellectual Campaign in Perspective," *Current Scene*, vol. iv, no. 11 (June 1, 1966); Merle Goldman, "The Fall of Chou Yang," *The China Quarterly*, no. 27 (July–September, 1966), pp. 132–48. Lu Ting-i's Hundred Flowers speech of May 26, 1956, and Mao Tse-tung's of February 27, 1957, on "contradictions" can be found in *Communist China, 1955–1959: Policy Documents with Analysis*, Cambridge, Mass.: Harvard University, Center for International Affairs and East Asian Research Center, 1962. Chou En-lai's *Report on the Question of Intellectuals* (January 14, 1956) was published by the Foreign Languages Press (Peking) in 1956. Chou Yang's speech was released by the New China News Agency on December 26, 1963. For documents on the period between 1962 and the Cultural Revolution, see *A Great Revolution on the Cultural Front*, Peking: Foreign Languages Press, 1965. Some important documents relating to the attack on the "black gang" can be found in American Consulate General, Hong Kong, *Current Background,* nos 784 (March 30, 1966), 786 (May 16, 1966), and 792 (June 29, 1966).

On the minor parties, in addition to Townsend (*supra*), see Harold C. Hinton, "The 'Democratic Parties': End of an Experiment?" *Problems of Communism,* vol. vii, no. 3 (May–June, 1958), pp. 39–46.

Material on the national minorities is rather scattered. Amrit Lal, "Sinification of Ethnic Minorities in China," *Current Scene,* vol. viii, no. 4 (February 15, 1970), is a useful survey. Some good general material is also contained in George Moseley, "China's Fresh Approach to the National Minority Question," *The China Quarterly,* no. 24 (October–December, 1965), pp. 15–27; his main point, however, misinterprets the situation. Paul V. Hyer has written a good political biography, "Ulanfu and Inner Mongolian Autonomy Under the Chinese People's Republic," *The Mongolia Society Bulletin,* vol. viii (1969), pp. 24–62. Two other valuable contributions are Paul V. Hyer and William Heaton, "The Cultural Revolution in Inner Mongolia," *The China Quarterly,* no. 36 (October–December, 1968), pp. 114–28; Daniel Ellegiers, "The Cultural Revolution in Tsinghai Province," *Courrier de l'Extrême-Orient* (Brussels), no. 11 (November, 1967), pp. 214–50. Developments in Sinkiang and Tibet must be followed largely from original sources.

13. Foreign Policy and Foreign Relations

It is almost axiomatic that no country's foreign policy can be fully understood in isolation from its domestic politics. It is almost equally true, although perhaps less obvious, that an essential characteristic of any political system, as of any individual, is its mode of interaction with others of its kind, or in other words its foreign policy and foreign relations. This is fully as true of China as of any other country.

The Two Strands

If there is a country where the old saw about politics stopping at the water's edge holds good, it is not China. Because of the high degree of secrecy with which foreign policy decisions are discussed and formulated in Peking, it is not possible to analyze the process from the "bureaucratic politics" perspective to the same extent as in more "open" societies. On the other hand, as in other aspects of Chinese politics and policy-making, two strands, the Maoist and the non-Maoist (in effect, the Chouist, at least in foreign policy), can be discerned, even if a bit dimly.

Mao Tse-tung's whole career and written output, and notably a series of occasional personal anti-"imperialist" statements that he has issued since 1963, testify to an intense interest in foreign policy, as well as a very limited knowledge of world affairs. He is mainly concerned with encouraging, through the Chinese example and Chinese propaganda, revolutions more or less Chinese-style in as many foreign countries as possible, against governments that in his eyes are under the control or influence of "imperialism" (mainly American), "reaction" (in effect, a catchall category), or "modern revisionism" (mainly Soviet). The qualification more or less refers principally to the fact that, at least since the beginning of the Cultural Revolution, Mao has held up as the model for the developed countries the Paris Commune of 1871, rather than the Chinese revolution, which he considers to be relevant primarily to the developing (colonial and semicolonial) countries. Mao regards it as a matter of principle to offer support (moral support, propaganda support, political guidance, arms, funds, and the like) to approved revolutionary movements and "people's wars" in other countries, within, however, fairly narrow limits imposed by considerations of risk and cost and the Maoist conviction that revolutions should be essentially "self-reliant" (meaning in particular that political decisions should be made by the local revolutionary leadership). Mao tends to assume that any government of which he disapproves is in a state of "antagonistic contradiction" with its own people, who therefore are assumed to be, or to be capable of becoming, revolutionary. Mao also has a tendency to apply the spirit and lessons (as he understands them) of the (pre-1949) Chinese revolution not only to post-1949 China but to the rest of the world. In China's case, he attempted during the Cultural Revolution to revive the spirit and political style of the Kiangsi and Yenan periods. At least in theory, he seems to believe that now as then the way to deal with a foreign military threat is to "lure the enemy to penetrate deeply," then annihilate him in a people's war. This tendency seems to have helped inhibit him from working out for export a coherent model of the essential features of China's "socialist construction" (since 1949), as distinct from its "socialist revolution" (before 1949). In a similarly straightforward, even simpleminded, way, Mao tends to see foreign policy as a projection of domestic policy; for example, his belief after 1957 that the Chinese national and petty bourgeoisie had shown themselves to retain "reactionary" tendencies clearly predisposed him to view national bourgeois governments abroad (in India, in particular) as also necessarily "reactionary." Conversely, he has occasionally talked about, and even tried to promote, foreign developments in order to facilitate desired domestic policies; this could be called the backdrop effect. Important examples of this tendency are the "East wind has prevailed over the West wind" line of 1957–58 (as a backdrop for the launching of the Great Leap Forward), the furor of 1965–66 over Vietnam (as a backdrop for the launching of the Cultural Revolution), and the exploitation in 1969–71 of the (actual) Soviet threat and the (alleged) Japanese threat for purposes of domestic post–Cultural Revolution mobilization and stabilization.

For reasons of political necessity, Chou En-lai concedes an important role to Maoist considerations and influences in foreign policy as in domestic politics and may even approve of them up to a point. As Maoism influences his behavior, so his views appear to have influenced Mao; this his been especially clear since the great enhancement of Chou's political role that began with the end of the Cultural Revolution. Whereas Mao regards the promotion of revolution, in the long run at any rate, as the highest priority abroad, Chou appears to assign a higher priority to China's national interest as viewed from a much less ideological perspective. He stresses diplomacy more than propaganda. He is much less prone than Mao to like or dislike a given foreign government for largely ideological reasons. His philosophy seems to be to avoid antagonizing, at the very least, any government that is not a direct threat to the C.P.R. (as the United States was until about 1969, and as the Soviet Union has been since 1969) or a close ally or satellite of such a threat. Such governments are normally the targets of Chou's official hostility, but he is quite capable of wooing non-Communist opposition leaders in countries whose governments he dislikes and of trying by diplomatic gestures to loosen the ties between the source of the major threat and its allies. There have been many examples of the latter technique: Japan, the United States's most important ally in Northwest Asia (from the standpoint of American commitments and bases, in particular), and Thailand, the United States's most important ally in Southeast Asia (from the same standpoint). (South Vietnam is a special case in that the American military presence there has been perceived in Peking, since 1966 at any rate, as a threat to North Vietnam rather than to the C.P.R., and since 1969 as a declining factor.)

It is reasonably clear that the two strands coexist and interact in Chinese foreign policy and foreign relations and that on occasion (notably during the strategic debate of 1965–66) other views are offered by members of the Party leadership and may exert an independent influence on the policy actually adopted. On the whole, however, the details of the policy-making process are rather obscure because of the secrecy already mentioned. The problem is less serious than it might appear. The policy-making process itself, for practical purposes, can be "black boxed": in other words, we not only cannot know for sure but do not really need to know what actually goes on inside the leadership at such times, since we know the outputs (policies) from foreign as well as Chinese sources and since, especially with the advantage of hindsight, we can form a fairly clear idea of the inputs (the objective situation, perceptions, considerations, and so forth) that contributed to determining the shape of the policy in question.

Objectives and Instrumentalities

For reasons that are uncertain but may include differences of viewpoint within the leadership along the lines just discussed and reluctance to appear as interested in anything that resembles intervention in other countries' affairs, the C.P.R. has never indicated publicly and systematically what its foreign policy objectives are. The latter must therefore be inferred from Peking's record and, to a lesser extent, from its propaganda statements as well as statements dealing with particular policies. In fact, this procedure can produce a result that has a high probability of being essentially correct.

Peking is concerned like any other regime with safeguarding its own security against possible border probes, strategic attacks, or other less dramatic threats (see Chapter 9). The military means employed are deterrence (conventional and now nuclear also), pre-emption on occasion, and defense if everything else fails. The political means employed are caution when a strategically superior power is or may become the adversary, and occasional backing down when the alternative is perceived as an unacceptable risk (as in 1953, in the last stage of the Korean War).

Peking is concerned with achieving national unification as a matter of dignity and principle. It remembers with some bitterness the "unequal" treaties by which the major foreign powers (other than the United States) annexed portions of the Manchu dynasty's tributary system in the late nineteenth and early twentieth centuries, but this is not the point. Peking has no serious intention of securing, or even demanding, the return of these territories, and is even prepared to compromise its remaining serious border disputes, those with the Soviet Union and India, as it has in signing boundary treaties with other neighbors (Burma, Nepal, Pakistan, Afghanistan, and the Mongolian People's Republic). The point is rather that Peking claims all territory, and only territory, to which the Nationalists had a serious claim in the immediate pre-1949 period. This criterion excludes the Mongolian People's Republic, whose independence under Soviet tutelage Peking has recognized *de jure,* however reluctantly, and which the Nationalists recognized in 1946, even though they withdrew recognition in 1952. It definitely includes Tibet and Taiwan; since Tibet was "liberated" in 1950–51, Taiwan is left as the main area to which the goal of national unification remains to be applied. Peking's desire for the "liberation" of Taiwan is all the keener because the island has been the Nationalists' main base since 1949 and has been protected by the United States against Communist attack since 1950. "Liberation" by military means being impractical for this reason, Peking has confined itself essentially to political approaches, in particular efforts to pressure or persuade the United States to abandon its commitment to the Nationalists and the latter to reach an accommodation with the mainland.

There is also a more complex series of objectives relating to the enhancement of Peking's influence in various environments.

The first of these is Asia, which for obvious geographic, strategic, cultural, and historical reasons occupies the highest place in Peking's calculations among the regions of the world. At the minimum, Peking would like to see Asia free of the military presence and politico-economic influence of non-Asian powers, and in particular free of bases and forces belonging to such powers and directed actually or potentially against the C.P.R. This attitude applies most definitely to the United States. There is probably little meat in recent speculation that Peking privately would like the United States to stay on as a military presence in Asia to counterbalance the Soviet Union. Peking believes that the United States can do the counterbalancing, and should maintain strategic parity with the Soviet Union for the purpose, from farther away (the continental United States and Western Europe, in particular), and should leave Asia before the Soviet Union and/or Japan are in a position to fill the ensuing partial vacuum. Reluctantly, Peking must make one major exception to this rule: the Soviet Union is obviously an Asian as well as a European power in the full territorial sense, and there is no way in which Peking can safely or effectively challenge, let alone undo, this situation in the foreseeable future. Similarly, Peking must deal with, even though it resents, those regional (that is, purely Asian) states that are, or are capable of becoming, its rivals. Until the Sino-Indian border war of 1962 demonstrated its relative weakness to the world, India was such a rival, and in very recent years it has given some signs of becoming one again by virtue of the strengthening of its armed forces, Mrs. Indira Gandhi's leadership, Soviet support, and the defeat of Pakistan. Since about 1960, Japan has increasingly emerged as the C.P.R.'s major Asian rival, objectively and potentially even if not in terms of current intent; Peking's basic approach to this problem has been to try to manage it in order to minimize the chances of Japan's becoming what Chinese propaganda has occasionally—although seldom since 1971—said it had already become, a military menace.

In view of these problems and complications, and others far too numerous to mention here, it is obvious that Peking can hardly entertain seriously the idea of having Asia as its exclusive sphere of influence without competition from extraregional, still less regional, rivals. Neither as a state nor as a revolutionary influence is Peking in a position to impose its will, regardless of what it is, on any other Asian state, except at the cost of probably unacceptable military risks and political consequences. Even if the United States withdraws from Asia, the Soviet Union and Japan will remain to balance the C.P.R. On the other hand, China will always be there too, and by virtue of its size, population, central location, cultural tradition, prestige, potential power, and revolutionary dynamism, is bound to play a major role in Asia. In the middle term, by means of various pressures and blandishments, some of which are discussed below, Peking can reasonably hope to encourage a considerable degree of accommodation to its own wishes of the foreign policies of at least some of the Asian states, and perhaps of the domestic policies of a few. In the long run, Peking (or at least the Maoist constituency) probably hopes, although how seriously it is hard to say, that Communist-led and China-supported (within the limits of risk, cost, and "self-reliance") "people's wars" will bring Peking-oriented regimes, not necessarily satellites, to power in all or most of the other Asian countries. For the foreseeable future, however, Peking must be content to operate in Asia as one of its major powers and as an important revolutionary influence, without being in a position to dominate it. This means, in effect, continuing to accept grudgingly the presence as rivals of the Soviet Union, the United States, Japan, and, to a lesser extent, India, and to regard the Sino-Soviet border, Northeast Asia, and South Asia in decreasing order of urgency as areas of major concern. It means cultivating the goodwill of regional states capable of being helpful as against China's rivals; in the past, these have included in particular Indonesia (from 1960 to 1965), North Korea, North Vietnam (which to be sure is a rival of Peking's to some extent), and Pakistan. It means promoting and sustaining revolutionary activities where it appears militarily safe and politically useful (as in South Vietnam), but not to anywhere near the point at which such activity would take priority over such considerations of national interest as those just discussed.

With respect to the rest of the Third World (the Middle East, Africa, and Latin America), the situation is significantly different. Peking's knowledge of and interest in these regions, although far from negligible, are much less than in the case of Asia. For these reasons and because of the Third World's vastness as compared with the C.P.R.'s resources (or those of any other power), Peking realizes that it must be highly selective in making major efforts to exert influence in the Third World. There is one exception, or near exception, to this—propaganda, which, being relatively cheap, Peking uses wholesale in the Third World as elsewhere. From the viewpoint of China's national interest, the Third World obviously cannot pose threats to China's security, whether of regional or extraregional origin, in the way that Asia can. Similarly, the risk to China of realistically possible action tends to be much less in the Third World than in Asia; no actual or contemplated Chinese action has yet produced a threat of American or Soviet military retaliation except in instances relating to Asia. On the other hand, the economic cost of any given Chinese action or program tends to be greater in the Third World than in Asia. The potential for acquiring political influence is about the same; the greater instability of many of the local Third World governments (by comparison with which most Asian governments are relatively stable), and the fact that China is not feared to the same extent as in Asia, are roughly balanced by the greater difficulty for the C.P.R. of bringing its foreign policy instrumentalities to bear on a Third World country beyond its Asian periphery and its lack of significant ethnic and cultural affinities outside Asia. In the Third World, as in most other regions, the C.P.R. has been effectively preceded by the United States and the Soviet Union and finds one of them, or more commonly both, in active competition with it for influence. This means that the C.P.R. can hope, barring blunders of its own, to exploit the resentments that the two "superpowers" inevitably tend to create and to lend some substance to its contrasting claim to a disinterested championship of the "small and medium states" as against the "superpowers." In particular, Peking has been remarkably successful since 1969 in picking up diplomatic recognitions and support for its entry into the United Nations in the Third World, and it can hope to cultivate future support from Third World countries in the United Nations with reasonable success.

In the revolutionary field, the same Maoist principles ("revolutionary" peoples against "reactionary" governments, "people's wars," and so on) obviously apply in theory to the Third World to the same extent as to Asia. In some ways, the Third World seems to offer even more attractive revolutionary opportunities than does Asia. A wave of "people's wars" in the Third World, for example, might tend to distract the "superpowers" from Asia, where their presence and activity are of course highly inconvenient to the C.P.R. That many Third World governments are more unstable than the Asian average tends to create in Peking a recurrent sense of revolutionary opportunity in the areas beyond Asia, and on occasion to tempt Peking into overplaying its hand by working too hard to ripen immature revolutionary situations. It did this in sub-Saharan Africa in the early 1960's, was rewarded by a series of military coups in 1965–66 that greatly reduced its influence in the region, and since then has been much more cautious and selective in Africa. This trend is a reminder of the rather obvious fact that Peking has virtually no reason to hope that it will ever be in a position to "dominate" the Third World.

Another important environment within which the C.P.R. seeks to promote its basic foreign policy objectives (security and influence) is the international Communist movement and its inner core, the "Party-states" in which Communist Parties are in power (sometimes known officially as the socialist camp and unofficially as the Communist bloc). From the point of view of national interest, Peking's main concern is to try to cope with the Soviet Union as rival and threat (in the latter connection, Peking has often used the term social-imperialism to refer to the Soviet Union since the invasion of Czechoslovakia). Much of the job of coping with the Soviet Union, to be sure, must be done bilaterally (through diplomacy, efforts at politico-military deterrence, and the like) or in other ways lying outside the scope of the international Communist movement, notably through seeking a positive political relationship with the United States that may help to reduce the Soviet propensity to put pressure on China. Within the international Communist movement, Peking has cultivated from time to time other socialist states that shared its resentment of the Soviet tendency to try to dominate the socialist camp and the international Communist movement; this has been especially true of Albania since 1960, and of Romania and Yugoslavia since about 1968. In the long run, Peking may hope, after building up a stronger bargaining position, to reach a satisfactory *modus vivendi* with the

Soviet Union, as it seems to be in the process of doing with the United States.

Such an outcome would require, however, in addition to other things, a decline in the vitality of the ideological component in Chinese foreign policy-making, and perhaps a further decline on the Soviet side as well. Beginning in 1957, Mao Tse-tung became obsessed with the danger of "revisionism" in the international Communist movement as a threat to anti-"imperialist" unity, and after 1960 he increasingly identified the Soviet leadership as the major source of "revisionism." As the alternative, Mao offered, or claimed to offer, original Leninism, of which he insisted that the CPC was an orthodox exponent. With the support of other dissident Parties, he neatly avoided being steamrollered by a pro-Soviet majority within the movement by gaining acceptance of the requirement for unanimity on any authoritative ideological or policy decision by the international Communist movement as a whole. From 1963 on, the CPC encouraged the formation of "Marxist-Leninist" anti-Soviet splinter parties in some thirty countries where the regular Communist Party was firmly under the control of pro-Soviet elements. Since the fall of Khrushchev in 1964, which rather went to Mao's head, the CPC has tended to advocate his "thought" rather than Marxism-Leninism per se as the alternative to Soviet "revisionism." Whatever appeal this approach might otherwise have had was greatly dimmed by the excesses of the Cultural Revolution, which in Castro's words "made a laughing-stock of socialism." It is significant that the only foreign Communist Party to have a Cultural Revolution of its own, in imitation of the Chinese, was the Burmese, and that the results were disastrous: the leadership killed itself off to a large extent. Since the invasion of Czechoslovakia, the CPC has made friendly contact with the leaderships of some Communist Parties that are "revisionist" and hostile to Moscow. Another sign of the CPC's growing ideological flexibility within the international Communist movement is that it was not officially represented at an Albanian Party Congress held in 1971.

For reasons that include the CPC's highly independent performance, the over-all trend within the international Communist movement is away from subordination to any power center or single ideology (or at least any foreign version of Marxism-Leninism, whether Soviet, Chinese, or something else) and toward what is sometimes called national Communism. This trend is obvious in the case of the major Asian Communist Parties—the North

Korean, the Japanese, and the North Vietnamese. Moscow and Peking no longer try to dominate foreign Communist Parties—except to some extent in the case of Soviet influence over the ruling Parties of the "northern tier" countries of Poland, East Germany, and Czechoslovakia—so much as to seek their support in the Sino-Soviet dispute. As a result of these trends, other Communist Parties are sometimes in a position to play Moscow and Peking against each other, a situation that would have seemed impossible until about a decade ago. It is obvious, then, that the CPC is no more likely to "dominate" the international Communist movement, ideologically or organizationally, than the C.P.R. is to dominate Asia or the Third World.

The C.P.R. says officially that it does not aspire to become a "superpower" like the "imperialist" United States or the "revisionist" and "social-imperialist" Soviet Union, which allegedly oppress other countries and peoples when possible. Instead, the C.P.R. apparently aspires to be what might be called a revolutionary great power. While continuing (mainly but not exclusively through propaganda) to support revolution on the part of peoples whose governments it considers reactionary, it demands a voice in the settlement of all major questions among existing governments, reactionary or not. It has always demanded, and now controls, China's permanent seat on the United Nations Security Council in lieu of the Nationalists, and it is prepared, broadly speaking, to establish diplomatic relations with any government that does not also try to maintain them with the (Nationalist) Republic of China. Although it probably does not expect and is not likely to achieve parity with the "superpowers" in economic and military strength, it certainly aspires to parity in political influence through giving leadership to the small and medium states. It tries to oppose what it has claimed, since about the time of the Nuclear Test Ban Treaty, to be a tendency toward collusion between the two "superpowers," and indeed it tries to play them against each other (by means of the invitation to President Nixon, for example).

The preceding discussion of foreign policy objectives has included some comments on instrumentalities, but a more systematic commentary on this subject may be helpful. Probably the most important, and certainly the most widely used, is propaganda, including cultural relations. Its main aim is to establish, to the extent possible, a sense of affinity between the Chinese "people" and the "people" of all other countries, especially those whose governments Peking considers reactionary, and to cultivate popular opposition to those governments, at least on issues of interest to China. Among the elements in foreign countries (or at least in some of them) to which Peking addresses itself in this way are local Communist Parties, overseas Chinese communities, and elements of the New Left. Peking must be careful, however, for some of these groups are vulnerable to political reprisals and cannot be expected to take a strongly pro-Chinese line. This tendency to address itself to other peoples over the heads of their governments helps Peking to avoid diplomatic crunches with foreign governments, as a rule by claiming that the issues lie not between the Chinese and the foreign government in question but between the latter government and all "peoples" (including the Chinese and its own). Even with governments it dislikes, Peking claims to be willing to practice what it calls the "Five Principles of Peaceful Coexistence," under which in theory conflicts between the governments are assumed to be unnecessary, but Peking assumes no obligation not to encourage the people of the other country to put pressure on their government along lines favorable to Chinese interests. This is not to say that Peking is incapable of effective intergovernmental diplomacy: its recent dealings with the United States are enough to demonstrate the contrary. The point is that Peking prefers to engage in formal diplomatic negotiations only when it has no effective choice because the potential gains are great and/or the lack of negotiations would be risky (as was true in its dealings with the United States), or when its position is overwhelmingly strong, or when the questions on which there is agreement exceed in importance those on which there is disagreement. Where disagreement prevails, or the Chinese position is weak, Peking prefers if possible to avoid negotiations while trying to build up a favorable international climate (especially in the other country) through propaganda in particular. The recipients of Chinese economic and military aid are selected in order to reward and encourage friendly governments, and the aid programs and trade as well are naturally handled by Peking in ways that are intended to promote, or at least not to obstruct, Chinese political objectives with respect to the country in question.

In summary, Peking chooses its friends and enemies and its policies, strategies, and tactics toward them (in combinations that vary from case to case) on the basis of shifting mixes of ideological (or Party, or revolutionary) and national (or state) considerations. The principle is simple and virtually universal. The practice is more complex and more interesting.

The Record to 1965

The first decade (1949–59) of the C.P.R.'s foreign policy was a period when Peking regarded the United States, in collaboration with a possibly resurgent Japan, as a serious threat and the Soviet Union as its only effective ally and source of aid. Then as later, the Third World (including Asia) was regarded essentially as a testing ground for the Maoist revolutionary strategy and a field of maneuver against the United States (and after about 1958 against the Soviet Union as well).

Aware, although unadmittedly, that it had not actually beaten Japan in 1945, and overestimating the chances of U.S. intervention to restore the Nationalists, as the "imperialist" powers had intervened against the Bolsheviks after 1917, the CPC genuinely regarded the United States as an aggressive threat after 1949 and in any event was determined to allow its citizens no contact with it that might corrupt them ideologically. The CPC banged down the bamboo curtain on the highly tentative moves the U.S. Government was making until early 1950 to "keep its options open" and find some way of having at least a polite relationship with Peking, in spite of Republican criticisms at home.

This promising adversary relationship was pushed toward the point of no return when, in January, 1950, Peking joined, to exactly what extent is not certain, with the Soviet Union and North Korea in planning a North Korean invasion of South Korea, which would among other things serve to keep off balance the American-Japanese alliance that Peking insisted was in the making. As part of the over-all planning to cope with this situation, as well as for other purposes, Stalin gave Mao the alliance and some of the aid he had been seeking and demanded the leading role on the Communist side in Northeast Asia, in return for which he conceded (temporarily, as it turned out) to the CPC a similar position with respect to Communist activities in Southeast Asia.

General MacArthur's advance toward the Manchurian frontier in October, 1950, in pursuit of the beaten North Korean Army, created in Peking's eyes a serious threat to Chinese security, one serious enough to constitute a strong argument for pre-emptive action. Furthermore, since Stalin was reluctant either to accept the crushing of his North Korean satellite or to intervene on its behalf, he favored Chinese entry into the war and supported it with military aid. The CPC regarded intervention as a promising way of strengthening its own position at home and abroad, the risks being presumed to be acceptable in view of the existence of the Sino-Soviet alliance.

Chinese defeats in early 1951, following initial successes, and the dangerous situation in the United States created by the crisis over the recall of General MacArthur, disposed the Soviet Union toward an armistice in Korea from the spring of 1951 on, but Peking and Pyongyang had to suffer more defeats (in April and May) before agreeing to negotiate. The negotiations were then spun out for two years, while fighting continued, in the hope of achieving the best military and political terms attainable, given the absence of a Communist victory. During 1952, Peking increasingly preferred to keep the war going rather than accept its opponent's position on repatriation of prisoners (see Chapter 9). The death of Stalin early in 1953 and the ensuing confusion among his successors deprived Peking of essential support, and, under an American nuclear threat, it had to sign an armistice in July that incorporated the other side's principle of voluntary repatriation of prisoners. The fact that the armistice has not yet been followed by an international political settlement of the Korean conflict and the general situation on the peninsula (its division, in particular) is one reason Peking and Hanoi are reluctant to see a cease-fire in South Vietnam that is not tied directly to a political settlement.

From early 1948 on, the CPC preached the "way of Mao Tse-tung," including "armed struggle," to the former colonial countries of Southeast Asia, and refused to concede the independence and neutrality in the cold war of the region's new governments. Except perhaps in Malaya, Chinese influence and support played a role of varying, but not decisive proportions in the Communist insurgencies that broke out in Burma, Malaya, Indonesia, and the Philippines in 1948. By about 1951, however, Peking perceived that these revolts had no chance of success and that active support for them was incompatible with cultivation of the goodwill of neutral Asian governments, notably the Indian, whose support would enhance the C.P.R.'s international stature and would be helpful as a supplement to the Sino-Soviet alliance in case the United States threatened to attack China. The cultivation of neutral Asian (in fact, Afro-Asian) sympathy reached its peak at the Asian-African Conference held at Bandung, Java, in April, 1955, at which Chou En-lai represented the C.P.R. with brilliant success.

Even the Communist "armed struggle" in Vietnam, which had begun in 1946, proceeded under some Chinese influence and with some Chinese aid, although Peking was careful to keep its role as quiet as possible in order to avoid a possible second crunch with the United States (France being a NATO member) as long as the Korean War lasted. On the other hand, this was a war that could be supported without alienating neutral Asian opinion, and after the end of the Korean War, Peking increased its flow of aid to Ho Chi Minh's forces. The latter's successful siege of the French fort of Dienbienphu in the spring of 1954 led to another round of threatening behavior by the United States. For this reason as well as others, the Soviet Union and the C.P.R. refrained at a number of points from giving full support to the maximum demands of Ho Chi Minh's representatives at the Geneva Conference, which met from May to July, 1954, in order to work out a settlement of the Indochina crisis. Ho Chi Minh got considerably less than he wanted, but the C.P.R. got what it wanted most—a provision in the main agreement barring foreign (American were what Peking had in mind) bases and forces from the Indochina countries—even though it failed to persuade the United States to sign the agreement.

Peking had been infuriated when, in June, 1950, the U.S. Government, mainly in order to get Republican Congressional support for intervention in Korea, extended American protection to Taiwan and thereby made its "liberation" by military operations from the mainland practically impossible. By 1954, American military aid to the Nationalists had assumed such proportions that Peking became afraid of a possible attack and in September initiated a kind of forestalling action involving the use of aircraft, ships, and artillery bombardment against certain Nationalist-held offshore islands. The main effect of this was to drive the Nationalists still closer to the United States: they signed a treaty of alliance at the end of 1954. Peking then tried negotiating with the United States at the ambassadorial level, beginning in August, 1955, in an effort to weaken the American commitment to Taiwan. When this ploy failed to produce the desired result, the CPC began in 1956 to urge the Nationalists publicly, but without effect, to make a deal with it.

After Stalin's death in 1953, Mao increasingly felt and displayed a sense of seniority and superiority to Stalin's quarreling successors. He gave some support to Khrushchev, who went out of his way to cultivate Peking and seemed to the CPC to be the most acceptable of the contenders. But after 1955, as Khrushchev's position grew stronger, he increasingly ignored and even went against Chinese interests. This was especially true at the Soviet Twentieth Party Congress in February, 1956, where he implied publicly a fear of American nuclear power that rendered unlikely active Soviet support for the C.P.R. over Taiwan and for revolutionary movements in the Third World. Khrushchev's "secret speech" attacking Stalin outraged Mao and helped to embolden his colleagues to take action aimed at curbing the "cult of personality" within the CPC (see Chapter 3).

Although the CPC favored a moderate loosening of Soviet controls over Eastern Europe, it was shocked by the strong anti-Soviet trend that Khrushchev's "secret speech" helped to let loose, especially in Hungary. Accordingly, Peking supported, and may have urged ahead of time, the Soviet intervention in Hungary, lectured Tito publicly on his ambivalent attitude toward it and toward Marxism-Leninism (as defined in Peking), and sent Chou En-lai to the Soviet Union and Eastern Europe in January, 1957, to argue for clearer recognition of Soviet political leadership over Eastern Europe, and indeed over the socialist camp and the international Communist movement as a whole. This line was greatly strengthened in late 1957, when Mao tried to use Soviet successes in missilery and space as the basis for arguing for still firmer Soviet international leadership that might promote Chinese interests, among others, and might help Mao improve his own weakened domestic political position (see Chapter 3).

The leftward shift of Peking's outlook in 1957–58 of course led to the Great Leap Forward at home. Abroad, it gave rise to intensified propaganda against "imperialism, reaction, and modern revisionism," and to some action against these demons as well. Peking not only began, for the first time in public since 1952, to urge armed struggle against "imperialism" but also proceeded to outdo the Soviet Union in giving political support and military aid to the Algerian National Liberation Front, the main movement then actually engaged in an anti-"imperialist" (in this case, anti-French) armed struggle. Partly to lend credibility to its own enhanced anti-"imperialist" militancy and spur others in the same direction, Peking precipitated a military crisis in the Taiwan Strait in August, 1958, but, as in 1954, the main effect of the operation was to tighten the ties between the Nationalists and the United States as well as to expose the Soviet Union's lack of enthusiasm for such behavior on the part of Peking. In the light of enhanced Chinese militancy, India appeared increasingly as the principal "reactionary" power because of its bourgeois leadership, its receptivity to American and Soviet aid and influence, its efforts to give guidance to the Third World, its sympathy for the Tibetans (see Chapter 12), and its disagreement with Peking over the proper location of the Sino-Indian border. The flight of the Dalai Lama to India in March, 1959, led to sharpened Chinese propaganda attacks on Indian "reaction" and to some armed clashes along the border; Khrushchev displayed an attitude toward this episode that Peking interpreted as pro-Indian. "Modern revisionism" was represented in Mao's eyes mainly by Tito; accordingly, in May, 1958, the Chinese press launched a propaganda offensive against him that led to a ten-year chill in Sino-Yugoslav relations.

The 1959–69 decade was marked primarily by Peking's adoption of what is called in this study the dual-adversary strategy. American "imperialism" and Soviet "revisionism," although of course differing from each other in nature, were held to be the enemies not only of China but of the "revolutionary people of the world" to roughly equal degrees. Political struggle against both of them, sometimes with military overtones, was regarded as obligatory and expedient. There was a tendency, although not an unbroken one, for the United States to decline in Peking's eyes as an active threat to China after the Taiwan Strait crisis of 1958 and the death of John Foster Dulles in 1959. On the other hand, Peking's difficulties with the Soviet Union tended to grow more serious, even though it did not begin to perceive Moscow as a major active threat to China until almost the end of the decade. As in the earlier period, the Third World (including Asia) was regarded as the major field of maneuver against the two "superpowers," as well as the principal testing ground for the Maoist revolutionary strategy.

As the decade began, a crisis was in progress in Laos in consequence of the Eisenhower Administration's effort to create a pro-Western regime there instead of the neutral one envisaged in the Geneva Agreements of 1954. Peking and Hanoi naturally viewed this effort with alarm. The main result was that in the early months of 1961, North Vietnamese troops moved into the highlands of Laos, not only to counterbalance American efforts in the Mekong Valley but also to open up the "Ho Chi Minh Trail" to South Vietnam, where in 1959 Hanoi had begun to increase its involvement in Viet Cong insurgency. In 1961–62, a major international conference on the Laotian crisis met at Geneva; the Chinese delegation played a leading role in working out an agreement reaffirming the principle of Laotian neutrality.

Peking was perturbed by the Kennedy Administration's adoption of the doctrine of "flexible response" and its addition to counterinsurgency in opposition to Communist-supported "wars of national liberation." The main theater for American counterinsurgency efforts was, of course, South Vietnam. Being reluctant to become involved in another military confrontation with the United States, Peking was rather unenthusiastic about Hanoi's growing support after 1959 for insurgency in South Vietnam. In the spring of 1963, however, a bargain was struck: Peking increased its propaganda support for the insurgency and allowed weapons of Chinese origin to be used in South Vietnam, and Hanoi gave limited support to Peking's side in the Sino-Soviet dispute. Peking had some nervous moments at the time of the Tonkin Gulf crisis of August, 1964, but on balance it felt reassured by President Lyndon Johnson's rather dovish line on Indochina during the Presidential campaign of that year, as compared with that of his opponent.

From Peking's perspective, there were two main bright spots in the Third World in the early 1960's. One was Indonesia, whose increasingly leftist government under President Sukarno was on good terms with its powerful Communist Party (the PKI) and formed a close relationship with Peking in 1960–61 based on a common anti-Western outlook and an understanding that Djakarta would not unduly harass Indonesia's large Chinese community. On this basis, Peking gave strong support to Djakarta's successful politico-military campaign to regain West Irian (Western New Guinea) from the Netherlands and its unsuccessful campaign to crush the new state of Malaysia after its formation in 1963. Djakarta in return loudly endorsed Peking's and Hanoi's foreign policies. The C.P.R. and Indonesia worked hard for and hoped to dominate an Afro-Asian Conference (the first of its kind since 1955) to be held at Algiers in June, 1965.

The other seeming bright spot was sub-Saharan Africa, which after the wave of decolonization in 1960 Peking expected to be the scene of numerous "armed struggles" against "neocolonialism," meaning in effect indigenous governments alleged with or without justification to retain ties with "imperialism." By all odds, the most important target was the former Belgian Congo, but neither Peking nor local revolutionaries succeeded in establishing an effective foothold there. Peking did succeed in establishing embassies in several adjacent countries, as well as several in West Africa (notably Ghana, Guinea, and Mali), and in using these to varying degrees as centers for helping to train African revolutionaries from various countries with governments unacceptable to Peking and sometimes even from the host countries. It was an unusual instance of Peking's seeking, at least during the period prior to the Cultural Revolution, to promote revolution in ways that obviously endangered a growing relationship with governments that were neither initially hostile to the C.P.R. nor genuinely close to the United States or the Soviet Union. The explanation is undoubtedly Peking's exaggerated sense that Africa, as Chou En-lai said in 1964, was "ripe for revolution."

By the early 1960's, India had become easily the most disliked of Third World states in Peking's eyes. New Delhi, in addition to being ideologically distasteful and relatively pro-Soviet, had rejected a Chinese compromise proposal on the border dispute in 1960. The essential point was that New Delhi had decided against leaving Peking in *de facto* possession of a disputed area at the northeast corner of Kashmir across which the Chinese had built a military highway in 1956–57. Under domestic political pressure, the Indian Government persuaded itself that it could occupy this area and push the Chinese out without a fight. But Peking was determined to hold the area because of its military importance and from an unwillingness to be humbled by a government it intensely disliked. At some point in the summer of 1962, in fact, Peking decided to use the issue as a means of turning the tables on the Indians, whose troops were advancing in the disputed area in spite of numerous warnings to stop, and of inflicting a humiliating defeat on them that would enhance Peking's and damage New Delhi's standing in the eyes of the world, the Third World in particular. Peking felt the need for such a success, not only to teach the Indian Army a lesson and protect the highway, but also because Peking had been feeling itself under severe external pressure for the past several months and was furthermore about to launch a major domestic movement, the Socialist Education Campaign, for which a backdrop of a victorious external confrontation would be useful. Indochina had been in turmoil as usual, American troops had been sent to Thailand, the Soviet Union had been inciting dissident tribesmen to flee from Sinkiang to Soviet Central Asia (see Chapter 12), and, worst of all, the Nationalists had been giving signs of a possible intent to attack the mainland. All these crises passed away, although in the latter situation not until after Peking had heavily reinforced its troop strength opposite Taiwan in June. That left the Indians as the sole available targets of Peking's dangerous mood. Between October 20 and November 20, accordingly, Chinese forces launched two brilliantly successful attacks against poorly prepared Indian troops in the eastern and western sectors of the frontier. Then the PLA broke off combat and withdrew approximately to its previous positions; it had more or less achieved its objectives, but it will be recalled that one of these was not the seizure of additional territory. The fighting had begun almost simultaneously with the eruption of the Cuban Missile Crisis, and at first Peking and Moscow gave each other declaratory support in their respective confrontations. Peking, however, interpreted the Soviet Union's subsequent decision to withdraw its missiles and bombers from Cuba in the face of a virtual American ultimatum as capitulation to American "imperialism" and a "Munich"-like betrayal of Castro; in retaliation, Moscow shifted its line on the Sino-Indian border crisis somewhat in favor of India.

Growing hostility to Khrushchev and to Soviet "revisionism" was the main single hallmark of Chinese foreign policy during the early 1960's. Peking's objections were usually those just mentioned in connection with the Cuban Missile Crisis: the alleged Soviet tendency to appease American "imperialism" and not to give active support to anti-"imperialist" revolutionary movements and "oppressed" countries. Toward the end of the period, Khrushchev's supposedly "revisionist" domestic policy also came under Chinese attack.

Even though in Peking's eyes Khrushchev had displayed deplorable softness toward "imperialism" in 1959, notably by visiting the United States, the quarrel remained barely below the propaganda surface until April, 1960, when, in an effort to disrupt Khrushchev's forthcoming summit conference at Paris with the three major Western powers, Peking unleashed a barrage of propaganda in various forms against him (without naming him in public, however). Khrushchev retaliated by cutting off economic aid to China in the summer of 1960. In November–December, 1960, the two sides aired their differences on "imperialism" and revolution before the often astonished delegates of nearly all the world's Communist Parties at a major conference in Moscow. By that time, another issue had arisen. Khrushchev was having a row with Albania rather similar, although of course on a smaller scale, to the one he was having with China and cut off aid to it in the spring of 1961. Peking stepped in with economic and military aid and with political support against the Soviet Union and Albania's adversary, Yugoslavia. The Albanian issue was debated publicly and unprecedentedly by Khrushchev and Chou En-lai at the Soviet Twenty-Second Party Congress in October, 1961. During the next few years, in addition to the Indian and Cuban crises already mentioned, other issues were added to the growing pile of Sino-Soviet differences. By signing the Nuclear Test Ban Treaty in 1963, the Soviet Union (in Chinese eyes) compromised with "imperialism" and made it more embarrassing for Peking to proceed with its own nuclear-weapons program, as it was determined to do. In 1963–64, Peking raised, for the first time in public, the highly sensitive question of the Sino-Soviet border dispute and left the dangerous (for itself) impression that it might make a serious claim to some Asian territories long since controlled by Russia. Khrushchev tried with little success to arrange another conference like the one of 1960 for the purpose of disciplining or expelling the Chinese, and may even have been contemplating some form of military pressure against them, but these schemes were frustrated by his overthrow in October, 1964. Peking, for its part, opposed the idea of the conference, encouraged the formation of anti-Soviet "Marxist-Leninist" Parties in various countries, and loudly denounced Khrushchev and all his works.

Setbacks, Red Guard Diplomacy, and the Sino-Soviet Crunch

Although the Maoist dual-adversary strategy continued in effect until about 1969, important developments that complicated its application and eventually led to its modification began in 1965.

In November, 1964, and February, 1965, Khrushchev's successors, Brezhnev and Kosygin, approached Peking with an offer of a compromise. Ideological issues ("revisionism," for example) were to be de-emphasized, normal economic relations were to be resumed, and the two regimes were to cooperate on international questions (Vietnam in particular). The offer aroused some interest in Peking and did so again when it was brought back in somewhat different form by a Japanese Communist delegation a year later, but it was vetoed each time by Mao Tse-tung, who had become addicted to his campaign against Soviet "revisionism" and was unwilling to compromise with it. He feared that "united action" on Vietnam, which Moscow was demanding, would enhance Soviet international influence and encourage Mao's "revisionist" colleagues. All Moscow got was an agreement on the shipment of Soviet military equipment by rail across China to North Vietnam.

The escalation in Vietnam came as an unpleasant shock to

Mao, who had predicted as recently as January, 1965 (in an interview with Edgar Snow), that the United States would do no such thing. A strategic debate over the implications of Vietnam for Chinese security and military policy promptly began in Peking (see Chapters 3 and 9). The winning position, which can be considered the Maoist one, was expressed by Lin Piao, who insisted that China should not intervene directly in the Vietnam conflict beyond supplying arms and logistical support to Hanoi, should not cooperate with the Soviet Union (beyond, apparently, minimal observance of the agreement on rail shipments), and could either deter the United States from a strategic attack with its own embryonic nuclear force, or if necessary cope with an American attack through a "people's war." This rather primitive position represented, in effect, a classic statement of the dual-adversary strategy.

The C.P.R.'s actual role in the Vietnam conflict was compatible with Lin's position, at least once the more hawkish Chief of Staff Lo Jui-ch'ing had been purged early in 1966. Peking sent arms and supplies to North Vietnam, as well as some 50,000 railway engineer troops to help keep the two rail lines to China open, and tried with little success to discourage Hanoi from fighting above the guerrilla level. When Hanoi decided, in the spring of 1968, to negotiate in an effort to capitalize on the post-Têt mood of discouragement in the United States, Peking objected at first, but privately and of course ineffectively.

At first, both Peking and Washington were nervous about the obvious possibility of a Sino-American war like the one in Korea. In order to ensure against one, the two sides reached a tacit understanding in the spring of 1966 to the effect that the United States would not take military action against China as long as Peking did not increase its current level of involvement in the Vietnam conflict, and vice versa. Peking was also impressed by signs of a shift in American official and public opinion in the direction of a desire for better relations with the C.P.R. These trends alarmed the Soviet Union, which began to fear Sino-American collusion to its disadvantage; until after 1969, at any rate, this fear had little substance.

The year preceding the outbreak of the Cultural Revolution saw some major Chinese setbacks in the Third World. Antagonism toward China's demands for support of its foreign policy at the forthcoming Afro-Asian Conference was a major reason the conference was never held. Worse still, Peking's friend Sukarno involved himself in an attempted Communist coup against the

Indonesian military leadership on September 30–October 1, 1965; it failed, and the result was a huge disaster for Sukarno, the PKI, and Peking's interests in Indonesia. When an Indo-Pakistani war over Kashmir broke out in August, 1965, Peking was able to do nothing for Pakistan, which got the worst of the fighting, beyond inciting it to continue the losing struggle and trying to frighten India with the specter of another border war. In 1965 and early 1966, a number of military coups in sub-Saharan African countries, including Ghana, weakened or eliminated the Chinese presence, which had acquired the reputation of being subversive in purpose; since then, Peking has been more cautious and more selective below the Sahara.

The approach and outbreak of the Cultural Revolution brought a sharp worsening of Sino-Soviet relations. Peking boycotted the Soviet Twenty-Third Party Congress in March, 1966, after the Soviet Party circulated a "secret letter" denouncing Chinese behavior. Moscow was enormously distressed by the Cultural Revolution, which clearly challenged the Leninist principle of control by the Communist Party apparatus; both sides had withdrawn their ambassadors by mid-1966, and Moscow probably contemplated military intervention but refrained when it could find no organized anti-Maoist force with which to cooperate.

During the first year of the Cultural Revolution, Red Guards kept constant pressure on the Foreign Ministry for a more militant foreign policy along lines indicated by the dual-adversary strategy. In response to these pressures, all Chinese ambassadors except Huang Hua in Cairo were recalled for political indoctrination. Red Guards staged violent demonstrations against foreign embassies in Peking, along the Sino-Soviet border, and even in Macao and Hong Kong. Maoist elements among the Chinese community in Rangoon did the same and produced a serious crisis in Sino-Burmese relations. For four days (August 19–22, 1967), Red Guards and other militants seized control of the Foreign Ministry and burned the British diplomatic mission's compound in retaliation for a controversy involving Hong Kong, before being evicted by force. After that, Red Guard diplomacy, as it was often called, tapered off, even though the Cultural Revolution did not come to an end for another year.

Peking was shocked by the Soviet invasion of Czechoslovakia on August 21, 1968. If Moscow could use force against one Communist regime of which it disapproved, it might do so against another, even one as formidable as the Chinese. The so-called

Brezhnev Doctrine seemed to claim the right to do exactly that. In November, 1968, Chou En-lai began to seek a limited counter-weight against possible Soviet pressures by taking steps to open ambassadorial talks with the incoming Nixon Administration in February, 1969. An upsurge of Maoist militancy, probably orchestrated by Lin Piao, frustrated this move; the scheduled talks were canceled by Peking almost at the last minute. Lin, evidently with Mao's approval, prepared to parallel this slap at American "imperialism" with one at Soviet "revisionism" in a way that was logical enough, given the tenets of the dual-adversary strategy. Incorrectly assuming that the Russians would be preoccupied with a crisis then in progress over West Berlin, Lin planned a limited military action that he apparently intended to proclaim defiance of Soviet "revisionism" and provide a suitable backdrop for his own formal announcement as Mao's heir at the approaching Ninth Party Congress. Such, seemingly, were the origins of the famous clash on the Ussuri River on March 2, 1969.

When the Russians retaliated, unexpectedly and with over-whelming force, at the same spot on March 15, Lin's political star began to fade. The unmistakable evidence of Soviet determination to have border negotiations and of a huge buildup of Soviet forces near the frontier left diplomacy as the only effective Chinese option. The situation inevitably made Chou En-lai indispensable and enhanced his political influence correspondingly. He was under severe Maoist pressure not to negotiate, however, and agreed to do so (on October 6, 1969) only after the Russians had applied severe pressures along the border and uttered a variety of threats of invasion and/or a "surgical strike" at China's nuclear installations, and after Chou and Premier Kosygin had talked at the Peking airport on September 11, just before the expiration of what amounted to a Soviet ultimatum to negotiate.

The Sino-Soviet border talks, which began in Peking on October 20, 1969, and have continued intermittently, have proceeded in secrecy interrupted occasionally by misleading leaks by one side or the other. Peking wants an agreement on a cease-fire and a withdrawal of troops from the frontier and from disputed areas by both sides, and the incorporation in a formal new boundary treaty of a Soviet admission in principle that the earlier treaties were "unequal" and therefore in some sense invalid. On the other hand, Peking is not actually demanding the territories lost under the "unequal treaties," which would be a foolhardy thing to do; it insists, however, that, at some points in Central Asia and along the Manchurian frontier, the Soviet Union has occupied pieces of territory not ceded under the "unequal treaties" and that at least some of these must be returned. The Soviet Union is willing to make some minor adjustments of this sort but declines to give up its major source of leverage on Peking by agreeing to a cease-fire and troop withdrawal in advance of a boundary settlement, and will not concede that the earlier treaties were "unequal," if only because to do so would weaken the Soviet position on certain other territorial issues in the Far East and Europe.

Even in the absence of a boundary agreement, the Peking talks have been valuable to the C.P.R. as an additional incentive to the Soviet Union not to go to war. Chou En-lai's approach has been to manage the Soviet Union, in this and other ways, while not yielding on anything that he or his Maoist colleagues regard as a matter of principle. He succeeded in arranging an exchange of ambassadors with the Soviet Union and must have been pleased that Moscow sent a major political figure and friend of Brezhnev's, V. S. Tolstikov, as its ambassador in October, 1970. Soon afterward, the two sides agreed to increase their mutual trade, which had fallen off to almost negligible levels. It is likely that Lin Piao objected to Chou's relatively conciliatory approach to China's Soviet problem, as well as to Chou's diplomatic opening to the United States, and that his attitude, as well as the fact that he was strongly objectionable to Moscow for several reasons that included his role in the first clash on the Ussuri, formed an important part of Chou's case against him. Meanwhile, however, Chou was working to strengthen China's nuclear deterrent (in particular by testing and deploying intermediate-range missiles) and its conventional forces (by modernizing their equipment and gradually withdrawing them from politics), and to prepare the population for a "people's war" (by civil defense measures, stockpiling, and the like). Most important of all perhaps, Chou was working to strengthen the C.P.R.'s international position and relationships, in ways to be discussed shortly, in order to make it as politically disadvantageous as possible for the Soviet Union to resume pressures or launch an actual attack on China.

In spite of Chou's skillful management and the decline of overt Sino-Soviet tension since 1969 (Brezhnev has proposed the signing of a Sino-Soviet nonaggression pact), the situation remains very tense. The Soviet military buildup has continued to the present and, by the end of 1971, had reached a level of about forty-four divisions, with the most modern equipment. This is not the place to consider why the Soviet Union is behaving in this manner (there are a number of probable reasons, some of which have nothing directly to do with China); what is important, especially from Peking's point of view, is the fact, not the reasons. It was against a backdrop of threatening Soviet propaganda statements and disturbing Soviet diplomatic moves (notably the August 9, 1971, treaty of friendship with India and the West Berlin agreement of September 3, 1971) that Chou made his final move against Lin Piao (see Chapter 4).

The Soviet Union is competing vigorously with the C.P.R. for influence in Asia, the rest of the Third World, and in Europe (especially the Balkans). It has vaguely proposed a "collective security system" for Asia, supposedly including China, which Peking has denounced on the plausible suspicion that it must have an anti-Chinese purpose.

Post–Cultural Revolution Normalization and Great Power Politics

A swing back toward normality in China's foreign policy and foreign relations after the Cultural Revolution was inevitable. That it has gone farther than might have been expected is due mainly to Peking's sense of the Soviet threat. Shortly after the Ninth Party Congress, Peking began to send ambassadors to nearly all the countries (India and Indonesia are prominent exceptions) where it had had them before the Cultural Revolution. Beginning with Canada in October, 1970, the C.P.R. has established diplomatic relations with nearly thirty other countries; in no instance has Peking permitted the other country to maintain any sort of formal relations with the Nationalists, but it has allowed some variations in the degree to which the other country has endorsed Peking's claim to Taiwan. An important feature of the normalization campaign was a revival of Peking's long-dormant interest in admission to the United Nations, and, on October 25, 1971, Peking was elected to China's seat with American support, and Nationalist China was expelled in spite of American efforts to keep it in.

In its propaganda, Peking still maintains the dual-adversary strategy and claims to be opposing both "superpowers." In fact, however, it has tilted strongly toward the United States. One reason for this, and the U.S. Government would like to think the only reason, is Peking's fear of the Soviet Union. But Peking also knows that the Nixon Administration is eager, for domestic purposes, to get help in reaching a political settlement for Vietnam, believes China could be useful toward this end if only it were willing, and is in the process of reducing the American military presence in Asia and the Western Pacific in part on the theory that previous American administrations had overrated the Chinese threat to Asia. Hence, there are vulnerabilities in the American position, and Peking has been trying to play on them, not only to achieve a positive political relationship that might help to counter-balance the Soviet threat, but also to exploit the rift between the United States and Japan, get concessions on Taiwan and possibly on Vietnam, and promote American military withdrawal from the region before the Soviet Union or Japan is in a position to fill the vacuum. Given these overriding objectives, Peking has not allowed itself to be deflected more than temporarily by anger over the American intrusion into Cambodia in the spring of 1970, American air support for the short-lived South Vietnamese invasion of Southern Laos in early 1971, and the American bombing and mining campaign against North Vietnam that began in May, 1972.

Peking became aware shortly after President Nixon's inaugura-tion that he claimed to want to "wind down" the war in Indo-china, to improve relations with the C.P.R., and indeed to visit it. Unless convinced of his basic sincerity, Peking would probably have been unwilling to try to establish a positive relationship with him, even in the face of the Soviet threat. Peking did become con-vinced as Nixon reduced American ground forces in South Viet-nam and made a number of gestures toward Peking, of which the stopping of the Seventh Fleet's largely symbolic Taiwan Strait patrol in late 1969 was probably one of the most important. Am-bassadorial talks with the United States were resumed briefly in December, 1969, and, in February, 1970, Peking began to indicate privately an interest in having President Nixon visit China. A series of intermediaries, including President Ceausescu of Romania, took a hand in carrying top-level messages back and forth between Washington and Peking. Ceausescu visited Washington in October, 1970, and it was then that President Nixon first publicly called the C.P.R. by its official title, a significant gesture. It will be re-called that it was also in October, 1970, that a Soviet ambassador reached Peking. The evidence therefore points to that month as the one in which Chou En-lai's policy of soothing the Soviet Union while tilting toward the United States began to bear demonstrable results over the probable opposition of Lin Piao. It is interesting that Lin was last seen in public on June 3, 1971, during Ceause-cu's visit to Peking. The famous secret visit of Dr. Henry Kissinger (July 9–11, 1971) and the public invitation to President Nixon followed soon afterward. By April, Chou had already began to cultivate American public opinion and please his Maoist colleagues by launching a campaign of "people's diplomacy" centering on invitations to China for an American table-tennis team, journalists, biological scientists, academic radicals, Americans of Chinese descent, and a few others, as well as cultivation of favorably disposed groups in the United States.

The projected Nixon visit to China was rendered more urgent in Chou's eyes by the tension in Sino-Soviet relations during the summer of 1971, and was complicated by the crisis over the purge of Lin Piao in September. By late October, however, when Kissinger visited Peking for the second time, the Nixon visit became practically irreversible. It aroused a great deal of puzzlement and discontent in China, especially among the Maoists. In spite of repeated briefings explaining Peking's reasons for inviting Nixon (as well as the official version of Lin Piao's fall; see Chapter 4), Chou did not gain the full legitimacy that he wanted for the Nixon visit until Mao received Nixon on the first day (February 22, 1972).

The main purpose and effect of the Nixon visit—apart from its disturbing impact on the Soviet Union, Japan, Taiwan, and some other Asian allies of the United States—was to improve the understanding on each side of the other's attitudes and objectives. In addition, a number of specific issues were explored, and some of these were mentioned, with an indication of whether agreement had been reached, in the so-called Shanghai Communiqué issued at the conclusion of the visit. This document, remarkable in spite of its seeming blandness, stressed the American interest in stability as opposed to the Chinese interest in revolution by "oppressed" peoples and the agreed point that neither side wanted to "dominate" Asia and the Pacific or would combine with a third power against the other. The Chinese side reiterated its propaganda support for North Korea and North Vietnam and its demand that all foreign troops withdraw to their own countries (Soviet forces should withdraw from the Mongolian People's Republic, that is; not merely American forces from the Far East). The United States made some significant concessions on Taiwan by failing to reaffirm its defense commitment to the island, by coming close to recognizing it as part of China, by endorsing in effect, although not by that name, Peking's Five Principles of Peaceful Coexistence (one of which is "noninterference in the internal affairs of other states," a principle that the United States knows Peking considers to cover the American presence on Taiwan), and by agreeing that American troops would ultimately be withdrawn from Taiwan. On the other hand, by adding that this would be done "as the tension in the area diminishes," the United States gave the C.P.R. an incentive to promote peaceful outcomes in Korea, the Taiwan Strait, and Indochina in order to hasten the withdrawal of the 8,000 American military personnel currently on Taiwan, a withdrawal Peking greatly desires.

To be sure, Peking was in no mood or position to put direct pressure on Hanoi for a settlement on anything like American terms, pressure that if applied would probably drive Hanoi into the arms of the Soviet Union. Still, Peking had begun to establish a relationship with the United States that clearly transcended in importance its relationship with North Vietnam, and one that it would not likely allow to be disrupted by the absence of a settlement for Indochina. Contrary to its attitude until recently, Peking would apparently now prefer a political settlement rather than "protracted war" in Indochina, mainly in the higher interest of its relationship with the United States and the ultimate "liberation" of Taiwan. This became clear in May, 1972, when the Nixon Administration mined the major North Vietnamese ports and intensified its bombing campaign in retaliation for a major North Vietnamese invasion of South Vietnam at the end of March. Clearly both the C.P.R. and the Soviet Union felt that Hanoi had gone too far, although they proceeded predictably and competitively to step up their military aid to North Vietnam within the limits imposed by the bombing and mining, but neither allowed its improving relationship with the United States to be jeopardized by the crisis, if only because to do so would play into the other's hands.

Japan has always been an important part of Peking's calculations, and this has never been truer than since the end of the Cultural Revolution. Japan is an obvious candidate for the demon role in Chinese foreign and even domestic policy, now that Peking's relations with the United States are improving and inasmuch as it is unsafe to insult or provoke the Soviet Union except in the most general terms. Many Chinese understandably dislike Japan, are rather overawed by its recent economic performance, and fear that in the middle term it might rearm on a large scale (as it is not now doing) and become a serious rival of China's in such sensitive areas as Korea and Taiwan. Peking has become concerned over Japan's large share of China's external trade and would apparently like to divert a larger share than at present to Western Europe, the United States, and even the Soviet Union (see Chapter 11).

All this is true and important, but none of it explains why Peking's expressed concern over Japanese "militarism" should have peaked in 1971 and declined in 1972, even as this alleged demon was regaining jurisdiction over Okinawa from the United States. The explanation seems to stem from the basic unpopularity of the Nixon visit in China. Chou En-lai could and did argue, although rather indirectly, that by inviting Nixon, the C.P.R. was helping to split the United States from Japan, and that Japan was the major menace to China, whereas in reality Chou regards the Soviet Union as the major menace and the United States as the best counterweight to it but finds it inexpedient to say so publicly. The retirement of Japanese Premier Eisaku Sato in July, 1972, and his replacement by Kakuei Tanaka has brought to power a man much more disposed to conciliate Peking, in the hope of increasing Sino-Japanese trade and for reasons of domestic politics and foreign policy. Peking has succeeded in exerting, indirectly at least, a profound influence on policy-making in Japan and in giving the Japanese Government a greater sense of stake in improving its relations with the C.P.R. than in trying to fill, in any sense, the partial vacuum left by the United States through its disengagement from Asia under the Nixon Doctrine.

Peking had a windfall when Prince Norodom Sihanouk of Cambodia, after his overthrow in March, 1970, took refuge in China and became a source of leverage for Peking on the Communist coalition in Indochina (North Vietnam, the National Liberation Front, the Cambodian National United Front, and the Pathet Lao). Peking has both supported and quietly competed with Hanoi, for example by cultivating feelings in Thailand favorable to neutrality and better relations with the C.P.R. More important, Peking has endorsed Hanoi's immediate demands regarding South Vietnam (in particular, immediate American withdrawal and a neutral coalition government with Communist participation) but has shown no real enthusiasm for Hanoi's (often unstated) further objective of reunification under North Vietnamese control; such an outcome would make an already troublesome partner into a serious rival for influence in mainland Southeast Asia. With regard to Korea, on the other hand, Peking favors reunification under Pyongyang, following American withdrawal, because a unified Communist Korea would not be a serious rival for Peking, and a vacuum in South Korea left by the United States and not filled by Pyongyang would tend to draw Japanese influence in even more than is already the case.

If Hanoi has been playing a strong hand in Southeast Asia, Pakistan, Peking's closest friend elsewhere in Asia, has been playing a losing one. Peking disapproved (quietly at the time, more openly in recent months) of the barbarous behavior of the Pakistani army in East Pakistan after March, 1971, but for the sake of its over-all relationship with Pakistan, Peking gave political support to Rawalpindi first against the movement for independence for Bangladesh and then against Indian intervention supported to some extent by the Soviet Union. Peking postponed indefinitely what had begun to look like a cautious improvement of its relations with India, without however being able to give Pakistan anything more effective than propaganda support; even then the strongest Chinese statements came exactly as the Pakistani forces in East Pakistan were surrendering on December 16, 1971. Distances, logistics, snow-filled passes, six Indian divisions along the Sino-Indian frontier, and the belief that the Soviet Union might retaliate if the C.P.R. took military action in support of Pakistan combined to prevent Chinese intervention. Since then, Peking has followed Pakistan's lead by withholding recognition of Bangladesh, and on August 25, 1972, vetoed its application for admission to the United Nations.

Since the end of the Cultural Revolution, Peking has exchanged diplomatic recognitions with several Middle Eastern countries (Turkey and Iran, for example) and has considerably increased its level of activity in the region. Its high card is varying degrees of local disenchantment with the two "superpowers," as manifested for instance in Egypt's expulsion of its Soviet military advisers in August, 1972. Another card, although hardly one peculiar to Peking, is hostility to Israel. In this connection, Peking has been giving rather extensive military aid to the Palestinian guerrillas, whose performance, however, has been unimpressive against the Jordanian army, to say nothing of the Israeli army. Peking has also been supplying military aid to guerrillas along the Persian Gulf. China is not yet in the market for Middle Eastern oil and may never be, because it is short of foreign exchange and because it appears to have sizable reserves within its borders and on the East China Sea continental shelf, which may become the object of serious international rivalry.

Although Peking has encouraged anti-Soviet tendencies in Albania and Romania since the early 1960's and has greatly improved its relations with Yugoslavia since the Russian invasion of Czechoslovakia, it has not made major inroads into Eastern Europe. The Soviet Union ultimately looms too large over the region for that. Everyone knows, as Chou En-lai pointed out in an interview with a Yugoslav correspondent in the summer of 1971, that China cannot give effective support to an East European country if it becomes involved in a confrontation with the Soviet Union, given Moscow's post-Czechoslovakia self-confidence.

The Soviet Union's remarkable recent improvement of its relations with West Germany worries Peking greatly. Its fear, quite possibly a realistic one, is that Moscow may be settling issues in the West in order to turn eastward and devote more attention to managing its China problem, whether by military means or otherwise. Peking is, of course, most anxious that this should not happen. Although not in a position to promote tension in Central Europe, or between the Soviet Union and Western Europe, it is improving its own relations with the Common Market countries, encouraging them to play an active role in international politics as a counterbalance to both "superpowers," and urging the United States not to reduce further the level of Soviet concern over Western Europe by withdrawing its forces from the area, even though Peking wants it to do so from the Far East.

FURTHER READINGS

Because the literature on Chinese foreign policy is fairly large, this list must be highly selective.

Two brief general works by Australian authors are Arthur Huck, *The Security of China: Chinese Approaches to Problems of War and Strategy*, London: Chatto & Windus, for The Institute of Strategic Studies, 1970, New York: Columbia University Press, 1970; and J. D. Simmonds, *China's World: The Foreign Policy of a Developing State*, New York: Columbia University Press, 1971. Somewhat more detailed is Harold C. Hinton, *China's Turbulent Quest: An Analysis of China's Foreign Relations since 1949*, rev. ed., Bloomington: Indiana University Press, 1972, New York: Macmillan, 1973. Still more detailed, but now dated, is Harold C. Hinton, *Communist China in World Politics*, Boston: Houghton Mifflin; London: Macmillan, 1966. Somewhat more specialized, and highly useful, are Peter Van Ness, *Revolution and Chinese Foreign Policy: Peking's Support for Wars of National Liberation*, Berkeley: University of California Press, 1971; James Chieh Hsiung, *Law and Policy in China's Foreign Relations: A Study of Attitudes and Practice*, New York: Columbia University Press, 1972; and Herbert Passin, *China's Cultural Diplomacy*, New York: Praeger, 1963. There is an important series of articles in *The China Quarterly* written by A. M. Halpern from a psychological perspective and based largely on content analysis: "Communist China and Peaceful Coexistence," no. 3 (July–September, 1960), pp. 16–31,

"The Chinese Communist Line on Neutralism," no. 5 (January–March, 1961), pp. 90–115, "The Foreign Policy Uses of the Chinese Revolutionary Model," no. 7 (July–September, 1961), pp. 1–16, and "Communist China's Foreign Policy: The Recent Phase," no. 11 (July–September, 1962), pp. 89–104. Some interesting and valuable information on the background of foreign policy-making can be found in Ross Terrill, *800,000,000: The Real China,* Boston: Little, Brown, 1972. Dated but still useful is A. Doak Barnett, *Communist China and Asia: Challenge to American Policy,* Mystic, Conn.: Lawrence Verry, 1960. See also Tang Tsou, ed., *China in Crisis,* vol. ii, Chicago: University of Chicago Press, 1968; and Melvin Gurtov, *China and Southeast Asia—The Politics of Survival: A Study of Foreign Policy Interactions,* Lexington, Mass.: D. C. Heath, 1971.

A valuable pioneer study of the Chinese role in the Korean war is Allen S. Whiting, *China Crosses the Yalu: The Decision to Enter the Korean War,* New York: Macmillan, 1960 (reprint, Stanford, Calif.: Stanford University Press, 1968). A comparable study of another early episode is Melvin Gurtov, *The First Vietnam Crisis: Chinese Communist Strategy and United States Involvement, 1953–1954,* New York: Columbia University Press, 1967. Peking's role in the Geneva negotiations of 1961–62 on Laos is covered in Arthur Lall, *How Communist China Negotiates,* New York: Columbia University Press, 1968. The Indonesian crisis of 1965 is perceptively treated in Sheldon W. Simon, *The Broken Triangle: Peking, Djakarta, and the PKI,* Baltimore: Johns Hopkins University Press, 1969.

Standard works on Sino-Soviet relations are Donald S. Zagoria, *The Sino-Soviet Conflict, 1956–1961,* New York: Atheneum, 1964; William E. Griffith, *The Sino-Soviet Rift,* Cambridge, Mass.: The MIT Press, and London: Allen & Unwin, 1964: and *Sino-Soviet Relations, 1964–1965,* Cambridge, Mass.: The MIT Press, 1967. On the Sino-Soviet border dispute and related problems, see Dennis J. Doolin, *Territorial Claims in the Sino-Soviet Conflict: Documents and Analysis,* Stanford, Calif.: The Hoover Institution, 1965; and Harold C. Hinton, *The Bear at the Gate: Chinese Policymaking Under Soviet Pressure,* Washington: American Enterprise Institute, and Stanford, Calif.: The Hoover Institution, 1971. Current Soviet policy toward China is well traced in Vernon V. Aspaturian, "Moscow's Options in a Changing World," *Problems of Communism,* vol. xxi. no. 4 (July–August, 1972), pp. 1–20.

On China and the United States, the most useful source is the essays and documents in Roderick MacFarquhar, ed., *Sino-American Relations, 1949–71,* New York: Praeger, 1972.

On China and Africa, the best book is Bruce D. Larkin, *China and Africa, 1949–1970: The Foreign Policy of the People's Republic of China,* Berkeley: University of California Press, 1971.

14. The Taiwan Question in Chinese Politics

Although not in the same sense as Korea or Vietnam, China is a divided country. Its civil war is not yet over; the Nationalists, driven from the mainland in 1949, have established their base on Taiwan under the protection of the United States. The decision to extend this protection has not only strongly influenced U.S. relations with the Republic of China, it has also introduced the biggest single irritant into the United States's inevitably difficult relationship with Peking.

Historical Background

Of Taiwan's current, rapidly growing population of about 14 million, some 12 million are Taiwanese, people whose families have lived on the island for several generations or several centuries. Their ancestors came originally, in almost all cases, from the nearest mainland province, Fukien, across the Taiwan Strait, and the Taiwanese today speak a dialect of Fukienese. In connection with current political disputes, the question inevitably arises: Are the Taiwanese Chinese? Some Taiwanese leaders, eager for autonomy, and some foreign observers answer no. Most Chinese, however, say yes, and logic appears to be on their side. Ethnically and culturally, and in spite of half a century of Japanese rule, the Taiwanese must be considered Chinese. They are as much Chinese as the Okinawans are Japanese, and, on May 15, 1972, although with mixed feelings, the Okinawans reverted to Japanese jurisdiction after twenty-seven years of American rule. It does not necessarily follow that all or most Taiwanese wish to be ruled from the mainland; at present, they almost certainly do not. Nor does it necessarily follow that all predominantly Chinese communities should belong to a single state; Singapore is an example of another possibility. In reality, apart from a few articulate and educated spokesmen, the wishes of the majority of Taiwanese cannot be ascertained in the absence of a free plebiscite, which it is impractical to hold in view of the opposition of the Republic of China.

The Japanese captured Taiwan, against considerable local resistance, in 1895 and developed it into a reasonably prosperous tropical colony producing sugar, camphor, and other primary products for the Japanese market. Once conquered, the inhabitants gave little trouble, and relations were far better than between the Koreans and the Japanese. Economic and literary levels were high for an Asian country. The island served as a major training ground and base in connection with Japanese operations against Southeast Asia at the beginning of World War II.

Being more nationalist in fact as well as in name than its predecessors, the Kuomintang developed an interest in recovering Taiwan as well as some other neighboring areas that had been lost to various "imperialist" countries. This interest grew as relations with Japan worsened. Accordingly, at the Cairo Conference (November–December, 1943) the Republic of China's American and British allies promised that Taiwan would be restored to it after the war.

The Nationalists therefore occupied the island in 1945. As in other areas taken from the Japanese at the end of the war, carpetbagging Nationalist officials and generals misruled the island outrageously. A series of demonstrations was met by a massacre of Taiwanese by Nationalist troops on February 28, 1947. The situation was so notorious that Chiang Kai-shek removed the governor and in 1949 appointed as governor the able and honest Ch'en Ch'eng (later Premier and Vice President), but the memory of this episode lingers among the Taiwanese.

The situation was further complicated by the arrival from the mainland in 1949 of more than a million refugees—officials, military personnel, dependents, and others—who are usually referred to collectively (together with similar individuals already on the island) as mainlanders, in contradistinction to the indigenous Taiwanese. Actually, of course, they come from many mainland provinces and are far more heterogeneous than the Taiwanese. The most eminent of these mainlanders was President Chiang Kai-shek, who during a year of nominal retirement came to Taiwan in 1949 and then resumed the Presidency of the Republic of China on March 1, 1950.

Those were difficult and chaotic years, but under Ch'en Ch'eng's supervision and with some American advice an ambitious program of land reform was undertaken. The Republic of China was deter-mind not to let peasant discontent threaten its political position, as it had on the mainland. Land belonging to former Japanese owners was sold at reasonable prices to the cultivators. A similar approach was adopted with respect to land belonging to Tai-wanese landlords, who were compensated mainly with industrial bonds issued by government-owned enterprises formerly belonging to Japanese owners or the Japanese colonial administration.

As with respect to the other "lost" territories, the CPC at first was somewhat less nationalist than the Kuomintang. In 1936, in an interview with Edgar Snow, Mao Tse-tung seemed to imply that the Taiwanese were not really Chinese and should be inde-pendent, rather than part of China, after the defeat of Japan. This relaxed attitude changed during the 1940's as the CPC drew closer to power and as the Nationalists first occupied Taiwan and then made it their major base. In early 1950, the PLA was preparing to "liberate" the island through an amphibious operation in conjunc-tion with some sort of cooperation from supporters on Taiwan. The latter aspect of the plan was frustrated by Nationalist pre-ventive action, and the amphibious operation was spoiled by the movement northward of many of the troops involved because of the impending outbreak of the Korean War and by the extension of American protection to Taiwan on June 27, 1950.

The Republic of China Since 1949

As compared with its generally poor record on the mainland prior to 1949, there can be no doubt that the Kuomintang has done substantially better on Taiwan since then. The island, being much smaller, is far more manageable than the huge chaotic mass that the Kuomintang was trying to govern before 1949. Taiwan's location is far more favorable than most of the mainland's to external contacts, especially trade and investment. The Japanese left behind an impressive infrastructure, including a predominantly literate and educated population. The Nationalist leadership has learned some lessons, or what it takes to be lessons, from its defeat on the mainland. One of these is that its effort on the mainland suffered from poor leadership, although of course Chiang Kai-shek's numerous mistakes are not discussed and probably not even considered in this context; accordingly, there have been some purges, and even more retirements, of senior civil and military officials who contributed heavily to the disaster on the mainland.

Another (correct) lesson learned is that inflation contributed to defeat, and therefore only bills of small denominations are printed (to avoid an inflationary psychology), and inflation has been prevented with reasonable success. Finally—a factor seldom acknowledged publicly by the Republic of China as having contributed to its performance on Taiwan—there has been American aid and protection, approximately $1.5 billion in economic aid until 1965 (when the program was terminated) and $2.5 billion in military aid since 1950.

The Republic of China has maintained officially since 1949 that one day it will "return to the mainland" and eliminate the "Communist bandits," who are repeatedly claimed to be about to collapse. The facts that they have not collapsed, and that their already great military superiority has been increased by the acquisition of nuclear weapons, have rendered the scenario of a reconquest of the mainland by the Nationalists increasingly incredible, even to its most ardent champions, especially since the United States has made it clear that it has no intention of supporting such an operation. Accordingly, the official myth has shifted its base to the proposition that the "return" will be primarily a political process, the nature of which is understandably left vague. Even this slightly less implausible version of the myth is not taken seriously by many people on Taiwan. The purposes for which it continues to be proclaimed appear to be to maintain President Chiang Kai-shek's self-image as the savior of the Chinese tradition from Communism, to rationalize the virtually supreme political power he and his son exercise over the regime and the island, to justify the maintenance (partly for purposes of patronage) of a large party and state apparatus and military establishment on a scale more appropriate to the whole of China than to Taiwan, and to mobilize support on Taiwan and elsewhere.

The second and third of these suggested motives can be used as themes for a brief discussion of the Nationalist political system since 1949.

President Chiang Kai-shek's prestige is roughly as real and as effectively unchallengeable on Taiwan (although almost certainly not on the mainland) as Mao Tse-tung's on the mainland. The sense of rivalry between the two men is very real, and each seems determined to outlive the other. Like Mao in recent years, Chiang cultivates the aura of an elder statesman (he has been elected to five six-year terms as President of the Republic of China under the 1948 constitution, most recently in 1972) and prefers not to attend to administrative matters. He leaves these largely to others, of whom his elder son, Chiang Ching-kuo, has become increasingly the most important and is clearly marked as his father's heir. A complex secretive man in rather poor health, the younger Chiang has long been the major power in the army's political apparatus (inherited from the Kuomintang's days under Soviet tutelage), the party's Youth Corps, and the island's internal security mechanism (centering in the Taiwan Garrison Command). He has repeatedly taken action against possible rivals among the mainlander elite and against political and intellectual dissent among the mainlanders and the Taiwanese. In the mid-1950's, he and his father purged K. C. Wu, the able and honest governor of Taiwan Province who had demanded liberalization of the political system; and General Sun Li-jen, a respected commander who was too close to the American military and had evidently been expressing skepticism about the "return to the mainland." In 1960, a mainlander editor, Lei Chen, was imprisoned for trying to start a genuine opposition party, as contrasted with the two tame parties the Kuomintang permitted to exist. In 1970, Henry Kao (Kao Yu-shu), a popular Taiwanese independent who had been elected Mayor of Taipei and then appointed by the central government when the post was made appointive in 1968, was impeached by the Control Yuan (see below) on a dubious charge of corruption in office. On the theory that the civil war is still in progress, certain emergency legislation bordering on martial law is in effect; the number of political prisoners is believed to be several thousand. Thus rivalry, dissent, and attempted freedom of action on a scale that could conceivably jeopardize the power and authority of the ruling establishment are severely dealt with; below that level, however, a gradually increasing amount of political freedom has been permitted. Both propositions are true, and both are important; the second will be examined in more detail shortly.

The Kuomintang is obviously not in a position to recruit new members on the mainland, but only among the mainlanders and Taiwanese on Taiwan and among supporters elsewhere. Nevertheless, it behaves for formal purposes very much as though it were still in power on the mainland; it should be remembered that because of the party's reorganization by Soviet advisers in 1923–24 (see chapter 2), its organization and functioning fairly closely resemble those of a Communist Party. The Party Congress meets every five years (the Tenth was held in March–April, 1969) but does little of importance beyond electing a Central Committee (formerly referred to as the Central Executive Committee), whose membership is in fact selected by Chiang Kai-shek. There was a considerable injection of new, younger blood into the Central Committee at the Tenth Party Congress. Chiang Kai-shek also controls nominations to the Central Standing Committee, a more important policy-making body comparable to the CPC's Politburo and nominally elected by the Central Committee. This top-level machinery of the Kuomintang is dominated by Chiang Kai-shek and in turn dominates the government at the national (or quasi-national) and provincial levels.

At the central level, the National Assembly (whose membership is aging since elections obviously cannot be held on the mainland) has as its main function the election (essentially rigged) of the President and Vice President of the Republic of China. The cumbersome governmental structure inherited from Sun Yat-sen's blueprint and the days of power on the mainland consists of five Yuan (branches): the Executive (or cabinet, whose chairman is usually called the Premier), the Legislative (a parliament with somewhat limited powers), the Judicial, the Examination (to supervise recruitment to the civil service), and the Control (to detect and prosecute violations of the law by public officials). The members of the Executive and Control Yuan, as well as those of the National Assembly, were elected in 1946–49; the members of the other Yuan have been appointed by the President when and as he has seen fit. Of the Yuan, by far the most important is the Executive, which concentrates on matters of administration and development and in recent years has come to include an increasing percentage of younger, better-trained men of real technical competence.

At the center, the most important recent trend has been the increase of the already impressive power and influence of Chiang Ching-kuo. The difficult problem, for him, of what to do about his respected senior, Vice President Ch'en Ch'eng, was solved by Ch'en's death in 1965. From Defense Minister, the younger Chiang was made Vice Premier in 1969, with special responsibility for economic development; since the island's economy was growing at a rapid rate, this was a role in which he could hardly fail to appear to advantage. In 1972, shortly after the beginning of his father's fifth term as President, he was named Premier. He has brought an increasing number of Taiwanese (not dissidents, of course) into high government positions and appears to be improving the performance of the formerly ineffective bureaucracy. He would apparently have little difficulty in succeeding his father, in fact and probably as President also, except in the unlikely event that others in the military and civilian leaderships who resent his rise and fear his capacity for ruthless action were to combine against him.

The tattered army that crossed to Taiwan in 1949 has since been built up, with American advice and aid (stopping short of major offensive weapons systems)., to a force of some 600,000 (including a small but efficient navy and air force) that appears capable of defending the island against any likely attack by conventional forces and perhaps of making a limited landing on the mainland under optimum conditions. The rank and file is composed overwhelmingly of Taiwanese conscripts; the upper commissioned ranks, however, are still dominated by mainlanders. About 60,000 of the best troops garrison the offshore islands, principally Quemoy (Kinmen), which is opposite the Fukienese port of Amoy. The Nationalist presence on these islands has little military utility but links the Republic of China to the mainland and inhibits a "two Chinas" outcome; it is therefore basically acceptable to the CPC, pending the "liberation" of Taiwan itself. Some of the Nationalist military apparently favor acquiring nuclear weapons, but such a step seems unlikely, and if it is actually taken, the weapons will probably be used mainly for bargaining with the Communists rather than for fighting them.

The Kuomintang has given acceptable Taiwanese an increasing share of its own nominations for positions in the five Yuan and for various elective offices (membership in the City Council of the capital city of Taipei, for example). It is mainly at the provincial level and in the rural areas that the Taiwanese majority can exercise at least some of the functions of self-government. Even there, the provincial governor continues to be appointed by the President, although the provincial assembly is popularly elected and the Kuomintang is the only party effectively active in provincial and local politics. Nevertheless, there have been reasonably free elections at the *hsien* (district or county) level since 1950, with the qualification that non-Kuomintang candidates are normally elected only when not opposed by Kuomintang candidates. The functioning of this system without serious popular discontent is to be attributed not only to efficient controls but also to the prosperity in which the rural economy has been basking, thanks to central government policy, American aid, and the growth of the economy as a whole.

There is no question that the educated elite among the Taiwanese, including students, contains a sizable number of individuals who bitterly resent the central government's presence, without which they would presumably be in charge, and who would much prefer autonomy or independence for the island, under their own leadership and perhaps under foreign protection (preferably Japanese, possibly American). These people naturally resent the role that the United States has played in keeping the Republic of China in power in and over the island. Their point of view, however, does not appear to have spread to the rural Taiwanese to any significant extent. Since visiting Americans, not so much officials as scholars, students, and journalists, tend to come into contact with educated Taiwanese, they often form an exaggerated impression of the level of discontent and the iniquitous effects of American policy. The organized movement for Formosan (preferred by its supporters to "Taiwanese") independence has been weak and for obvious reasons has had to function largely outside the island. It remains to be seen whether discontent among educated Taiwanese can be reduced by Chiang Ching-kuo's tendency to bring some of their leading members into higher administrative positions; the probabilities and the initial indications are negative.

In the long run, and barring some change in the general political situation, the cleavage between mainlanders and Taiwanese appears likely to grow less rather than greater. They have many problems in common; students of both groups when abroad, for example, often take anti-Kuomintang positions and in many instances are unwilling to return to Taiwan. Some Taiwanese who are prosperous business or professional men are better off financially than most of the mainlanders. In student movements, labor disputes, and the like, there is a tendency for the difference between mainlanders and Taiwanese (who in most cases can communicate with each other because of the widespread knowledge of Mandarin, the official language) to be less important than other differences. There is, in effect, an establishment that is predominantly mainlander but includes a growing percentage of Taiwanese and that by no means includes the entire mainlander community.

There is no doubt that over-all conditions on Taiwan have improved since 1949. In spite of land reform, the 1950's were a tense and difficult decade. Friction between mainlanders and Taiwanese was still acute in the aftermath of the 1947 massacre. The myth of the "return to the mainland" had sufficient vitality to inhibit effective planning for the island, apart from treating it as a temporary base pending the recovery of the mainland. In spite of the 1954 mutual security treaty with the United States, American support was still not considered dependable. The 1958 Taiwan Strait crisis was something of a turning point, and the 1960's were a much pleasanter decade. American support now seemed more reliable; economic aid was terminated in 1965 because the U.S. Government no longer considered it necessary in view of the island's striking economic progress, but military aid was continued. The government paid less attention to the "return to the mainland" myth and more to improving its administration of Taiwan. Under the influence of prosperity, relations improved between mainlanders and Taiwanese (apart from educated dissidents). By the end of the decade, in addition to a prosperous agriculture, the island had a flourishing and rapidly growing light industrial sector benefiting from substantial investment by overseas Chinese and by Japanese and American firms. The island's foreign trade roughly equaled that of the mainland (about $4 billion per year).

This prosperity, in fact, was probably Taiwan's main asset as it entered the 1970's, a decade that promised to be nervous. Chiang Kai-shek's advanced age meant that his leadership, for good or ill, might end by death or retirement at any moment, with possibly unsettling results in spite of the care taken to smooth the way for his son's succession. The loss to Peking of the United Nations seat in 1971 and of a growing number of diplomatic relationships was a serious prestige and morale problem. Worst of all, perhaps, the Republic of China's generally good commercial and diplomatic relations with the United States and Japan appeared to be in some danger as both countries began to give a higher priority to improving their relations with Peking. If in fact this trend should go so far as to weaken the ties between Taipei and Washington and Tokyo, and above all the American commitment to give military protection to Taiwan, and if the Republic of China leadership were still unwilling to accommodate with Peking, it might have to seek the patronage of the Soviet Union, perhaps in cooperation with India; there is some slight evidence that Taipei is considering at least keeping this option open. One outcome that it does not appear willing to tolerate is any trend that would lead to its eventual overthrow by the Taiwanese; at present, such a contingency seems remote.

American Policy Toward Taiwan

From mid-1949 to mid-1950, American policy was one of "letting the dust settle." Having failed to save the Nationalists on the mainland from the Communists and their own mistakes, the U.S. Government now proposed to give them no further military aid or support (apart from continuing diplomatic recognition for the time being) and not to interfere if the PLA went ahead with its plan to "liberate" the island.

The Korean War changed this, mainly because in order to get Republican Congressional support for intervention in Korea, the Truman Administration had to reverse itself on Taiwan. On June 27, 1950, it was announced that the United States would prevent an attack across the Taiwan Strait by either party to the Chinese civil war; since the Nationalists were in an even poorer position to do this than the Communists, the effect was unilateral protection of Taiwan. This was soon followed by a great increase of American military aid in the form of arms and training. In addition, the United States acquired logistical (not combat) bases on the island and until 1971 conducted reconnaissance activity from Taiwan against the mainland. The United States supported the Republic of China's position in the United Nations, treated it formally as the government of all China (apart from maintaining the ambassadorial talks with Peking after 1955), and in general tried with diminishing success to "isolate" Peking diplomatically and commercially. In February, 1953, the Eisenhower Administration "unleashed Chiang Kai-shek," meaning that the prohibition on a Nationalist attack on the mainland was nominally removed. At the end of 1954, a mutual security treaty—a defensive alliance, valid indefinitely unless abrogated by either party—was signed by the two governments.

American support for the Republic of China was not, however, entirely unqualified. In a complicated move apparently connected with the negotiation of a peace treaty with Japan, the U.S. Government announced in 1950–51 that it regarded the legal status of Taiwan as "undetermined," meaning that the island was not necessarily considered part of China, even though it was being protected by the United States as the base of a government recognized as being that of China. The U.S. Government still officially holds that the status of Taiwan is "undetermined." Statements by John Foster Dulles in 1954 and President Kennedy in 1962 made it clear that the U.S. Government did not consider itself committed to support a Nationalist attack on the mainland. American willingness to defend the Nationalist-held offshore islands, as distinct from Taiwan, was conditioned, under the Formosa Resolution of 1955, on a finding by the President that a given Communist attack on the offshore islands was part of an attack on Taiwan. Since the Communists have never seriously launched such an attack, apart from shelling Quemoy intermittently since 1958, the Resolution has never been tested, and it was admitted by the U.S. State Department in 1970 to have become a dead letter; in other words, the U.S. Government would not now consider the Resolution a sufficient basis for involving the United States in the defense of the offshore islands, although the security treaty obligating the the United States to defend Taiwan is still in force.

The escalation of the Vietnam war in 1965 increased the importance of Taiwan to the United States as a logistical and reconnaissance base. It was probably more important, however, that the United States did not try to use the island as a combat base, for example by stationing B-52s there; that was done in Thailand instead. By the time the approaching reversion of Okinawa to Japanese jurisdiction was beginning to make that island useless as an American nuclear base, and voices in the Pentagon were recommending the transfer of nuclear weapons from Okinawa to Taiwan, the Nixon Administration was in office and much more concerned with improving its relations with Peking. The proposal was accordingly vetoed.

The Nixon Administration has, of course, maintained its diplomatic relationship with the Republic of China, supported it (unsuccessfully) in the United Nations, kept the security treaty in force, and continued military aid. But it has also begun what may turn into a process of letting the Republic of China down gently by improving American relations with Peking, making certain concessions relating to Taiwan (see Chapter 13), and publicly urging Peking and Taipei to settle their differences by political means (by agreeing either to unite or to leave each other in peace as "China" and "Taiwan"). The United States has failed to support the Republic of China's claim to the resources of the continental shelf and to the Tiaoyüt'ai (in Japanese, Senkaku) Islands, which are claimed by Peking and Japan (by the latter as part of the Ryukyus) and threaten to become the object of a major international dispute. All this is a far cry from the spirit of American China policy in the 1950's and 1960's.

Peking's Search for Leverage

Since the Kuomintang established its base on Taiwan in 1949 and came under American protection in 1950, Peking's policy toward the island has revolved around a search for leverage sufficient to persuade or compel the United States to withdraw its forces and protection and recognize the Taiwan issue as an internal Chinese problem, and the Kuomintang to reach an accommodation that would be regarded as a "liberation" of the island. Peking is entirely serious about "liberating" Taiwan, for reasons of national dignity, although the issue has been useful for mobilizing support at home and sympathy abroad. Peking has no desire to deal directly with the unpredictable Taiwanese, nor does it want another power, especially Japan, to move into the protector's role if the United States should abandon it.

Peking's intervention in the Korean War gave it for a while the greatest leverage it has had, at least until recently, and it listed the withdrawal of American forces from the Taiwan areas as one of its demands on the United States. But the leverage proved inadequate in view of Peking's failure to win a victory in Korea, except in its own propaganda.

The increase of American military aid to Taiwan in the 1950's and the signing of the security treaty between the United States and the Republic of China were, of course, most unwelcome developments in Peking's eyes. As already mentioned, it opened talks with the United States at the ambassadorial level in 1955 and tried to use American prisoners, whom it was then holding, as leverage for weakening the American commitment to Taiwan, but without success. Peking, of course, rejected a repeated American demand that it agree to a "renunciation of force" in the Taiwan Strait, on the ground that it had every right to use force to finish its civil war if it chose. At the same time, Peking began to encourage Chinese on the mainland with relatives on Taiwan to write to those relatives, praising conditions on the mainland and urging unification. In 1956, Peking began publicly to urge the Nationalist leadership, including Chiang Kai-shek, to return to allegedly secure lives and jobs on the mainland and to accept an "autonomous" status for Taiwan (presumably similar to that of the Autonomous Regions on the mainland). The existing situation was attributed in Peking's propaganda to an American policy of creating "two Chinas," an outcome known to be as unacceptable in Taipei as in Peking. These public offers were supplemented with continuing lower-level contacts, mainly via Hong Kong. There were no important takers, except for some Kuomintang-oriented Chinese leaders living outside Taiwan. Nevertheless, Peking apparently persuaded itself that there was a good chance for "peaceful liberation" of Taiwan, and this was one reason it was initially reluctant to crack down on its "blooming and contending" critics in 1957 (see Chapter 3).

Since then, Peking has aimed its search for leverage more at the United States than at the Kuomintang, apparently on the assumption—probably correct—that there is virtually no chance of an accommodation with the Nationalists while Chiang Kai-shek is alive and in power. But little could be accomplished unless an American administration interested in improving relations with Peking came into office. The Kennedy Administration never really felt such an interest, largely for domestic reasons, and the Johnson Administration was too preoccupied with Vietnam to take major initiatives toward China. It was left for the Nixon Administration, for a combination of domestic and foreign policy reasons (see Chapter 13), to give priority to an improvement of relations with Peking, although without intending to abandon its basic commitment (diplomatic recognition and the security treaty) to the Republic of China. Since the American concessions on Taiwan in the Shanghai Communiqué (see Chapter 13), apart from the pledge to withdraw American military personnel from Taiwan eventually, were more verbal than substantive, Peking obviously does not regard them as going far enough, although it is prepared to be patient as long as there are some signs of movement in what it considers the right direction. Moreover, it is not likely to jeopardize its potentially valuable new relationship with the United States because of Taiwan any more than because of Vietnam. It is possible that Peking will use the United Nations as a platform from which to increase its international support and put additional political pressure on the United States for further concessions on Taiwan.

Peking wants to deal directly with the Kuomintang on the future of Taiwan, and with no other foreign power when and if the United States withdraws from the controversy. Peking will have no part of any "two Chinas" or "one China, one Taiwan" outcome, nor does it want the Formosan independence movement or any other Taiwanese group to come to power on the island; on these issues, the Kuomintang is in full agreement. For historic and current reasons, Peking is very worried that Japan may become an economic patron and even a political and military protector of Taiwan; it has put pressure on Japanese firms to reduce their dealings with Taiwan, with some effect, and has made it clear to the Japanese Government that any improvement in the relations between Peking and Tokyo is contingent on Japanese noninterference in Taiwan. Since about 1968, when the Soviet correspondent and informal envoy Victor Louis visited Taiwan, the Soviet Union has established some contacts with the Kuomintang and with Kuomintang-oriented Chinese outside Taiwan. Peking is naturally concerned about this and views it as a Soviet effort to promote "two Chinas"; it is probably, however, nothing more than a way of putting pressure on Peking, at least for the time being. It is possible, but only barely, that if the Kuomintang became desperate, it might turn to the Soviet Union as it did in 1922.

In 1971, Chou En-lai publicly promised that "liberation" would not lead to a decline of living standards on Taiwan, an interesting statement because it was the first official admission from Peking that Taiwan was not the hell that mainland propaganda had painted it. Obviously, Peking is trying to cultivate a state of mind on Taiwan that will be receptive to unification after Chiang Kai-shek's death or retirement and that will be willing to cut the Republic of China's current ties with the United States without establishing new ties with some other power. What are the actual chances for an explicit accommodation between Peking and Taipei? This is one subject among many on which China specialists sharply disagree. In view of the intensely nationalistic political coloration of both leaderships, their conviction that Taiwan is part of China, the relative impotence of the Taiwanese, and the apparent determination in both Peking and Taipei that, whatever it may be, the island's future shall not be determined by the Taiwanese, any agreement to live amicably and separately as "two Chinas" or "one China, one Taiwan," in which case the Taiwanese as the majority would probably eventually acquire a preponderant political voice on Taiwan, seems very unlikely. But there is, of course, the alternative possibility of unification through an agreement that would leave Taiwan at least formal, and perhaps real, autonomy. A cautious vote can be cast in favor of this scenario as the most plausible, even though few people on Taiwan are actively in favor of it. Both Chinas are already changing as they anticipate the deaths of their grand old men, and, after that, further changes are likely that may make the current confrontation seem more or less archaic. The current trend toward détente between North and South Korea, which until recently were outspokenly hostile to each other, suggests that in the Far East, more than in most other areas, politics can take some surprising turns. The mainland appears to be evolving in a less ideological direction, and Taiwan is not the only Chinese-inhabited area differing politically and economically from itself that the mainland will want to absorb; there is also Hong Kong, which from all indications will revert to China before the end of this century. By that time, or even earlier, the problem of Taiwan's relationship with the mainland may become much less intractable than it appears now.

FURTHER READINGS

The China Quarterly, no. 15 (July–September, 1963), is devoted largely to articles on Taiwan; the quality is generally good. For background on Chiang Ching-kuo, see the interesting article by Allen S. Whiting, "Mystery Man of Formosa," *The Saturday Evening Post*, March 12, 1955, pp. 26–27, 116–18. A good article on recent political trends is J. Bruce Jacobs, "Recent Leadership and Political Trends in Taiwan," *The China Quarterly*, no. 45 (January–March, 1971), pp. 129–54.

A good general survey of conditions on Taiwan is "Background Papers on Taiwan, Department of State, August 3, 1971," *United States Relations with the People's Republic of China*, Washington, D.C.: U.S. Government Printing Office, 1972, pp. 361–85.

For sympathetic accounts of the Formosan independence movement, see George H. Kerr, *Formosa Betrayed*, Boston: Houghton Mifflin, and London: Eyre & Spottiswoode, 1966; Douglas Mendel, *The Politics of Formosan Nationalism*, Berkeley: University of California Press, 1970; Peng Ming-min, *A Taste of Freedom: Memoirs of a Formosan Independence Leader*, New York: Holt, Rinehart & Winston, 1972; and Peter P. C. Cheng, "The Formosa Tangle: A Formosan View,"*Asian Survey*, vol. vii, no. 11 (November, 1967), pp. 791–806.

On American policy toward Taiwan, see Jerome Alan Cohen *et al.*, *Taiwan and American Policy: The Dilemma in U.S.–China Relations*, New York: Praeger, 1971; William M. Bueler, *U.S. China Policy and the Problem of Taiwan*, Boulder: Colorado Associated University Press, 1971 (sympathetic to the Taiwanese); *United States Foreign Policy: Asia*, Washington, D.C.: U.S. Government Printing Office, 1959 (the so-called Conlon Report; the section on Northeast Asia, by Robert A. Scalapino, is the first important published policy document to have recommended a "two Chinas" policy for the United States); Kenneth T. Young, *Negotiating with the Chinese Communists:*

The United States Experience, 1953–1967, New York: McGraw-Hill, 1968 (on the ambassadorial talks); and Allen S. Whiting, "What Nixon Must Do To Make Friends in Peking," *The New York Review of Books,* October 7, 1971 (deals with American military activities in Taiwan and other parts of Asia).

There is no detailed recent study of Peking's Taiwan policy. Chou En-lai's remark regarding living standards on Taiwan was made in an interview with Seymour Topping of the *New York Times* on June 21, 1971 (see Seymour Topping, *Journey Between Two Chinas,* New York: Harper & Row, 1972, pp. 399–400).

15. *The Outlook*

It is hard enough to understand the present and the past from which it grew, especially that of a country as complex as China. It is obviously much harder to perceive the shape of the future with any reliability. The prediction record of China specialists since 1949 has been generally poor, at least in the political sphere, for several reasons. They have often tended to project smooth curves from the present, without allowing sufficiently for shifts of power and policy resulting from little-understood leadership conflicts in Peking. (The alternative of building various models of the future embracing a wide spectrum of possibilities, without much regard for probability as determined on the basis of reality, is no better.) There has sometimes been a tendency to overapply the lessons of China's past, or occasionally those of the Soviet experience, in forecasting China's future. Some mistakes have resulted from taking the regime too much at its propaganda self-valuation, which is always bullish in big things. Conversely, some analyses have erred by overlooking the regime's basic strengths, underrating the possibilities for political and economic development, and forgetting the absence of any effective alternative. With pitfalls like these in mind, the comments that follow are offered in a distinctly tentative spirit.

Domestic Outlook

The possibility of a clash between Chou En-lai and the Maoists, with disastrous results for Chou, seems to be taken seriously in Soviet and Chinese Nationalist propaganda. In the eyes of the Maoists, however, Chou and his team appear to be the only current alternative to, and a much lesser evil than, a weakening of central authority that would probably lead to a further upsurge of military power in the provinces; everyone remembers that this was the result of the last open large-scale struggle within the Peking leadership, the one in 1966 that paved the way for Lin Piao's drive for power. Furthermore, it is by no means certain that even Mao could purge Chou at this stage, in the unlikely event that he should decide to do so.

The more probable alternative is Chou's survival at the head of a "collective leadership" (under Mao's general supervision until his death) that includes the leading Maoists but follows largely pragmatic policies aimed at political stabilization and pragmatic development. The chances for significant progress along these two lines appear reasonably good, always assuming that there is no resumption of serious conflict within the Party leadership. The Great Leap Forward was an even more traumatic experience than the Cultural Revolution for most Chinese, but within a year after its termination, the country was well on the way to recovery (as became clear later; it was not entirely obvious to the outside world at the time). Recent reports by foreign travelers, even if their usual tendency toward bullishness is somewhat discounted, certainly paint a predominantly favorable picture of conditions only a short while after the end of the Cultural Revolution; that they were allowed to enter China and to travel more widely than before suggests that the regime considers domestic conditions to be improving.

Even if it is conceded that the immediate future looks reasonably encouraging from the perspective of essentially pragmatic leaders like Chou En-lai, there remains the question of the impact of Mao's death, assuming that it occurs before Chou's and in the middle of a trend resembling at least approximately the one sketched in the preceding paragraph. There is no doubt that, even though no one really expects him to live ten thousand years (the literal translation of *wan-sui*, the Chinese equivalent of "Long live"), the passing of a leader as dominant as Mao is bound to have a profound psychological effect on many people. This is likely to pass, however. The important, and difficult, question is the extent to which Chou En-lai's current power and influence, especially in his dealings with the regional and provincial military leadership, depend on the general knowledge (or at least the assumption) that he has Mao's support. There is no doubt that Mao's approval is one of the highest cards in Chou's hand, as was true (outwardly at least) of Lin Piao until not long ago. On the other hand, Chou's experience, knowledge, brilliance, administrative ability, diplomatic skill, and pragmatic objectives for China clearly command widespread assent and support within the Party, the PLA (including even some of the regional figures, in all probability), and the non-Party public. His loss would be a serious setback for China, not only at home but abroad as well, a loss that could hardly be afforded while the Soviet threat is still real and the new relationship with the United States is not (or not yet) an adequate counterweight. It seems likely, therefore, that Chou's position as effective head of a "collective leadership" is capable of surviving Mao's death. It is obviously in his interest that the dead Mao should help him to reinforce his position, as the live Mao has done. He is therefore unlikely to launch a program of "de-Maoization," as Khrushchev launched one of de-Stalinization; in any case, there is much less incentive in the sense that Mao is far less feared and hated than Stalin was, and even appears to have genuine popular support. Indeed, Chou's legitimacy, whatever his exact title, would be impaired were he to take the lead in an overt attack on Mao's memory. It is likely, however, that in continuation of current trends, Mao's "thought" will be interpreted moderately and pragmatically, as is perfectly possible, and its more radical aspects confined largely to meaningless slogans or even ignored altogether. The dead man, as distinct from his "thought," is likely to be treated with great reverence, as Sun Yat-sen has been.

In the middle and long-term perspective, however, the problem of possible warlordism remains. The present trend is toward co-opting the regional and provincial military leaders into the new Party apparatus by making them secretaries of provincial Party committees (as well as chairmen, vice chairmen, and members of provincial revolutionary committees). As of late 1972, no military man in such a position has been replaced by a civilian, although some have been replaced by other military men. There is an obvious possibility, therefore, that these provincial military leaders will pay only lip service, if that, to directives from Peking and will increasingly go their own way, much as provincial military strong men under the Nationalists accepted titles but little else from the central government. This possibility cannot be ruled out, but the chances for it appear less than those against it. Much has changed in China since 1949. There is a greater degree of national unity, psychological and actual, than ever before. Communications have been significantly improved, and modern weapons (which would be needed on a sustained basis by anyone trying to maintain independence from the center) are produced in only a few places and under central control. Chinese today are probably even more convinced than in earlier times, because they have seen more evidence, that national disunity leads through weakness to foreign pressure and perhaps even domination. The warlords of the 1920's have a bad image, in China and abroad, partly because they were subject to foreign influence and helped to prevent China as a whole from being able to stand up to external (mainly Japanese) pressures. It is unlikely that a local PLA commander, especially in view of the intensive political indoctrination to which he has inevitably been subjected, would want to play such a role. There has been plenty of bargaining by the regional military with the center, and vice versa, but little direct defiance and no discernible drift toward systematic and successful defiance that over a period of time would constitute warlordism.

The military will probably continue to play a significant, although possibly declining, political role. Milovan Djilas has predicted for all Communist countries a future of rule by a coalition between the (governmental) bureaucracy and the military leadership. This prediction is not necessarily valid, of course; even in the Soviet Union, the current trend is rather toward a coalition between the Party apparatus and the military. (Soviet propaganda often claims to see a similar trend in China by asserting, with great exaggeration, that a militarist, expansionist Maoist-military coalition is in power.) Still, the current importance in Chinese politics of Chou En-lai and Yeh Chien-ying, and their close relationship to one another, certainly suggest the possibility that Djilas's forecast may prove accurate for China. The alternative of a centralized military dictatorship, presumably wearing Communist labels, as distinct from informal provincial warlordism, seems rather unlikely, especially in view of the fate of Lin Piao. The Chinese and the Marxist-Leninist traditions are strongly against military dictatorships. In any event, the growing complexity of modern societies tends to make difficult and discourage military takeovers except in the more backward countries, and China is not really one of them.

One obvious possible political future is the restoration of a more or less orthodox Leninist Party apparatus dictatorship, such as essentially existed in China from 1961 to 1965. This is presumably the outcome the Soviet leadership would prefer. But it appears a somewhat improbable outcome, partly because the Cultural Revolution gave it a bad image in China. Furthermore, the political power of the bureaucracy and the armed forces has probably become great enough to act as an effective countervailing force sufficient to prevent the restoration of a full-blown Party apparatus dictatorship, benevolent or otherwise. The main way in which a Party apparatus dictatorship might emerge is if the new apparatus, in the context of an impressive economic and technological advance, joins with the technicians to institute what might be called a computerized dictatorship; there seems to be a trend in this direction in the Soviet Union.

There are four other possible futures that deserve mention but appear to be of a low order of probability. One might be called neo-Maoism, meaning a resurgence of Maoist fundamentalism as the dominant ideological and political influence; Maoist fundamentalism has been ebbing since its high point in 1966–67, and there is nothing in sight that seems capable of reversing the trend, given Mao's advanced age and the nonexistence of any Maoist successor of comparable stature. Another is a more or less non-ideological technocracy under a coalition of governmental administrators and technicians; the political forces at work in China, including the still considerable political power of the army, are too strong to make such an outcome very plausible. Another is "revisionist" Communism of the Yugoslav variety; social discipline in China is too strict and effective, and the fear of anarchy through relaxation too great on the part of the elite, especially since the Cultural Revolution, to permit such an outcome, at least for the foreseeable future. For the same reason, the theoretical possibility of an "open" or pluralist society and political system, with legal freedom for opposition political movements and viewpoints, appears to be virtually out of the question; there is no basis for it in the Chinese tradition, pre- or post-1949, and certainly none in the Marxist-Leninist tradition.

Whatever the actual outcome, it will probably be roughly describable as national Communism Chinese-style. It will probably retain Marxism-Leninism and the "thought" of Mao Tse-tung as its officially ideology, or at least as the basis of its ideology. The leadership will probably be, at least in form, a kind of grand coalition in which elements of the New Party apparatus, the bureaucracy, the security system, the armed forces, and the technicians and intellectuals all participate, but to different degrees. The security system is likely to grow in power, if only as an offset to the political power of the armed forces, but probably not to the proportions of a "Stalinist" police state. The main key to influence, for any individual in any of the systems, is likely to be "expertness" rather than "redness." It may be that, in addition to technical competence, the qualifications of a candidate for a leading position in any field will include a determination not to permit any erosion of the control of the elite as a whole over the "masses." Almost the only outcome that it seems possible to rule out is some sort of collapse that would lead to the overthrow of the Communist system or even the breakup of the country. While not inconceivable, such a scenario is supported by no evidence or consideration of plausibility, at least under anything like current conditions. The C.P.R. appears to be there, in one form or another, to stay.

External Outlook

Chinese foreign policy, like domestic policy, seems likely to move in the direction of partial (not complete) deideologization. Its essence will probably be increasingly effective participation in what seems to be an emerging multilateral balance of power in the Far East, the other main participants being of course the United States, the Soviet Union, and Japan.

There are several possible futures for what is probably China's most important external relationship, the one with the Soviet Union. The two most interesting and potentially the most important, although not necessarily the most probable, lie at the extremes: reconciliation and war. There are many disadvantages and risks for China in the current confrontation with the Soviet Union, and it is very likely that Chou En-lai would like to move, without concessions of principle and from a position of strength rather than weakness, away from it to some more positive relationship such as he seems to be achieving with the United States. Unfortunately, he is dealing with a Soviet leadership that appears to have an irrational fear and hatred of China; by the time the current Soviet leadership has given way to a younger one that might be more conciliatory, Chou will presumably be gone. Nevertheless, an approximation of a reconciliation is not out of the question, but probably not on an ideological basis or as a close alliance like the one in effect from 1950 to about 1953. At the other extreme, given current Soviet attitudes toward China and the level of the Soviet military buildup near the Chinese border, a Sino-Soviet war is an obvious possibility, even though the arguments on both sides for its undesirability are virtually overwhelming. The most plausible forecast, although it cannot be made with much confidence of accuracy, is that the Soviet leadership will review from time to time the arguments for and against war with China, but will decide each time that the arguments against going to war have the edge, especially since China's nuclear deterrent will presumably grow in size and effectiveness.

Peking's relationship with the United States has lost the element of tension that has entered Sino-Soviet relations. It should be possible for the United States and the C.P.R. to work out a relationship acceptable to both countries, especially if there is progress toward a settlement for Indochina and one for Taiwan that Peking regards as tolerable, even if not ideal; the Taiwan question may become solvable through a changing relationship between Peking and Taipei (see Chapter 14).

There is obviously the possibility of a serious adversary relationship between China and Japan, as there has often been in the history of the Far East. To date, however, although Peking has often appeared tactless to outside observers in its treatment of Japan, Chinese policy has used about the right combination of stick and carrot to maximize its leverage on Japanese official and public opinion, with help from declining American influence due to the Nixon Doctrine and the economic dispute. There is a good chance that Peking will continue to handle its relations with Japan with skill, if not necessarily always with tact. Certainly Peking is anxious not to alienate Japan to the point of driving it to form what might amount to an anti-Chinese combination with the Soviet Union. And a cooperative relationship between China and Japan, as long as it stopped short of a combination aiming at domination of Asia, could have some very beneficial effects on Far Eastern stability; certainly the converse has been true in the past, namely, that Sino-Japanese tension has been a frequent occasion of trouble and war.

FURTHER READINGS

An informed and intelligent appraisal of Communist Chinese experience, combined with a look at the future from the perspective of the early Cultural Revolution period and some key documents, is A. Doak Barnett, *China After Mao,* Princeton, N.J.: Princeton University Press, 1967. The reference to Milovan Djilas is to his article "There'll Be Many Different Communisms in 1984," *The New York Times Magazine,* March 23, 1969. Future politico-military relations in China are discussed in William W. Whitson, ed., *The Military and Political Power in China in the 1970's,* New York: Praeger, 1972. For an example of alarmist Soviet analysis of the result of the Cultural Revolution as a Maoist-military coalition, see O. Lvov (pseud.), "The Political Maneuvers of the Mao Tse-tung Group," *Pravda,* January 11, 1969.

Appendix:
A Note on Research in Chinese Politics

A useful survey of the "state of the art" in Chinese studies in the United States, with special reference to the training of specialists, is John M. H. Lindbeck, *Understanding China: An Assessment of American Scholarly Resources*, New York: Praeger, 1971. For a left-wing analysis of this question, see David Horowitz, "The China Scholars and U.S. Intelligence," *Ramparts*, February, 1972, pp. 31–9.

An excellent bibliographical introduction to the study of Chinese politics is Michel C. Oksenberg, "Sources and Methodological Problems in the Study of Contemporary China," in A. Doak Barnett, ed., *Chinese Communist Politics in Action*, Seattle: University of Washington Press, 1969, pp. 577–606. A detailed bibliography of works in several languages (including Chinese) is Peter Berton and Eugene Wu, comps., *Contemporary China: A Research Guide*, Stanford, Calif.: The Hoover Institution, 1967. *The Journal of Asian Studies* publishes an annual *Bibliography of Asian Studies*, which of course includes many published sources (in Western languages only) on contemporary China. The best source for keeping track of current Western research in progress is *The China Quarterly's* semiannual *Modern China Studies International Bulletin* (London).

Most research on Chinese politics is based to one degree or another on original Chinese sources (in Chinese or in translation). It is sufficient for the purposes of this essay to mention sources available in English translation. It should be noted that many pamphlets and other materials are published in English in Peking by the Foreign Languages Press; these are available from China Books and Periodicals, 2929 24th Street, San Francisco, California 94110; and 95 Fifth Avenue, New York, New York 10003. The most important English-language periodical published in Peking is *Peking Review*, a weekly that carries translations of important policy statements and propaganda articles from the Chinese press for foreign consumption. The major newspaper, the *People's Daily*, and the major theoretical journal, *Red Flag*, do not publish English-language editions. They can be followed fairly well in the (indexed) translations published by the American Consulate General, Hong Kong (principally *Survey of the China Mainland Press*, as well as *Current Background* and *Selections from China Mainland Magazines* and its predecessor, *Extracts from China Mainland Magazines*), and by the Union News Agency, Hong Kong (*Union Research Service*). Current translations of Chinese radio broadcasts (which overlap the press to a considerable extent) are published by the Foreign Broadcast Information Service (Washington) in *Foreign Radio Broadcasts* and by the British Broadcasting Corporation in *Summary of World Broadcasts*; the former has the important advantage of carrying the full texts. Other Chinese publications, including some specialized ones, are translated, published, and indexed by the Joint Publications Research Service (Washington). Anyone using these sources and serials with reasonable care will be able to do adequate work in original Chinese sources, for almost any likely purpose, without having to know Chinese.

He should, however, also be familiar with and make use of the work of others in the same field. Among secondary sources, we may begin with the foreign English-language press. *The New York Times*, *The Washington Post*, *The Christian Science Monitor*, and *The Baltimore Sun* all have good China coverage based on the rich resources of Hong Kong and carry (as of course do many other newspapers) wire-service material originating in Peking. The Toronto *Globe and Mail* has a correspondent in Peking whose valuable dispatches are reprinted in some of the newspapers mentioned earlier. No one need have any intellectual qualms about using the material in reputable newspapers like these, but with the same critical judgment that should be applied to any sources (including this book). The main problem is that they lack an index (except for *The New York Times*) and are cumbersome and time-consuming to use, unless one happens to have built up a clipping file, as this writer has for the past twenty years. The *Far Eastern Economic Review* carries journalistic articles on China but has declined in quality in recent years from its former high standard; it publishes a valuable yearbook on Asia.

Individual books and articles on Chinese politics will not be discussed here, with a few exceptions, since a great many are listed at the end of the substantive chapters. But something needs to be said about the major periodicals devoted to contemporary China (or Asia).

The most useful of these, by and large, is *The China Quarterly* (London), which carries not only articles and book reviews but valuable chronologies and documentary excerpts. Another English-language periodical, published in Brussels, is *Asia Quarterly*, which is relatively new.

The most valuable periodical published in the United States that fairly regularly carries articles on contemporary China is the monthly *Asian Survey* (Berkeley: University of California); the first number of each year contains articles dealing with developments in China and Taiwan during the preceding year.

In Hong Kong, in addition to the Chinese press translations already cited, some periodicals deserve mention. One is *Current Scene,* published monthly by the United States Information Service and carrying valuable signed articles (usually by American scholars), unsigned articles (usually of even greater value, by "The Editor"), book reviews, and chronologies. Another is *China News Analysis*, which is rather in the nature of a newsletter and is edited by the Rev. L. La Dany, S.J.; it is very well informed as to detail and always interesting, but somewhat subjective and not at its best in political analysis.

There is a vast repository on Taiwan of information of various kinds on Chinese Communism before and since 1949, but it is difficult for even the student who reads Chinese and who can go there to use it, and still more difficult for the student who can do neither. Published analyses of mainland developments emanating from Taiwan nearly always include some obligatory propaganda, but are nevertheless sometimes valuable, for the reason indicated. The most useful and accessible English-language periodical dealing with the mainland and published on Taiwan is *Issues and Studies* (Taipei).

The substantial Japanese output of published analyses of contemporary China is hardly accessible to the student who does not read Japanese. As for press coverage, a few of the major Japanese newspapers publish English-language editions; there is also *The Japan Times*. The American Embassy, Tokyo, publishes translations of the Japanese press, but they are hard to find. Occasional Japanese articles on contemporary China appear in the English-language periodical *Pacific Community* (Tokyo), and Japanese-language periodicals sometimes print abstracts in English of the major articles. In all frankness, it cannot be said that the non-Japanese-reading student is missing very much. Japanese sources are generally well informed as to fact, but no better than many others (except on matters to which there is a specific Japanese aspect), and the interpretation is usually not the best.

Soviet sources on China present a special problem. Most, of course, are in Russian, and nearly all contain a good deal of propaganda. The Soviet press can be followed, not altogether adequately, in *Current Digest of the Soviet Press* (New York), which is indexed. The Soviet radio output is accessible in *Foreign Radio Broadcasts.* Pamphlets on Chinese affairs (as well as other matters, of course) are published in English translation by the Novosti Press Agency Publishing House (Moscow). Occasionally a study of more substance appears in English; a recent example is B. Zanegin, A. Mironov, and Y. Mikhailov, *Developments in China*, Moscow: Progress Publishers, 1968. For a good summary and analysis of some Soviet writings on China, see Klaus Mehnert, "Mao and Maoism: Some Soviet Views," *Current Scene*, vol. viii, no. 15 (September 1, 1970). In general, Soviet China specialists are considerably more objective and better informed than their (necessarily) somewhat propagandistic output would suggest, but they admit privately that Chinese studies (traditional, modern, and contemporary) are more advanced in the United States than in the Soviet Union.

Even this brief outline, in combination with the reading lists at the end of the chapters, is enough to indicate that there is a vast literature on contemporary China in English, to say nothing of other languages. Assuming the student has access to a major library or research collection, the problem is not so much to find material (except on very specialized or sensitive topics) as to avoid drowning in what is available. Much of it, however, is of poor quality, but an effort has been made to strain out substandard material in the process of compiling the reading lists in this book, although it should not be assumed that any title omitted is necessarily considered by the writer to be substandard.

Index